THE NORTH YORKSHIRE MOORS RAILWAY

THE MEMOIRS OF A HERITAGE RAILWAY MANAGER

BERNARD WARR

AMBERLEY

First published 2019

Amberley Publishing
The Hill, Stroud,
Gloucestershire, GL5 4EP

www.amberley-books.com

ISBN: 978 1 4456 9149 7 (print)
ISBN: 978 1 4456 9150 3 (ebook)

British Library Cataloguing in Publication Data.
A catalogue record for this book is available from the British Library.

Typeset in 10pt on 14pt Celeste.
Typesetting by Aura Technology and Software Services, India.
Printed in the UK.

Contents

Prologue

I got married in 1969 and my new wife and I lived in Bristol, where I worked for the British Railways Divisional Civil Engineer, based in Temple Meads station. My wife's family lived in the East Riding of Yorkshire in the village of Melton and my grandparents lived in nearby Hull.

In that first year of marriage we holidayed in the East Riding for a couple of weeks. We decided to take a day out and travel through the North Yorkshire Moors and admire the scenery. The memory of exactly where we travelled on that day escapes me now

Grosmont tunnel in July 1969. (Bernard Warr)

some fifty years later, but what sticks in my mind was that the car (loaned to us by my father-in-law) broke down in North Grimston with an overheating engine and I had to call on the AA from the red call box in the centre of the village. After about half an hour a very friendly patrolman arrived in a Ford Anglia van and sorted the problem out in no time.

And so that was that. The trip to the North York Moors was soon forgotten about and we returned to Bristol and carried on with our lives.

Only recently whilst sorting through some old colour slides did I come across one of railway interest. It showed some long-disused rusty railway tracks disappearing into a tunnel and through the tunnel can be seen a small signal box. Where could it be, I wondered. My first thought was that it was somewhere in Devon as I had toured many closed and nearly closed lines there in the mid-1960s. I was fairly certain it was near Bovey Tracey but despite an internet search I wasn't able to pin it down. Then one day everything 'fell in to place' and I realised where it was. It was Grosmont tunnel, photographed from the road through the village.

How the memories came flooding back! The railway from Pickering to Grosmont across the spectacular scenery of the North Yorkshire Moors. How closely my life had been intertwined with this line and how little had been written about that period of the railway's history. It seems hard to imagine now but e-mails and mobile phones were still twenty years away; computers were enormous and had air-conditioned buildings all to themselves; Railtrack, Network Rail and privately owned train operating companies were all in the future and the Middlesbrough to Whitby branch still had a weekly pick-up goods train. I resolved to do something about recording my experiences, which I hope the reader will find entertaining.

Bernard Warr
Market Rasen
Lincolnshire
April 2019.

CHAPTER 1

The First Visit

We drove into Newtondale Gorge from the Levisham village direction. This was new territory to me. Despite many years' interest in what we now call heritage railways I had not had the opportunity previously to visit the newly opened North Yorkshire Moors Railway. A family holiday for a week in Scarborough in early September 1975 provided the chance I had been waiting for.

The day was warm and sunny and big, fluffy, white clouds were scudding across the blue sky. In the family Morris Marina with me were my wife of six years, Wendy, and our children Jolyon, who was approaching four years old, and Samantha, who was just two.

Levisham station and the railway into Newtondale in September 1975. (Bernard Warr)

As far as Wendy was concerned the journey was being undertaken 'on sufferance' as a further example of her grudging support for my rather peculiar (in her view) interest in old steam trains. I had deliberately chosen to head for Levisham station as the starting point for our railway journey as the timetable I had picked up in our hotel showed only a diesel railcar service between Pickering (High Mill platform) and Levisham. I reasoned that we were here to sample a steam train, not something available every day on BR!

As we passed over the lip of the gorge, the whole vista of Newtondale opened up before us. Nothing can quite prepare for this first sighting – it was breathtaking. I pulled the car into the side on the narrow road and we looked down on this mighty gorge carved out of solid rock by millions of gallons of water thousands of years before. Like some miniature railway we could see Levisham station, the railcar from Pickering already standing at the Down platform. We watched as the signalman came out from his cabin and collected the single-line token from the driver and as the passengers disgorged on to the platform.

Way in the distance amongst the thick pine forests we could see a plume of steam from a large black engine. Presently the sound of its deep whistle reached our ears. Time to go. We drove down the winding, single-track road that went obliquely down the side of the cliff and round in a broad arc to face the railway.

Presently we came to the station and drove into the station yard. The engine whistle was becoming more urgent and louder now. We collected our flasks and sandwiches and made our way onto the same Down platform, now vacated by the railcar, which seemed to be standing and waiting a little way down the line towards Pickering, beyond the outer home signal.

'Black Five' No. 5428 rolls into Levisham station in September 1975. (Bernard Warr)

Then the steam engine was upon us. The great black beast glided slowly past and off the end of the platform until its last coach was clear of the level crossing. Strange, I thought, do all the trains on this railway carry advertisements? This one certainly did, an enormous circular sign with the words SKF Bearings emblazoned on it covering the whole of the smokebox door.

We boarded the nearest coach and arranged ourselves around a convenient table. Presently the engine passed on an adjacent track, making for the northern end of the train and its tender-first run to Grosmont. I noted the number 5428, a 'Black Five' of the former LMS Railway, now carrying the name *Eric Treacy*. I was pleased to see that we were to be hauled by an engine designed by Sir William Stanier. Although he had deserted the GWR (God's Wonderful Railway!) he turned into a disciple of good Swindon engineering practice as taught to him by the company for which I still have such an innate fondness.

The Down starting signal cleared, the guard's whistle blew and the driver acknowledged with a short deep hoot that only an LMS engine can do.

We moved slowly out of the station on to a long left-hand bend and into the pine forest. As we climbed up through Yorfalls Wood my mind drifted back to where this interest in old railways had started. I remembered a warm summer day back in 1966 and a ride out in a friend's car down a leafy Devon road.

I remembered coming upon the town of Buckfastleigh and pausing at the gated approach road to the long-closed railway station. The surprise of seeing Brunswick green engines and chocolate and cream coaches slumbering in the warm afternoon sunshine. My friend Nigel, whose car it was, was entranced. We got out to have a closer look.

The gate was padlocked but a notice proclaimed that this was the Dart Valley Railway Ltd. A smaller typewritten notice advised that the company intended to reopen the Totnes to Ashburton branch line as a tourist attraction and were looking for volunteers to help bring it back to life. Anyone interested in helping should write to Mr R. D. N. Salisbury, Hon. Sec. of the supporters' association. My interest was awakened and I made a note of the contact address.

I duly wrote to Mr Salisbury, paid my one guinea membership fee and became member ninety-seven of the fledgling Dart Valley Railway Association. I learnt that restoration working parties were held every Sunday and I decided to have a go. Another Sunday two weeks later found me alighting from the maroon and cream Devon General bus from Exeter and entering the Buckfastleigh station yard. I had been warned to dress in old clothes as the work tended to be 'physical' and dirty!

On arrival at the station I found a small gang of people waiting to start work who were in the charge of a grey-haired old gentleman whose accent had a rich Devon burr. He introduced himself as Ashley Burgess and explained that he was the recently retired British Railways Permanent Way Inspector from Totnes. He had been responsible for maintaining the branch when British Railways had been in charge and he was now a volunteer, keen to help get the trains running again.

He explained that the task for the day was to get the points working. It seemed they had lain derelict for four years since the last goods train had run and the moist Devon air had

Buckfastleigh station on the nascent Dart Valley Railway in April 1966, with engines and carriages in the yard and plenty of weeds to remove to get to the point rodding. (Bernard Mills)

caused the rods and cranks to rust up solid. When the various locomotives and carriages had been moved up the branch from Totnes the point rodding had had to be disconnected and the points moved with a crow-bar (which I now learnt was called a 'slewing-bar' in railway parlance) and then 'clamped' with a big, lockable 'G' clamp.

We set to work with a will, starting from the signal box and working outwards. The technique I learnt was to soak the crank pivot in a light oil, disconnect the rodding from each end of the crank and gently tap the crank arms alternately with a sledgehammer (being careful not to snap off the brittle cast-iron crank-arm). If this failed to produce a result, then a propane torch was produced and the pivot gently heated. More gentle tapping was usually enough to allow the crank to be moved and released from its pivot. It was then a simple matter of cleaning and greasing the components, reassembling them and moving on to the next crank.

At some point in the day we must have broken off for lunch but Ashley was a hard taskmaster and didn't let us sit around for long! At the end of that first day I suppose we must have dealt with about six or seven cranks and got thoroughly dirty in the process. There were no washing facilities then so I had to travel back on the Exeter bus as I was. Despite this I felt an extreme sense of having done something useful, something that would help bring this little railway back to life. I resolved to come again the next week.

The deep whistle of the Black Five interrupted my reverie and I watched as our train rolled over Kidstye Crossing, climbed out of the forest and, as the trees gave way to open ground with scrubby grass, marsh and fast-flowing streams, passed into Northdale.

I went back to the Dart Valley Railway many times in that far-off summer of 1966. The p-way gang that I seemed to have joined attended to all sorts of problems on and about the railway. We cut back the rampant undergrowth; we mended fences; we oiled fishplates; we hammered keys back in; we packed joints; we freed more point rods and cranks and we cut back the undergrowth again.

I don't think I realised it at the time but the interest that was growing in me, this respect for something built more than a hundred years before, the sheer engineering excellence that had gone into making even a simple branch line such as this, was to become an enduring passion that would change the whole direction of my life.

Unfortunately, my days of living in Devon were coming to an end. My employer, the National Provincial Bank, decided that my career as a banker would be helped if I moved to a larger branch. By the close of 1966 I was installed in their main branch in Bristol, some 80 miles away from the railway I had come to love.

Undeterred, I set about forming a support group for the Bristol area and was successively its secretary and then chairman. As a group, we organised many working parties to the railway and even on one occasion went to help the Great Western Society at Aschurch with stripping the paintwork on 0-6-2T No. 6697.

My involvement with railways took a serious turn in 1968 when I saw an advertisement in the *Bristol Evening Press* in the Situations Vacant column. 'British Railways, Bristol Division wishes to recruit a Technical Officer to assist in the maintenance of track and bridges'.

I had by then become convinced that banking was not a career that I could see myself following for the rest of my days. But this advertisement, well it raised the prospect of something altogether more interesting and satisfying. I rang for an application form.

Three weeks later saw me entering the Divisional Civil Engineers Offices to keep an interview appointment for the job. As I walked through the sun-bleached mahogany entrance doors my eyes lit up when I saw the mosaic on the floor – the pattern was the GWR Roundel as used on its coaches, locomotives, publicity and its buildings. The old company might have been swept away twenty years before but here I was coming for a job within the hallowed portals of Bristol Temple Meads station. The spirit of Brunel was all around me!

Eric Treacy disturbed my reverie once again as his deep whistle announced our arrival at Fen Bog, the point where the Lyke Wake Walk crosses the railway. I noted the remains of the loop at the summit of the line, where all trains had terminated before services were extended to Pickering. Our train rolled on through Moorgates in country that was less dramatic and gentler than we had seen so far.

My mind went back to that interview. There was a short wait, during which time I noted that unlike the offices of the Bank that I was used to, these were rather shabby and badly needed a fresh coat of paint. Presently I was shown into the office of R. T. Jones, who, I learnt from a notice on his office door, was the Assistant Divisional Engineer (Permanent Way).

R. T. Jones proved to be a man in his late fifties with thinning grey hair, a bushy grey moustache and an upright, military bearing. He wore a tweed suit that had seen plenty of use, I noted, as he welcomed me and put me at my ease.

'Now, tell me young man, why does anyone who has a good job with a bank want to come and work for a ramshackle organisation like British Railways?' he asked.

'Well actually, sir, [the Bank had taught me to be very respectful] I am quite interested in what you do here. For about the last three years I have been working as a volunteer on the Dart Valley Railway down in Devon.'

'And what sort of things have you been doing as a volunteer?'

'Mostly I have been working on the track dealing with all the regular routine maintenance. I have scraped paint off old bridges and re-tarred them and I have spent much time cutting back the trees and shrubs that grow profusely where we don't want them,' I responded.

'So if you've worked on the track, then you must know Ashley Burgess?'

'Oh yes sir, he taught me all I know!'

'What about Dick Dunwiddy and Bob Saunders?'

'Yes I know them both. Dick is the retired Stationmaster who still lives in Station House and organises much of the volunteer effort. Bob Saunders is a director of the Company, I've met him a few times but I don't know him that well.'

'You're probably wondering how I know these people; well, I used to be the District Engineer at Plymouth and the Ashburton Branch was on my "patch". Ashley was my Permanent Way Inspector at Totnes.'

I warmed to this man and was quite enjoying the turn that the interview was taking.

'So tell me more about what you have done on the track.'

I did, and we talked for perhaps three quarters of an hour. We talked about the Dart Valley Railway; about his career on the Great Western and British Railways; about our mutual acquaintances and finally, with a look at the clock on the wall, he said that he couldn't make any promises about the job but he would write to me when he had made his decision.

Within a week I received a letter inviting me for a medical examination and two months later, in July 1968, I became the newest employee of British Railways.

Eric Treacy came to a stand. I looked out of the window and noticed that we were alongside another track, obviously once the Down line, now a loop of some sort. Presently we set off again and rolled into a station, which the running-in board proclaimed to be Goathland. We had crossed over to the Down line platform and I noticed that in the Up line platform stood another train, presumably returning to Levisham and Pickering. A few people got off the train and with a blowing of whistles and a wave of the guard's green flag we resumed our journey. Now the scenery changed and became much more dramatic. The brakes came on almost as soon as we left Goathland to check our descent of the 1 in 49 gradient. We seemed to be perched on the side of a cliff as we crossed a deep ravine over the Eller Beck and passed through Darnholm, Thomason Foss and Beck Hole. After the cottages at Esk Valley the gradient eased and we rolled past a new locomotive depot and into the short Grosmont tunnel, coming to a stand on platform three of Grosmont station. This proved to be an interesting place; we waited on the platform to see the engine 'run round' the train. Bit of a surprise here as a line of washing was stretched across the 'back road' between the adjacent house and the station shelter. However, this was obviously a regular occurrence as a 'toot' from the loco whistle summoned the lady of the house, who promptly moved her washing line to let the engine pass. As *Eric Treacy* disappeared into the tunnel to replenish its tanks at the loco shed the washing was put back across the track.

Grosmont station stands at the junction of the Esk Valley line from Middlesbrough and the Whitby & Pickering Railway. In the 'V' of the junction stood a fine North Eastern Railway pattern signal box comprising a wooden superstructure, cantilevered out over the running lines, and standing on a brick base. It had become disused with the closure of the line to Pickering and was now in a sorry state. The closure had also resulted in simplification of the junction track layout with the result that the track on platform two had become a siding and at the end of it was a Gresley buffet car painted in green and cream. We made our way in to the coach for drinks and sandwiches.

Suitably refreshed we set out to walk through the old 'horse tunnel' to see the engine shed. This tunnel was the original, built to provide a single line of railway along which horses provided the motive power. We found it a bit dark and dingy inside with the occasional wet patch. As we emerged into the daylight again we were immediately confronted with the new engine shed that was still in course of construction. Beyond the shed was a row of workman's cottages and beyond this all manner of steam engines large and small with visitors able to walk amongst them at will. Needless to say, my wife's patience with this engine gazing was wearing thin and the rough cinder tracks were providing a steady stream of cinders in the children's shoes – time to make our way back to the station.

Another trip through the tunnel saw us back on the platform awaiting the return train to Levisham and, much to my wife's relief, the relative comfort of our hotel in Scarborough.

So, what had I learnt from this excursion? Was this new and undeveloped railway capable of exciting my passion for railways; could it fill the void left in my life by my recent relocation so far away from the Dart Valley Railway; was there an outlet here for my thirst for railway civil engineering? As we motored back to Scarborough I pondered these issues and decided that this new railway looked promising and I needed to investigate its potential further.

CHAPTER 2

Getting to know who's who

I wasted no time in joining the NYMR Preservation Society and I wrote a letter to the railway's offices in Pickering explaining my background in civil engineering and my experience as a volunteer bridge engineer and general civil engineering factotum to the Dart Valley Railway. For good measure, I mentioned my training as a guard and offered to help. I sat back to see what the reaction would be.

I didn't have to wait long; within a matter of days I received a very nice letter from Arthur Dytch, who was acting as General Manager for the fledgling railway. In it he thanked me for

High Mill Level Crossing in 1978. The car park was accessed by a gate to the left of the blue van. (Bernard Warr)

my interest and invited me to meet him at Pickering to discuss in more detail how I could best be deployed. Arthur Dytch was the former Assistant General Manager (Technical) of British Rail Eastern Region and upon his retirement had moved to Pickering. Somehow or other he had been persuaded to help with the management of this infant railway.

I drove up to Pickering for the meeting and upon arrival followed the signs to the car park, which was just on some rough ground north of the station, alongside the track, accessed by crossing the railway at High Mill level crossing.

The volunteer car park attendant directed me to a small path that led from the far corner of the car park to the station, crossing the Mill Stream Bridge on its way. I was very courteously received by Arthur Dytch and he suggested that we should adjourn to a carriage on platform two where we could talk undisturbed. There was no run-round facility in the station so the service train, a DMU, was using the platform nearest to the station building and platform two was being used as a siding. We talked for some time in this makeshift but very comfortable meeting room and concluded that I could be of most use to the railway as a civil engineer. He explained that the line's civil engineering needs were taken care of by Nigel Trotter, on a volunteer basis, and he was employed by British Rail in a similar capacity. He would arrange for Nigel to make contact. If I also wanted to help out as a guard, he explained that I would need to pass the guard's qualifying examination with an NYMR inspector as they couldn't rely on other railways' accreditation. He suggested I might like to contact the York Area Group, who ran regular training courses for guards. This all sounded very promising and I agreed to await contact from Nigel Trotter and contact the York Area Group directly to take matters forward.

Nigel duly made contact and we met up later the same month. A chartered civil engineer and former British Rail management trainee, he was working for the BR Regional Chief Civil Engineer in the Soil Mechanics section in York at that time. He had access to civil engineering records for the line going back many years and, in the time that he had been honorary civil engineer for the NYMR, had come to know the infrastructure well and could talk with authority on where the problems were to be found.

It became clear that with my background in railway bridge renewal and maintenance I could be of use in defining and organising future bridge maintenance needs. In the coming few months I learned that four bridges needed their waybeams renewing and within a couple of years an underbridge would probably need rebuilding.

The reader may be wondering what on earth a waybeam is. Victorian railway bridge designers were very adept at designing simple structures that supported the running lines on substantial longitudinal timbers (timber being cheap and plentiful). These timbers of square or rectangular shape and about 12 in. by 12 in. (300 mm square) sat either in a 'U' shaped trough girder or on cross girders attached to the main beams. The drawback to this arrangement was that even the best timbers tended to decay over time and after ten to fifteen years, new timbers were required. On the NYMR the run-down of maintenance activity in the final years of British Rail ownership led to several bridges needing replacement waybeams all at the same time.

Inspecting Bridge 15 in Newtondale in February 1976. (Bernard Warr)

The railbus stopped on Bridge 27 at Goathland whilst the inspection takes place. Although this inspection in February 1976 was on the pretext of including the bridge in a painting programme, the author is not aware that this was ever carried out. At the time of writing (March 2019) the bridge is scheduled for reconstruction. (Bernard Warr)

Bridge 30 was one of the largest structures on the railway and needed constant maintenance to keep it serviceable. Most of the load is carried on a central main girder beneath the deck level with transverse cross girders running under the track to the side girders. The timber waybeams carried the track over the cross girders. The bridge was rebuilt in 2010. (Bernard Warr)

CHAPTER 3

Getting my hands dirty

Having established myself in a civil engineering role on the railway, I was also interested in re-engaging with train operations by carrying on from where I had left off with the Dart Valley Railway and becoming a qualified NYMR Guard.

Arthur Dytch had made it very clear that to be an NYMR Guard I would need to pass an examination with their inspector. Enquiries revealed that a guards' training course was about to start in March 1976. I signed up for that and started attending the sessions. These proved to be a bit irregular in nature but they did include a session away from the

Watching the signalman at work in a modern (for 1976) box controlling York yard. (Bernard Warr)

classroom looking at the more hands-on side of the work. This was undertaken in York and a group of four of us were put through our paces on buckeye couplers, use of the brake stick and the shunting pole. We were also able to visit two signal boxes:

We were also privileged to be shown inside the main York Station power signal box opened in 1951, which had replaced seven mechanical boxes. Inside, it had a hushed cathedral like atmosphere with subdued lighting, which allowed the illuminated track display to dominate. As with all railway technology things moved on and by 1989 the power box was replaced by the IECC (Integrated Electronic Control Centre), which in turn was replaced in December 2018 by the York ROC (Rail Operating Centre).

There followed further practical training on NYMR trains and the course culminated in passing the guards' inspector on Sunday 23 May.

Whilst I had been following the guards' training I could not but pick up on the general air of gloom that seemed to have descended on the railway. I tried to find out what had caused this and it seemed to relate to the financial position. The previous year's results had been disappointing; in fact, there had been a small loss. There was considerable uncertainty about the NYMR's ability to continue to operate the full line to Pickering and many felt that a railway from Grosmont to the summit at Eller Beck was a more sustainable option. To improve financial liquidity certain items of stock were put up for sale.

The view inside the York Power Box showing the track display screens and the operator's console. This 1951 box was at the time one of the largest route-relay interlockings in the world, with its relay room 46 metres long by 10 metres wide, containing nearly 3,000 relays. (Bernard Warr)

To relieve some of the pressure on Arthur Dytch in his honorary role as General Manager the Trust Council decided to appoint a Line Manager and set about seeking suitable candidates. Unfortunately, this came too late and on 7 April Arthur Dytch wrote to Richard Rowntree, the Trust Chairman, and resigned his position as General Manager. His dissatisfaction with most of the departmental heads wasn't generally known at the time but his inability to get them to perform as managers and to get volunteers to be able to see the bigger picture led to his disillusionment.

The search for a Line Manager was successful and John Besford took up the responsibilities of the new post from 3 May. The lack of suitable office accommodation at Pickering station resulted in the purchase of a Portakabin, which was sited at the northern end of the up platform.

The new Pickering office 'suite' located at the north end of the station by Bridge 7 over the Mill Stream. The building contained two individual offices with a reception area between them. (Bernard Warr)

Pickering fuel supplies – water for steam engines in the United Molasses tank and red diesel (with supply pipes to fit both the DMUs and the Class 24) in the Mex Fuel Oil tanker. (Bernard Warr)

During the winter of 1975/76 a new turnout was laid at the south end of the station to allow locomotives to be able to run round their trains. Storage for water and diesel fuel was also provided by means of two tank wagons.

Also made available from Easter 1976 were two camping coaches at Goathland. They had originally been DMU buffet cars but were converted to provide accommodation for four adults in two compartments and up to four children in a further compartment. Cooking was by Calor gas and hot water fed the shower, kitchen and toilet. These proved to be a popular attraction and quickly booked up, providing an additional income stream for the railway's struggling finances.

Having passed the guards' exam, I suddenly found that my services were much in demand. John Hardy, the Grosmont stationmaster, was responsible for rostering guards and I agreed to let him roster me for one day each alternate weekend. I would have liked to do more but with my wife's view of my railway activities I had to strike a delicate balance to keep the peace!

Most of my turns were on trains starting from Pickering and these were mostly on the DMU. NYMR owned two-car Class 100 sets built by the Gloucester Railway Carriage & Wagon Company. There seemed to be reliability problems with these sets and we were sometimes down to a single operational two-car set. When things got bad the Class 24 Diesel loco was provided to haul the two sets as a normal train.

Working as a guard I came into contact with many more people. DMU drivers I had already met in different capacities were Dick Oxlade, Frank Carrington and Les Barwick and new faces (to me) were Bill Smith, Andy Teasdale and Dave Birtles. I was also rostered

The south end of Pickering station showing the new (in 1976) connection between the Up and Down lines to facilitate a locomotive running round its train. Beyond the buffer stop the line originally crossed Bridge Street and the new Council car park and carried on to Rillington Junction and Malton. (Bernard Warr)

A general view of Goathland, in May 1977, looking north. The two camping coaches are in the centre of the picture behind the tarpaulin-covered engine. (Bernard Warr)

to work from both Goathland and Grosmont on other occasions and worked with many of the steam crews including Chris Cubitt, Mick Hewitt, Andy Newman, Ian Storey, Norman Ash and Kevin Gould.

Trains arriving and departing from Pickering had to negotiate two sets of level crossing gates each way. Neither set of gates was controlled by a signal box so the train guard was required to open the gates to let the train through and then close them again after the train had gone over the crossing. High Mill crossing, just north of the station, was very quiet and had only a single pair of gates to open but New Bridge Level Crossing, about another 1,000 yards on, comprised a pair of very substantial wooden gates across a road busy with lorries to and from the nearby quarry. Stopping this flow of traffic to close the gates was not appreciated by the lorry drivers!

Things were easier when there were plenty of volunteers about and if the guard was lucky both crossings could be manned and the train wouldn't need to stop. Contrast that with a quiet Wednesday in October when hardly anybody was about. Levisham Signal Box would be 'switched out' so the railway from Pickering to Goathland would be worked as 'one engine in steam' (OES). At Goathland there would be a signalman, usually Tony Hart, and the same at Grosmont in the form of John Hardy. Apart from them and a few passengers it was quite a lonely place!

The hot summer of 1976 had taken its toll on steam train operation. With the moorland tinder-dry by the beginning of the summer holidays, operating steam trains south of Goathland was impossible because the risk of a serious and extensive moorland fire was too great. During the weekday operations, the DMU and the railbus operated between

Pickering and Goathland with a steam service between Goathland and Grosmont. To keep services running on the busiest day of the week, Sunday, a Class 08 shunter was hired from BR. Class 08 locomotives are not designed to run at the NYMR line speed of 25 mph. 15 mph is about the best they can do and so the timetable had to be adjusted accordingly. Unfortunately, on 1 August the 08 broke down in remotest Newtondale and had to be rescued by a steam engine. After this the railway decided that the 08s weren't up to the job and for the next two weekends a DMU was hired from BR, but this was expensive. Then, in early August the railway got lucky and discovered a serviceable Class 24 locomotive in a scrapyard in Stockton. Urgent discussions involving BR and the scrapyard owner, Mr Turner, cleared the way for the engine to come to the NYMR, initially on a free loan. Loco No. 24032 arrived at Grosmont under its own power shortly afterwards.

By the end of the year the financial position had deteriorated further and a loss of around £20,000 was expected. The blame was placed on the long hot summer keeping tourists on the coast and preventing steam operation south of Goathland. Other factors were the cost of hiring the 08 and the DMUs from BR and the high maintenance costs of the NYMR-owned DMUs. By January 1977 some coaches had been sold and the under restoration standard tank No. 80135 was sold to a member who promised to fund the remainder of the restoration and to keep it on the railway in a deal that was worth about £10,000 to the NYMR.

The new loco, No. 24032 (aka D5032), at Pickering shortly after its arrival on the NYMR in August 1976. This loco has many times been described as the engine that saved the railway from collapse by being available to keep services running over the fire-prone moors when steam engines were not safe to use. (Bernard Warr)

BR Standard Class 4MT 2-6-4T No. 80135 was sold to Jos de Crau, a benefactor of the NYMR, in 1977. (Bernard Warr)

The North Yorkshire County Council, who had part-funded the extension of the line right through to Pickering, decided to take a hand and commissioned a study into the viability of the venture, asking the consultants (Coopers & Lybrand) to recommend a way forward for the charity. The cost of the study (about £20,000) was to be shared between the County Council, the Countryside Commission, the English Tourist Board and the NYMR. The report was to be available later in 1977.

As far as civil engineering was concerned I joined the regular Sunday working parties that met in Pickering at 09.30 hrs. The task for the winter was to undertake a large re-sleepering project in Newtondale. 1,000 chaired concrete sleepers had been purchased and laid out lineside ready for installation. The task of the Sunday gang was to drive out the keys, tip out the rails, lift out the old wooden sleepers, lay in the replacement concrete sleepers, re-rail, ballast and restore and level the line. There were no mechanical aids to help us and it all had to be done by hand. A large workforce was essential as it took eight people to lift and carry one concrete sleeper! Muscles were a bit achey on Monday morning!

On Saturday and Sunday 11 and 12 December 1976 a party of officer cadets from RAF Henlow in Bedfordshire arrived on the railway to gain experience of working on a project as a team. The project agreed with the RAF was the replacement of the timber waybeams on Bridge 15 in Newtondale. The party arrived on the Friday evening and were accommodated in carriages in Pickering station with the buffet car being used for catering purposes. The area was at its wintery best with a thin layer of snow on the ground. They must have had good sleeping bags because, despite the cold, they were all very cheerful when the party left Pickering on Saturday morning.

On arrival at the site the cadets got their first taste of the sheer weight and size of railway engineering and the tools that go with it. First task was to remove the rails, so keys were knocked out, fishplates unfastened, put on one side and the rails tipped out. By lunchtime the chairs had been unfastened and the old waybeams removed. The deteriorating state of these timbers meant that they were difficult to remove in one piece and after the larger pieces had been carried away, shovels were needed to remove the remainder. An inspection of the metalwork revealed that the bridge was in quite good order so fitting of the new waybeams was started in the afternoon. It took ten cadets to lift each waybeam and care had to be exercised on the icy bridge deck as the timbers were carried in. Each timber needed a certain amount of trimming to ensure a snug fit against the cross-girders but by 16.00 hrs, when work stopped due to failing light, three of the six timbers were in place.

The party was back on site by 09.30 on the Sunday morning and the remaining three waybeams were fitted and in place by lunchtime. The chairs and the track were refitted in the afternoon and although fog was starting to close in the cadets could see their handiwork tested when the Class 24 arrived to run over the bridge.

The weekend was judged a great success by the RAF and the NYMR and it was hoped that it might be the first of many visits.

CHAPTER 4

On becoming a Driver

The NYMR owned two-car Diesel Multiple Units (DMUs), latterly BR class 100. They were constructed by the Gloucester Railway Carriage & Wagon Company in 1958. The four vehicles were 50341/56099 and 56097/51118 and were classified as Driving Trailer Composite Lavatory (DTCL) vehicles 56097 and 56099 and Driving Motor Brake Second (DMBS) vehicles 50341 and 51118.

In early February 1977, a note was circulated amongst the Pickering guards inviting those with at least two seasons' experience as a guard to consider training as DMU drivers. Training would start at the end of February. I had only one season's service as a guard on the NYMR but had several years guarding behind me on the Dart Valley Railway. In addition, a DMU driver was needed on most Sundays in the winter months to take the p-way gang out to their relaying site. As I counted myself a regular member of this gang I thought it would be useful if I could be trained as a driver. I approached Norman Ash and persuaded him of my case and he agreed to my joining the course.

This started on Sunday 27 February and was held in the lobby behind the Down platform in Pickering station. Chris Cubitt was there to teach us and I suppose there must have been about six of us in the group. The first two Sundays were concerned with the rule book and the components of a DMU. As we were all guards and had already passed the rules exam, the rules session was superficial and covered the differences between what we were used to and what was expected of a driver.

The second Sunday introduced us to the driver's controls, the components of the DMU and fault-finding. We were taught the principles of the epicyclic gearbox and fluid flywheel; how the diesel engine worked and the theory of the vacuum brake. We were taken round to the workshop further down platform 2 where a recently overhauled engine was on test. It was started up for us and run up. We were also able to see a stripped down gearbox and see at first-hand what we had been learning the theory of.

From the third Sunday onwards we were taken out for some practical training 'on the road'. At the end of this we given an individual assessment as to our suitability for the task. Fortunately, I was deemed fit to take the qualifying exam, which was to take place on Saturday 23 April.

I duly reported to Norman Ash in Pickering station at 09.00 hrs on 27 April. Here I learnt that the rostered driver had been given the morning off and it was up to me to prepare the set and drive it to Grosmont. I walked round the train and did the checks as I had been taught and then set about starting the engines. Everything, for once, worked as it should and I soon had both engines running and air pressure building up nicely. As departure time approached I settled myself in the driver's seat, depressed the Driver's Safety Device (DSD) on the throttle handle and raised the vacuum to 15 inches ready for a smooth departure. Norman took up his position on the secondman's seat where he could keep a close eye on what I was up to. Two beats on the buzzer from the guard was my starting signal, after a quick check that the single line token hadn't grown legs and 'walked', I engaged first gear, opened the throttle, released the brake and responded to the guard's signal with two beats of my own. We moved steadily out of the station and for once the gates at both High Mill and New Bridge were manned so I didn't need to stop.

On the approach to Levisham we were stopped for a few moments at the Down outer home signal awaiting the arrival of the southbound service from Grosmont. With this safely in the Up platform the signal cleared and I was able to drive into the station, stopping in front of the Down starter signal. With the token exchanged I could set off again and climb up through Newtondale, having to drop down to third gear for the steepest part. Soon we were past the summit of the line and rolling down past Moorgates and were given a clear run into Goathland station. Another token exchange and then the steep descent towards Grosmont. Heavy braking needed here to keep the train speed within the 25 mph limit. Presently we passed through Grosmont tunnel and rolled into platform 3 of Grosmont station. Norman had kept pretty quiet throughout the journey and after we had changed ends he announced that he would leave me to my own devices for the return journey and ride in the coach behind me.

Setting off from Grosmont with only me in the cab was a new experience. Any questions that arose or decisions needed would be mine and mine alone so I started the ascent of the 1 in 49 bank with some trepidation. However, the experience gained during training took over and after recognising that second gear was the best that could be achieved for most of the journey to Goathland, we were soon coming to a stand at that station's Up starting signal. The rest of the journey to Pickering was uneventful and as I came to a stand at the southern terminus, Norman came back into the cab, congratulated me on passing and asked me when I was available to drive!

No time was wasted in beginning my driving career. I quickly arranged a day's leave for the following Tuesday and spent the day thoroughly enjoying myself driving Diagram P1, which involved three round trips from Pickering to Grosmont.

The countryside was at its springtime best; the sun was shining and we were the only train active on the railway so no hold-ups.

I worked about fifteen driving turns in 1977 nearly all with two, three or four-car DMUs. The reference to Pickering Diagram P1 brings to mind the next time I was rostered for this turn was not until the autumn, Wednesday 19 October to be precise. I arrived at Pickering

Looking rather pleased with himself, the author is seen with one of the Gloucester RCW DMUs in Pickering station shortly after 'passing out' as a driver. (BW Collection)

just after 09.00 hrs as usual to begin preparing the set but instead of a DMU in the platform I found the single-car railbus, W79978. I set about preparing it for use and soon had the engine started. The cab was a bit small and could only be accessed from the interior of the vehicle, not a problem when all passengers had seats but, as I was to find later in the day, a bit difficult to get to when the coach had standing passengers.

The real surprise came after we had departed Pickering. I drove it as I would the DMU but whilst that was somewhat underpowered, the railbus was just the opposite. It took off like a scalded cat as the throttle was opened and I was soon having to shut off the power to keep within the line speed limit of 25 mph. I learnt that Brian Crouch had spent some time rewiring and refurbishing the vehicle and it was now akin to a sports car in the performance that was available. It certainly made easy work of climbing the 1 in 49 up from Grosmont. The only drawback was the seating capacity and at less than fifty seats some standing was inevitable, even on a low-season day such as this.

Another notable turn came on Wednesday 10 August when I was rostered as a secondman on the Class 24, D5032, with a view to driver training. I was keen to learn to drive the 'big' diesel and had badgered the 'powers that be' unmercifully and eventually had been given some instruction books to learn and was now being rostered as a 'secondman' to gain experience. Unfortunately, at weekends, when I normally volunteered, being rostered as a secondman meant that I was much more likely to find myself coupling and uncoupling the engine rather than learning to drive, simply because the rostered driver was also a volunteer and was reluctant to give up his turn, or part of it, to a trainee.

The railway was reasonably well placed for volunteers at weekends but it was a different matter on weekdays. Most days a full-time member of staff had to drive. I reckoned that I would have a much better chance of getting behind the controls with someone who was doing the job day in and day out. I resolved to take a day off from my job and volunteer on a weekday. I duly signed on at Pickering station and waited for the rostered driver to arrive. When he did I was alarmed to see that he was another volunteer – so much for my theory! However, he let me check around and start up the engine, uncouple it from the south end of the train and work the ground frame to enable him to drive it on to the north end, where I coupled it back on to the carriages. Although somewhat disappointed that I still wasn't at the controls, I had overlooked the fact that the peculiarities of the timetable made it essential for the Pickering driver to change sets during the day so as to be driving the last train of the day into Pickering.

This changeover took place at Levisham on the first train of the day so twenty minutes into the day my fellow volunteer driver left the Class 24 to spend the rest of the day driving the DMU. I waited with 'baited breath' to see who would be taking over. It turned out to be Dick Oxlade, the building foreman.

'Aye up Bernard! What are you sitting there for?' he barked as he climbed into the cab and saw me sitting on the secondman's seat.

'I'm learning to drive the Class 24.'

'Hmm... well you won't learn much sitting there, better get in the driver's seat.'
I climbed across to the driver's seat – it was finally happening! I was getting to drive the Class 24!

No time for any nerves now because at that moment the signalman appeared at the cab window with the single-line token for the Levisham–Goathland section. I took it from him, read the inscription and gave it to Dick, who hung it on a convenient hook on the bulkhead.

'Don't touch the engine brake but release the train brake,' he instructed.

'Move the reverser to 'FOR' and make sure your foot is on the 'deadman's' pedal' he continued. I did as he said. At that moment, the guard's whistle sounded and I put my head out of the cab window to see the green flag and acknowledge his signal. I checked the down starter, noted it was 'off' and put my head back inside.

'Rightaway,' I said.

'Move the throttle to REV'. I thought we wanted to go forwards – oh I see what he means, no graduations on the throttle arc but as it used the same quadrant as the reverser it was convenient to use the directional marks. I did as he said – nothing happened.

'It's not moving!'

'Try taking the engine brake off,' he laughed. I did as he said and after a moment the train started to move. This is it, I thought. At last I'm driving the 'big' diesel!

Once we had left Levisham station limits I was able to open the throttle some more and listen to the throaty roar of the Sulzer diesel engine as we climbed up into the forest. On we went past Yorfalls Wood and into Newtondale, climbing all the time. As we approached the

Photographed on 25 September 1977 are (left to right) Bert Kemmenoe, Steve Dew and Martin Foster. Bert was there to gain experience as a trainee driver, Steve was the train guard and the author was the rostered driver. (Bernard Warr)

summit of the line at Eller Beck our speed increased so I shut the throttle and we coasted all the way to the Goathland outer home signal, keeping the speed in check using the train brake. The signal cleared and we gently rolled down to the inner home signal, where we stopped, uncoupled from our train, moved forward to the Up platform and coupled up to a Pickering-bound train ready to return.

Dick let me drive all day and I have never forgotten the thrill of handling that mainline diesel for the first time.

Despite this enjoyable first taste of 'big' diesel driving it was not until the following January that I was able to start formal training and I was finally passed as fit to drive the type on 15 April 1978 at Grosmont.

With the coming of the end of the operating season our attention turned to track maintenance once again. Considerable numbers of 'chaired' concrete sleepers had been purchased through the summer and with the beginning of the 'close' season these were laid out on the lineside ready for installation. By the end of January 1978, 1,000 sleepers had been installed in the Milepost 16 area and work started on changing 1,500 sleepers round the Kingthorpe reverse curves. This latter task was completed in late March just before trains were due to start running again.

The Coopers & Lybrand report into the feasibility of the NYMHRT, commissioned by the North Yorkshire County Council, was received in the autumn of 1977. The contents were not widely communicated to those of us working on the 'front line' and probably

Class 24 diesel D5032 arriving at Pickering with a train from Grosmont in April 1978. Note the colour light signals waiting to be erected each side of the line. (Bernard Warr)

with good reason. The report was critical of several areas, including governance, general management, lack of engineering expertise amongst senior management, commercial management, operating capacity, susceptibility to major engineering failure of diesel traction, lack of cohesion between the commercial department and marketing, financial management and long-term financial (particularly capital) planning.

The report praised what had been achieved so far, the funding that had been raised, the enormous input of volunteers and the contribution to the economy of the region. If the railway was to survive and grow urgent action needed to be taken without delay. The report included a twenty-five-point plan of areas where urgent improvement was needed. Very near the top of this list was the need to recruit a suitably qualified and experienced Chief Executive with 'his role, authority and responsibility ... clearly defined.'

At the very top of the list was the recommendation that: 'Steps should be taken to improve the committee and management structure of the Trust along the lines suggested by the Consultants, particularly by the creation of a Railway Board with sub-committees responsible for specific activities.'

Little was heard about any reorganisation of the Trust Council but one aspect of the twenty-five-point plan that was taken on board was the need to find some permanent back-up for the unreliable DMUs. John Bellwood, Chief Mechanical Engineer at the NRM, was approached about the possibility of help with the problem. I learnt from Nigel Trotter

Lunch break on a typical Sunday's re-sleepering at Kingthorpe in March 1978. A good turnout of volunteers with rails tipped back in and the steel keys laid on the sleeper ends ready to be driven in to the chairs. (Allan Birkin P. Way archive NYMR)

in January 1978 that the NRM were amenable to this request and were planning to lend the NYMR their preserved 'toffee apple' Class 31 diesel, D5500. As I was then being trained as a diesel driver I looked forward very much to being able to drive this new 'acquisition'. The loco, I learnt, was likely to arrive after Easter when the NRM had fitted new batteries. D5500 duly arrived on Friday 7 April, two weeks after Easter. In addition, the Management Committee had held discussions with the owner of the Class 52 diesel-hydraulic loco D1048 *Western Lady* and at their meeting on 18 February 1978 agreed they were prepared to enter into an operating agreement for him to bring the loco to the line.

CHAPTER 5

Rebuilding Bridge 10
at Farwath

Earlier, mention has been made of the condition of Bridge 10, where the railway crosses the Pickering Beck at 10m 36c. In January 1978, I was invited to a meeting in York to discuss the organisation of the reconstruction of this bridge with Nigel Trotter and Roger Bastin. As I had undertaken this type of work on many occasions, during my time with British Railways, I was asked if I would take on the role of Resident Engineer and organise the whole of the site work. I readily agreed to this proposal and was assured that all would be ready for the work to be undertaken during March, before the 1978 season began.

Unfortunately for the bridge reconstruction, the company selected to cast the concrete beams let us down badly on the delivery date. Instead of being able to carry out the reconstruction in March, as we had planned, we were dismayed to find that casting of the concrete beams didn't take place until March, so to allow sufficient time for the concrete to 'cure' and reach its full strength we had to postpone the work until May. We decided to undertake the main reconstruction over two days (18 and 19 May), which would mean that no trains would be able to run between Levisham and Pickering during the blockade. To facilitate this, we also needed an occupation the previous Friday, 12 May, to unload the concrete girders and remove the parapet girders and walkways. Fridays were selected as the best days to do the work because there was no timetabled services on these days at that time of year.

On Thursday 4 May, the BR 'pick-up' goods train delivered two wagons containing the concrete bridge beams for Bridge 10. These were tripped up to Goathland and the following Sunday I drove up to inspect them and check them for dimensional compliance. All was well.

For a railway that had only been open for five years the NYMR could call on significant plant and equipment from its own resources, which served us well in this project. The main lifting and placing of the beams was to be undertaken by the 25-ton steam crane, already on an extended loan to us, from the NRM in York. Also available and based at Pickering was

Safely stored in the Goathland 'depot' siding on the downside, these are the new concrete beams for Bridge 10. The two parapet upstand beams are nearest the camera and the two centre beams can be seen in the next wagon. Sunday 7 May 1978. (Bernard Warr)

NYMR crane power 1978-style! On the left is the Grosmont-based NRM 25-ton steam crane, formerly the Middlesbrough breakdown crane, and on the right is the 5-ton diesel crane from Pickering. (Bernard Warr)

a 5-ton diesel powered rail crane, normally used for handling concrete sleepers. To provide enough man-power to undertake the job we had to rely on the MPD at Grosmont and the regular permanent way gang.

To ensure that everybody knew what was expected of them, I drove to Pickering on Wednesday 10 May, met up with Les Barwick and caught the train through to Grosmont where Kim Malyon (new shed master) and Dick Oxlade (our in-house builder) joined us for a final briefing on the two occupations. We 'ironed out' the last-minute questions and I felt at the end of it that everyone was as well briefed as they could be.

On Friday 11 May, I drove to Levisham station and met up with the works train that had come through from Grosmont. The Class 31, D5500, was in charge and had the two wagons of concrete beams and the 25-ton steam crane in the consist.

I took up a possession of the line from Levisham to Pickering at 09.30 hrs and, once the loco had run round the train and we had shunted the crane match truck to the north end of the crane, we set off to propel the train to the site. On the face of it the task for the day was quite straightforward – remove the timber walkways and parapet girders, store them safely for re-use and then off-load the new concrete bridge beams. As with so much railway work of the period, we were still using Victorian methods of working and Victorian equipment to do it with! So, having arrived on site we placed the first wagon containing the two deck beams on the bridge and set up the crane to lift them out.

Friday 12 May 1978, D5500 arrives at Levisham with the works train and prepares to 'run-round' and propel the train to the site at Farwath, about 2 miles towards Pickering. Steam crane seems to be burning some 'smokey' coal! (Bernard Warr)

With the first wagon on the bridge the crane's outriggers are packed with timber to reduce the load on the track and keep it stable when slewing. (Bernard Warr)

Preparing to lift out the first parapet girder. (Bernard Warr)

The 25-ton steam crane lifts out the first of the concrete deck beams and places it on the waiting temporary timber bed. (Bernard Warr)

The first of the upstand concrete beams is lifted out of the wagon and placed across the bridge opening to provide a temporary walkway. (Bernard Warr)

With the first beams lifted out, we then had to reform the train and return to Levisham to shunt the second wagon to be next to the crane before returning to the site to offload the two outer upstand beams.

With these two beams off-loaded the day's work was done and we were able to reform the train and despatch it back to Grosmont. I was able to give up the occupation just after 7 pm.

Work started up again on the following Wednesday when Les Barwick took up the occupation of the Pickering to Levisham section and despatched the 5-ton diesel crane to site (it was a very slow mover!). I drove to Levisham the following morning and joined up with the works train that had come through from Grosmont. It had been intended that two hoppers of ballast should have been delivered by the pick-up goods to Grosmont, but this didn't happen for some reason and ballast had to be delivered by road to Pickering, where it was transhipped into five-plank wagons and brought up to site by the Pickering shunter, Stanton No. 44. Both trains were on site by 10.00 hrs and work commenced.

After setting up the steam crane, the first job was to remove the rails and waybeams and then fit closure rails to allow the crane to get as close to the bridge as possible. In no time at all the old bridge was being lifted out.

The next task was to lower the concrete bedstones to accommodate the greater thickness of the concrete bridge deck. The two cranes made short work of lifting the concrete beams out and a single course of masonary was removed from each abutment.

The old bridge deck is lifted out on Thursday 18 May 1978, prior to being cut up for scrap. (Bernard Warr)

Bedstone removed from the Pickering abutment (resting on railhead above) and a course of stonework removed. (Bernard Warr)

Rebedding the concrete bedstone on the cut-down Levisham abutment. (Bernard Warr)

With the evening shadows lengthening, the first of the centre beams is craned in. (Bernard Warr)

With all four beams in place the final job for the crane (and for the day) was to replace the parapet girders. The Up-side girder was tackled first. (Bernard Warr)

With both the bedstones re-bedded at their new level a hard rubber bearing strip was glued to each one ready for the new concrete beams to be laid on them. By now we were well into the evening but there was a determination to get the bridge in place before dark.

As darkness fell I rode on the materials train back to Levisham, where I collected my car, drove to Goathland and spent the night in the volunteers' sleeping coach. Up at 06.30 hrs the following morning, I met the works train coming up from Grosmont. Norman Ash was driving and he asked me if I would take my car through to Pickering so that I, rather than he, could take the Class 24 back to Pickering from Grosmont after the works train had been returned. I agreed and went to Pickering to ride up to site with Les Barwick on the shunter.

We were all on site by about 09.45 and spent the morning waterproofing the bridge deck and building ballast retaining walls at the bridge ends. In the afternoon, we replaced the track and ballasted it by hand.

By 17.30 hrs the members of the team from Grosmont had finished their allotted tasks and I joined Norman Ash on the footplate of D5032 and returned the works train to Grosmont. I brought the loco back to site 'light engine', arriving at about 19.00 hrs. The track-work was finished by 22.00 hrs and I returned to Levisham with the loco to drop off some members of the p-way gang who had their cars there. At the time that I had set off for Levisham, the Pickering works train headed for home followed by the 5-ton crane. As this was such a slow machine I had to proceed cautiously as I headed for Pickering but I eventually caught it up just before New Bridge crossing where Les was waiting with the

Ballasting the bridge deck by hand whilst Nigel Trotter enjoys a refreshing cup of tea! Note the first of the brick ballast walls by Nigel's feet. (Bernard Warr)

The track is now reinstated across the bridge and the remaining ballast awaits unloading. The Pickering shunter, Stanton No. 44, just gets into the picture. (Bernard Warr)

works train. We crossed over together and made our sedate way in to the station. The track possession was given up just after 11 pm and I drove my car back through Levisham and stayed the night at Kidstye Farm with Neil and Libby McDonald. I drove home the following morning.

The successful completion of a civil engineering project like Bridge 10 was a great morale booster and showed us what we were capable of when we put our minds to it and all pulled together. John Besford, the acting General Manager, was quick to write to me and congratulate me on the success and the punctuality of the project. This was much appreciated.

CHAPTER 6

The search for a Chief Executive

With the opening of the 1978 operating season I found myself being regularly called upon to drive the DMUs from Pickering and even though Richard Munn, a new technician was being employed, their reliability left much to be desired and it was rare to have an operable 4-car set. After I was passed to drive the Class 24 things improved and more often than not I was finding this loco attached to the DMUs.

In March the position of the new Chief Executive was advertised widely. I felt that with my management background and my knowledge of the NYMR, I was ideal for the job (well I would, wouldn't I?). I applied and received a very encouraging response from the President of the Trust, Lord Downe. It seems, however, that the other 150 applicants also got the same response. After two months' delay I received a further letter from Richard Rowntree, Chairman of the Trust, advising me that I hadn't been shortlisted. I didn't have much time to think about this outcome as the letter came the day I started on the reconstruction of Bridge 10. What he didn't say was that prior to this letter being written, the Trust Council on 29 April had agreed to offer the post to a 41-year old applicant, married and although 'not a professional railwayman but has an interest in Railways and a most excellent record in the engineering industry'. (Quotation is from the Management Committee Newsletter No. 46, May 1978.) When he told his wife that they were about to move to Pickering so that he could take up his new job, she is reported to have refused point-blank. This was a bit of a set-back for the new CEO and upon reflection he decided to refuse the offer.

The Sunday after the Bridge 10 reconstruction, I was driving the Class 24 again and had Steve Dew as guard. Unusually, I was rostered to have a secondman with me but such sexist titles were not appropriate and second person would have been more apt. My second person turned out it to be Rosemary Beasley, a member of the Trust Council, who was already a qualified guard and was now starting to make the moves to become a driver. In her capacity as a guard I had worked with her regularly. I don't think her presence on the engine was altogether coincidental. We had a two-hour layover in Goathland and Rosemary quizzed me on my application for the CEO post and in particular was I still interested? I confirmed that I was.

Things started to gain momentum from that point on. I was driving the Class 24 again on Tuesday 30 May and had Norman Ash as my secondman and Rosemary Beasley as guard. I learnt that Bill Smith (or Captain W. G. Smith VRD RNVR to give him his full title), another Trust Council member and man of influence in NYMR matters, was keen to speak to me. I gave Rosemary my home telephone number to pass on. I duly spoke to him in the evening and he was very enthusiastic and thought that many Trust Council members would back my appointment. He asked to see copies of the correspondence that had passed between Lord Downe, Richard Rowntree and myself. I posted these the following day.

At 10 pm the following evening I received a telephone call from Richard Rowntree inviting me to attend for an interview the next Sunday afternoon at Wycombe Estate Office. I readily agreed.

After this my home telephone seemed to get very busy! Bill Smith rang the next evening to say that he had spent four days trying to get hold of Lord Downe and had just succeeded in tracking him down. He told me that he had spent half an hour putting my case across. I told him that I had been invited for interview, which he was pleased about, but his worry was that the people on the interviewing panel were not of his choosing and couldn't be relied upon! He gave me some tips for dealing with them.

On the Friday Bill Smith rang me four times at the office to give me hints and tips on what I might be asked and how to respond. On the Saturday, I was rostered for the Class 24 from Pickering with Chris Cubitt as secondman and Rosemary Beasley as guard. We seemed to spend every spare moment discussing the interview and even what we needed to do once I had got the job! After I had got home Bill Smith rang again and then on the Sunday morning to say that he had been speaking to Richard Rowntree, who shared the news that there were no other suitable candidates and therefore, in Bill's words, 'the job was mine for the taking'!

Wykeham Estate Office proved to be the former LNER Wykeham station on the Scarborough to Pickering railway, closed to passengers in 1950. It seemed to me to be a very appropriate place to be interviewed for a railway manager's job and I duly turned up just before 3 pm. The interview panel comprised Lord Downe (President), Richard Rowntree (Trust Chairman), Nigel Trotter (NYMR Volunteer Civil Engineer), Richard Whiteman (NYMR volunteer driver) and Les Barwick (NYMR volunteer permanent way inspector). The interview lasted about one and a half hours and ranged across many aspects of the railway, particularly safety and operations. I had expected to be quizzed on strategic and tactical management issues but little was forthcoming on these issues. The most incisive questioning came from Lord Downe. By 16.30 the interview was over and I was told that the Chairman would be in touch.

Later that evening Richard Rowntree rang to say that the panel were unanimous in recommending my appointment as Chief Executive to a special Trust Council meeting that had been arranged for 25 June. In a somewhat euphoric state I rang Bill Smith and told him the news. He professed to be 'over the moon and hadn't felt so happy about NYMR affairs in a long time'. I had to admit to being pleased myself!

CHAPTER 7

Into the 'Whirlwind' of managing the railway

Where to begin!

The NYMR was clearly in a mess financially; it lost £20,000 in 1976 and had just about broken even in 1977. To try and make ends meet some items of rolling stock had been sold, including coaches and BR Class 4MT 2-6-4T No. 80135, the only steam engine that it owned. Fortunately, the purchaser of these items had agreed to keep them on the railway and had taken over the financing of the locomotive's restoration up to a certain limit. In 1978

Basking in the Goathland afternoon sunshine in May 1979 is the NELPG-owned LNER K1, No. 2005. Although carrying LNER livery the locomotive was actually built by the North British Locomotive Company in Glasgow and was delivered to the newly created British Railways in 1949 with the number 62005. (Bernard Warr)

LMS Class 5 *George Stephenson,* owned by Ian Storey but operated by NELPG. Seen here at the south end of Goathland loop in May 1976. (Bernard Warr)

takings were better than in the previous year but no control over expenditure seemed to have been exercised and the increased revenue was being frittered away through poor budgetary control by individual departments.

Locomotives provision was a 'minefield'. Most were in the ownership or control of the North Eastern Locomotive Preservation Group (NELPG), who maintained them and received a fee for every mile operated. The locos concerned were NER T2 0-8-0 No. 2238, NER P3 0-6-0 No. 2392, LNER K1 2-6-0 No. 2005 and LMS 'Black' 5 4-6-0 No. 4767. This last loco was owned by Ian Storey but operated under the NELPG umbrella. Others were individually owned.

Lambton 0-6-2T No. 5 had been purchased for preservation by a couple from Derby and Lambton 0-6-2T No. 29 by a consortium of NYMR and NELPG members. Both arrived on the line in 1970.

GNR J52 0-6-0T No. 1247 was owned by Bill Smith and had been the mainstay of the steam service since I had been a member. Unfortunately, at the time of my arrival as GM, it was out of use following a derailment at the Grosmont trap points, although repairs were underway.

As far as diesel engines were concerned there was the Class 24, D5032, whose continued loan was shortly to be confirmed by the owner, Mr Turner. Also available was the recently arrived Class 31 D5500 from the NRM and in the 'pipeline' was the Class 52 diesel-hydraulic D1048 *Western Lady.* The two-car Gloucester RCW Class 100 DMUs were more use as coaching stock than traction units.

Lambton No. 29 departs Grosmont on 28 April 1973 shortly after the official re-opening of the railway. Fireman Don Robertson is collecting the single line token from the Grosmont signalman, John Hardy. (Bernard Warr)

Lambton tank No. 5 is seen crossing the gated High Mill Crossing in Pickering in October 1978. No. 5 was built in 1909 by Robert Stephenson & Hawthorn of Darlington, Works Number 3377, for Lambton Collieries, which in 1924 became Lambton, Hetton and Joicey Collieries. No. 5 was employed all its working life hauling coal transfer trains over the colliery 'main lines' around Wearside. (Bernard Warr)

Veteran GNR J13 class (more commonly known by the LNER designation of J52) 0-6-0 No. 1247 seen in May 1976 at Goathland having just arrived with a service from Grosmont and will shortly head into the Down loop to allow the loco to run round and return to Grosmont. No. 1247 was built in 1899 by Sharp Stewart & Co. to a design by Henry Ivatt. Withdrawn after sixty years' service it was privately preserved by Captain Bill Smith and thus became the first engine to be purchased from BR, straight out of traffic, by a private individual. (Bernard Warr)

Bill Smith was convinced that, although he was a member of that organisation, NELPG was seeking to take over the supply of locomotives to the railway and was critical of them at every opportunity.

Other locomotives potentially available included 0-6-0ST No. 47, *Moorbarrow*, 0-4-0ST No. 15 *Eustace Forth*, 0-6-0T No. 20 *Jennifer* and 0-6-0T No. 30 *Meteor*. However, these four were all a bit small for anything larger than two-or three-coach trains.

As already pointed out by the Coopers & Lyebrand report the railway was critically short of coaches and more needed to be sourced. In all there were thirteen coaches that were fit for operation. Four of these were non-corridor stock, of which one was the Great Western saloon. By use of the four-car DMU it was just possible to put together three four-car sets and be able to strengthen these as necessary with the non-corridor coaches. Not that the track capacity infrastructure was much better. At Goathland the up-starting signal needed to be passed to get a five-coach train in clear of the catch points at the north end. Similarly, at Levisham a five-coach train had to be signalled into the head-shunt to clear the level crossing at the north end.

Working conditions for many of the two dozen permanent staff were rudimentary in the extreme. At Grosmont a repair and servicing shed had been erected on the south side of the

Moorbarrow and *Eustace Forth* await their turn for restoration in Pickering station yard in 1978. Note the stockpiled sleepers in the background. (Bernard Warr)

No. 20 *Jennifer*, owned by Graham Binns, in steam near Goathland in June 1978. (Bernard Warr)

Superpower at Levisham on a wet day in May 1979 with Southern S15 No. 841 *Greene King* leading LNER (BR) K1 No. (6)2005 into the Down platform, both running tender first. The crossover from the Up line to the single line can be seen alongside the second coach and the Up starting signal is located just before this out of frame to the left. (Bernard Warr)

Platform two in Pickering station, photographed in April 1978. The combined C&W and DMU maintenance workshop (behind the large stone wall) is entered through the white door in the red-brick building. Complete engines were moved in and out through these doors. Note the pile of spare carriage brake blocks on the platform to the right of the white door. (Bernard Warr)

tunnel, largely by the 'in-house' builder Dick Oxlade. There was also a terrace of cottages that were used for staff accommodation and messing facilities. NELPG was in the process of constructing a storage shed on the site of Deviation Signal Box.

At Pickering, all carriage maintenance was being carried out in the open, as were the servicing and repairs to the Class 100 two-car DMUs. An undercover workshop located on platform two provided stores and basic facilities for small items for both departments. As I had seen when I was training to drive the DMUs, complete engines and gearboxes were somehow being removed from the train and taken inside this building for attention. Despite the hardships the staff were still working with enthusiasm.

Pickering station boasted a large bookshop that produced quite good financial results. Unfortunately, the floor level in the shop was a step down from the platform level and this seemed to have necessitated the provision of a porch. There was also a window hatch serving teas and snacks in the capable hands of Mrs Brown and a separate kiosk selling tickets for the train.

In the former booking office was a store for the bookshop and an office for the Commercial Manager and his assistant. Over on platform two, in addition to the workshops already mentioned, was a small, rather decrepit building behind the large stone wall at the south end. This was part store and part signing-on point and used by train crews. It was not uncommon to find rodents in residence and the building had become known, predictably, as the 'rat house'.

Platform one at Pickering station in April 1978, showing (left to right) the refreshment servery, the shop entry porch and the booking office kiosk. (Bernard Warr)

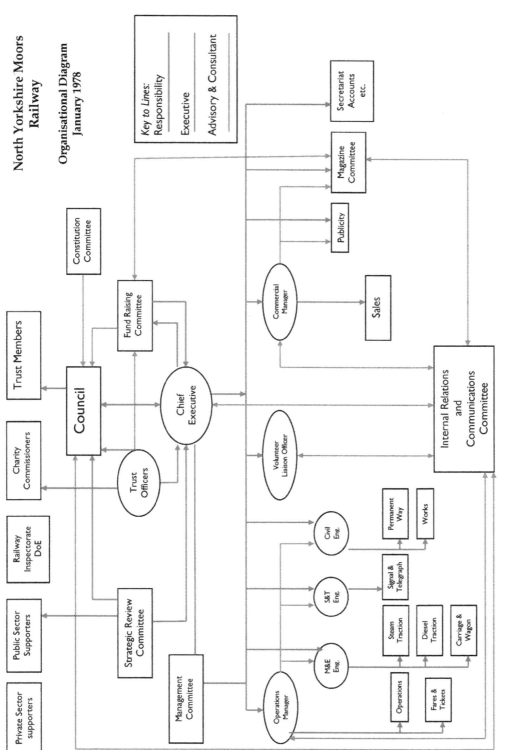

North Yorkshire Moors Railway

Organisational Diagram
January 1978

Key to Lines:
Responsibility

Executive

Advisory & Consultant

Private Sector supporters

Public Sector Supporters

Railway Inspectorate DoE

Charity Commissioners

Trust Members

Constitution Committee

Council

Fund Raising Committee

Chief Executive

Trust Officers

Strategic Review Committee

Management Committee

Commercial Manager

Volunteer Liaison Officer

Operations Manager

M&E Eng.

S&T Eng.

Civil Eng.

Operations

Fares & Tickets

Steam Traction

Diesel Traction

Carriage & Wagon

Signal & Telegraph

Permanent Way

Works

Publicity

Magazine Committee

Secretariat Accounts etc.

Sales

Internal Relations and Communications Committee

This is a redrawing of the organisational chart issued to CEO candidates in 1978. The original was, as was the practise at the time, hand drawn with separate colouring and was difficult to follow. (BW Collection)

Part of the information pack that I had been given when I was invited for interview was a chart which showed the governance arrangements for the railway. It contained so many lines of reporting as to be meaningless. As an example, the Internal Relations and Communications Committee had six separate reporting lines. As far as I was aware it had never met! Before I had been appointed, Bill Smith had raised the issue of the unrealistic complexity of the official structure with the Chairman, Richard Rowntree, and with the President, Lord Downe. Neither had shown much interest in simplifying the structure or for that matter paid much heed to the Coopers & Lybrand suggestions on revising the railway's governance and management.

The supreme decision-making body on the railway was the Trust Council. This comprised forty-two members, all elected by the general membership of the Trust. The main qualification for getting elected was to be well known! In consequence, anyone expecting quality debate and strategic thinking would be disappointed!

My early impressions of the Trust Council were that it was more of a 'talking shop', a place where members could express their views on all manner of subjects and try to get agreement for their chosen course of action. It needed to be well chaired with a firm chairman who would not allow deviation from the main topic. Unfortunately, we didn't have this and very often the 'any other business' item took the longest time to get through.

Sitting somewhere above and to one side of the Trust Council was the (non-elected) Strategic Review Committee, membership of which comprised the President, the Trust Chairman, the Management Committee Chairman, the Treasurer and myself as General Manager. Meetings seemed to be held under conditions of semi-secrecy and indeed for the first one that I attended in July at Wycombe Abbey, Bill Smith warned me not to arrive at the same time as him! This meeting was an opportunity for me to update these senior trust officers on the current problems facing the railway, which included the lack of coaching stock, minor collisions and derailments and the financial situation. We discussed the sale of the track bed from Pickering to Moorgates to North Yorkshire County Council for £27,000 (following a revaluation from £15,500) and the cost of a lease back. We further discussed the need for a new governance organisation and revisions to the management structure. We broke up after a couple of hours and had sherry with Lord and Lady Downe. All very civilised but I formed the view that this was a million miles away from what the railway was all about.

The previous Saturday I had attended the management committee meeting, which lasted for five hours and didn't achieve very much, whereas the Saturday after the SRC meeting I attended a Volunteers' meeting in Goathland, which was with 'real' people who had issues that could be resolved quite easily and proved to be productive!

One of the first things I did after I was appointed to the role was to prepare a new timetable for 1979. I was keen to have an hourly service from both ends of the line, and make these services leave at the same time each hour. I had originally planned for this to be at half-past the hour from Pickering, but as the Commercial Manager pointed out, this would miss the connections at Grosmont for Whitby. I changed the departure time to twenty minutes past the hour to overcome this, with the resulting departure from Grosmont at ten minutes to the hour. In the peak season, there were trains at 10.20 hrs from Pickering and hourly until 17.20. Four departures from Pickering were planned for steam haulage.

Knowing how controversial the timetable could be, I circulated the draft extensively from early August and invited comment. I received many suggestions on the detail, some of which I was pleased to incorporate, but most people welcomed the new proposals. I released the final version in September.

One of the projects that I had to get involved in when I took on the GM role was promoting the Railway's own lottery. This was in the days before the National Lottery and the Chairman, Richard Rowntree, was convinced that the railway would make a lot of money out of the venture. I was less convinced. A Special Projects Co-ordinator, Dennis Milnes, had been appointed and he was trying to get some major department stores and the like to sell the tickets for us. We had printed 80,000 tickets for the first lottery and the Chairman was convinced that we would make £12,000 from this. However, Dennis Milnes was never able to sign up the 'big name' outlets that were needed so sales were through our own efforts on the trains, in the station shops and through the area groups. In the end, we managed to sell 13,000 tickets and incurred a loss of £640. After that, despite Richard Rowntree's faith in the idea, I was unable to recommend to the Trust Council that we try again.

After I had been in post for a few days it was clear that the administration of the business had been neglected; in fact, it was pretty well non-existent. Nobody could give any reliable financial information, other than to say that we were carrying more passengers than ever before. When I asked about costs and departmental budgets I got blank looks. I enquired who authorised payment of bills and was told that the Treasurer did all of that and a chap called John Hammond looked after the paybill. There were no personnel records although I did find that John Craven had some information. I decided to start from scratch and create a new file for each employee and gather as much information as I could and keep it under secure conditions in my office.

I had no permanent secretary but had a mountain of mail flowing in each day and although two very excellent ladies came in part-time to help (Margaret Bennison and Marjory Hare), the call of the ladies' golf club was a more inviting proposition! Royd Scurrah knew of the wife of one of the existing members of staff who might be willing to help and promised to ask if she was interested in helping out until a permanent appointment could be made. She agreed and took over the role whilst I advertised. Wyn Heron was one of several who responded to the advertisement and she was offered and accepted the role in early September.

At the end of September John Besford left the railway's employment. He had originally been appointed to hold the fort whilst the search for a chief executive took place. I was quite keen to keep him on as he could have been a useful deputy but I was unable to persuade Bill Smith of this so I was told to end his temporary employment.

The grants that we had received from the English Tourist Board resulted in our coming to the attention of the Department of the Environment. I was advised that Ken Marks MP, Under Secretary of State at the DoE, wanted to visit on Saturday 29 July 1978. I was naturally happy to facilitate such a visit and met Mr Marks and his party in Pickering in the morning and showed them the new Tourist Information Centre and the shop and in the afternoon we met again at Grosmont to view the shed.

During my time on the Dart Valley Railway in Devon I had been involved in the operation of some evening dining trains, which were marketed as 'Champagne Specials' and had proved very popular. I was hopeful that we could do something similar on the NYMR and the opportunity arose in a small way in July 1978 when I was approached by Edwin Craggs, a trained chef and enthusiastic volunteer, to enquire if I was interested in running a Sunday lunch service on the train. I liked the idea but was a bit hesitant about what vehicle we would use, mentally noting that the Dart Valley had two very comfortable GWR Super Saloons for their luxury catering, but we had nothing like this. However, Edwin assured me that he had been cooking lunches in the static buffet car in Grosmont station for some weeks and if I could arrange for C&W to get this buffet car mobile again then we should be able to use it. I agreed to talk it over with Ron Rothwell, our C&W expert, to see if it was possible.

The Under Secretary of State at the DoE, Ken Marks MP (on left), emerges from the original tunnel at Grosmont in conversation with the author. (BW collection)

Ken Marks MP discusses loco restoration with the author inside Grosmont shed in July 1978. (BW Collection)

Ron wasn't entirely enthusiastic but he agreed to go and have a look. When he came back he was remarkably positive and said that provided some minor work was undertaken it should be possible as a 'one-off'. We agreed that he would go ahead and do this. I spoke to Edwin and we initially agreed on Sunday 6 August although, because of Edwin's shifts, we subsequently put this back to 13 August.

On the day all went according to plan. The buffet car was attached to the north end of the train at Pickering using the Stanton No. 44 shunter as the station pilot. The coach was fully booked with twenty-four people all paying £4.50 each for an excellent lunch taken whilst the amazing NYMR scenery slipped past. When it was all over many people asked when we would do it again. This was a bit of a difficult question to answer as the buffet car was not in the best of health. However, with our fingers crossed behind our backs, we said that we did plan to operate dining specials regularly and we would be in touch with everyone who had travelled on this inaugural catering journey.

Another catering venture that was started in 1978 was the evening 'Disco' trains. These provided music and dancing and included an on-train-made steak and kidney pie with peas and potatoes – all very tasty. I travelled on one at the beginning of July from Grosmont. The consist from the south end was a 20-ton brake van to house the petrol-driven electricity generator for the lights and the sound system; next was a BG (a railway van, as big as a

The Grosmont buffet car, after further refurbishment, was used more regularly for dining in 1979. Here it is seen at the beginning of September with a Grosmont–Pickering dining special leaving Goathland. (BW collection)

coach but without seats and windows) suitably decorated and then four ordinary coaches. Apart from the music, dancing and food there was a bar, which was also popular. The train I tried out didn't return to Grosmont until 00.45 hrs so the bar takings were considerable. This particular evening there were 170 people in the party and takings were about £600. Several more similar trains had been booked up to the end of October and to improve winter cash-flow I authorised the marketing of even more through the winter. These were all for pre-booked parties and seemed to catch the imagination of evening revellers in the area. All the trains up to the end of the year loaded well and brought in similar amounts of income.

Chapter 8

Making Changes

As anyone who manages a business will know, it always pays to keep on the right side of the regulators. In our case, it was HM Railway Inspectorate and the inspector who had responsibility for preserved railways was Major Peter Olver. It transpired that he was a close friend of John Boyes, our volunteer Signal and Telegraph Engineer. A telephone call from Major Olver advised that he would like to come and visit the railway in early September and look over a variety of items, which he listed for me. He said he would be staying overnight at Kingthorpe Hall with the Chairman, Richard Rowntree, and could I meet him off the London train in York the previous day and take him to Kingthorpe. I readily agreed and so the afternoon of 6 September saw me on York station meeting the 16.02 arrival from the capital. On the journey to Kingthorpe we had an interesting discussion on the potential issues that he might have with the NYMR which proved to be food for thought.

The following day I collected him from the Chairman's house and took him to Pickering where I had the GW Inspection Saloon waiting with the Class 24 as motive power. During the day, we looked at the major re-sleepering that we had undertaken at Kingthorpe reverse curves and the reconstructed Bridge 10 at Farwath before making our way to Levisham to inspect the proposed lengthening of the Up platform line and the re-positioning of the Up starting signal. Major Olver was pleased with what he saw and we agreed that John Boyes would keep him advised as the work proceeded. Pressing on, we looked at the re-sleepering at Milepost 16 and then on to Goathland to inspect the Up home signal route indicator. The day was finished off at Grosmont inspecting the new shed occupation crossing that had been established to facilitate road deliveries of loco coal. With a satisfactory inspection over, John Boyes drove Major Olver back to York.

Throughout August the railway was exceptionally busy, probably helped in part by the poor weather! Takings for the season up to the beginning of September stood at over £215,300, a 40 per cent increase over 1977. Free publicity in the form of television programmes and an article in the *Guardian* newspaper no doubt helped. In view of this

The beginning of the single line northwards from Goathland showing the over-run sand drag, the Up home signal and just to the left of the signal is the reverse side of the Up route indicator. The purpose of this indicator is to show drivers of trains in the Up direction which platform they are being routed into. (Bernard Warr)

increase in revenue my predecessor, John Besford, in agreement with the Treasurer, had authorised some further capital works including the erection of the water tower and crane at Pickering; the resurfacing of the Up platform at Goathland and improvements to the volunteer accommodation at Grosmont.

In my early discussions with the Trust Treasurer, Derek Sawyer, he made it clear that he did not want to carry on trying to exercise control over individual departments' spending. As regional director for the Midland Bank he already had a very demanding 'day' job and had found that whilst setting a budget for the railway was the easy part, getting the spending departments to 'live' within that budget seemed well-nigh impossible. I agreed that I should take over this responsibility, together with setting the budget in the first place. As a first step, I provided a 'cash-flow' forecast for the coming close season and on into the 1979 main operating season. Upon enquiry, it soon became clear that there was no form of accounting system in place and the Commercial Manager's assistant, Bill Craze, was doing his best to collate the income received with the spending figures provided by the Treasurer and produce the basic figures to do the VAT returns every three months.

To bring some semblance of order to the financial affairs of the Trust, with the Treasurer's help, I invited a firm called Kalamazoo Business Systems to demonstrate their accounting systems to us. Before the advent of the personal computer, paper-based accounting systems were popular amongst small businesses that did not necessarily number professionally trained accountants amongst their staff. I liked what was demonstrated to us and placed an order for the system. I asked the Commercial Manager to find me a suitable candidate to employ as a part-time budgetary control assistant. A suitable person was quickly found and it soon became apparent that no departmental heads were containing their expenditure within the budgets set by the Treasurer. The reasons needed to be established and I entered discussions with all of them to establish a basic budget for 1979. Because of the unbudgeted expenditure in 1978, the big increases in income (43 per cent at the end of the season with turnover exceeding £250,000 for the first time) were not sufficient to allow any new projects to be started.

The ongoing negotiations for the Class 52 diesel-hydraulic locomotive to come to the railway on the service agreement were finally concluded and D1048 was delivered to Grosmont by a BR Class 31 diesel, No. 31123, on Friday 6 October. This was a 'no scheduled services day' so, taking advantage of this, a gauging trip to Pickering was arranged to check clearances from lineside structures. This was entirely successful and the loco reached the buffer stop at the south end of Pickering station without incident.

The locomotive fleet was further increased with the arrival of a Southern Railway Type S15 4-6-0, which had acquired the name *Greene King* in recognition of the brewery of the same name that had sponsored the restoration by the Essex Loco Society. The loco came under its own steam from Peterborough on Saturday 9 December 1978.

At the Annual General Meeting of the Trust held at Goathland on 28 October 1978 there were several changes to the Trust Officers. Richard Rowntree (under pressure from Capt. Smith) had decided to step down as Chairman and Capt. Smith had put his name forward. As there were no other candidates he was elected. Also, elected to a Trust officer post for the first time was Rosemary Beasley, who became Trust Secretary. Rosemary was a very popular and enthusiastic volunteer guard and later DMU driver and her appointment was well received.

On Saturday 21 October, we received a large party of Ffestiniog Railway supporters from the Manchester area. We laid on a special train from Grosmont to Pickering and return. The original intention was to have the Q6 head the special but for one reason or another the engine could not be made available. Instead we used Lambton No. 5, piloted by GNR J52 1247, on the southbound run and the newly arrived Class 52 D1048 *Western Lady* on the return. All participants were reported to be very happy with the NYMR experience, particularly the Grosmont–Goathland section!

BR (WR) Class 52 diesel-hydraulic D1048 *Western Lady* stands in platform three at Grosmont on Friday 6 October 1978 immediately after delivery. (Bernard Warr)

D1048 passes Pickering yard on its 6 October gauging run. Note the newly erected colour light Down starting signal to the right of the loco, the BG 'Disco' coach on the left and the newly erected water crane. (Bernard Warr)

Finally through to the buffer stop adjacent to Bridge Street, Pickering, D1048's crew prepare to return to Grosmont. On the ground is Commercial Manager Royd Scurrah with Peter Pickering, Norman Ash and, in the cab, Kim Malyon. (Bernard Warr)

GNR J52 pilots Lambton No. 5 into Pickering station with the Ffestiniog Special on Saturday 21 October 1978. (Bernard Warr)

Since taking up the role of Chief Executive/General Manager in August I had found that it was very easy to work every day of the week! One of the difficulties was taking responsibility for the safe operation of the railway on a day-to-day basis. Whilst it was clearly my responsibility, I felt that I needed some back-up to allow me to take the occasional day off. To this end, with their agreement, I set up a panel of volunteers experienced in railway operating to take charge and be the 'responsible officer' (RO) for the days when I wasn't available.

John Bruce, at that time well known as the volunteer signalman at Goathland, was one of this panel and was the designated RO on the last day of regular services on Sunday 30 October. By chance, although it was my day off, I went down to Pickering station to see the last steam train of the season depart into the gathering night. A telephone call from John about two hours later brought the unwelcome news that the loco, Lambton No. 5, had been derailed on the depot siding trap points at Goathland whilst undertaking some

Lambton No. 5 back on the rails in the depot siding at Goathland after being derailed through the trap points that can be seen in front of the locomotive. On the adjoining down platform line can be seen the Class 24, D5032, with the breakdown train. The derailment was caused by a misunderstanding between the signalman and the driver and the subsequent inquiry was unable to determine who was responsible. (Bernard Warr)

Measuring up the trap points to check for gauge. (Bernard Warr)

shunting. Fortunately, no one was injured, the breakdown train had been summoned from Grosmont and the loco had now been 'jacked and packed' back on to the rails. As there were no injuries and the loco had been re-railed, no useful purpose would be served by my going to Goathland that night so I said that I would come up on Monday morning and would arrange for an official enquiry to determine how this had come about.

Back in August a film crew from BBC Leeds had been on the railway filming for a programme to show a day in the life of the NYMR. The resulting film was screened by BBC Leeds in the *Close up North* series at 22.15 on Friday 10 November. Unfortunately, the programme was not picked up by BBC Newcastle so most of us were unable to see it. However, Chris Wright, the producer, agreed to arrange a private showing for all of us who were interested. This took place in Egton on the evening of Saturday 30 December.

The Coopers & Lybrand feasibility study, published in 1977, had amongst its twenty five action points the provision of a carriage maintenance shed at Pickering station. The capital cost was estimated to be around £45,000 for a structure 150 feet (46 m) long by 40 feet (12.2 m) wide with an open veranda 30 feet (9.2 m) long and 40 feet (12.2 m) wide at the north end. As an outright purchase this was completely beyond the railway's means. I had wondered if there was some sort of leasing deal that I could come up with that might allow us to go ahead and get the C&W and Diesel maintenance staff at Pickering into dry and warm working conditions.

After discussion with Bill Smith he offered to provide such a building through a leasing company that he was a director of. We discussed it with Derek Sawyer and he was enthusiastic and confirmed that the leasing charges that Bill quoted were affordable. The proposal was approved by the Trust Council on 28 October 1978. I entered discussion with the local planning authority (LPA) about our proposals and said that we were of the opinion that we did not need separate planning permission as operational railway buildings on operational railway land were regarded as permitted development. The LPA didn't agree with this interpretation and at a meeting I had with their head of Planning in December insisted that we make a formal application in the usual way. This I did and on 8 January 1979 Rydale District Council, the LPA, refused the application. An appeal against this decision was lodged. There was considerable delay and by the end of August 1979 we were still awaiting the planning inspector's decision.

One of my self-imposed duties was to try and bridge the gulf between the 'ordinary' volunteer and those who were seen to be managing the railway. As a former volunteer myself, I was ideally placed to appreciate the volunteer viewpoint and I made it my business to keep in touch with the 'grass roots' of the organisation. The main vehicle for this strategy was the regular volunteer meetings held around the railway and in their own

In May 1979, J52 No. 1247 takes water from the temporary supply at the United Molasses tank wagon in Pickering yard. The site for the proposed C&W workshop was alongside here where the two tank wagons and the railbus are standing.

areas by the area groups and NELPG. In 1978 I attended ten such meetings and found them very useful. At these meetings, many people wanted to speak to me and give their point of view on where we were going wrong or as a question that usually started with 'why don't we...?' I didn't have all the answers but that didn't seem to matter; many people I spoke to seemed to feel better having just got matters off their chests!

Despite Bill Smith's quite negative attitude towards NELPG, I found all the people that I came across to be very dedicated to keeping their engines in good working order and very willing to listen to what the NYMR wanted from NELPG's locos. In early October, I was able to 'hammer out' an agreement with the group that would give certainty to their use in 1979 and the years following. By this agreement NYMR would make regular use of locos Nos 2005 (K1), 4767 (Black 5) and 2238 (T2) and between them would be guaranteed a share of 3,000 miles running and paid a rate per mile using the Historic Loco Agreement. In addition, where two locos were needed in the peak season, at least one of these would come from this trio. I attended a NELPG general meeting in Newcastle on 17 November and was able to announce the details of this agreement, which was very well received. Unfortunately, Bill Smith was less enthusiastic and thought I should concentrate on Nos 80135, 841 and 1247, all of which were on the Service Loco Agreement where no mileage payment was made but the NYMR was responsible for all maintenance including the ten-year overhauls. To my mind this was a too onerous burden for the NYMR.

At around the time of the AGM the volunteer marketing and public relations 'guru', John Tindale, decided to give up the role. This left Royd Scurrah, the Commercial Manager, holding this particular baby. Just before Christmas a new volunteer, Duncan Barclay, appeared who was occupying a similar role at Flamingoland, just down the road at Kirby Misperton. He was keen to come and work for us so I agreed a trial and then the prospect of a job if he was any good. Little did I know then that he would get the opportunity to prove his worth very quickly, as we shall see.

One final change I made before the year end was to promote Norman Ash from driver to Traffic Manager with day to day responsibility for operating and safety.

CHAPTER 9

Some Winter Challenges

In the run-up to Christmas we had tried out a new type of service aimed at children. On a train running from Pickering to Levisham and back a dedicated band of volunteers had built a grotto for Father Christmas to occupy and purchased, wrapped and labelled sufficient presents for all the children booked on the services. Each child with its parents visited the grotto, told Father Christmas what they really wanted on 25 December and were given the interim present that our volunteers had prepared. Services were moderately successful but suffered from inadequate publicity (hence the need for Duncan Barclay) and poor weather.

New Year's Day 1979 with No. 841 *Greene King* on what became the 'snow special', awaiting departure from Goathland. (Bernard Warr)

D5500 bringing up the rear of the same train. The icicles give some clue as to how cold it was even after travelling from Pickering. (Bernard Warr)

On New Year's Day, we had planned to run a service the full length of the line using the Class 31, D5500, and the S15, *Greene King*, both of which were capable of providing steam heat for the carriages. In addition, we planned to use the DMU if there was sufficient demand. Our plans took a bit of a knock when snow started to fall on Sunday 31 December. It intensified on New Year's Day and temperatures remained below freezing. We managed to run two round trips with the steamer and the diesel but cancelled the DMU departures. Unfortunately, loadings were light because, despite good pre-publicity, the roads were almost impassable so few people managed to get to us.

The weather got worse as the week progressed and we received many calls from prospective customers who wanted to get to Whitby (the road over the moor was blocked). In discussion with members of my team, we felt that we could do ourselves a great deal of good with the local community if we put on a service. Duncan was set on to 'get the word' out and he did us proud! We had decided to start the service on Friday 4 January and he communicated this to all the local news media. On the morning of the first day we got word from the BBC in Leeds that they were sending over a film crew to film the afternoon service. In addition, many national newspapers were taking stories from us featuring 'the only railway in the country' that was still running (I don't think this was true but it made a good headline!).

Turning the plan into reality was something else. The Class 31, D5500, was at Pickering at the south end of the coaching set. As the only person in the station qualified to drive it, it was down to me to get it into action. Despite the sub-zero temperature the engine started easily and the steam heat boiler fired up when asked. What was giving trouble was the air system and I couldn't get air pressure to build up. Presently the Class 24, D5032, arrived from Grosmont and coupled on to the north end of the train. In discussion with Norman Ash, who was driving it, we decided that condensation in the air system had frozen and the various air operated control systems wouldn't work until the pipes had warmed through a bit. At 10.30 we set off slowly through the deep snow but despite this managed to reach Grosmont by about mid-day. To our great joy the air system on D5500 had come to life and we could make the return trip to Pickering without bringing D5032 to the front of the train.

The BBC were waiting for us at Pickering and we were filmed on arrival. They were very keen to film from the cab so the cameraman, the presenter, Norman and I all squeezed into the cab. On this second trip the weather had deteriorated and it was snowing again. When we got to Goathland the film crew asked if I would drive (GM getting his hands dirty seemed newsworthy!), which I did through to Grosmont.

The BBC did us proud and we made the main evening news programme (*The Nine O'clock News*) with a lengthy slot and the regional programmes from Leeds and Newcastle.

We operated the service until Saturday 12 January, by which time the road over the moor was open again and demand for our services dropped off. Whilst it ran, we carried Calor gas to remote settlements, groceries to the activity centre at Stape (more of that anon) and we carried RAF personnel to Eller Beck for the short (if cold) walk to Fylingdales Early Warning Station.

At Pickering, during the operation of the snow services in January 1979, Class 31 D5500 takes on fuel, whilst Class 24 D5032 awaits its turn. (Bernard Warr)

The winter weather set in and the sub-zero conditions (with plenty more snow) were with us until March. Getting around became hazardous, hard packed snow became frozen solid on roads and pavements. The effect on the masonry structures on the railway gave us some concern; water penetration in masonry and brickwork is never welcome but add in a deep and long-lasting frost and trouble will eventually show.

In late January, we received a rather unusual request from a householder in Pickering. He was about to move to a house close by Levisham station but the state of the roads meant that it was too dangerous to try and get his removal van up and down those tortuous narrow roads between Lockton and the station. Could we help? After some thought we decided that it could be done, so on the appointed day in early February we marshalled a short train comprising the Disco coach (a BG) and a regular BSK. After his removal men had loaded his worldly goods into these two vehicles we set off for Levisham on a clear and frosty morning. Once there, the train was stopped across the level crossing and the gentleman's furniture and other possessions were loaded on to a handcart and wheeled slowly to the house by the removal men. In no time at all we were on our way back to Pickering having earned ourselves some 'brownie' points with the local community and being paid for doing so.

After another bout of heavy snow in February, a call came in to the Commercial Manager, Royd Scurrah, from the Outdoor Pursuits Centre up in Newtondale. Their food supplies were getting low; the road out was impassable and did we have any trains that were passing that could bring out fresh supplies? The easy answer was to say 'no', we had no trains running, but that wouldn't have been helpful to them or to our reputation. On the day in question I was the only qualified driver at the Pickering end of the line and so Royd asked me if I was prepared to help. We had the trusty 0-4-0 DE shunter, Stanton No. 44, which had a buffer beam that went almost down to the track and would act like a sort of snow plough. I said that we would try and reach them and we agreed on Kid Stye crossing for a meet up point. Royd took down the list of supplies that were needed and went to a grocery shop just round the corner from the station to obtain them.

I brought the loco into the platform and as soon as Royd returned with the supplies I put them in the cab and set off. The fresh blanket of snow had completely obscured the running lines so I had to make my way fairly slowly. Royd opened High Mill and New Bridge gates for me and I pressed on into the 'winter wonderland' with the snow being 'rolled up' before us by the deep buffer beam. The journey was uneventful and after about an hour I arrived at Kid Stye crossing where the group leaders were waiting. The groceries were soon unloaded, payment made and with their thanks ringing in my ears I set off back towards Pickering. In this direction, I could at least see where the track was, having already cleared the snow away on the outward trip. After about another hour I was back in Pickering and able to resume my proper job. Both the furniture removal and the Outdoor Pursuits Centre trip found their way into the local papers and earned us positive publicity.

One final tale from the snowy start to 1979. Having an operational Class 52 diesel on the railway was a big attraction for enthusiasts (myself included!). An enquiry had been received from Railway Pictorial Publications Railtours for a trip behind *Western Lady*.

A snowy Pickering yard on 18 March 1979 as some of the tour participants admire and photograph D1048, resplendent in her new coat of BR green. (Bernard Warr)

We responded positively and a booking was taken for a train from Pickering to Goathland and return. (The Goathland–Grosmont section wasn't available due to ongoing re-sleepering.)

The train started from Kings Cross behind a Class 40 Diesel (No. 40119) and was due to detrain the party at Malton for a road transfer to Pickering. On the day more snow fell, rendering the Malton to Pickering road impassable to the coaches. The decision was taken to carry on to Scarborough and then take the coaches from there to Pickering. Our train was due to leave at 14.00 hrs but as the party was only just arriving in Scarborough at this time we had to re-time it to 15.10 hrs.

A little earlier than this I had gone home to have lunch and when I came out of the house in Westgate to return to the station I could hear the Western's Maybach engines ticking over quite clearly – it reminded me of Newton Abbot in the 1960s!

With all the passengers safely on board we set off pretty well on time on our revised timetable. We were soon bowling along and presently came to Levisham, where we had promised a photo stop.

Once everyone was back on board we set off for Goathland and marvelled at what a good snow-plough the Class 52 made as we passed through snow filled cuttings around Abbots House.

The much deeper snow can be seen in the Goathland photograph opposite below. The return to Pickering went without incident.

Despite the weather the train was back in to Pickering within a minute of the revised timetable and the very satisfied party left by road to join their train for London at Malton.

The view from the cab of D1048 in Levisham facing a massive 'gallery' of photographers keen to take photographs that could (as it turned out) never be repeated. (Bernard Warr)

At Goathland the Class 24 was used to facilitate the loco run-round and D1048 is seen ready to return to Pickering. Standing in front of the engine, amongst others, can be seen a bearded John Hardy, Murray Brown and Nigel Spetch. (Bernard Warr)

With steam leaking out from between the carriages, *Western Lady* enhances a very wintry day as she prepares to complete the journey back to Pickering. (Bernard Warr)

When the thaw finally came the extent of the damage to the railway became apparent. I reported to the Trust Council that the severe winter weather had damaged the railway in many ways. It had caused burst water pipes at all stations; frost damaged the road surface at Levisham Station Crossing; caused a serious cutting slip south of Darnholme, depositing slurry, trees and scree on to the line; and melting snow had caused ballast to be washed out from under the track in various places, all of which had had to be repaired.

Towards the end of 1978 I had become aware that we might be eligible for a grant from the European Regional Development Fund (ERDF) towards our infrastructure costs on the basis that we were contributing to increasing tourism in the area and therefore economic activity. I held several meetings with colleagues at North Yorkshire County Council and was able to put together a grant application. By May it had got the approval of the Government Office in Leeds and was eventually approved by London and Brussels, netting us 30 per cent of our approved infrastructure costs each year.

Further help came from the National Parks Committee of North Yorkshire County Council in the form of a proposal to finance the building of a new halt in Newtondale to facilitate walkers accessing the forest trails. The site chosen was at Yaul Sike Haul (yes really!) just north of Kid Stye Farm. The site was chosen because there is a right of way crossing the line here but there is also an underbridge to keep walkers off the track. It was to be a request stop and to be called Newtondale Halt. Late in 1978, I visited the closed station at Warrenby with Nigel Trotter. This turned out to be a not very old steel structure that would be easy to dismantle and transport to our site. John Boyes volunteered to handle the purchase on behalf of the railway. It would of course need planning permission for its erection.

CHAPTER 10

The 1979 Season gets underway

Mention was made earlier of my desire to emulate the luxury dining trains that I had experienced on the Dart Valley Railway. Our early trials with the Gresley buffet car serving Sunday lunch the previous August had demonstrated that there was a market out there to be exploited; all we needed were suitable vehicles. The opportunity came in late December when Pullman parlour cars appeared on the BR Tender Lists. We had no money for such purchases but after a discussion with the Chairman, he told me to go ahead and bid and if successful his 'in house' finance company would lend us the money.

I arranged for Ron Rothwell, our Carriage and Wagon Engineer, to go and examine them. One was at Doncaster (E328 *Opal*) and the other was at Newcastle (E327 *Garnet*) reflecting their final use on the Hull Pullman and Tyne-Tees Pullman respectively. Ron's assessment was positive but he pointed out that they were fitted with 'Commonwealth' bogies and BR wanted these back. We discussed this for a while and I suggested that we could remove the bogies from the two camping coaches at Goathland (which never moved anyway) and place them on a nest of sleepers. Much to my surprise, he agreed that this was feasible so I went ahead and put in a bid. The bid for both was accepted and we paid the BR invoice and arranged carriage to Grosmont, Bill Smith's finance company reimbursing the cost in due course.

The two vehicles arrived on the line in early February and came complete with a wagon for us to return the bogies. This was a bit of a surprise (and disappointment) as I was hoping we might be able to put off returning the bogies until the following winter! The coaches looked to be in fair order but were of course in the BR version of Pullman livery: rail blue above the cantrail, silver below and no names displayed.

With both vehicles now on the line a swift resolution of the bogie issue was needed. I asked Ron to come up with a plan to have the vehicles ready for use by the end of July. He looked at me as though he thought I had taken leave of my senses but, after I had got him down from the ceiling, I asked him to tell me what he would need to make this plan happen. He went away to think about it.

When he returned, he listed all the other work he had to do to get the carriage fleet ready for the new season, which started on 14 April, Easter Saturday. He was confident that he could get help from Les Barwick and his p-way volunteers to help get the bogies out from under the camping coaches and build nests of old sleepers to replace them, recognising that this had to be done before the first visitors arrived to use the camping coaches. What he was lacking was competent C&W engineering skill. Apart from himself there was no one else on the railway that he had confidence in that would be able to do a good job.

He had a solution though; his son John Rothwell had recently left the British Rail Engineering carriage works at York and he was available to help. The drawback was that he needed to be paid as he had no other source of income. We discussed how this father and son duo might work for a time and I agreed to offer John a temporary job to get the Pullmans into service.

The Rothwell duo and helpers did a splendid job and had the two coaches ready for service in early August. Utilising the Gresley buffet car as a kitchen, we now had the ability to run a quality dining train service.

In the peak season timetable was a Thursday evening National Park Scenic Cruise normally worked by a two-car DMU from each end of the line. We replaced the 19.15 hrs Pickering departure with the Pullman diner set on 16 August and with only limited advertising this was well patronised and appreciated by our new-found dining customers. We ran the service on the remaining Thursday evenings of the peak timetable with equal success and so began the legendary NYMR Pullman dining services that are still running forty years later and have become the biggest money-spinner in the railway's history.

Swapping bogies at Grosmont in May 1979 using the NRM steam crane. The coach in the foreground is No. 15709, a CK used as a camping coach at Goathland and later as volunteer accommodation. The coach by the shed is E332, a second class Pullman parlour car, which was a non-runner and was to be used as the Grosmont station buffet. (Bernard Warr)

One of the advantages of having a direct connection with the BR network is that trains can move over the connection from one system to the other. Reference has been made elsewhere to the weekly 'pick-up' freight that ran to Whitby and delivered various goods and commodities to us, ranging from concrete bridge beams to carriages and even locomotives. There was one other annual visitor that is well worth mentioning and that is the weed killing train. Keeping trackside vegetation under control is a mammoth task for any railway organisation. British Railways let area by area contracts to have its permanent way treated and this was undertaken by the successful contractor providing a train with spraying equipment, chemicals, water and a specialist crew to operate it. The only BR contribution (apart from paying for it) was to provide motive power for the ensemble.

The NYMR was no different and when the contractor was dealing with the Whitby branch we would arrange a trip from Grosmont to Pickering to get our permanent way treated. In May 1979 we used D1048 *Western Lady* to undertake this duty.

Towards the end of 1978 I was approached by Ian Armstrong in his capacity as Teesside Centre Chairman of the Stephenson Locomotive Society. He told me that the centre would be celebrating its seventieth anniversary in 1979 and he was keen to hire a celebratory train on the NYMR. He had already lined up the well-known and respected railway historian and author O. S. Nock to undertake book signing sessions at both Grosmont and Pickering.

On May 23 1979 D1048 *Western Lady* stands at the north end of Pickering station having just run-round the weed killing train in preparation for the return run to Grosmont. On the left in front of the locomotive is Les Barwick, permanent way inspector, discussing the plan with driver Norman Ash and secondman Peter Smeaton. (Bernard Warr)

The weed killing train surges through Northdale and approaches Fen Bog on a warm May 23 1979. (Bernard Warr)

He reminded me that in May 1979 the GNR J52 No. 1247 would be eighty years old and it would also be twenty years since our Chairman, Bill Smith, had made history by being the first individual to buy a steam engine from BR.

No. 1247 is a member of the LNER J52 class of 0-6-0 saddle tank engines. She is the only one left out of an original 129, and was built for the GNR by Sharp, Stewart & Co. in Glasgow in 1899 to meet a design by H. A. Ivatt. The locomotives were intended for shunting and short freight workings. Bill Smith always referred to her as 'The Old Lady' and she was the shed pilot at the Kings Cross Top Shed as BR No. 68846, where she acquired this affectionate name.

In discussion with Ian Armstrong and Bill Smith we decided that we should make something of an event of the occasion and invite further celebrities in addition to O. S. Nock. We would serve a meal in the Great Western saloon, prepared by our embryo Pullman catering experts, for the VIP party. I was left to make the arrangements. I set about finding more people who had been involved in the sale and handing over of No. 1247 to Bill Smith back in 1959.

I started with Peter Townend, the former shed master at Kings Cross. Peter accepted our invitation and put me on to Colin Morris, the Divisional Maintenance Engineer who had actually presented the engine to Bill Smith. Colin also accepted our invitation and suggested that we should invite Geoff Huskisson, the former Kings Cross Divisional Manager. He supplied me with an address for Geoff and he also accepted the invitation. To round off the mechanical engineering presence I invited John Bellwood, CME at the National Railway Museum, whose generosity and goodwill had resulted in NYMR being able to borrow so many items from the NRM.

To get some interest from the railway press we invited John Slater, editor of the *Railway Magazine,* and Michael Harris, editor of *Railway World.* Both accepted and Michael Harris asked if we could get some time together to discuss a major article that he was preparing for the August edition of the magazine.

In addition to Ian Armstrong, the SLS party included Dr. K. Greenalch, past Vice-Chairman of the Teesside group, and Mr A. G. F. Davies, the Teesside Centre Librarian.

The train planning went ahead without any hitches and the Special Train Notice (STN) was issued a few days in advance. The special train was to be the 12.00 hrs from Grosmont with the Great Western saloon marshalled next to the engine, No. 1247. Unfortunately, the GW saloon was in primer as the volunteer who was tackling the repaint had left!

The celebratory meal was taken on the outward journey.

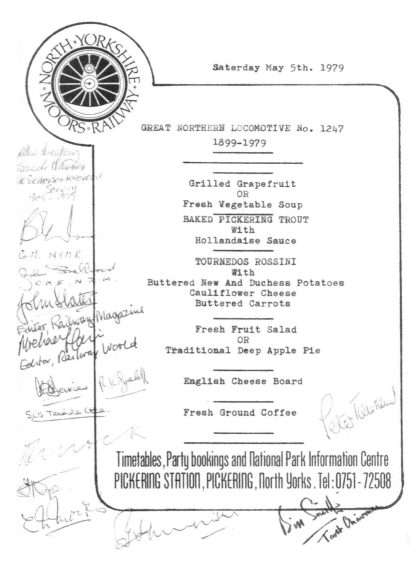

The menu for the celebratory meal taken in the GW saloon. Most of the guests exchanged signed copies of the menu such as this one as a memento of the day. (BW Collection)

Saterday May 5th. 1979

GREAT NORTHERN LOCOMOTIVE No. 1247
1899-1979

Grilled Grapefruit
OR
Fresh Vegetable Soup

BAKED PICKERING TROUT
With
Hollandaise Sauce

TOURNEDOS ROSSINI
With
Buttered New And Duchess Potatoes
Cauliflower Cheese
Buttered Carrots

Fresh Fruit Salad
OR
Traditional Deep Apple Pie

English Cheese Board

Fresh Ground Coffee

Timetables, Party bookings and National Park Information Centre
PICKERING STATION, PICKERING, North Yorks. Tel: 0751-72508

Prior to leaving Grosmont Mr Nock kindly did a book signing session in the station shop. On arrival at Pickering the saloon was left in the down platform and Mr Nock was again prevailed upon to do a book signing session in Pickering shop, whilst the rest of us socialized! Our trusty station shunter, Stanton No. 44, re-attached the saloon to the front of the 16.00 hrs for the return journey to Grosmont.

Having returned to Grosmont I had arranged for a special presentation to be made to the Trust Chairman, Bill Smith, by Geoff Huskisson, thereby reprising their roles from 1959. Bill Smith knew nothing of this in advance and he was pleasantly surprised.

Judging by the letters of appreciation that I received afterwards all participants seemed to have a good time and thoroughly appreciated the opportunity to take part.

From time to time the railway was asked to provide facilities for television and film companies to film sequences. In 1978 we played host to the filming of a Martini advert but in June 1979 I was approached by Granada Television, who were about to film the Evelyn Waugh novel *Brideshead Revisited* starring Jeremy Irons and Anthony Andrews. Craig McNeil from Granada Television came to see me in early June. He had been scouting around the NYMR looking for suitable locations and had been enchanted when he came across Levisham station. He described it as ideal for the film but it would need to be renamed and would have to take on a Southern Railway persona. He estimated that it would take two or three days to set up, do the filming and then clear up afterwards.

The party about to leave Grosmont behind No. 1247 and eagerly anticipating the first course being served. Some well-known faces here with Peter Townend and Bill Smith on the left, Ian Armstrong and O. S. Nock at the far end (with their backs to the engine) and John Bellwood sitting next to the author on the front right. (SLS/BW collection)

Some of the party in conversation in the saloon at Pickering. From left to right; John Bellwood, Ian Armstrong, the Author, O. S. Nock, Colin Morris, Peter Townend and Geoff Huskisson. (SLS/BW collection)

With Stanton No. 44 having shunted the saloon on to the stock for the 16.00 hrs departure, a highly polished No. 1247 prepares to attach to the train. Driver Keith Gays can be seen in the cab. (Bernard Warr)

J52 No. 1247 ready to depart Pickering for Grosmont with the 16.00 celebratory special. Note the GW saloon still in primer! (Bernard Warr)

Geoff Huskisson, former Divisional Manager Kings Cross, 'hands over' No. 1247 to Bill Smith a second time in a recreation of the events of twenty years previously. (Bernard Warr)

The presentation over, the group assemble in front of the engine. With Peter Smeaton and Keith Gays on the footplate we have (left to right) Geoff Huskisson, Peter Townend, John Bellwood, Colin Morris, The Author, Ian Armstrong, O. S. Nock, Bill Smith, John Slater, Dr Greenhalch, Mr F. Hope and Mr A. G. F. Davies. Although on the author's camera, the photograph was taken by Michael Harris, editor of *Railway World* magazine. (BW Collection)

The difficulty for the railway was being able to fit the filming in around our normal services. With an hourly service in operation this was a bit of a challenge and I seem to recall that we redrafted the timetable for the day's filming to give them maximum use of the station whilst maintaining our busiest trains. The day selected for the actual filming was a Friday, which was the quietest day of the week for us. The date selected was Friday 29 June.

The lack of Southern Railway vehicles was overcome by re-badging GNR J52 No. 1247 as a Southern 0-6-0 tank engine, No. 436, and hiring in from the Vintage Carriage Trust a Southern 'Birdcage' Brake Third, No. 3554. This was originally purchased by the Keighley & Worth Valley Railway but later sold to the VCT for a nominal £1 but in need of a full restoration. The VCT made a fantastic job of the restoration, as can be seen in the following images.

Levisham station had to be transformed into Melton Carbury. The film company did a very convincing job by building an awning in front of the existing passengers shelter and adding quite convincing valances to this and the adjacent signal box. A new 'running in' board was also provided. After they had finished it was all taken away again and the railway received a nice facilitation fee.

The only Southern Railway vehicle on the NYMR at the time was S15 No. 841. This was 'too big' for the film makers as they thought a tank engine would give a more rural image. However, as can be seen here, No. 841 did get used for filming and was adapted with the platform that can be seen attached to the second carriage to film the actors from outside the train. (Bernard Warr)

Standing in Levisham station yard on Friday 29 June 1979 is the VCT Southern Railway 'Birdcage' Brake Third, 3554, with the mock Southern J52 No. 436. (Bernard Warr)

Levisham becomes Melton Carbury for one day. Southernisation has overtaken the station's former authentic LNER livery. (Bernard Warr)

Very careful dressing of the set provides a convincing backdrop for the actors awaiting their next call. Note that the Down platform was also given the same treatment where it could appear in shot. (Bernard Warr)

Keith Gays brings mock Southern J52 class No. 436 and 'birdcage' coach into Melton Carbury Up platform under the watchful eye of the signalman, John Russell. (Bernard Warr)

Despite my ambition to provide covered accommodation at Pickering for carriage maintenance being thwarted by Ryedale District Council's unwillingness to recognise that an operational railway building on operational railway land is permitted development, I still needed to acquire more coaches. BR had released very few during 1979 and those that had become available were too costly to consider. In early August, I heard that the Derwent Valley Light Railway in York was giving up its passenger operation and had three BR Mk I coaches up for disposal. I asked Ron Rothwell to go and have a look at them and he came back with a positive report. Although the price that was being asked was a bit more than I wanted to pay, I felt that the opportunity was too good to miss and so decided to go ahead with the purchase. I already had the finance available through a very generous benefactor, Jos de Crau, so was able to move quickly. The coaches were two Standard Corridor (SK) and a Brake Composite Corridor (BSK).

CHAPTER 11

Positive Progress

Earlier, mention was made of the radical revisions to the timetable for the 1979 season with the adoption of a 'clock-face' departure pattern from each end of the line. This approach was deemed to be a success and the Trust Council resolved to continue the approach in 1980. In conjunction with the NYMR, BR had introduced a joint ticketing scheme, which proved popular and produced additional revenue for both parties. Over 3,000 tickets were sold between July and September, at least half of which were to local people. The only slight downside to this was that some late running on our part resulted in missed connections at Grosmont.

In an attempt to reduce unemployment, the Government had introduced two schemes relevant to the NYMR. One was the Special Temporary Employment Programme (STEP) and the other was the Youth Opportunities Programme (YOP), both under the control of the Manpower Services Commission (MSC). The MSC Job Creation Scheme had proved to be of benefit to the railway and had provided employment for seven unemployed people. This scheme finished on 15 September 1978 and the employees had to be dismissed. However, four employees – Messrs Harper, Russell, Liddle and Anderson – were offered permanent posts. To replace the Job Creation Scheme, the MSC introduced a further STEP programme from 18 September and a new Work Experience Programme from 16 October 1978. Fifteen places of up to six months' employment were available on these schemes, all funded by the MSC. Like most Heritage Railways of the time the NYMR benefited from the resource that this funding allowed and at the end of each scheme hard decisions had to be taken on employing the full and part-time staff displaced by the ending of these programmes.

The new timetable had settled in very well and appeared to be liked by the crews and public alike. My desire to see more steam departures from Pickering proved to be in tune with customer expectation. The timetable called for four departures from Pickering during the peak season (30 July to 7 September) and up to three departures in the 'shoulder' period (29 May to 27 July). To augment these were regular diesel railcar or diesel-hauled services that connected with steam departures. We were stretched to be able to provide five-coach trains in the peak and even these were overloaded on occasions. The Thursday evening DMU service in July and August was also popular and even more so after the working became the Pullman dining service from 16 August. In planning the timetable for 1980 I proposed to the Trust Council that we should run a similar timetable to that used in 1979 but with some minor adjustments to improve connections to and from Whitby at Grosmont.

August 1979 proved to be a good month for publicity. The feature that I had discussed with Michael Harris of *Railway World* in May was published with the title 'A Line for all Reasons' and was a very positive assessment of what we had done and were still planning to do. The cover picture was an action shot of the S15 at Eller Beck. Not to be outdone, the *Railway Magazine* had a photograph of our railbus at Grosmont on the front cover, and an article on it by Murray Brown inside. Also included was a review of the Class 24 Diesel and a page of photographs of events on the NYMR. The BBC Television early evening news magazine *Nationwide* carried a feature in late July about our first female train driver, Rosemary Cubitt, who was interviewed and filmed in action and very credible she looked too!

It was becoming clear that we were reaching the limits of our line capacity but in the short-term there was little that could be done. We needed more carriages and the three from the DVR would help here but of course longer trains need longer platforms. Both Pickering and Grosmont could not handle more than five coaches and more than this would be off the platform end. We still had to tackle the extension of Levisham Up loop so that trains could be accommodated behind the starting signal but clear of the level crossing and the Up starter at Goathland needed to be moved to accommodate trains clear of the catch points.

For some years work had been going on at Pickering to install a multiple aspect signalling scheme (MAS) controlled from New Bridge signal box. When completed this would allow more trains between Levisham and Pickering but completion was still two to three years away.

With no resolution in sight of the planning difficulties for the new carriage maintenance shed, I decided to look at other alternatives both in another part of Pickering yard and north of New Bridge where there was an existing embankment wide enough for two lines of rail on the west side of the line. What was clear was that none of these issues would be resolved quickly.

My biggest concern was with departmental spending. Towards the end of 1978 I had called for budget submissions from all spenders. By and large and in conjunction with the Treasurer, I had been able to prepare a budget that all were happy with. Fortunately, the estimate I had set for income was conservative and as the season developed it became apparent that the upward trend in passenger numbers seen in previous years would be repeated in 1979. However, the late 1970s were a time of high inflation and this brought pressure on our spending budgets as income was rising faster than expected and could not be accommodated.

Where I had difficulty was with the spending that was totally outside the agreed budget. In particular, the Pickering signalling scheme was 'gobbling' money at an alarming rate and

I had to speak to John Boyes to get him to slow down his spending to the agreed level. Similarly, track re-sleepering costs were spiralling and I formed the opinion that if material became available at a good price then Nigel would place an order, whether or not budget was available.

This situation goes to the heart of the difficulty that a heritage railway manager faces. Unlike an employed subordinate, there is no effective sanction that can be used against a volunteer manager who chooses to ignore a general manager's instructions.

In June, fuel became a potential problem. Coal, the lifeblood of any steam railway, was shooting up in price, as was diesel oil. To make matters worse the various tensions in the oil supply world resulted in shortages and our suppliers advised us that they could only supply 90 per cent of the previous year's total. A very dry summer and a shortage of diesel oil could make the operation of our services very difficult. Whilst we had no way of controlling the weather we could do something about the income. From the beginning of July, we introduced a modest fare increase. Not an ideal action to have to take, but, as most of the income is received in the peak season, we would have been foolish not deal with the price inflation that we were experiencing. For the record, annual inflation reached over 15 per cent in August 1979 and as a result most of our passengers were sympathetic to the fares increase we had introduced.

CHAPTER 12

A Personal Crisis

In 1979 I had been married for ten years but my relationship with my wife was not, for reasons that I don't need to go into here, very satisfactory or even marginally happy. The extra burden that the General Manager role placed on me, particularly the time commitment, was the 'final straw' as far as my wife was concerned and we decided that we would separate and go our own ways. Shortly after this decision had been taken I met someone else that I admired and came to care for who also worked for the NYMR. My wife and I had already agreed that we would sell our house in Pickering and purchase two smaller properties to allow us to live independently of each other. The property sale went ahead quickly and we purchased the two properties as planned, taking up residence in July.

None of this had any impact on the railway or my ability to do the job but unfortunately others didn't see it this way. The first inkling that I had that there was trouble ahead was when I was invited to Kingthorpe Hall to have coffee with Richard Rowntree, the former chairman. At this meeting, he informed me that the 'whole of Pickering' was appalled at the fact that I had set up home with a woman that I was not married to and he was concerned that it was reflecting badly on the NYMR. I told him that I thought my private life was no concern of his (or the 'whole of Pickering') and my new partner and I had gone to great lengths to ensure that we were not seen together on the railway. He warned me that if I didn't dismiss my new partner from her job on the railway things could go badly wrong with my own position. I was shocked at this outdated (I thought) moral stance.

It became clear that Bill Smith, my guide and mentor up to this point, shared the same view. He became distant and critical and found fault with everything that I was trying to do. On one occasion, he rode with me to Levisham on Stanton No. 44 to take some wagons back that had been brought to Pickering so as not to interfere with the filming of *Brideshead* by Granada TV. It was clear that he had a thing about my driving, no matter what the circumstances, and wrote to me quite formally shortly afterwards and suspended me from driving. Relations were not improved when I pointed out to him that as Chairman he didn't have the authority to suspend me from driving without going through the normal disciplinary channels. However, in an effort to make amends I did agree to refrain from driving for the time being.

A regular Trust Council meeting was due to take place in Goathland on the evening of 31 August. Amongst other things, I was seeking approval of several items to do with the future carriage shed and the role of the diesel maintenance section. I was surprised and disappointed when the Chairman spoke in his usual eloquent way against most of the things I was trying to do, with the result that I did not get the approvals I was seeking. At the end of the meeting he called an impromptu special meeting and asked all staff, observers and non-Trust Council members to leave. I checked with him that he didn't want me to remain and he confirmed this. On the way back home I thought to myself that he's probably finding ways to get rid of me, no surely not, I worried.

The following morning, I had a pre-arranged meeting with Bill Smith to discuss the electricity supply to Grosmont Shed. However, the meeting didn't quite turnout as I expected. I was stunned to hear him say that, at the special meeting, there had been an immediate call for my dismissal and a motion to this effect had been carried with only three votes against. He said that further discussion had resulted in a revised proposal being approved, which called upon the Chairman to come and see me and invite me to resign my post. He said, 'Don't fight it Bernard, if you do they'll call another meeting within a week and throw you out.' I said that I found this all very difficult to believe to which he responded with, 'It wouldn't be so bad if it was only the volunteers who were against you but it's all the staff as well!' He left me to think over what he had said. Why I didn't ask for reasons the Trust Council wanted me to resign, I don't know; I clearly wasn't thinking straight. I felt let down; for the previous three years, I had put my heart and soul into working for the NYMR, first as a volunteer then as an employee and now I seemed to be expected to just give it all up. Amongst the Trust Council were many that I thought of as friends and I just couldn't believe that they along with the staff were so against me. Finally, feeling totally demoralised by the turn of events, I did as Bill Smith had asked and wrote out my resignation.

CHAPTER 13

Fighting Back

The day after my meeting with Bill Smith was strangely quiet. The 'phone didn't ring and no one called at my house. Eventually at about tea-time the phone did ring and it proved to be Chris Cubitt. He said that the Trust Council hadn't wanted me to resign, the motion of no confidence that they had passed was meant as a warning. I told him that I knew nothing of a motion of no confidence as Bill Smith had told an entirely different story and I had been forced to resign or face the 'wrath' of the Council if I resisted.

Pondering what to do next I went into the office for the last time on Monday and Tuesday 3 and 4 September. There were many glum faces and no sign of the staff 'all being against me' as Bill Smith had claimed.

In the meantime Bill Smith didn't waste any time in replacing me and installed the organiser of the failed railway lottery, Dennis Milnes, as interim General Manager. The whole situation didn't sit well with most staff and, having seen how easily the GM could be disposed of, they feared for their own jobs. A branch of the National Union of Railwaymen (NUR) was established quite soon after.

As I had been so seriously misled by the Chairman I wrote individually to each member of the Trust Council and asked to be able to withdraw my letter of resignation and to address their apparent concerns over my conduct. This was arranged for Friday 12 October and was to be held in the Memorial Hall in Pickering.

In the meantime, the press got wind of the story and called on the railway to find out what was going on. Had the GM left his wife? Had he run off with another woman? Had he been sacked? What was happening? One reporter, perhaps more persistent than the rest, found his way to my front door. At first I would only talk 'off the record' but having laid out the whole story for him I was persuaded to let him publish it. Not thinking that it would be of much interest outside Pickering, I expected the story to appear in the local weekly newspaper, the *Gazette*. How wrong can you be? When the following day's *Daily Mail* dropped through my door I was shocked to find that the story was on the front page! Not to be outdone, every other national daily from the *Sun* to *The Times* gave the story similar treatment. The headline writers had a field day; 'Rail Romance Runs off the Rails!' was one, 'Rail Romance hits the Buffers', was another. Now my phone was ringing constantly, mostly with friends and colleagues from both the NYMR and other railways expressing sympathy and support. Others were less impressed. This became apparent when I attended the Special Trust Council meeting on 12 October. I was given a frosty reception and they voted twenty-four to seven to not allow me to withdraw my letter of resignation. This also was reported in the press.

I took legal advice, which suggested that if I could satisfy an Industrial Tribunal that I had been coerced into giving up my job then this would have been constructive dismissal. If I could then show that there were no grounds to terminate my employment, then the dismissal was unfair and I could be reinstated by the tribunal. As my future employment prospects could depend on getting these rulings, I decided to go ahead and take the NYMR to an Industrial Tribunal.

The tribunal was held in Leeds over five days in January and February 1980. At the end of the hearing my resignation was held to be a constructive dismissal and despite the railway raising twenty five reasons why I should be dismissed the tribunal ruled that separately or together they did not warrant dismissal and should have been dealt with in other ways. The dismissal was therefore unfair. I was asked if I wanted to be reinstated into the post but I decided it would be impossible for me to work with Bill Smith and many members of the Trust Council again and so declined the invitation.

After the initial flurry of media interest the story was not allowed to rest. Throughout the five days of the tribunal hearing, the press were there in force together with their photographers. As observers of the hearing they could report what they heard and express their own opinions to their readers. Happily, for me they were very supportive of my case and there was considerable jubilation at the result.

CHAPTER 14

Back to Volunteering

The NYMR was in a bad state in early 1980. Morale amongst staff and volunteers was at a low ebb and money was short. The interim management introduced after my departure seemed incapable of controlling expenditure and costs exceeded all expectations. A new General Manager was appointed but he lasted for only a few months and was asked to leave for 'health' reasons. He was replaced by a Line Manager whose experience of railway operating appeared to be limited. An ill-thought-out reorganisation of the mechanical engineering function resulted in many failures and general unreliability of the diesel fleet. The Trust Council found that by degrees their authority for running the railway had been subsumed by an unelected Management Board led by the Chairman.

Just before the 1980 season began I was invited to put my name forward for the drivers roster. I wasn't surprised to get a note back from Keith Gays, who was doing the rostering, telling me that he had been instructed not to roster me for driving at all during 1980 – no reason given but the conclusion was obvious. If I couldn't drive, then I could help in other ways; I was a qualified guard so I offered my services to the guards roster clerk and was accepted.

The 1980 season was an unmitigated disaster. Trains were late, suffered break-downs or were cancelled altogether. Minor accidents abounded. Inflation was rampant; fares had been increased by a massive 28 per cent but income only rose by 17 per cent. The permanent staff came close to 'working to rule' and at one stage were considering an all-out strike over pay and a new grading system.

Word of the parlous state of safety on the railway reached the ears of the Railway Inspectorate, who wrote an urgent letter to the Trust Chairman, placing responsibility squarely on his shoulders, and they followed this up with a visit to emphasise the point. However, despite all this pressure the Trust Chairman still found time to continue his personal vendetta against me, refusing to allow me to return to driving and even threatening to call an extraordinary general meeting of the Trust to bar me from membership! Inevitably, even he had to recognise the damage he was doing to the Trust and, prior to the 1980 AGM, he quietly resigned. Within weeks of the AGM, I was reinstated as a driver!

Jubilant at being reinstated as a driver, the Author is seen alongside Class 31 D5500. (BW collection)

CHAPTER 15

Epilogue

The fortunes of the NYMR gradually recovered from the low point of 1980 under the careful and considerate guidance of the new Chairman, Michael Pitts. I continued as a driver for a few more years before I started a canal boat hire company in Manchester which, as can be imagined, took up most of my free time and energies. I did come back to volunteer on the line and was elected to the Trust Board in 2013.

The 'wild west frontier' type railway described in these pages is long gone! The enterprise has developed into one of the most successful heritage railways in the country, if not the world, carrying over 350,000 passengers a year. It is unique amongst heritage railways in that it runs over an additional 6 miles of the national network to provide services from Pickering right through to Whitby.

WHEN YOUR NUMBER'S UP

MERITOCRACY GOES TO WAR

Raymond S. Ross

Raymond S. Ross, Ph.D.

First Page Publications
Livonia, Michigan

First Page Publications

12103 Merriman • Livonia • MI • 48150
1-800-343-3034 • Fax 734-525-4420
www.firstpagepublications.com

Library of Congress Control Number: 2005902776

When Your Number's Up/R. S. Ross

ISBN # 1-928623-57-3 (soft cover)

Library of Congress Control Number: 2005925594

When Your Number's Up/R. S. Ross

ISBN # 1-928623-60-3 (hard cover)

Ross, Raymond S. 1925–

Summary: Account of the battle scenes, war adventures and personal stories of four soldiers in theArmy Specialized Training Program (ASTP) who are sent to an armored infantry division for active overseas duty.

First Page Publications
12103 Merriman Road
Livonia, MI 48150

Other Books by R. S. Ross, Ph.D.:

Persuasion: Communication and Interpersonal Relations

Persuasión: Communicación Y Relaciones Interpersonales (Translation)

Understanding Persuasion (4 editions)

Small Groups in Organizational Settings

Relating and Interacting (w/Mark Ross)

Essentials of Speech Communication (2 editions)

Speech Communication: Fundamentals and Practice (11 editions)

Contributing Author:

The Air Force Staff Officer

The Communication Arts & Sciences of Speech (Keith Brooks)

Communication Probes (Wayne Pace)

TABLE OF CONTENTS

Chapters

PREFACE

"The front is a very small club." British General Sir Brian Horrocks put it well. Less than 14 percent of our forces in World War II bore the brunt of mortal combat.

An even smaller club was composed of the country's brightest teenagers—the 140,000 high-IQ soldiers, assiduously tested, judiciously selected, and then protected by the Army Specialized Training Program (ASTP). The deferential treatment for this less than 2 percent of the army would come to a shocking halt in the wake of battlefield casualties and charges of elitism. Among these special young men were Bob Dole, Henry Kissinger, Gore Vidal, Ed Koch, and many other recognizable names of today. [1]

This is a narrative account of how a few of them fared when thrown into an armored infantry company of a hard charging armored division. Military writer Jim Mesko describes their combat expectations. "Due to their mobility, the armored infantry often saw a great deal more combat than their (foot) infantry counterparts. When there arose the need for quick reaction to a German counterattack, tanks and armored infantry were often rushed into the breach." [2]

When Your Number's Up is drawn from the author's battle experience as an ASTP armored infantry squad leader and from the recollections of men who were comrades in arms. The title is drawn from the squad's fatalistic maxim—"It's up!"

Major events of the war are depicted as they happened. However, since this story is more narrative than memoir, I found that changing most names and some unit numbers made my recollections less personal and less painful and more likely to be true.[3] Also, it was less likely to cause distress to the relatives and friends of those men who died. Key characters are drawn from life but not always from single individuals. They are combinations of the characteristics of the men to whom I answered or who answered to me and therefore belong to the composite order of architecture and portrayal.

This narrative is based on the combat adventures of the 8th Armored Division during three major battles in the European Theater of Operations: France, the Ardennes, and Germany. More specifically, the story deals with the 58th Armored Infantry Battalion, especially the 3rd Squad, 2nd Platoon of Company B. Some minor battle actions and fire-fights are out of order for purely literary reasons. While a B-17 crew was picked up in no man's land, the B-17 flight (chapter 42) was contrived for purposes of historical review.

Twenty-seven men went through the ranks of the twelve-man 3rd Squad. The very real names of the men who were wounded or killed in action are found in the epilogue. Also listed are the men who figured prominently in this story and/or influenced what I've written.

Finally, a paean of appreciation to my editorial assistant and business agent, the charming Ricky, who waited for me to come home.

RSR
ASTP, S/Sgt., WWII

[1] Louis E. Keefer, *Scholars in Foxholes: The Story of the Army Specialized Training Program in World War II* (Jefferson, North Carolina: McFarland & Company, Inc., Publishers, 1988).

[2] Jim Mesko, *M-3 Half-Track in Action* (Carrollton, Texas: Squadron/Signal Publications, Inc., 1996), p. 43.

[3] See General Norman Schwarzkopf, Foreword, in Edward B. Atkeson, *Tale of Three Wars* (Carlisle, PA: Army War College Foundation Press, 1997), p. v.

BACKGROUND

This narrative is a war story drawn from the author's World War II experience as an armored combat infantry squad sergeant. It chronicles the fate of some of the country's brightest teenagers—the 2 percent of the army who survived multiple batteries of tests to qualify for the Army Specialized Training Program (ASTP).

This higher education program would provide the army with the rocket scientists, engineers, medical personnel, and language translators needed for a very long war. When the war turned ugly and infantry casualties mounted, draft boards came up short. To solve the problem, the ASTP was abruptly and ingloriously ended.

There was no time to save America's best minds for the future—they were needed *now*. Harsh critics of the program put it bluntly: these protected whiz kids, these elitist bookheads, these smartass rich kids are going *up front*—and so they were marched off to brutal frontline combat.

Twelve hundred ASTP men from the University of Illinois were sent summarily to an armored division alerted for overseas duty. The division was a mix of semiliterate "depression army" officers and noncoms. The interpersonal and emotional adjustment problems between these two disparate types were eventually resolved.

This account centers on the plight of four of these "bookworms" who were assigned to an armored infantry squad. The men already in the squad range in age from seventeen to thirty-six. Few have finished high school. This unusual squad was sent to France, where they joined General Patton's 3rd Army. After one vicious battle in the Saar, trouble in the Ardennes demanded their presence in Holland, where they joined General Simpson's 9th Army, then under the control of British Field

Marshall Viscount Montgomery. They relieved the stalled British 7th Armored Division, the famous "Desert Rats," and were promptly thrown into a hellish battle in the Ardennes region of Holland.

When his squad leader was wounded, ASTP Private Zachary Gates assumed leadership and was promoted to staff sergeant in the field. The story narrates the march of events of his squad from that day on.

> One day one of their number would write a book
> about all this, but none of them would believe it,
> because none of them would remember it that way.

> From *The Thin Red Line*
> James Jones

1

A WORLD AT WAR

In 1940, high school sophomore Zachary Gates was playing varsity basketball for Milwaukee, Wisconsin's Bay View High School. Like everyone else, he kept an ear tuned to the radio. What would become the most horrendous war in history had erupted one year earlier. That isolationist America would become involved seemed obvious with the initiation of the draft in 1940. Zach and all of his teammates and friends gave a sigh of relief when the announcement came that the draft was limited to men over twenty-one years of age who would serve for a period of twelve months.

The 1939 German blitzkrieg attack on Poland killed 125,000 Polish soldiers and civilians. Rumors surfaced that ten thousand Jews had been sent to internment camps. History would later call them extermination camps.

By April of 1940, Denmark and Norway were overrun. In May of 1940, 136 German divisions attacked Holland, Belgium, Luxembourg, and France. Emboldened by Hitler's overwhelming success, Italy declared war on England and France.

By 1941, the Axis powers of Germany and Italy controlled most of Western Europe and North Africa. Flushed with victory, the German army invaded Russia. By October 1941, they occupied six hundred thousand square miles of the Soviet Union and were within sixty miles of Moscow.

On December 7, 1941, Zach Gates, his school, and indeed all of America were shocked beyond belief when the Japanese attacked Pearl Harbor. On this day of infamy, their sneak attack sank or damaged eight battleships and killed twenty-four hundred Americans. The Army Air

Corps lost 188 planes that never got off the ground. Guam, Wake, Philippines—all were overrun. At the same time, the Japanese were attacking Bangkok, Tarawa, Makin, and more. Hitler, delighted with the Japanese victories, declared war on the United States on December 11, 1941.

Sixty million people would be killed before this, the most catastrophic war in history, ended. Even in its last days, the June 1945 battle for Okinawa raged. The casualties were horrific: 109,000 Japanese soldiers and 3,500 Kamikaze pilots were killed; 150,000 Okinawins died. The Americans suffered 12,250 men killed in action plus another 36,000 wounded. The Navy lost 30 ships and 5,000 sailors.

In the hellish years between 1939 and 1945, 27,600 lives were lost each and every day. The impact of this overwhelming struggle has been described as second only to the birth of Jesus Christ.

*****

By 1942, the draft age had been lowered to eighteen, with all men serving for the duration of the war. Seventeen-year-old Zachary Gates knew it was time to consider his military options.

Not all men were fit for duty—40 percent were rejected for being too short (under five feet), too light (less than 105 pounds), having flat feet, or not meeting other hastily established standards.

The small, standing regular army was over-age, poorly equipped, and under-trained when they, plus green draftees, were sent to Africa in 1942. Their encounter with the wily Desert Fox, General Rommel, and his experienced German Wehrmacht became a near disaster.

And so it was that our young men would soon face aggressive, but more discriminating, selection systems plus more extensive training. By 1942, intelligence and mental quickness were given more importance. Special programs were developed to seek out these exceptional young men. The brightest high school students were encouraged to take a battery of War Department tests. Those with exemplary scores would be eligible for a special army program allowing them to enter college after completing basic training.

*****

Life could not get much darker for Bay View High School's isolationist basketball coach and counselor Art Meyer as the war moved into December 1942. He called his star senior forward, Zachary Gates, to his office. "Zach, have you taken all of those War Department tests?"

"I still have two or three to go. Mr. Meyer, what are these tests all about?"

"If you're smart enough, you get to go to college and learn how to design and handle weapons still on the drawing boards."

Zach's expression was uncertain as he considered other options. "Coach, my Uncle Bob flies P-40s in the Pacific. I'm considering the air corps."

Coach Meyer frowned. "Zachary, you haven't heard today's news. One of our graduates was just shot down and killed flying a Curtiss P-40. A *Warhawk* they called it."

Zach swallowed hard. "I didn't know that. Anyone I might know?"

"Perhaps—he has a brother in your class, one Gus Landorf. Let's see—"

Zach's jaw dropped. "Not Bill Landorf..." he gasped.

"Yes. Do you know him?"

Zach felt a sharp pang of loss. "Yes. He was my counselor at Boy Scout camp."

"I'm sorry, Zachary."

Zach's expression was one of stark disbelief. "You're sure it was Bill Landorf?"

"Yes, I'm very sure. Zach, take this Army Specialized Training Program if you can get into it."

Deep sadness overcame Zachary. "I don't know, Coach... Rumor is you need an IQ over 135."

"135 sounds high. Officer Candidate School is only 110." Coach Meyer shuffled some papers. "Not to worry, Zach. You'll make it either way."

"I just don't know, Coach."

"Zach, how about no decisions until we see how you do on the tests. Dr. Fox will let you know."

"Yeah...thanks, Mr. Meyer."

*****

"Dr. Fox, you wanted to see me?"

Dr. Fox, the vice principal, had recently arrived from the University of Illinois where he had taken retirement. "Yes, Zach. Congratulations. I have good news. You qualified exceptionally well for the Army Specialized Training Program."

Startled by his high test scores and wrestling with the air corps option, Zach asked in a toneless voice, "Will the army program allow me to graduate in June?"

"You will probably be on furlough, but yes, keep working on your valedictory commencement speech."

Zach struggled with yet another force—his parents had made their position clear after the loss of Bill Landorf. His throat went dry. "Dr. Fox, have you heard any more about this program?"

Dr. Fox closed his office door. "Some of my colleagues at Illinois were academic advisors on this new program. The announced purpose of ASTP is 'to provide the continuous and accelerated flow of high grade technicians and specialists needed by the army.' I'm told those who qualify are labeled 'officer material' and are considered the cream of our manpower barrel."

"Would I be part of a large group, Dr. Fox?"

"Not if my Illinois grapevine is accurate. They're projecting only 140,000 men."

"That sounds like a big group."

"Not when you consider the army's manpower goal for 1943 is eight and a half million men. The ASTP represents less than 2 percent of that figure—a very special group indeed."

Zach's interest was piqued. "Do you know the curriculum, Dr. Fox?"

"Yes, and Zach, I highly recommend you take this program."

"Yes, sir."

"You will do four years of engineering in a little over two years. The War Department needs smart, well-trained people to research and utilize new, complicated weapon systems. Of course, if the war goes badly, you may be handed a rifle." Dr. Fox paused and looked at some documents. "The good news is I think you will go to the University of Illinois. First you'll have to finish thirteen weeks of basic infantry training at Camp Hood, Texas, a godforsaken place from all reports." Dr. Fox stood up. "There is one more thing you should know. Not everyone in the War Department is happy about protecting what some call a meritocracy."

The word was new to Zach. "Meritocracy?"

"Yes, Zach, that's a system in which the intellectually talented are chosen and protected or moved ahead of others."

Zach looked perplexed. "You mean an *elitist* group?"

"Yes. You would hopefully be protected from frontline combat." Doctor Fox paused. "Not everyone appreciates the manpower needed to build a new bomb or rocket." He stood up and walked to the window facing Lake Michigan. "Your basic training is apt to reflect that."

Zach's lips drew taut over his straight white teeth. He ran his hand through his slightly tousled hair and his face took on a worried look. "Meritocracy," he said quietly, and stood up. He sighed audibly. "Thank you, Dr. Fox."

*****

Zach's proud parents convinced him that he should follow his advisor's advice. "Zach, if it doesn't work out, you can always transfer to the air corps, since it is a branch of the army."

And so it came to pass that high school senior Zachary Gates was among the favored 2 percent who were sworn into Secretary of War Henry Stimson's Army Specialized Training Program (ASTP). They were told they would be trained in university programs to meet the future specialized needs of the military in such areas as engineering, mathematics, language, and medicine. Zachary Gates was indeed on furlough when he delivered his commencement speech in June of 1943.

*****

Basic Training

Fort Worth, Dallas, Waco—city names called out by the conductor on the long, hot train ride to Texas—finally *Gatesville*, the hastily named town at Camp Hood's ominous main gate. The train chugged to a halt just inside the gate. "This looks…" Zach paused, "unprovidential."

His new friend from Milwaukee, John Brenner, cracked, "Unprovidential? They don't know that word in this embryonic camp— try ominous or forbidding."

An older, regular army private 1st class with a clearly hostile attitude ordered the boys off the train and marched them unceremoniously to South Camp Hood—a treeless disaster of rushed construction located in the worst part of this primitive, sprawling camp. The rough, grid-like roads were loose sand and gravel. One-story tar paper shacks with leaky roofs and see-through siding became barracks. Only the smaller North Camp had a few newer two-story barracks with toilets and showers. The ASTP cadet shacks had neither, utilizing instead a company latrine building with open toilets and open showers.

There were no company mess halls here. Instead, a one-thousand-man battalion mess with unending lines was served in a giant circus tent. KP started at 0330 followed by breakfast at 0430.

Undrinkable, brackish water became a serious problem for this hurry-up camp. One dozen fifty-gallon lister bags full of the same water treated with an evil-tasting chemical called halazone plus a touch of chlorine were the camp's way of solving the problem. These bags hung in full sun causing the daily block of ice to evaporate in a few minutes. The awful water and the unrelenting heat led to scores of the nation's brightest soldiers passing out daily from heat exhaustion. It was a grand place!

The ASTP *Yankee* recruits looked tired and scared when taken to their company area. Fear turned to near panic when they met their basic training *Führers*, two hostile, old-army, evil-looking "good old boys" from the Deep South—Sergeant Robert E. Lee Trincado and Corporal P. E. "Pig" Hancher. Basic began with bitter, deep-seated ill will.

"Yo…Ten-shut…I said tenshut goddamn it. You assholes are fuckin' draft dodgers to this here cadre. This ain't no Boy Scout camp, and this ain't no volleyball game. We are in a world war…YO…and we are losing it. We don't need your fucking brains; we need your guts if you got any."

This nasal, southern voice came from Buck Sergeant Robert E. Lee Trincado—two hundred pounds of unlimited authority controlled by a two-ounce brain—a leftover from the dropout depression army of the thirties. His sycophant assistant was pig-eyed, yellow-toothed Corporal "Pig" Hancher, a carbon copy of Trincado in attitude but half as bright and twice as ugly because of two broken front teeth. Now it was his turn.

"Yo…Suck it up…You're still at atenshun. We aim to make you chicken fairies suffer for three months—most of you won't make it to your free rides. You'll be dead or in infantry repple depples where you belong. This is armored infantry and we take no shit from nobody. The tank destroyers hate your guts so keep your noses clean.

If you fuck-offs are caught anywhere near North Camp and that 92nd nigger division, your ass is fried! This is a segregated army and we and J. B. Hood aim to keep it that way!

One more thing. Unless you want preacher's clap, stay off the cadre crapper marked VD. If you have any questions, save 'em for the fuckin' chaplain. Oh yeah…welcome to Camp Hood, the biggest latrine in the whole state of Texas. Now fall out and report to your barracks' leaders."

The profane, insulting orientation over, the sun-cooked recruits were dispersed to their assigned barracks. Each windblown, leaky building held one platoon. Over-and-under bunks and footlockers were the only contents. Two bare electric light bulbs worked some of the time.

Hard-smoking, hard-drinking "good old boys," all privates 1st class were in charge of each barracks, a clear reminder that even one stripe makes a difference in "this-here-army." A former corporal, now a lieutenant, served as the company commander. He was rarely seen because, according to Sergeant Trincado, "He's alles chasin' cock in Gatesville."

Barracks number three drew thirty-year-old Private 1st Class Jeremiah Rugger, a short, wide man, muscular in a grotesque way. His neck was too thick. His arms were too long. His big, foul mouth was encased in a pox-scarred face.

"Okay, boys…gimme some attention…goddamn it, TENSHUT. I am

Private 1ˢᵗ Class Jeremiah Rugger…YO…I called tenshut…I give orders…I assign the details…and you take 'em…or you're in deep shit. I am cadre…I am with Trincado and the Pig—this ASTP is bullshit…and we ain't cutten you fuck-offs no slack. Fuck with me and you're SOL. Now locate your bunks and prepare to stand inspection. Damn it, nobody moves till I say dismissed. Dismissed."

Those who survived this discriminatory training developed a close kinship. Zachary and his lower bunkmate and fellow Milwaukeean, John Brenner, had become as brothers. The three young men in the adjacent bunks had gone through most of the trials with John and Zachary, forming a kind of five-man survival club. Tom "Sandy" Sander, son of a California professor, was short in stature but long on guts and brains. His two-hundred-plus IQ was tops in the unit. Zach and the others had stood up for him in some heavy confrontations with the sadistic cadre. "I owe you guys," he said sincerely. Quiet Ken Whedder was especially loyal to Zachary, who had dragged him off the live fire course when he was overcome with heat exhaustion.

Stu Sloan, the fifth man of the survival club, did not survive. He became delirious during a live fire exercise conducted in 115 degree heat. He struggled to his feet—30-caliber rounds tore through him—and he hung on to life until the twelfth week. He was not alone. The heat and harassment took its toll. After thirteen weeks, two out of every ten men washed out, dropped out, or were in the hospital. Most of them would be sent to infantry replacement depots.

Zachary Gates was judged the coolest under "basic" fire and harassment by this tight group of five. He felt deep sadness burdened with guilt about Stu Sloan's death. *We should have gotten to him sooner…we could see it coming on.* The four remaining survival group members had made Gates their consensus leader. They vowed to stick together no matter what was ahead.

*****

Basic finally came to what Sandy Sander called, "an ignominious and execrable end."

Ken Whedder grinned. "I think he means it was wretched and detestable."

Zach grunted and walked quietly to the front of the barracks where he surveyed the sprawling, steaming camp. He felt a roar of rage as he pondered the barbaric training rituals, then a strange bewilderment laced with guilt overcame him. *All this crazy training and now we go to the University of Illinois. There's a war on…I should have gone air corps.* His torment was broken when Ken's voice echoed across the length of the barracks. "Gates, get your ass over here!"

"Yeah, yeah."

"Okay, all together—good-bye Camp Hood, good-bye Pig, good-bye Rugger and bully Trincado. May we *never* meet again."

2

UNIVERSITY DUTY

After brutal Camp Hood with its sadistic cadre, the no-Pullman, three-day train ride to Champaign, Illinois in August 1943 became a sleepy stroll in the park. "Champaign Central Station" awakened the train passengers. A one-mile march followed, from the station to the University of Illinois ROTC armory, a huge building built around a quarter-mile track. An odd collection of army vehicles and equipment stood nearby—a jeep, three six-by-sixes (two-and-a-half-ton trucks), a halftrack, a tired tank, and several artillery pieces in varying sizes. The armory, hockey rink, and fraternity row were located on the Champaign side of the campus. The sorority houses stood on the Urbana side of these twin cities. The four friends were assigned to a room in the Alpha Epsilon Pi house, a far cry from Camp Hood's tar-paper barracks.

"We're still together," John Brenner cheered as he dropped his duffel bag on one of the four beds in the room.

Zach stared out of the window at the serene campus. He looked away, shaking his head and feeling guilty. "What a tragedy Stu Sloan didn't make it…"

"Fall out," sounded from outside. The house "brothers" lined up on the sidewalk facing the athletic fields in three ranks of ten each. A pleasant-looking man appearing to be about sixty-five years old faced the soldiers. Captain's bars were attached to his Class A officer's uniform. Tom Sander on Zach's left whispered, "He should be wearing a bird or a star. Who is this guy?"

"Attention," asserted the captain. "At ease," followed quickly. "I'm Captain Fred Mason, your house mother." Laughter spread across the ranks as Captain Fred raised his hand. "Make that house father. I'm here to keep you on schedule and out of trouble. You work with me and I'll be the best CO you ever had or may get again. Any questions?" None were asked. "Very well. Organize your gear and return to this assembly area at 1700 hours for mess call. Dismissed."

"This guy is interesting. How can we find out about him?" John Brenner asked. Zach found the university telephone book on one of the four student desks in their room. "Mason, Fred. Here it is—Ph.D., emeritus professor of military history, lives here in Champaign."

"I thought emeritus meant deceased," Ken Whedder said.

"No, birdbrain, it means retired with distinction. It's an honor," Tom "Sandy" Sander chided.

"How come you're so smart?" Ken shot back.

"Because I'm ASTP. Also because my dad is a professor at UCLA."

"How old do you think he is?" John asked.

"Older than he looks. Professors teach until they're seventy, longer if they can," Sandy replied.

"Judas, this guy could have been in the Spanish-American War as well as World War I," Zach observed.

Indeed, Captain Fred had served in both wars as an infantry battalion commander. A permanent commission had been awarded to him by Teddy Roosevelt himself. A widower, this was his way of once again serving his country.

*****

Class schedules were the next order of business. There were no free elections here and no long registration lines. They could take it or leave it, with all classes part of the mechanical engineering curriculum.

"My God," Ken said. "Twenty-nine hours in one term."

"What's your first class, John?" Zach asked.

"Monday, physics. Jesus, 0700."

*****

The boys' first-floor room was adjacent to Captain Fred Mason's office. They soon discovered he was writing his third book on military history and he was happy to share his insights about war with them. What a welcome diversion that was from the grind of mechanical engineering for the foursome.

John looked up from his study desk. Zach's head was up as he stretched. "I'll bet the old man is still in his office. Should we see if he's ready for a mini-seminar on who's winning the war?"

"Why not? I'm studied out."

Captain Fred motioned them in as newscaster Gabriel Heater was signing off. Zach asked warily, "Can we get a review of the news, Captain Fred?"

Captain Fred turned off the radio. "Well, the one piece of good news is that we landed on a strategic island in the Solomon Islands. Not so happy is the news from New Guinea where twelve thousand Aussies have been killed. Over in the CBI theater—China-Burma-India—the Japs have completed the Burma-Thailand railroad which greatly strengthens their position."

"So what about the ETO (European Theater of Operations)?"

"The Russians are holding their own. That American-designed T-34 tank of theirs is making a difference. The scary news is the Germans have established over fifty secret weapon sites, 'snow slides' I think they are called, from which to fire their V1 and V2 rockets."

"What next?" John said, shaking his head.

"Jet airplanes!" the captain announced.

"Jet airplanes! What are jet airplanes?" John gasped.

"No propellers, flies like a rocket at incredible speeds. If they have many of these, we're in for a very long war," Captain Fred intoned.

John's mouth turned down. "We're going to get in this fight yet, Zach," he mumbled.

Captain Mason stood up. "We'll see...we'll see. Good night, boys."

*****

Back in their room, John picked up an envelope. "Zach, this is for you. It was in with Tom's stuff."

Zach started reading. "Oh my God."

"What now?" John cried out.

"Bud Henner, one of my best friends, was shot down over New Guinea."

"I'm sorry, Zach. Any details?"

Zach exhaled with a low moan. "The whole B-25 crew was lost..."

John put his hand on Zach's shoulder. "I've lost five or six class-mates...I know how it hurts."

"Thanks, John....Poor Bud."

"Zach...perhaps it's just as well you didn't go air corps," John said in an uncertain voice.

*****

At the next seminar, Captain Fred stood waiting at the door. "I'm sorry about your friend, Zachary."

"Thank you, Captain Fred."

"I see you brought Tom and Ken."

"We're anxious to hear about your role in World War I, Captain. We're not very clear on how we got into that war in the first place," Tom said.

"That's an interesting story. We were a Johnny-come-lately as you probably know. World War I started in 1914 for a number of reasons. One big one was the expansionist ambitions of William II of Germany. The precipitating cause was the assassination of Archduke Franz Ferdinand of what was then Austria-Hungary. This took place in Sarajevo, Serbia, what is Yugoslavia today. War was declared on Serbia by Austria-Hungary and all hell broke loose. Russia declared war on Austria, Germany declared war on Russia, and France and England declared war on Germany. The casualties were enormous even before we entered in late 1917."

"What was our policy from 1914 to 1917?"

"Strict neutrality according to President Wilson, isolationist according to others."

"Then how did we get dragged into it?" John asked.

"The sinking of the *Lusitania* was part of it. There were 124 Americans among the twelve hundred who lost their lives."

"Was that the spark that did it?" Tom asked.

"No, and this is the bizarre part. The German foreign minister to the United States wrote a coded note to the German ambassador to Mexico. This note was intercepted and decoded by British intelligence. Are you ready for this?"

"I'm not sure, Captain. What was in the note?"

"It said if the United States and Germany were to go to war, Germany would seek an alliance with Mexico. And get this. Germany would give them Texas, New Mexico, and Arizona."

"So then we declared war."

"Right. April 6, 1917."

"But were we ready for war?"

The history professor became animated. "Hell, no! We had a standing army of only two hundred thousand men, only four million by 1918, about half of whom went overseas. We were ripe for slaughter."

"Did we take enormous losses?" John asked.

"About fifty thousand killed in action (KIA). Nothing like the rest of the Allies, but most of our boys were not on that thin front line of battle. As I recall, you boys were especially interested in North Africa because of John's uncle, Colonel Grimes. Well, try this. Was he 1st Infantry Division or was he 1st Armored?"

"1st Armored, sir."

"Well, in this war, the 1st Infantry Division in Africa alone spent more time in mortal combat than it did in all of World War I, even if one includes all of the training time, travel time, and down time. Those few of us, however, who were front line in World War I, even for short periods, took unreasonable casualties. One U.S. commander reported that his unit had ten Americans killed for every one German they eliminated."

Zach interrupted. "Was that, in part, General Pershing's fault?"

"No. He did the best anybody could. He was a very good man, still is. He's eighty three now. He was forced to play second or third fiddle to Marshal Ferdinand Foch, the French supreme allied commander. Thanks to the insistence of President Wilson, by August 1918 Pershing had organized a separate United States 1st Army. Black Jack Pershing proved that Americans could fight by routing the Germans from the Saint-Mihiel salient."

"Did you know General Pershing during the Spanish-American War?"

"Believe it or not, I did. He distinguished himself as a leader in Puerto Rico at both the Kettle and San Juan Hills battles. Pershing was a real soldier, and he became a hell of an organizer, or we would all have been foreign army replacements in World War I."

"We could use him in this war," John said.

"You boys should also know that three of our outstanding generals in this war were division or battalion commanders in World War I. MacArthur led the 42nd, the Rainbow Division, George Patton was aide to General Pershing and then became the United States tank brigade commander, but that's a separate story, and George C. Marshall was my C.O. in the 1st Division. I must also add the name of T. R. Roosevelt."

"T. R. wasn't in World War I, was he?"

"No. Poor T. R. died in 1919 at age sixty. I speak of Theodore Junior, who was a major in World War I and commanded the 1st Battalion of the 27th Infantry. He distinguished himself in several battles including the offensives at St. Mihiel and Meuse-Argonne. He was gassed, wounded twice, and received every medal but the Congressional Medal of Honor. A great soldier like his father."

"Is he still alive today?"

"Oh very much so. You're not up to date on the African campaign. It was Brigadier General T. R. Roosevelt who led a first wave combat team in the invasion at Oran, Algeria, in 1942."

"Then he must have been with the 1st Infantry Division."

"Right, the Big Red One. They were called upon for another landing at Gela in Sicily this year. Roosevelt was again up front, this time with a cane. We'll hear more of him if his health holds out."

"That's fascinating," John declared.

"I'll say. What about Eisenhower in World War I?" Ken asked.

"Ike was left stateside, where he ran training camps and learned the diplomacy and organizational skills for which he is known. Vice President Truman, as you probably know, was an artillery captain in World War I."

"I knew about Truman, but not the others. Since Patton is already famous for his exploits in Africa and Sicily, we'd like to hear more of his World War I story," Zach said.

"He was one bold warrior, even then, but that's a long story for another time."

*****

Back in their room, Tom was slapping his head. "Damn, I meant to ask Fred about this."

"About what?"

"My dad sent me some just-released news on New York—November 10, 1942."

"So what's so important about old news?"

"A German U-boat planted ten mines in the harbor."

"That's a crock!"

"No, really. It happened five miles east of Ambrose Light. The harbor was closed for forty-eight hours."

"What happened to the mines?"

"Let's see…they swept them—but get this, five have never been found."

"What next? Hit the sack, guys," Zach ordered.

*****

The heavy engineering program ground on for another three weeks before the seminar met again to discuss tanks. "If you men get to the ETO, you will see the best tanks in the world, and all but one are German," the captain announced.

"You mean the Churchill?" Zach asked.

"No. That's a good, forty-ton tank, but the similar sized Russian T-34, the one I mentioned earlier, will, I think, prove to be the best tank in this war."

"I haven't heard anything about the T-34," John commented.

"You may never see one. They are all on the Eastern Front. The T-34 is the reason the Germans developed the Panther, and I will not be surprised if they try for an even bigger Tiger."

"How much bigger can they get?" Ken asked.

"I would bet ninety to a hundred tons."

"Wow! The lesson seems pretty clear—bigger and better tanks and motorized infantry to work with them," Zach concluded.

"You've learned the lesson. Class dismissed."

*****

Just past midterm, the crammed engineering curriculum began taking its toll. Almost 25 percent of the men in the frat house were lost—three who just were not cut out for engineering, three for psychological or emotional overload, and one for medical reasons.

The war seminars became less frequent until final exams were finished. The survival group managed two or three hours on the latest Italian campaign, and were into their second session on the organization of the German army when rumors of the ASTP program's demise started. Large battles loomed in the ETO. "An invasion," Captain Fred said, nodding his head.

Indeed, manpower was needed and the draft was coming up short. Older, married men were being drafted and seventeen-year-olds were encouraged to enlist.

*****

Alas, two weeks into the second term, all classes abruptly ceased. The informal war seminars came to an unexpected and inglorious end. The ASTP program was summarily cancelled. The "Whiz Kids," the "Smartass Rich Kids," or the more generously called "Bookworms" were handed orders labeled A.I.R. "Air Force?" Ken asked hopefully.

Captain Fred entered the room. "Sorry, boys, that's Armored Infantry Regiment."

Zach's end-of-basic-training bewilderment returned. A knot tightened in his stomach as he again stared out at the pleasant campus. He felt cold shivers as he thought of what lay ahead. *Oh, a line outfit is going to love draft dodgers!*

LINE OUTFIT

Swamp Land

"We've been on this damn train for over thirty hours," Zach grumbled.

"Yeah, it's getting dark again," John replied.

Zach stretched. "Where the hell are we going?"

"Secret stuff—who knows?" Tom said, looking out of the window.

"Well, I'm pooped. Another day of K rations will do me in," Ken griped.

"Get some sleep," Zach directed.

"On these racks? Even a Camp Hood bunk would look good right now."

"A shower and shave would help too."

The complaining stopped when the train started to hiss, groan, creak, and finally screeched as the brakes engaged. Zach cupped his face to the window. "Nothing, not a light anywhere."

"What time is it?" Ken asked.

"2330, that's 11:30 P.M.! This is crazy. There's nothing out there. It looks like swampland," John speculated.

A conductor dropped a step out of the coach door. A tall, fiftyish officer stepped into the dim light at the front of the car.

"Jeez, a light colonel," Tom whispered.

"Yeah, and in combat gear," Ken mumbled.

"Look at his helmet just above the red ribbon," Zach observed.

"Cripes, a cross—he's a chaplain!" Tom sputtered.

The train car went silent as the chaplain spoke. "Welcome to Louisiana and to the Red Army. I'm Father MacArthur, 18th Armored Division chaplain, and you're going to need me, because you are on maneuvers and we're under attack from the Blue Army. I must visit the other cars. 1st Sergeant Otto Furk will explain."

A scowling Furk entered the train and strode down the aisle, glaring at the tired troops.

"Why is his lip all puffed up?" John whispered.

"Snuff, I think."

"Yeah, his teeth are yellow."

"Judas, I thought we left these Neanderthals at Camp Hood," Zach groaned.

Sergeant Furk threw up his hands when he saw the wrinkled, mismatched uniforms. He said nothing as he walked briskly to the front of the car. There, a toothy stooge corporal greeted him with a box of red ribbons. Corporal Ludolph Kolchak's eyes raced over the motley troops. "Holy shit, Sarge. Sad-sack assholes, all of 'em."

"Ain't that the truth. Give the bookheads ribbons. I'll take the right side," he growled as he handed Zach a ribbon.

Tired from three days on an aging troop train, Zach frowned and said, "Thanks, Sarge. I always wanted a red ribbon."

"Shove it up your bookhead ass, and here's another to stuff in your big mouth. *And* wipe that chicken-eatin' grin off your face. We ain't taking any shit from you fucking bookheads. Corporal Kolchak, get this asshole's name."

The bookworms had just met their worst nightmares, 1st Sergeant Otto Furk and Corporal Ludolph Kolchak, both regular training cadre who were now scheduled for overseas duty. Clearly, thirty-year-old, uneducated Otto Furk wanted "real soldiers" and not smartass shitheads. His crony, Ludolph Kolchak, would prove himself a greater menace, as his blind hatred for the ASTP men was unforgiving. A big man, his short-tempered and often violent behavior was well known.

The situation was about to worsen. "Dismount and line up in a column of twos next to your coach. You're in B Company," said Corporal Kolchak. The thirty weary bookworms watched a jeep appear out of the swampy night forest carrying a large box of steel helmets and liners. "One size fits all," Corporal Kolchak barked. "Put your ribbon on it and wear it or I'll have your ass!" He then stormed down the line.

One struggling private dropped his tennis racket and garrison hat. "Judas, I'm carrying all this shit and they give me a fifty-pound helmet."

"Goddamn it, straighten your helmet!" the beady-eyed corporal snarled as he reversed field.

Sergeant Furk returned. "Get these assholes moving, Corporal."

"Yes sir, Sarge. They got a shitload of junk…"

Furk dropped his head after looking again at the broken uniforms, this time burdened with everything from tennis rackets to fancy lug-gage and briefcases. His teeth clenched. "Lose all this shit—NOW! One bag per man. That's a direct order! This is the army, not some fuckin' comedy hour. Corporal, move 'em out."

The men were marched a half-mile down a narrow, moonlit trail to a clearing where three GIs were setting up pup tents. Kolchak stopped. "Okay, big shots. This is it! These real soldiers will show you how to set up your hotels, two to a tent and no screwing around. Fall out!" the corporal shouted as he strode off.

Zach approached two of the "real soldiers." "Hi, guys, thanks for the help."

"Yeah, be sure to line 'em up or Sergeant Furk will have all our asses."

"We learned to set these up in basic," Ken replied.

"Good, then we're outta here. Good luck. The Blue Army is infiltrat-ing this area."

"The guy said, 'Good luck,'" Sandy observed. "They don't all hate us."

"This Sergeant Furk even looks like Trincado and Pig Hancher. Remember them?" John groaned.

"Heh, it's cool out here. Did we get any blankets?" Sandy asked.

"Here comes a jeep with some kind of load."

"One to a customer," a smiling corporal shouted while chewing on a cigar. He dismounted and helped distribute the blankets. "I'm Corporal Jim Wing, company clerk, Captain Brunner's driver, and the brain behind headquarters." Wing, a tall, affable man in his early-twenties with an infectious grin and savvy Irish eyes, assessed the ASTP additions with a note of acceptance. "My uncle almost went to college and he's okay."

Seeing that Wing did not seem hostile, Zach approached. "Corporal, when do maneuvers end and what's our main camp?"

"Christ, didn't anybody tell you anything? We're ending maneuvers this week, and then we go back to Camp Polk to fit you guys into the ranks."

"That's a big help. Are we on alert for overseas duty?"

"Top secret, but such rumors are flying—gotta run—oh, this is Louisiana."

*****

A loud whistle announced reveille at 0600 hours. At best, the men had four hours of fitful sleep in the small pup tents.

Corporal Ludolph Kolchak glowered at the men crawling out of their tents. *"On your feet, bookheads. This ain't no goddamn fraterni-ty house."* The men, in their sweat-stained, wrinkled, Class A uni-forms looked like they had been dragged through the swamp. "Jesus Christ! You look like real shitheads! *ATTENTION.*"

The men slowly formed a rank and stood straight. Kolchak went over to a tech sergeant who was studying the men. Kolchak turned abruptly. "This is our platoon sergeant, Russ Grinnell."

"Good morning, men. At ease. Welcome to B Company and the 2nd platoon." Russell Grinnell was pushing forty, an Iowa farm boy who attended Iowa State for two years before dropping out to help run the family farm. He was among the first men drafted and his affable lead-ership style had earned him five stripes. He repressed a smile, and in a strong, clear voice continued, "We will march to our company field headquarters at 0700, where you will meet Lieutenant McNutt. He will direct you to the trucks which will take you to Camp Polk. Maneuvers are officially over at 1200 hours today. Any questions?" The look on Kolchak's face said, *There better not be any.*

Camp Polk Adjustments

Camp Polk was not a Fort Knox, but almost the Waldorf compared to Camp Hood. The twelve hundred ASTP men (10 percent of the divi-sion) were joined by three hundred former aviation cadets. "I guess they just don't need any more pilots," Ken said.

The TO (Table of Organization) called for fifty-six men in the 2nd platoon. The ranks were filled by sixteen ASTP men and four or five air corps cadets. When the squad assignments were completed, the four ASTP friends managed to stay together. They were joined in the 3rd Squad by former Air Corps Cadet Stan Goldman. The men called him a grounded butterfly. The squad was led by unstable acting ser-geant Ludolph Kolchak. Big, forbidding, but "good guy" Bruno Nitchke was the assistant squad leader. Like Bruno, most of the young Camp Polk squad members had not finished high school. All were a little intimidated, a little suspicious, but very curious about Stan and these four different bookworms. What the eleven men had in common was a frenetic fear of Ludolph Kolchak.

The first test for the new men in this unusual mix of soldiers was a rifle maintenance drill. The squad would have four hours to disassem-ble, clean, and reassemble an M1 Garand rifle. Corporal Kolchak marched the squad over to the first open crate where each man was ordered to extract a rifle.

Private Stanley Kosinski was first up. Polish farm boy Stosh was one of several new seventeen-year-olds in the platoon, a good kid who left high school in his senior year. He stopped and looked into the crate. "I'm not putting my mitts in there. It's all axle grease."

"It's *not* axle grease. Now pull out a goddamn rifle," acting Sergeant Kolchak ordered.

"Yuck," Kosinski grumbled as he fished out an M1 Garand covered from barrel to butt with a heavy coat of cosmoline.

"Commence fieldstripping," ordered Platoon Sergeant Russ Grinnell. "Now hear this. Every part must be free of every other one. If you lose parts, you'll be digging holes for the duration."

Quickly, the 3rd Squad began their work—all except the four bookworms. Kolchak was furious. "Insubordination! I'll have you Einsteins court-martialed."

Sergeant Grinnell rushed over. "What's the problem here?"

"Sergeant Grinnell, we've never even seen an M1 before," Zach explained.

"What? Didn't you men have basic training?" Grinnell barked.

"Yes, sir…"

Kolchak interrupted. "Russ, they had basic training without rifles. They fieldstripped their fucking books in the ASTP."

"Put a sock in it, Kolchak. Explain yourself, Gates."

"At Camp Hood we were issued English Enfields and a few Springfields and Craigs. These are the first M1 Garands we've seen."

Grinnell shook his head. "Corporal, have these men observe soldiers who know the M1."

"Okay, Russ. These boneheads better be fast learners."

The embarrassed boneheads walked over and watched the more experienced squad members deftly disassemble the new, sticky M1s, putting each part in a linear order. "Thanks, guys. We've got it," Zach said, signaling his buddies.

The four bonehead rifles were quickly fieldstripped. Kolchak frowned in disbelief. Grinnell smiled and shook his head again. "Now comes the hard part," he announced. "Each part must not only be clean but absolutely dry—that's *DRY*. Signal when you're ready for a parts' inspection. More rags are available."

Nobody passed the first *DRY* parts inspection. The slightest glisten of grease on a single nut or bolt meant failure. "There must be an easier way," Sandy griped. "Yeah, but this is the army way," grinned Ken.

Finally, every part was bone-dry and had passed inspection. "Your next assignment is to finely lubricate each and every part. Then see how fast you can reassemble your rifle," Russ Grinnell instructed.

Everybody groaned and groused. "Why so damn dry if we're going to grease them up again?"

"To make sure you get the feel of each part and can do this in the dark. Oil 'em up," the sergeant ordered.

Reassembly of the Garand rifle with its many small parts was a slow, tedious process even for an experienced rifleman. To everyone's surprise, Zach was the first soldier done. Kolchak and Grinnell inspected the rifle, pulling back the slide, trying the safety, easing the trigger back, and looking down the barrel. "Well done, Gates," Grinnell mumbled in surprise. Seconds later, John, Ken, and Sandy had also finished ahead of the rest.

"These bastards lied. They must have done this before," Corporal Kolchak sputtered.

*****

Sergeant Grinnell called attention. "All right, men. If you've assembled your rifle, memorize its serial number, and get cleaned up for mess call. You four bookworms, see me in my quarters. Dismissed."

The bookworms looked at one another. "What now? I thought he said well done."

They assembled in Sergeant Grinnell's room in the front of the barracks. "At ease, men. Sit down. The bunks are okay. Now explain how you did that."

"Did what, Sergeant?"

"You know damn well WHAT!"

"I think I can explain," John offered.

"Okay, Brenner, so explain."

"Well, it's a little complicated," John stammered.

"Uncomplicate it NOW, Private Brenner."

"Yes, sir. You see, sir, Private Gates has something like a photographic memory."

"What kind of bullshit are you shoveling, Brenner?"

"I can explain it, Sergeant," Tom Sander said.

"Okay, try me, Private Sander."

"Back at Illinois, we took some anatomy tests for medical school. Gates aced them because he could memorize charts and sequences like a camera. He memorized the rifle coming apart in a systematic order and simply reversed it for assembly. We just followed his lead."

A bewildered but impressed Sergeant Grinnell stared at the group and shook his head. "You guys really are some kind of nuts. Get the hell out of here."

*****

Stosh Kosinski sat nursing a badly bruised cheek. Zach approached. "What happened, Stosh?"

"Corporal Kolchak hit me...I dropped my clean rifle."

"What?"

"He banged me; it's really sore."

Zach stormed into the platoon sergeant's room at the front of the barracks, breathing fire. "Grinnell, that son of a bitch—"

"Hold it right there, Gates—I know about Kosinski. It will be addressed. The inspector general is visiting us tomorrow to clean out all nut cases before we go overseas. So cool down and tell it to the IG. Get out of here!"

The inspector general did get an earful and many changes were made in the TO. Ludolph Kolchak was summarily demoted and transferred, escaping a court-martial only because of time in service. 1st Sergeant Otto Furk received only a reprimand and a lecture—he too was saved by his long tenure.

The 3rd Squad gave a sigh of relief. "That sadistic Kolchak is a real lunatic. I knew he was going to hurt somebody," Brenner sputtered while clenching his fists.

Even the battalion commander was replaced for incompetence. Major George Hartman, a West Pointer who had served in Italy with the 1st Armored, took command and succeeded in inspiring much-needed confidence.

Among the air corps additions was Staff Sergeant Norm Ricks, twenty-one, a track star at North Carolina University before he was drafted. Grinnell had used his influence to have Ricks assigned to replace Kolchak as 3rd Squad leader. Ricks related well to all of the men. The bookworms were especially delighted. Bruno Nitchke was promoted to buck sergeant—the bookworms were still trying to figure him out. Zach Gates, Stosh Kosinski's hero, was also the appointed psychologist in the squad. "Bruno is a good guy. Every squad should have a Sergeant Nitchke...he's just a little defensive...he'll come around. You'll see."

"I like the beak," stammered Stosh Kosinski. "He chewed out Kolchak real good." Stosh referred to Lieutenant McNutt, a gung-ho citizen soldier and bar owner from New Jersey with a prominent nose.

Jim Wing was dismayed that the IG let 1st Sergeant Otto Furk escape. "Now I've got to do all the thinking for B Company," he griped when far away from headquarters.

The new 3rd Squad quickly developed a camaraderie under the lead-

ership of Norm Ricks. After the Stosh incident and the rifle demonstration, the bookworms were much more understood and accepted.
The few weeks left before embarkation gave the 3rd Squad—indeed
the whole battalion—a chance to show off and even have some fun.

*****

"A *track* meet?" Stan Goldman asked with a note of surprise in his
voice.

"Yeah, Butterfly. Major Hartman sold it to the whole division to kill
time before we go."

"A track meet?" the former cadet repeated.

"Yeah, dumbbell, the BC knows Norm Ricks is the fastest man in
the army," track driver Corporal John Naylor declared.

"The battalion should look real good. This guy Franks in A
Company was a speedster in high school," John Brenner added.

"What about Gates? He's pretty good," Stosh offered.

"Yeah, your big buddy can run," Tom Sander smiled.

*****

Some of the events were similar to standard track meets. Most, such
as wall scaling, close order drill, and shoot-and-run were not.
Companies A and B did very well in all of the dashes, thanks to Franks
and Ricks. One open event was a two-hundred-yard run across the
drill field. One thousand men lined up and waited for the gun. Norm
Ricks was first across, Jack Franks was third, and the only other battalion point getter was Gates, who finished forty-fifth. "You did good,
Zach," Stosh cheered. "You finished ahead of 950 guys."

"955," Ken Whedder corrected.

"Yeah, 955."

The most interesting event was the tire-change race. In this event,
three men drove a jeep across the drill field, changed all four wheels,
and then raced back to the other side. The team was allowed one man-
ual jack, two tire wrenches, and one spare wheel. Each wheel had to
be on a different axle when they crossed the finish line. Each company could have only one team. Lieutenant McNutt was in charge of the
event since most of the points scored so far were from men in his 2nd
Platoon. "Okay, men, I need some fast tire changers who are willing
to practice and then practice some more."

"I worked in a gas station, Lieutenant, I'm pretty fast," offered a kid
from the mortar squad.

"Very good. I need two more."

The men were assessing one another—Russ Grinnell raised his hand. "Unless the bookworms have a better idea."

Norm Ricks responded. "Zach Gates has a wild idea."

The lieutenant moved in front of Zach. "Okay, Gates, be brilliant."

"Yes, sir, but my idea has to be tested…and kept secret," Zach replied.

The platoon rolled their collective eyes. *What have these whiz kids dreamed up now?*

"Let's hear it, Gates."

"Pete Clovitch in our 2nd Squad is the strongest man I've ever met—"

"So?"

Zach turned to Clovitch. "Pete, do you think you could lift the front end of a jeep?"

"I think so, Gates. Why?"

"If you can hold it up long enough for two fast guys to change the tires—"

"I get it, Gates—brilliant," McNutt cried out.

"Well, it's up to Pete, and we can't let the other teams know what we're up to," Zach insisted.

*****

Pete Clovitch could not only lift the front end, he could hold it long enough for his other two lightweight teammates to quickly spin off the nuts and simultaneously switch the tires. They then proceeded to repeat the operation on the rear end of the jeep. No problem. Pete was a veritable Paul Bunyan. They won hands down. Protests were coming in from all parts of the division, but the umpire could find nothing in the rules to outlaw the procedure. Strongman Pete became the hero of the 85th Battalion and the talk of the division. Battalion commander Major Hartman was delighted and personally congratulated McNutt and the winners. He took Lieutenant McNutt aside. "Lieutenant, did you think up this crazy idea?"

"No, sir, it was one of our bookworms."

"Point him out."

"Private Gates, sir, over there."

The BC stood directly in front of Zach. "Well done, Private Gates. Now save some of those creative ideas for combat."

"Yes, sir."

4

EMBARKATION AND SEAFARING

"What the hell is POE?" Nitchke demanded.

"Port of Embarkation—that's where we get on a boat," Tom Sander quipped.

"I know what embark means, bookworm."

"Sorry, Sergeant. I think we have two weeks left to load up and get some kind of training, 'T' Series they call it."

"Shit, not more lectures."

"Fraid so, Bruno; maybe some training films just for you," Sandy cracked while backing away.

"This better be good," Bruno grumbled.

Training Series

"T" Series did open with films. Most were perceived by the men as corny. However, the series ended with two lectures by a young West Point lieutenant colonel who had seen action with the 1st Armored Division in Africa and Sicily. His voice carried high credibility and the troops paid close attention. Even Bruno was all ears.

Colonel Crane explained, and then used pictures to vividly illustrate, the tactical advantages of an armored division. The advantages he stressed were 1) maneuverability 2) firepower 3) quick dispersal and 4) independence. After sharing several graphic combat illustrations regarding those advantages, he turned to a discussion of the kind of personnel needed to man a first-rate armored division—that caused a real stir.

Stosh nudged Zach, his eyes urgent. "He's talking about us, huh?" he whispered.

"Yeah, shh…"

Stosh persisted in a soft voice. "He sounds a little like you bookworms."

"Right, now pipe down."

The first requirement was *mental mobility,* which Colonel Crane explained as being adaptive and creative in finding solutions to rapidly changing combat circumstances. Stosh was really getting into the articulate colonel's lecture. "Like the tire race, huh Zach?"

"Yeah, like that. Now be quiet."

The second desirable characteristic was *daring* which the colonel explained as *audacity*—the ability to take a chance and boldly stun the enemy with actions they do not expect. He quoted George Patton's motto, "*L'audace, l'audace, toujours l'audace*—bold, bold, always bold."

The colonel then spoke of General Grant, who said, "In every battle there comes a time when both sides consider themselves beaten; then he who continues the attack wins." Zach leaned over to John and whispered, "James J. Corbett, 'Fight one more round.'"

"Who's he?"

"The boxer."

"Oh yeah."

Next came tactics. *Offense,* he stressed, becomes the main mission of armor. To the officers and noncoms, he emphasized giving latitude to well-trained and experienced subordinates in getting their mission accomplished.

Quick dispersal, they learned, referred to getting out of the way of an assault by an overwhelming force. A voice was heard from the crowd. "He means retreat like hell."

"*Retreat* is not the correct word," said the young colonel. "We prefer *retrograde movement.*"

Independence was clarified by Crane reviewing the difference between an infantry division with all of its attached units and an armored division with its own tanks, artillery, engineers, ordinance, and even a medical battalion.

A single armored infantry platoon working with a platoon of tanks, he explained, was like a small army. "You have five tanks, five halftracks, and fifty-six infantrymen (instead of thirty-six), plus twenty-seven tankers, a mortar squad, and a machine gun squad. You also have two officers and two platoon sergeants, an outfit big and strong enough to independently give fits to the enemy."

Next came *tank infantry coordination and cooperation.* "The infantry must ride on, hide behind, and protect the flanks of their big brothers. In marching fire, they must know how to fire the freewheeling 50-caliber gun mounted on top of the tanks. When S-2 (intelligence) says there are no German tanks, the men may have to ride their halftracks into the fray with guns blazing."

John leaned over. "What about panzerfausts?"

"Ask him; it's Q and A time."

Colonel Crane responded quickly. "If they have panzerfausts, you walk. If they have antitank guns, you leave your tracks behind."

Port of Embarkation

Camp Polk became a busier, more confused place than usual. New recruits were coming in to fill the soon-to-be-vacated barracks. Only TAT, the gear To Accompany Troops, had been delayed. Some Sherman tanks were backed off the flatbeds to be refitted with the newer 76 mm guns. The halftracks stayed put.

The division finally boarded the troop trains and headed east—destination Camp Kilmer, New Jersey. Three days of a deliberately devious route was devised to confuse the enemy. The troops thought it a joke. "Any German or Japanese spies are probably more amused than confused," cracked John.

The winding trip ended at the railroad sidings of Camp Kilmer in Brunswick, New Jersey, reclassified as a port of embarkation (POE) camp. Here, the camp personnel took their duties very seriously, starting with practice drills on a mocked-up ship called *Rock and Rye*. Most of the troops had never been on an ocean cruise, so they found the bell calls, the "Now hear this," the life jackets, and the lifeboats fascinating. The drills were realistic to the point of loading the boats and lowering them to the pavement some twenty-five feet below. These drills took on a sense of urgency when the men were told that two ships in the last convoy to leave New York had been sunk.

The making of wills was revisited and finally executed for those who had put the whole idea out of their minds. "Avoidance," Zach called it.

"What's next, Sergeant?"

"The gas chamber. Get your masks and fall in at the two sealed barracks."

"I hear this is a real pain," John said, as a base sergeant barked orders.

"All right, men, carry your masks. I say carry your gas masks. Do not put them on until I give the command. I want you to get a good whiff of each gas so you'll be able to identify it." The doors were sealed and a small cloud of chlorine gas was released. Widespread choking and coughing ensued as breathing became very difficult.

"*Affix gas masks*," the sergeant shouted. The gas masks worked and the red-eyed troops settled down and looked at one another through their goggle-eyed masks.

"That was chlorine. I hope you'll recognize it if you meet it again." The troops were sure they would. Chlorine had been used successfully by the Germans in World War I and was considered a major threat again. The exercise was repeated with tear gas, choropicrin gas, and, finally, the deadly mustard gas. In the mustard gas demonstration, a small part of each soldier's arm was left exposed. A minuscule drop caused a painful burn. To inhale it was fatal. The value of one's gas mask became painfully clear.

The last test of pain and suffering before passes would be issued was the hypodermic injection—the dreaded shots.

"Why? We had a ton of shots in 1942," was the common cry.

"Yeah, I'm still hurting."

The nurse smiled sweetly. "Be brave. These are mostly boosters."

His Majesty's Transport Samaria

Duffel bags were piled ten high in the workhorse six-by-six trucks for delivery to the trains. The troops were loaded. Mess that evening was a box lunch eaten during the one-hour ride to Jersey City that was followed by a ferry ride across the Hudson River to the huge New York docks. A hard-working American Red Cross service unit supplied doughnuts and coffee. At last the ships came into view. Half of the 85th Armored Infantry Battalion was assigned to a small, tired, four-hundred-foot British transport named the HMT (His Majesty's Transport) *Samaria*. Three larger ships carried the rest of the division.

In single file, the men labored up the gangplank. Battalion commander Major George Hartman himself barked the last names of each and every one of his men. "Gates, Zachary S.; Brenner, John R.; Sander, Thomas P.; Whedder, Kenneth." And so it went, on and on into the night and on into the darkened hull of the ship. It was a moment of truth—there would be no turning back now.

The next morning, the HMT *Samaria* eased quietly out of pier forty-five at the Staten Island docks heading out to sea. The war-weary transport closed in on the convoy rendezvous area a few miles outside of New York, where a British-American naval team sorted out its escort duties. A reassuring sound came from a squadron of P-47 Thunderbolts roaring overhead. Stan Goldman, the surplus air force cadet, became the focus of attention. "Butterfly, how far will they escort us?"

"Depends on their auxiliary gas tanks."

"So?"

"Well, if these are P-47 Ds, they have a range of about nineteen hundred miles."

"So they'll be with us for about a thousand miles?"

"No. We're averaging twenty miles an hour at best, which means the planes are burning up gas just slowing down and circling. I'd guess about five hundred miles, max."

"And how far do we go?"

"A little over three thousand miles, if we're going to Southampton."

"You mean we're naked for twenty-five hundred miles?"

"Yup, except we do have two navies supporting us."

"Yeah, two destroyers are all I see."

"Well, they have depth charges."

"When are we out of the Thunderbolts' range?"

"I'd guess only three or four days."

"Then what?"

"Then the U-boats know it's safe to attack."

"That's just great. How many more naked days do we have?"

"I'm not sure. Ask Sandy. He's the brain."

"I'd guess the whole trip under these evasive conditions will take thirteen to fifteen days, so we have ten or eleven days of U-boats," Sandy replied cautiously.

*****

Sandy was right. On the fourteenth day of angry seas, the HMT *Samaria* pulled into Southampton.

Driver John Naylor was bent over. "I'm staying in Europe. I'll never get on a boat again. I have never been so sick in my life."

"Cut the crap. We're getting off this row boat," Sergeant Russ Grinnell shouted.

The Red Cross was serving coffee, British tea, and doughnuts on the dock. In appreciation, the men freely gave away their five-cents-a-pack cigarettes, not realizing cigarettes in England were worth their weight in gold. No wonder the joke about Americans: overpaid, oversexed, and over here.

The men marched to the train tracks area on the docks where the small, compartmentalized English trains were quickly loaded for the two-hour trip to Tidworth Barracks near Stonehenge. John was reading the mimeograph handed to him by a Red Cross worker. "It says here that Tidworth Barracks was designed by Kaiser Wilhelm of Germany for the purpose of housing Queen Victoria's troops...this is a strange country."

Stosh needed a moment to ponder John's report. "I thought the kaiser was on their side—Germany's, I mean."

John shrugged. "You're right and you're wrong, Stosh."

Stosh frowned. "Quit bullshitting me."

"I'm not bullshitting you. That happened in the Victorian Age, before World War I." *Thank you, Captain Fred.*

"Crazy. You bookworms are full of it."

The train stopped in the small town of Tidworth, and the division marched a short distance to the historic and pleasant looking two-story brick barracks. The grounds were landscaped and treed unlike so many of the hastily commissioned U.S. Army camps. Each barracks had a foreign sounding name reflecting the Victorian Age: *Bhurtpore, Delhi, Jellabad.*

"Not bad."

"Damn fine," was heard as assignments were made and the barracks started to fill.

"What about the three infantry battalions? Are we always last?"

"I don't like this. I hear trucks coming this way," Zach said.

Lieutenant McNutt arrived on the scene. "Attention men. We're being trucked up the road a few kilometers to Windmill Hill and Penning's Camp. Prepare to mount up."

"What's with this camp?"

"I hope it's not for tents."

The infantry battalions mounted up just as a light rain began to fall. Twenty minutes later, the rain increased as the convoy of trucks came to a halt at Windmill Hill. "85th, prepare to dismount," sounded up and down the column.

"Where the hell are the barracks?" roared Bruno. A short march up and over the hill answered his question. Laid out in neat, unending rows stood hundreds of pyramidal tents. The rain increased as the troops slogged through the muddy corridors and were assigned eight to a tent.

"Jesus, mud floors, no doors or sideboards—we might as well live in foxholes," Sergeant Ricks griped.

The squad unloaded their TAT equipment under the army cots and turned in for a rainy, drippy night. The next morning, all drivers were ordered front and center to begin the huge task of unloading the divisional vehicles now arriving in Tidworth, Plymouth, and Southampton. Two days later, the tanks, tracks, artillery, trucks, and jeeps marched into camp as the rain finally stopped. The preparations for the cross-channel move proceeded with great urgency. Last minute details were standard operating procedure and kept the division busy from morning until night. Preparing vehicles for combat, zeroing weapons, staff conferences, even lectures on how to act if taken prisoner—these were only part of this busy time. Divisional officers down to the battalion commanders were flown to France for battle orientation.

"Good grief, Zach. I thought we'd be in England long enough to see London," John complained.

ACROSS THE CHANNEL

Good-bye, Windmill Hill and muddy Penning's Camp. Advance units with divisional equipment had already departed, their destination secret. Rumors ran wild.

"Can't be Le Havre. The Germans still hold it...don't they?"

"Beats the shit out of me. Ask Zach."

"I'm pretty sure Le Havre fell in the middle of September or early October," Zach mumbled.

"One Mulberry is still working, isn't it?"

"Who knows with all this secret shit?"

"Is the port at Cherbourg ours?"

"Yeah, that fell on D-day."

John Brenner shook his head. "No, Cherbourg fell around July 1, I think."

"None of the harbors are 100 percent cleared. We're not all going to walk off without getting wet," Sander huffed.

"All the beaches are now clear of mines, aren't they?"

Lieutenant McNutt halted some of the rumors and speculations by explaining that they all could be correct, since heavy equipment would land one place, support troops another place, and infantry still another. He guessed the infantry would LCI (landing craft infantry) to Omaha Beach. Their tracks and trucks would be towed by the big LCTs (landing craft tank) to an area on the Cherbourg Peninsula.

Corporal Naylor, the 3rd Squad's track driver, looked worried. "Towed in what kind of LCT, Lieutenant?"

"Some really big barges called Rhino Ferries. Piece of cake, Naylor—unless the channel is rough."

"It's gonna be rough, Naylor. You'll have to swim," Goldman kidded.

"Not a chance—you guys better know how to swim."

McNutt raised his hand. "Maybe none of us will get wet. It depends on how close in the landing craft can get before they drop the front ramp."

"We don't cross the channel in an LCI, do we, Lieutenant?"

"I don't think so. The LCIs or smaller craft will probably come out from the beach to meet us. God only knows what ships are available to get us across the channel. Any more questions?" Not hearing any, McNutt turned on his heel and exited the area.

Bruno was uptight about the beach operation and bluntly confronted Zach. "Well, bookworm, don't you have a take on this?"

Zach wasn't expecting that from usually calm Sergeant Nitchke. He paused as the rest of the squad tuned in. "Yes, I do…a few months ago the Germans had fifty-five divisions, eleven of them armored, waiting for overlord. Some of our assault companies had 90 percent casualties in a matter of minutes on D-day. We should thank God no one will be shooting at us from the beach."

The squad became silent and, in a rare moment for the big buck sergeant, his voice caught. "I'm sorry, Gates."

The next voice sounded from Platoon Sergeant Russell Grinnell. "Check your final equipment and then hit the sack. We have a tough march tomorrow."

*****

The advanced divisional units cleared the Tidworth area and headed for the channel. The 85th Armored Infantry Battalion was next in line. Baker Company led the 85th through the Red Horse Area, Channel Base Section, and on to the ports of Weymouth and Southampton. The small, two-seat Piper Cubs called L-4s or "Grasshoppers" were escorted across the English Channel by the RAF. To attract less attention from U-boats, the critical 184th Signal or Communication Company was being secretly shipped over in a small, camouflaged boat.

The tanks were crossing four to each landing ship tank (LST), which in turn was towing the barge-like Rhino Ferries, much as Lieutenant McNutt had speculated. The heavy stuff was landing at the partially rebuilt ports of Cherbourg or Le Havre and at the remaining battered Mulberry harbor near Sword Beach. Two of the three infantry battalions would land on the Cherbourg Peninsula. The 3rd Squad with the rest of the battalion would land at still-ominous-looking Omaha Beach.

At Southampton, B Company boarded the Polish ship *Sobiesky*, a war-weary four-hundred-footer. Their halftracks and drivers were with the LSTs and Rhino Ferries. The air- and sea-escorted convoy could see the beaches. All seemed go, except for the critical signal company which ironically could not be reached. Since German submarines were operating in the area, new concerns raised the fear level.

Whedder stared out at the rolling sea. "Could they have been torpedoed?" he asked in a drained voice.

Sandy shook his head. "I doubt it. We would have heard some signal."

John agreed. "We have a ton of air and navy cover. What do you think, Zach?"

"I think they ran into a submarine—"

"What?"

"If they are taking evasive action, they wouldn't use the radio."

The worried mood changed when smaller craft came into view on their way to meet the ship. "They don't look very big," Staff Sergeant Ricks observed.

"No, they look like LCMs and LCVPs," 2nd Platoon Sergeant Grinnell replied.

"What's with all the new letters, Russ?" Bruno Nitchke growled.

"*Landing craft mechanized*, holds about three squads, same for the larger LCVPs, except they can carry a vehicle. I'm not real sure."

Lieutenant McNutt joined the group. "I think some of those approaching are what they call Higgins Boats. They all have drop fronts."

"Stand clear!"

Scramble nets made of heavy rope were lowered over the tall sides of the rolling *Sobiesky*. The climb down the net carrying a rifle, gas mask, and full field equipment became a nerve-jangling ordeal. The landing craft rose and then fell with each swell of the sea. Then it would swing away from the larger ship, creating a gap. A bone crushing collision followed on the return swing. The trick was to judge the right time to let go of the net. Hold on if there was a gap and let go when the landing craft was rising, thus shortening your drop. Confusion or panic on the nets could make for a long, leg breaking drop. If you missed the LCM altogether, you were crushed between the boats.

"3rd Squad, we're first off the net," Sergeant Ricks shouted as a landing craft approached. "Gates and Brenner first down. You can catch any stumblebums."

"He means take the point," John grumbled.

"Relax, John. Ambulances are waiting on the beach just for us." John and Zach made a near-perfect release and drop, shed their packs, and prepared to help those dropping with less good fortune.

The landing craft followed the swells, causing a series of rises and falls on the trip to the beach. One minute the beach would be in full view and then it would disappear. "Prepare to land," ordered the boat commander as he ran the craft hard on the beach and dropped the ramp front of the boat onto the sand. Cheering erupted. No wet feet for this group of soldiers as they filed off the ramp.

Tom Sander exhaled a huge sigh of relief as his feet hit the sand. "Now this beats D-day by a mile."

"Amen. Those poor bastards in the 1st and 29th Infantry took two thousand casualties doing this," Ken Whedder mumbled.

The 2nd Platoon moved up the beach toward a road some three hundred yards inland where they would rendezvous with their halftracks. En route were grim reminders of recent, terrible days on Omaha— burned-out vehicles, sunken LCIs, shell casings, craters, barbed wire, and hedgehog and tetra-hydra obstacles.

On the brighter side, some appreciative French citizens stood waving as the young soldiers looked for their squad halftracks and drivers. T/5 John Taylor was standing in the command ring of his halftrack "Babe," waving a pair of silk panties. "Where have you been hiding?" he yelled. "I've been partying for hours."

"Mount up," ordered Sergeant Ricks as the men entered through the rear door of the track.

"Where did you get the bloomers, John?" Stosh asked.

"A mademoiselle gave 'em to me, Stosh. She didn't need 'em."

"Jeez," Stosh stammered. Zach patted Stosh's back and said loud enough for everyone to hear, "Stosh, John has carried those around since Camp Polk. No girl wants him or his panties."

The B Company convoy headed west toward the Cherbourg Peninsula. "Where are we going, Sergeant Grinnell?"

"McNutt says we're going on a forced march to the Saar Region of France where we'll join Patton's 3rd Army to back up the veteran 94th Infantry."

"Any news on the signal company, Sergeant?" Zach asked.

"Not a damn word."

6

FRANCE AND
THE ARDENNES

The snowy, icy march ended near Eply, France, not far from Metz. The continuing December battle in the Ardennes was winding down. The 4th and 10th Armored Divisions had already pulled out of the Saar to help straighten out the bulge. This left the Saar vulnerable should there be a second German offensive.

Sergeant Grinnell returned from a company meeting. "Well, men, here it is. If there is a second attack, it will come here out of the Saar-Moselle triangle." He held up a map showing the two rivers. "It's our job to help the 94th give 'em a bloody nose before they get started. We're awaiting orders. Any questions?"

"What about the signal company?"

"Good news. Gates was right. They were taking evasive action; they're a day behind us."

"Was it submarines?"

"Yeah, and here's the bad news. The *Sobiesky*, the Polish ship that brought us to France, was torpedoed on her return trip to England. She was carrying a full load of wounded men from Normandy. All hands were lost."

There were no more questions.

*****

The signal company arrived the next day and the bloody-nose marching orders followed. The 7th Battalion led off taking most of the division's casualties in the first week. B Company and the 3rd Squad met only token resistance as they pushed through the 94th "grunt" Infantry. The German force appeared to have lost its momentum.

"We lucked out, Zach," Ricks said with a note of relief in his voice.

Nitchke came forward. "Yeah, they've had it. We can get the hell out of here."

Zach raised his hand. "Hold it...listen." Silence. And then an ominous, fluttering sound was heard overhead.

"*Mortars!*" Ricks shouted. "*Take cover!*"

The tracks had been left behind and so there was no real cover. The men hit the ground just as three large mortar rounds exploded on top of them. "*Run!*" Ricks shouted. "*They're on us.*"

Those still able ran toward a stone silo one hundred yards back. The mortar fire continued for another ten minutes and then ceased. "They've withdrawn..." Ricks said as he counted heads. "We're missing two—anybody hit?"

Tony Holter groaned from a gash in his left shoulder where shrapnel had hit him. Medic Bill Anders was on his way. "Hang in there, Tony. It's only a flesh wound. *Okay, let's go find Whitford and White!*" Ricks screamed as he started running back to the strike area.

"I found Bob Whitford," Stosh called in a broken voice. Whitford must have been only a few feet away from the explosion. His body had been torn almost in half.

Bill Anders just shook his head. "At least Holter will make it."

"I've got Bob White—he's alive!" Goldman shouted.

Anders rushed over. "This is bad. We'll need a stretcher."

*****

Now only nine men were left standing in the 3rd Squad. Ricks approached the four bookworms. "You guys were out front and did good—it will be duly noted."

"We're relieved," called Bruno.

B Company had twenty-seven casualties, light considering this was their first serious action. Also lost—not for wounds, but for dereliction of duty—was inept 1st Sergeant Otto Furk. After he was found drunk and fraternizing with a German girl, immediate demotion and a transfer to another battalion followed. Bob Klein, a veteran sergeant from A Company, replaced him as 1st Sergeant. A delighted Jim Wing cheered, "A straight shooter who can read and write. At last!"

No officers were lost, but B Company commander Captain Brunner remained on sick call for much of the action. He was expected back any day.

To the Ardennes

The 21st Army Group under Field Marshal Montgomery was stalled in a savage battle with the German 8th Parachute Division. To the dismay of General Patton, the division was pulled out of the 3rd Army and ordered north. Their mission—"*Unstick 'em!*"

A frigid, windy, icy day greeted Lieutenant Colonel Hartman's 85th Battalion as they mounted up for the 250-mile forced march to Holland. The big vehicles slowly crossed patches of glare ice and then charged the snowdrifts. "I say we let the limeys solve their own problem," griped Naylor as he fought the big wheel. Like Stosh Kosinski, John Naylor was a West Virginian. Working as a farmhand, he became a pro with heavy farm equipment and now with halftracks. Deeply religious, he prayed out loud during most of the harrowing journey.

Sergeant Norm Ricks stood up in the gun ring of his halftrack and surveyed the one-hundred-foot intervals between the halftracks. "This ice is bad. How the hell are the tanks staying on the road with their metal tracks?" he said to those shivering in the seats below.

"They're not," said T/5 Naylor, looking through his windshield. "On the left."

Raising his binoculars to his eyes, Ricks saw a tank off the road. "He's still upright. There's a prime mover trying to winch him back on the road."

"I thought those duckbills they put on the tracks were supposed to help," yelled Bruno.

"Only on snow. Nothing works on ice."

Naylor interrupted. "Hang on. We're going to slide around these guys." Ricks clutched the ring with both hands as Naylor deftly guided the big vehicle around the congestion, a maneuver which would become commonplace during the next three days.

When the convoy hit Luxembourg, the trip became even more interesting. The Allied lines were almost back to where they had been before the bulge on December 16, 1944. The Germans, in a strategic withdrawal capitalizing on the weather, now had only the last elements of their earlier large force crossing the convoy's path. The ice-delayed convoy met none of the major retreating units. Apparently they crossed into Germany or were hiding just to the west of the road, an unnerving thought, since the high roadbed made the vehicles sitting ducks for tanks in defilade positions. Only sporadic fire was engaged as the convoy moved into now-safer Belgium where the men relaxed and enjoyed the fuel stops and breaks for their portable, cold K and C rations. If a town was nearby, day or night, the grateful Belgians greeted the convoy with cakes and cookies. The troops rewarded them with cigarettes.

As the winter finally began to relent, B Company moved into still-hostile Holland, where the Germans were putting up a heavily dug-in defense to protect their German Rhineland. The 3rd Squad entered the small town of Linne, held by a British Armored Infantry Company. "Good luck, yanks—maybe you can move the stubborn bastards."

A house on the very edge of town was assigned to the squad. Exit the back door and you were in no man's land, forty or fifty acres of farmland with an ominous woods beyond. Improving weather, a comfortable house, and the arrival of mess trucks—things were looking up. One replacement arrived bringing the squad up to ten men. Private 1st Class Larry Cooper, a bold soldier who had been wounded while with the 4th Armored Division, seemed unusually anxious to get even with the "krauts." "What's his problem?" grumbled battle-weary Stan "Butterfly" Goldman.

*****

After a tense stand-down of three days, the Brits were gone. Attack rumors were abundant. "We go the day after tomorrow—get your shit together," ordered Platoon Sergeant Russ Grinnell. The first big battle test, under British control, was about to begin.

7

MARCHING FIRE

Linne, Holland
February 1945

Lieutenant McNutt stood briefing his 2nd Platoon the night before the battle. "Listen up. This is what we know. Our platoon will lead the battalion in an attack on the 24th Para Regiment of the German 8th Parachute Division. These krauts have been dug in for five years. They're tough parachute infantry who have stopped the British cold. We are going to mount tanks and run 'em out with a frontal attack."

Groans ebbed slightly when McNutt displayed a map. "This large farm in the middle of these open fields is our jumping off place. We're told that as of last night the krauts have abandoned the farm and retreated to the woods over here, a distance of one thousand yards. Our patrols and the Brits tell us they have elaborate trenches, dugouts, and concrete bunkers hidden in the woods. This area on the right flank is thought to be a minefield, and the areas at the fence lines are covered with concertina wire. We have to be at the farmyard at 0530. We jump off at 0600. Any questions?"

"Lieutenant, where is their main line of defense?"

"We're not sure. Probably two rows. One at the front of the trees and another back fifty to one hundred yards."

"Are we taking orders from our 9th Army?"

"No, not even from the 18th Armored. Our whole combat command is under the command of the British 7th Armored Division."

"What about squad orders?"

"You'll get those from Sergeant Grinnell and your squad leaders early tomorrow morning. Men! We're going to go through 'em like shit on a hot tin roof. First call 0430. Get some sleep. That's all."

Stosh Kosinski, who had just turned eighteen, seemed bewildered. "What's it mean, shit on a tin roof?"

"It's just a metaphor," said Corporal John Naylor.

Still confused, Stosh asked, "So what's a metaphor?"

"Ask your buddy Gates. He's a bookworm," Naylor grunted.

Still tired from patrolling the night before, Pfc. Zachary Gates reached back for some reserve energy. "It means it's going to be easy, like when we say, 'piece of cake.'"

"Oh, I get it. Thanks, Zach."

"You're welcome, Stosh. Now get some sleep."

"Who can sleep with those birds calling all night long?"

"Just some friendly night birds, not to worry."

"Ken Whedder says it's German patrols signaling one another."

"Whedder doesn't know shit. Go to sleep."

"He's a bookworm like you."

"Bookworms don't know shit about birds."

"Ken does."

"Yes, he does," said Ken Whedder, who had been listening.

"Okay, Ken, tell us about the birds," Zach grunted.

Before Ken could explain his theories, Sergeant Russ Grinnell entered the house. "2nd Platoon, SHUT UP! Get some sleep; you're going to need it!"

*****

At 0430, Staff Sergeant Norm Ricks faced his tired 3rd Squad. "Get your asses in gear and look alive."

"What's the word, Sarge?"

"I'll let you know. I'm meeting with Lieutenant McNutt and Russ Grinnell in five minutes."

"What about those damn birds we heard all night?"

"S-2 (Battalion Intelligence) says Whedder was right. The krauts probably know more about our mission than the brass. I'm out of here."

*****

Fear and apprehension were written on the squad's faces and showed in the phony, disinterested slouches of their bodies. Rifles were checked and rechecked. Bandoliers of M-1 clips were in abundance.

"One more bandolier and you'll fall down," said Tom Sander watching replacement Larry Cooper try to manage still another belt of ammo.

"Blow it out!" Cooper replied with a note of irritation.

"Sorry—be a hero," Sander shot back.

*****

Staff Sergeant Ricks returned from the squad leaders' meeting. "So what's the good news, Sarge?" Ken Whedder asked.

"The good news is we're going to learn about marching fire and rolling barrage."

"Meaning what?" Whedder asked nervously.

"Meaning that our tanks will attack on an even skirmish with all guns blazing," Norm Ricks replied matter-of-factly.

"That's it?" sounded Bruno.

"No, there's more. All three rifle squads will dismount our tracks and follow behind the tanks except for five 3rd Squad heroes who will ride the lead tanks and man their 50-calibers. Bruno—you and I will ride tanks one and two."

Bruno grunted. "RHIP, I suppose."

"You're right, rank does have its privileges...And if you're good with a 50-caliber, you get to ride tank three. That's you, Gates."

"Gee, thanks, but I'm better with an English Enfield."

Ricks didn't acknowledge the interruption. "Tank four is Goldman."

"Hey, Sarge, I'm an air corps butterfly—remember?"

"So am I, Stan—suck it up."

Eager Larry Cooper interrupted. "Ricks, I want that fifth lead tank."

"Are you ready for it, Cooper?"

"That's how I got shot up. I'm getting even."

"Okay then. Any questions?"

"What's with the rolling fire?" Zach asked through a dry throat.

"Our 406th Artillery Battalion, the guys who never miss, will cover us with HE (high explosives) as we move into the woods. They will keep the barrage rolling about two hundred yards ahead of us. Any more questions?"

Tom whispered to John. "What's with this guy Cooper? That's a suicide job."

"He's nuts."

Stosh overheard. "I saw him tearing up a letter from a girl."

"At ease, guys. Any questions?"

"What about the track?" Naylor shouted.

"Park it in the farmyard. Move up when we've secured the woods—whenever Captain Brunner says you can."

"What about enemy tanks?" Ken asked.

"S-2 and recon think they have withdrawn."

"Yeah, we've heard that before," grumbled Bruno Nitchke.

Mount Up and Move Out!

"Enough bullshit. We'll run right over 'em. Mount up!" called Sergeant Ricks.

"Like shit on a hot tin roof!" Stosh called out

Norm Ricks exhaled heavily. "Yeah, Stosh, like the lieutenant said."

The 2nd Platoon led off on a four-mile mounted march to a road two thousand yards south of Heide Woods. Here the terrain was mostly open, flat fields and pastures until it met the woods. The large farmhouse and several barns stood near the center.

Ricks looked in all directions from the ring of his 3rd Squad track. "Where the hell are the tanks?"

"Move out!" shouted Platoon Sergeant Grinnell.

The platoon of five tracks encountered no fire as they approached the farm. Perhaps S-2 was right for a change. Ricks, with his 3rd Squad in the lead, was not taking any chances. He signaled a halt and called for Lieutenant McNutt, who was following in a jeep. McNutt anticipated the question. "Good thinking. Dismount and check it out."

Ricks dismounted and sent Sergeant Nitchke and half of the 3rd Squad into the farmyard to make sure the buildings were clear. Stosh returned first, followed by a Dutch barge dog. "No one around, just Prinz here."

"Okay. Park the tracks and assemble on that tree-lined driveway," Lieutenant McNutt ordered.

While waiting anxiously for the platoon of tanks, Zach and Sergeant Ricks walked over to the men petting Stosh's dog. "Stosh, how did you know his name?" Zach asked.

"His tag. It says Prinz. Can he come with us?"

Just then the tanks rumbled into view. "No, Stosh, he'll be safer at the farm," replied Ricks as his heart began to pound.

The medics followed the five tanks and quickly set up an aid station in the farmhouse while Stosh introduced them to Prinz. "Take good care of him. He's a nice dog."

*****

The five lead tanks formed on a tight skirmish line. The quiet, apprehensive 3rd Squad dismounted and joined them. Zach opened the track's storage gear, grabbed an extra box of new, "liberated" blue goose explosive air force 50-caliber rounds, ran to the middle tank, and waited. The platoon had "acquired" them from a remote airfield in France when ammunition was scarce. They were designed to explode inside the new self-sealing gas tanks developed by the Luftwaffe. They were called "blue goose" because every fifth round, the one that exploded was painted blue. The other rounds were the same: tracer, armor piercing, and ball. No one was aware that this explosive ammunition was outlawed by the Geneva Convention for use by ground troops.

John and Ken approached Zach. "Be careful up there," John said in a dark voice.

"Like McNutt said, we'll—"

"Knock it off, Zach," Ken said with false anger but a worried tone.

Zach's voice caught. "Thanks, guys. I'll be just fine." *I hope I can do this when the bullets start flying.*

*****

The assembled troops waited uneasily for orders from their recently promoted battalion commander, Lieutenant Colonel George Hartman. It was Colonel George who had sold the bold marching fire and rolling barrage to the more conservative British. After an animated talk with the British liaison and a pale and seemingly confused Captain Brunner, the BC gave the order to move out.

The five "volunteers" mounted the lead tanks. Zach was breathing hard when he shook hands with the tank commander, Sergeant Bob "Flash" Gorden, who then disappeared into the tank and buttoned the hatch. The rest of the uptight 2nd Platoon took whatever cover they could find behind the tanks.

Company B followed, flanked about fifty yards behind. The objective—the woods one thousand yards away. Officers and noncoms were given great discretion—that was the colonel's way.

"Move out," ordered Lieutenant McNutt.

The big thirty-two-ton Sherman clanked slowly forward in line with the other four tanks. Zach threaded the ammo belt through the receiver on the 50-caliber machine gun and pulled the lever back to arm the lethal weapon. He checked the extra box of blue goose and secured it on the top of the turret, then checked his footing, making sure he could adjust to turret rotation. He started to perspire as the tank clanked on— nothing. Zach adjusted the sling on the rifle slung diagonally across his back. They had marched on line about one hundred yards when the first mortar fire started. Zach crouched behind the turret; his mouth went dry and his muscles tensed. The trailing infantry crowded close to the tanks for protection or quickly hit the ground. Zach held his fire. "Where the hell is the artillery?" he screamed out loud, feeling better for the yelling. As if he had ordered it, the promised rolling artillery barrage roared overhead helping disrupt the mortar fire.

Enemy small arms fire started when the lead tanks were within five hundred yards of the woods.

"*Commence firing!*" The marching fire order was in full effect.

Zach depressed the double trigger on the tank's 50-caliber and felt relieved—no turning back now! A curtain of fire marched from the tanks as each fired two additional 30-calibers from inside.

At almost the same instant, the German mortar fire restarted, dropping on the tanks and the rest of Company B, now seventy-five yards behind. At two hundred yards from the woods, German light machine guns started their rat-a-tat fire. Several foot soldiers were cut down. Bullets ricocheted off the turret.

"Bastards!" Zach shrieked and angrily returned fire. He glanced left—Norm Ricks was bent over the turret, his helmet off, his gun silent. Wounded, he rolled off the moving tank. Zach stopped firing and saw his friend and squad leader roll on the ground. Shocked and trembling, he was torn between conscience and duty. Flash Gorden, conflicted between proceeding or helping the doughboys, had stopped. Experience and discipline prevailed—the rule was clear. Continue the attack. A voice from within was clear and demanding—*Duty, always duty.* Zach pounded on the turret, indicating that he was still there, and shouted, "MOVE IT!" Flash still hesitated. Zach crawled over the tank commander's closed hatch and put his hand in front of the tanker's periscope. The tank started to move as Zach pointed a finger forward and then quickly returned to his gun. He squeezed the twin triggers, sending tracers at the now-closer sources of enemy fire. Then a loud explosion sounded—a panzerfaust had hit the tank on his right, and smoke poured from the engine cover. Cooper slumped over the handles of his tank's 50-caliber machine gun. The tank crew tumbled out of the trap door. Cooper slid grotesquely off to the side of the turret. His rifle sling caught in the 50-caliber's slide mechanism, holding him there.

Zach fought off a numbing fear. *I can do this, I can do this.* The tank rolled relentlessly forward. Zach clenched his teeth, fed a new belt into the machine gun, and was about to fire when antitank rounds fired at close range simultaneously hit the other two tanks, blowing off both Sergeant Bruno Nitchke and Stan Goldman. Some of the tank crews again escaped through the trapdoors as smoke poured out of one of the Sherman tanks. Through the smoke, Zach saw Nitchke and Goldman wave, indicating they were okay. Zach's tank stopped again, stunned by the sudden loss of the other two tanks. Zach pounded on the hatch cover until it cracked open. "On the right, damn it. I saw flashes. Fire before they reload."

The hatch snapped shut and the big gun swung right and fired. Zach fired in the same direction as the tank lumbered forward. Another badly aimed antitank round screeched over Zach's head. The tankers saw its source and fired three quick, high explosive rounds into the general area. The recoil from the rapid fire and the moving turret spun Zach to the ground. Brenner faced him. "You're not going back up there?"

"Got to. Give me a push." Avoiding the moving tracks, he climbed up the rear of the tank just as more machine gun fire erupted from the woods directly in front of the tank. Zach ducked behind the turret cover. The tanker manning the on-board 30-caliber racked the enemy machine gun emplacement, silencing it forever. Enemy fire became sporadic. The two remaining tanks moved up on line with Zach and paused, awaiting orders it seemed.

The turret popped open. Flash screamed, "Nobody's in charge!"

"What?" Zach yelled above the mortar and small arms fire. He moved to within inches of the tanker's face. "What do you mean?"

"I'm on the radio—you've only got one officer left. Hang on." Flash ducked inside as the radio squawked. "Your BC says whoever is in front is in charge."

"The colonel? You mean the captain?"

"No, he's down. Orders are to march and fire till they surrender or retreat."

"Okay, Flash, let's go."

The tank rumbled forward only a few feet when a hail of enemy small arms and machine gun fire resumed. The following infantry hit the ground. Zach, seeing the source, raked the area with deadly effect. The tank rolled on, spewing 30-calibers as it ground ahead. One squad of Germans had their hands in the air. The tank halted and Gorden's head appeared. "What now, General?"

Before Zach could respond, Lieutenant McNutt, the remaining B Company officer, caught up with Zach's tank. "Pour it on 'em till we get closer to the woods. When the artillery starts, we go on foot," he shouted. Zach nodded that he understood. The tank moved forward into a hail of German fire. The infantry hid behind the tanks. Zach again ducked behind the turret. From his perch, he could see McNutt had been hit. His bloody left arm appeared shattered, but he was alive. The gritty lieutenant was signaling forward with his good arm pointing in the direction of the incoming fire. Zach depressed the twin triggers as a German platoon struggled with their antitank gun. The tankers saw the gun and swung their big 76 mm to the left. Zach hung on as a loud, high explosive round tore into the bold German gunners. Zach regained his hold on the 50 and fired. Silence momentarily enveloped the battlefield.

Zach chanced a look back. Medic "Wild Bill" Anders had found Lieutenant McNutt. Zach waved as the increasing American artillery was now exploding in the woods some one hundred yards ahead of the 2nd Platoon. This silenced most of the mortar fire that was raising hell with the rest of the confused, stalled company. During the lull, the medics were able to bring up a stretcher-bearing jeep. They picked up the doughty lieutenant along with five other wounded men. Zach tossed a salute, thinking, *Why the Lieutenant and not me? Why Cooper? Why...?* Zach's trance-like state was loudly interrupted when he heard Grinnell's voice shouting, "Stay there, Gates. Plans have changed."

Platoon Sergeant Russ Grinnell usually brought up the rear. With McNutt down, he and a radioman were now up front and in command. The tanks had stopped some thirty yards from the woods. Zach waited. The far right flank was still exploding with German firepower pinning down the unprotected infantry and the mortar and machine gun squads who were moving up for the woods fight.

Russ Grinnell climbed aboard Zach's tank as the hatch opened. "Who the hell is running this show?" asked the tank commander.

"I am," Grinnell replied, jumping down. "Now head over there and unpin 'em."

The tank roared off to the right flank with Zach hanging on, stopped short, and fired its big gun.

"Go, go—go get 'em, Gates!" Grinnell shouted as the tank lumbered still closer to the action. Zach reloaded his last box of ammunition, the one from Babe, and fired. The trees exploded as the bootlegged air corps blue goose hit them.

Two panzerfaust teams exposed themselves to get a better shot at Zach's tank. Zach swung the 50-caliber in their general direction and fired two long bursts at very close range. The blue goose hit one of the rockets as it was released, exploding it right in the team's faces. The other team was literally torn apart by the lethal, exploding 50-caliber rounds. The tank commander stopped, overcome by the mayhem he saw through his periscope. The hatch opened. "What the hell are you shooting in that 50?" he called out.

"Move it, Sergeant. I'm a sitting duck up here!"

The hatch closed and the tank rumbled closer to the action. Zach resumed firing at anything that moved as the tank met the woods. One round blew off the top of a man's head, exposing and splattering his brains. Zach stopped firing. His body was soaked with perspiration and he felt sick. *I don't believe this is happening.*

A strange silence engulfed the battlefield as the tank stopped, the artillery lifted, and the German guns spoke no more. The three hatches on the tank opened and three heads popped out. "Have they had it?" the tank commander asked.

Zach regained control and his face grew cold. "There's a large bunker up ahead. Move up and put your gun in the opening. Then we'll see."

The tanker did just that. Immediately a whole company of stubborn German parachute troops came rushing and screaming out of the bunker and its connecting trenches. Hands in the air, they shouted "*Nicht schiessen*" and "*Geneva.*" Zach covered them with the 50-caliber while Sergeant Grinnell ran up and directed them to the rear.

Zach climbed down from the tank and approached the woods, now only ten yards away. There lay a dozen more blown-apart Germans, their bodies dismembered by the lethal air force ammunition. He choked out his next words. "We need medics here!"

Wild Bill Anders approached cautiously, gasping as he viewed the carnage. He turned to Zach, who was in a state of shock. "Gates, are you okay?"

Zach shook off a paralyzing sense of revulsion. "...I'm not sure, Bill...I thought I'd seen it all in France. How is the lieutenant?"

Bill looked away. "He'll make it, but he'll never use his left arm again."

Zach felt sick as Wild Bill pushed him away from the battle scene. "It doesn't get any uglier than this. Hang in there, Gates." With that, Bill ran to help the wounded, living up to his name.

The 3rd Squad men came running forward. Seeing the medics they thought Zach was down. Ken arrived first. "Where are you hit, old buddy?" he gasped through a winded voice.

"I'm okay...how's the squad?"

"Tom, John, and Stosh are okay. I'm not sure about the rest."

Sergeant Russ Grinnell came running. "Well done, Gates. The ambulances are on the way. We'll get to the krauts as soon as all of our guys are picked up."

Zach nodded while slowly surveying the torn apart, blasted battlefield. His stomach continued to retch. "What went wrong, Russ? If their antitank guns had survived, we could have lost this one."

"Thanks to you and Flash they were knocked out." Grinnell hesitated. "We lost our three lead officers and three tanks…and—"

"And what?"

"Captain Brunner went down."

"Jesus, what hit him?"

"That's not clear, but his runner and radioman became useless and all communication was screwed up."

"Thank God for our artillery," Zach choked.

"Yeah, the artillery and a few guys like yourself turned it around."

Two jeeps roared up. 1st Sergeant Klein jumped out of the first one. "Good work, Grinnell. You saved our asses." The BC followed. "Well done, Sergeant," he added quietly.

"Thank Gates, Colonel. He and his lead tank never stopped firing," Russ Grinnell replied.

At this moment, Zachary, leaning on the tank with one hand, was violently throwing up. Lieutenant Colonel Hartman dismounted his jeep and put his hand on Zach's shoulder, saying quietly, "You did good, son. Consider yourself promoted."

Hartman surveyed his strung-out battalion, the dead, the wounded, the burning Shermans, and the chaotic battlefield. "Except for Grinnell and a few smart kids, we could have lost this one." He took a deep breath, climbed into his jeep and signaled the radioman. After a short communication, he signaled Grinnell. "Sergeant, get your fine platoon out of this hellhole. We're relieved."

"Yes, sir." Russ Grinnell climbed atop Zach's tank. "Okay, Sergeant Gates. Back to the tracks. Lead us out of here."

An exhausted 2nd Platoon stood down in a Catholic monastery near Margraten, Holland, for ten days to recover and reorganize.

STAND-DOWN AT CADIER-EN-KEER

After the hellish battle in Heide Woods, the stand-down at the Dutch monastery was a welcome one—a critical one. It provided blessed time to grieve, to rest, and to replace. And also, to gripe. The riddle of Captain Brunner's collapse was never completely understood. Many were bitter, feeling he simply let the company down.

Stosh was among the angry. "Zach, what about this coward?"

"Easy, Stosh. Brunner was under a very heavy load. He lost all his frontline officers and a few sergeants."

"Well, I don't know…"

"We can all suffer an anxiety attack and lose it for a short time," Zach said softly.

"If you say so, Zach—I mean *Sergeant* Gates."

"Yeah, I say so, Stosh—thanks." Zach looked at his Pfc. stripe and felt dumbstruck over his sudden promotion. A young girl from the monastery was sewing on his stripes. *Maybe I'll feel more secure when I put the stripes on…*

*****

The word on Captain Brunner finally came down. He had, it was reported, suffered an anxiety attack, approaching a mild stroke. He was relieved of command and replaced by medaled 1st Lieutenant Ralph Black from A Company.

The Beak, 1st Lieutenant McNutt, respected leader of the 2nd Platoon and executive officer of Company B, would not return. His badly shattered arm led to his discharge from the army. He owned a bar back in New Jersey. An earnest, thoughtful Stosh worried how he would mix drinks with one hand. His replacement was veteran Platoon Sergeant Russ Grinnell—awarded a much deserved Battlefield Commission. Norm Ricks, promoted to five stripes, replaced Grinnell. Zach Gates, still a little tentative about his battlefield promotion, replaced Ricks as leader of the 3rd Squad.

The 3rd Squad had only two casualties, Norm Ricks and Larry Cooper. A bullet grazed Ricks's right shoulder, putting him in the hospital for ten days. Larry Cooper was not as fortunate. He died bravely manning his gun in the face of heavy fire. He was recommended for the Bronze Star. Tom Sander wondered what role Larry's "Dear John" letter played in his eagerness for battle.

There were only fifty-eight casualties in the battalion—light, considering the heavy action and high casualties among the enemy. Two of the five lead tanks were lost, but no tankers were KIA. Only four had to be evacuated.

The good news concerned Pfc. Tony Holter, who had been wounded a month earlier in France and would be returning to the 3rd Squad. Pfc. Ray White, also rapidly recovering from wounds, was expected to return in the near future.

And so the demands of war went inexorably on. In combat units, there was little time for grieving. Ordinance had vehicles and armaments to repair or replace and, perhaps more important, Company B had to shake down its many leadership and personnel changes.

Newly-promoted, thirty-year-old Lieutenant Russell Grinnell and just-returned Tech Sergeant Norman Ricks were back and accepted with little difficulty. Staff Sergeant Zachary Gates was still not quite sure how he would be received. At nineteen, he was the youngest staff sergeant in the company. While backing up the 94th Infantry Division in the Saar, he learned that the average age for all men in the 94th was twenty-six. A company clerk reported that more than four thousand of their men were over thirty. The young men in the 3rd Squad knew about the 94th. John Brenner was shaking his head. Zach listened from a distance. "The guys I met…" John turned serious. "They had no idea what their mission was—hell, they didn't even know what country they were in."

Stosh's face took on an urgent look and he blurted out, "They ain't got no bookworms."

"Or any butterflies," chided Goldman.

"I don't think we're being fair to the 94th," Tom Sander interjected. "They've been playing defense in the Saar, which is confusing politically and geographically. We play offense and have a greater need to know."

Stosh processed Tom's words before opening his mouth again. "Even their noncoms, all old guys, didn't know nothin'. We're smarter."

"If you say so, Stosh." Whedder smiled and directed the group's attention toward Zach. "We have a kid hotshot sergeant with more guts than all of us."

Stan stirred. "He's not too bright—playing target on top of a tank."

The group broke into laughter. Still uncertain of his role and how he was being received, Zach gave a half salute and walked away. *Why me? Bruno was next in line and he's twenty-three.*

*****

Mess call happened amidst a platoon of halftracks parked in the monastery courtyard as Zach stopped to talk to Grinnell and Ricks. Russ Grinnell was wearing a shiny gold bar on his collar and five stripes on his sleeves. The new lieutenant had given one of his oversized shirts with its five stripes to Norm Ricks. Zach's new shirt sported inexpert, hastily sewn stripes, one set lower than the other. The three stared at one another. Grinnell grinned. "We look like shit."

"The guys can use a good laugh," Ricks replied.

"A replacement didn't know what to call me," Lieutenant Grinnell chuckled.

"Well, congratulations anyway, Lieutenant. You earned it," Zach said.

"Thanks, Sergeant Gates. So did you."

Zach nodded but felt uncomfortable. He turned to Norm. "You're back early. How's the shoulder?"

"Sore, but improving every day. I had to get out of the damn hospital and keep you and Russ—oops, I mean Lieutenant Grinnell—out of trouble. How's the 3rd Squad doing?"

"I'll know better when the shit starts flying," Zach replied quietly.

"You'll do fine, Zach. You proved yourself in the woods."

"Thanks…I was lucky."

The three friends stood up and Norm patted Zach on the back. "Say hello to the squad, and Sergeant—"

"Yeah?"

"Lean to the left so your stripes line up."

"Grow into your shirt!" Zach waved and walked over to his halftrack where his three bookworms were chowing down. Today the bookworms were in rare form and trying to put their new leader at ease.

"Where'd you get the sexy shirt?" asked a grinning Ken Whedder.

"I think he's put on weight," cracked John Brenner.

"You're right, but only on the right side," Ken howled.

"So, Sergeant York, any orders for us?" Tom Sander asked.

"Knock it off, guys. I'm still adjusting."

"Relax, Sergeant. The whole squad is behind you," Stan Goldman reported, as the rest of the squad tuned in.

"How the hell do I replace Norm Ricks, the best squad leader in the company?" Zach asked, feeling better for saying it out loud.

"Zach, you already did—you earned it," Whedder said with a note of sincerity.

Zach inhaled audibly. "I still haven't talked to Bruno Nitchke."

"You didn't hear?"

"Hear what?"

"Bruno turned down a promotion in the 1st Squad."

"I didn't know that. Why?"

"Zach," Ken paused. "I don't think he wanted the added responsibility."

"Yeah, who does?" snorted Stan Goldman.

"He said he doesn't read too good," Stosh related.

Wild Bill, who felt like an ex-officio member of the 3rd Squad, gave Stosh a critical look. "Zach, it's clear to all of us that Bruno respects you and is comfortable where he is. He told me so himself. Loosen up."

Zach nodded appreciation. Tom patted him on the back and teased, "At least Stosh is happy about your promotion."

"Same is true of Corporal Naylor," said a serious John Naylor.

Zach was not quite sure what to say. The discussion ended when new Platoon Sergeant Norm Ricks arrived with two replacements, one short, the other tall. "Men, meet your squad leader, Sergeant Zach Gates."

They were an odd pair. Five-foot-six Elmo Becker at thirty-six was older than the battalion commander. He had somehow bad-mouthed his draft board and learned to regret it. He had good reason to be bitter. One of his legs was slightly shorter than the other, and he was the father of six kids—not a prime candidate for armored infantry—but Elmo was a tough old bird who had somehow survived infantry basic training. His other hang-up was a premonition that he would not make it home. Worse yet, he said so. Zach eyed the odd pair. "Welcome aboard."

Elmo Becker picked up a permanent nickname when Ken greeted him. "Welcome to the war, Pappy."

"That's better than Elmo," he grunted.

In sharp contrast to Pappy Becker stood John Bashford, a tall, athletic twenty-five-year-old. He was sporting new Pfc. stripes and carrying a deadly Browning automatic rifle (BAR), a welcome addition to any combat squad. The four-foot-long BAR weighed nineteen pounds, forty with a magazine and a bipod attached. It could be fired single shot or fully automatic. This rifle fired all types of 30-caliber ammunition at 550 rounds per minute. A big man like Bashford could fire it from the hip.

Zach studied the BAR. "Bashford, are you any good with that thing?"

"Oh yeah," the tall soldier replied matter-of-factly.

"Bashford earned a silver star with that 'thing' when he was with the 29th Infantry Division," asserted Sergeant Ricks.

Zach nodded and studied the serious-looking soldier. "I gather you were wounded and sent to a repple depple (replacement depot)."

"Stray bullet," Bashford replied without elaborating.

"How'd we get you, Bashford?"

"I asked for armor. You guys ride. Call me Bash."

"We're a lot different than the foot infantry."

"Yeah, thanks for the promotion."

"The Pfc. stripes go with the job. More risk, more rank, more money," Zach replied, feeling more confident about his role.

"I can live with that."

"The airborne or the rangers pay extra," Ricks quipped.

"I don't like heights, and the rangers walk."

Zach laughed. "Sounds about right. Welcome aboard. Any questions?"

Bash looked at the platoon's five halftracks all lined up. "Your platoons look bigger?"

"Yeah, five squads, fifty-five men, and five M-3 halftracks," Zach replied.

Bash nodded. "We had only three rifle squads of twelve men per platoon—sometimes we had a truck."

"We have three twelve-man rifle squads plus a machine gun squad of ten and a mortar squad of eight." Ricks paused. "Add a 50-caliber on each tank."

"That's firepower!"

"We're mean and we're big. There are three companies in a battalion."

"You guys can hurt somebody."

"Now add a Sherman M-4 tank and its crew of five."

"Have you heard enough?" Sergeant Ricks asked.

Bash cradled his BAR. "I feel like I'm joining a small army."

"I'll let Sergeant Gates try that one," Ricks quipped.

"Yeah, I guess we are pretty independent: three infantry battalions, three tanks, two mobile field artillery. Help me, Norm."

"Let's see. Add engineering, ordinance, and medical battalions."

Bash looked across the field at an M-8 six-wheel vehicle. "What about those guys?"

Ricks slapped his head. "*Right*, how could I forget our recon cavalry squadron? They are frontline recon—what else have we missed, Sergeant Gates?"

"We have smaller service units like quartermaster, supply trains, and MPs."

"Armor *is* something else," Bash remarked.

"Yeah, but we still attach independent units like tank destroyers or antiaircraft batteries," Ricks explained.

Bash grinned. "Doesn't sound like you guys do much backing up."

"You got that right. Have you seen an armored division in action?" Ricks asked.

"Oh yeah. It was back in the Normandy hedgerows. The 29th was under heavy fire and couldn't move. The 2nd Armored came crashing through with marching fire and saved our asses."

Ricks smiled. "Welcome to the armored infantry."

Zach shook Bashford's hand. "Where are you from, Bash?"

Bash paused, looked away, and said softly, "Virginia." He picked up his gear and took a step away. "I've got to unload this stuff," he said flatly and walked away.

Surprised at his behavior, Zach shrugged and looked at Norm Ricks. "What's with Virginia?"

"I didn't have time to brief you. His Virginia national guard unit were all together on D-day. It was a disaster. One town lost nineteen or twenty boys."

"Good God—all from the same town?"

"Yup. After he was wounded a second time, near Aachen I think, he asked for a transfer. I guess he thought it was time to leave all the bad luck and bad memories behind."

"I can understand that."

"Zach, I wouldn't press him about Omaha Beach."

"I hear ya...do the guys know?"

"No. Grinnell says we should keep it that way."

*****

On the eighth day of the monastery stand-down, the squad celebrated when Pfc. Tony Holter finally returned to duty. Zach was especially pleased, since the twenty-year-old jokester from Cleveland, Ohio was one of the best out-front scouts in the company.

On the ninth day of the stand-down, orders came down to move out and attack toward the Roer River and Roermond. Zach's leadership was to be tested.

Ken Whedder approached Zach with Tom Sander and John Brenner in tow. "Zach, before we go, we should thank Father Anselm, the CO of this monastery, for putting up with us."

"Yeah. He and Father Hetzi really went out of their way."

The small bookworm group entered the chapel, where they found Father Anselm praying. "Come in, my sons," he said in almost perfect English.

"Father Anselm, we will be leaving soon. We just wanted to thank you for all you've done."

The priest moved closer. "It was our duty, and I shall pray for all of you." The group shifted their bodies nervously. The father smiled. "What are your names?"

Zach hesitated. "Pfc....as you were, Staff Sergeant Zachary Gates."

"Pfc. Ken Whedder."

"Pfc. Tom Sander."

"Pfc. John Brenner."

Father Anselm extended his hand to each soldier. "I shall never forget you young Americans, and I shall pray for your safe return home. Godspeed my sons."

*****

After a late mess call, Lieutenant Russ Grinnell called for the 2nd Platoon to assemble. "This is what came down from the platoon leaders' meeting with Captain Black and Colonel Hartman. The battalion is a critical part of a very large 9th Army operation called GRENADE. The goal is to cross the Roer, push into Germany, and reach the Rhine River. The 18th Division will spearhead the operation. Four or five infantry divisions will follow if we are able to break out. Company B, led by our 2nd Platoon, has the mission of clearing the krauts out of the area west of the Roer River so bridges can be built and OPERATION GRENADE can have an assembly area."

Grinnell paused and Sergeant Ricks asked, "Lieutenant, can you tell us who we're up against?"

The lieutenant looked at his notes. "G-2 says it's the Para Lehr Regiment from the 8th Para Division. They think the 116th Panzers have withdrawn their tanks north and crossed the tributary bridges into Roermond on the west bank. We may have to deal with their rear guard. We don't know what kinds of weapons we'll run into. Probably some mobile artillery, plenty of mines, and dug-in automatic weapons."

"Sir, how far do we go?"

"Somewhere between three and five kilometers—all the way to

Roermond if things have dried up."

"Do we have backup?"

"A ton! Our battalion plus a company of tanks if it isn't too wet. Behind them, a battalion of grunts from the 35th Infantry Division."

"Sir, what's their mission?"

"Their mission is to find a bridge across the Roer and to establish beachheads across the river so the bridge companies can go to work. We have to clear the area ahead of them."

"How tough are these para guys, Lieutenant?" Sergeant Nitchke asked.

"I don't know, Bruno—they're all tough!" Grinnell asserted.

Stosh waved his hand. "Sergeant Gates knows about 'em."

"Okay, bookworm, let's hear it," Grinnell grinned.

Embarrassed, Zach hesitated, but he did not want to let down loyal Stosh Kosinski. He spoke softly. "I learned at Illinois that they're called *Fallschermjager,* which means parachute troops. We met some of them in Heide Woods. They are not SS, but they are among the toughest and most feared troops in the German Army. Ask the Desert Rats."

Russ Grinnell scowled. "Okay, so they're hot shots, but we're not green anymore. We'll hang 'em out to dry. I'll have the final word at 0530 tomorrow. That's all. Get some sleep."

$$*****$$

When Zach returned to the barn, Stosh approached him. "Sarge, Pappy can't sleep. He says he's not coming back from this battle."

"Damn, that's such a crock!"

"Right, Sarge. I'll tell him when we get back."

Zach shrugged, borrowed Stosh's copy of *Stars and Stripes*, the army newspaper, and joined the half-dozing John and Ken in the loft.

"What's new?" John asked.

"Pappy won't let go of his stupid death premonition."

"Well, it happened to Heller in the 1st Squad."

"Come on, John. That's baloney. When your number's up, it's up."

Aware that Zach did not take kindly to such premonitions, John murmured, "Sorry. What's new in *Stars and Stripes*?"

Zach mumbled, "Bullshit." Then he stared at the army newspaper. "In 'Combat Tips,' a 35th Infantry sergeant tells how to beat an S mine or Bouncing Betty."

"Yeah, what does he say about Schu mines?"

"Nothing, only about Bouncing Betty, which we haven't seen yet."

"Why is it called Bouncing Betty?"

"I guess it kind of jiggles as it dances out of the ground."

"What?"

"John, I don't know. Think of Betty Boop or Sally Rand."

"I get it. How are they tripped?"

"You run up on the stage and—"

"Come on—how are they tripped?"

"By a trip cord or just stepping on them."

"So what do we do?"

"He says hitting the ground is a mistake. This thing rises, jiggling slowly, and when it's five or six feet off the ground, it explodes, sending 360 ball bearings in all directions, including down. He says you can outrun them."

"How far do they carry?"

"A long way, but, according to him, they are only lethal for fifteen or twenty feet."

"What's the time on 'em?"

"He says you have five or more seconds."

"Sounds tricky."

"He outran two of them. All he got was a bunch of welts on his back and a ding in his helmet."

"Put Betty to bed!" Tom Sander yelled.

9

OPERATION
GRENADE: GO!

0500: The early morning air felt dark and cold when Norm Ricks gave Zach a shove. "Up and at 'em, Sergeant, and get your bums over to the cattle barn. Assembly at 0530."

Zach yawned. "Yeah, thanks."

"Move it, Gates, you're a squad leader now."

"I got it, I got it." He felt his muscles tighten as he laced and buckled his boots. *I can do this, I can do this.* He stood up to find smiling Sergeant Nitchke in his face. "We await your orders, Sergeant Bookworm."

Delegate, said a voice from Captain Fred. "Good! Have the men assemble in the cattle barn at 0530!"

Bruno turned on his heel shouting, "Attention, sad sacks! Sergeant Gates's orders: Let go your cocks and grab your socks!"

Zach shot Bruno a hard look and overrode him. "Now hear this. Cattle barn at 0530." Just loud enough to be heard, he added, "And don't forget your socks." The squad howled and Zach reconsidered when to delegate.

*****

Lieutenant Grinnell and Sergeant Ricks entered the barn. "Stand at ease—our immediate orders are the same. The other news is that once a bridgehead is established, our battalion will be first across." A collective groan filled the room. "That's it. The password is 'Bob' answered by 'Feller.' Move 'em out, Sergeant Ricks, and good hunting."

Ricks caught up with Zach. "Gates, are you ready to be lead squad?

Your scouts are the best in the company."

A tightness gripped Zach's body as the full impact of his responsibilities began to sink in. His eyes locked on Norm's. "Of course—I was taught by a master," he replied in as calm and flat a voice as he could muster.

Ricks slapped his good friend on the back. "The guys respect you, Zach—go get 'em."

The heavily armed 2nd Platoon moved out on foot with the 3rd Squad leading, accompanied by a radioman and medic Wild Bill Anders.

"Nothing's changed," griped newly returned Tony Holter. "I thought Grinnell and Ricks were your buddies."

Zach summoned his most authoritative tone. "Button it, Tony. You're lead scout."

"Like I said, nothing's changed." He grinned. "Except now we have a hard-nosed squad leader."

"You got it right, so move out!"

Off they marched into the eerie early light of no man's land. It was quiet—too quiet, it seemed. As the light slowly improved, the men could see open fields, broken fences, hedgerows, and a few dark, foreboding clumps of trees. The squad approached a small rise decorated by staggered trees. Zach signaled a halt and squinted at a small piece of aerial map. "Should be one of our outposts ahead."

"Unless the krauts have taken it," Holter said gloomily.

"I don't think so…check it out. I'll follow a few yards behind and cover you."

Tony moved boldly to within a few yards of the trees. Zach held his breath, raised his M-1…suddenly a shout of "Bob!" rang out from the outpost.

"Feller! For Christ's sake," Tony yelled back.

Zach slowly released his breath. The squad circled around the outpost and proceeded north; there was still no sign of enemy action, so the squad moved forward at a faster pace. Far ahead, a brilliant flare lingered over the brightening fields. Bruno moved up closer to Zach. "Now what, *mein Führer*?"

"They must have spotted a British patrol. They're way west of us." The flare burned out and German mortar fire followed. "I hope they ducked," Zach said. Then he ordered, "Move out!"

As the morning light brightened, the distant flares faded. Tony Holter moved forward more boldly and then stopped. He raised his hand. Zach moved forward leaving the rest of the squad frozen in place. "What you got?" he whispered.

"Somebody's watching us. I can feel the bastards."

Zach trusted Holter's instincts. "How far away?"

"Damn close. They were probably going to let me go through."

Instinctively, Zach gave the down signal and the frozen troops quickly went prone. *Now what the hell do I do? Be creative. Attack!* "Tony, are they within throwing range?"

"You mean grenades?"

"What the hell do you think I mean?" snapped Gates, beginning to feel the tension rise from his stomach to his throat. "Can we hit 'em or not?"

"I think so. See the shrubs on the left?"

"Yeah. What about the two small trees in front of us?"

"My gut says the shrubs."

"Okay. Have you got two?"

"Yeah."

"We throw all four on my signal."

"Hold it, Sarge. Here comes Bruno."

Bruno approached in a low crouch. "What's the holdup? The guys are scared shitless."

"Bruno, we're going to throw four grenades. If we receive fire, have the guys return fire. We'll duck."

"Got it. Thanks for letting me know," he said with a touch of sarcasm. "Anything else?"

"Yeah, give us your grenades and fall back." *Next time inform your second in command, rookie.* Zach's pulse began to pound. "Tony, are you ready?"

"Yeah."

"Okay, throw!"

Zach counted down the fuse times—five, four, three. The tearing sound of a machine gun erupted from the German gun positions—two, one. Four quick explosions followed by richochets from the grenade fragments ended the gunfire from the shrubs, but firing continued from the area near the two trees. Bruno started to bring up the rest of the squad.

"Damn, he's too soon. Tony, throw Bruno's grenades now."

"Shit."

"What?"

"These are goddamn smoke grenades."

"Throw 'em, damn it. Give me one!"

Two duller explosions this time followed by heavy smoke blinded the German machine gunners. Bruno's group came running. "Fire at the smoke, Bruno, hit the smoke!" Zach yelled.

The squad moved up, firing into the smoke. The machine guns went silent. Zach raised his hand. "We got lucky or they fell back. Anybody hit?" A long pause—Zach hated that wait period as the men checked on their buddies. Finally, Bruno called out, "All accounted for."

Blessed relief oozed from every pore as Zach moved the squad forward. It turned out only one of the six enemy gunners was still alive. He was taken prisoner and sent to the rear. The squad spread out and prepared to advance. Blunt Bruno caught up with Zach. "My smoke grenades saved your ass."

"Yeah, dumb luck," Zach replied, and reflected silently on the action. *We lucked out. We should all be history*.

*****

The squad edged forward, followed closely by the rest of the platoon as the morning sun lit the sky. The action farther north and west had stopped. A small stream glimmered as the sun grew larger. Suddenly, rifle fire erupted from the vicinity of the stream. The 2nd Platoon hit the dirt, expecting machine gun fire or worse. Instead, the battlefield went deathly quiet. Zach listened intently. Did he hear German voices or was it his imagination? The whole platoon froze. Tension built. Time seemed to have stopped. Bruno broke the paralyzing quiet with an uneasy whisper. "What's going on? No mortar fire, no Screaming Meemie rockets?"

Zach grabbed him. "We're too close. They're afraid of hitting their own guys."

Lieutenant Grinnell brought the rest of the platoon forward, and they dropped prone. Zach crawled over to Grinnell, who whispered, "Anybody hit?"

"No, sir. How about the platoon?"

"Two down, 2nd Squad. I'm not sure how serious."

Zach raised his head and surveyed the area. "Shit."

"What?"

"I'm missing Pappy Becker again."

"Well, find him!"

Goldman signaled. "I got him, Gates. Jeez, you don't think it's another Keller premonition?"

"Shut up," Zach replied, and crawled over to Stan and Pappy.

"Where are you hit, Pappy?"

"In the hip. Blood is running down my legs. I've had it."

"Not so damn loud, soldier." Zach took a closer look. "Christ, Pappy, a stray bullet hit your canteen."

"But my hip hurts."

"It's a scratch, soldier. If I hear any more premonition shit from you, I'll have you really shot!"

Holter was out front standing up. "The krauts are retreating across the river," he shouted.

"We hold here!" Lieutenant Grinnell ordered as Norm Ricks moved up.

"Now what? Shouldn't we be going after them?" Zach asked Sergeant Ricks.

"Russ thinks they set mines. How you doing so far?"

"I'm scared shitless, but I'm putting on my Patton act," Zach grunted.

"You're learning, bookworm. Good luck."

The lieutenant moved up. "Sergeant Gates."

"Here, sir."

"Our orders are to clear the area to the stream. Move out, but beware of mines."

Zach nodded and headed toward the river with his squad following close behind. He stopped abruptly. A slow, fluttering grenade was rising directly in front of him—*hello* Bouncing Betty. Zach stared transfixed as the grenade reached its apogee, shaking, spinning, taunting him. His lips went dry and he began to sweat. Combat experience directed, *hit the dirt, Mother Earth will protect me.* Another voice intruded, *run, run like hell.* The lesson from "Combat Tips" overcame instinct and past experience. He commanded his wide-eyed, terrified squad to "run, run!" Then came the explosion! Hundreds of ball bearings came flying at the fleeing soldiers. Zach sprinted at full tilt. *I need distance, the hell with the minefield, one crisis at a time.* He felt several painful stings to his back and legs. He faltered…then slowly regained his equilibrium. He stopped and surveyed his squad. Half were on the ground twisting and moaning. The other half were standing and rubbing multiple bruises.

"Medic!" Zach shouted. Wild Bill was already picking his way through the mine field. "I heard at least four muffled explosions," he said as he attended to the downed men, most of whom were now sitting up or standing. "You guys were lucky. I can't believe this," Bill said, shaking his head. Miraculously no one was critically wounded.

"Thanks for the 'run' order, Gates," Tom called out as he got off the ground, rubbing several large bruises on his backside. All of the men were swearing and nursing multiple welts and bruises, but otherwise were not seriously hurt.

Bruno Nitchke had a ding in his helmet and several large welts on his left shoulder. "That Betty packs a mean punch," he snorted.

"Thank you, *Stars and Stripes*," Zach murmured as his heartbeat finally slowed.

*****

Ricks brought up the rest of the platoon screaming, *"Where the hell is the radioman? We're almost to the river!"*

"I'm over here, Sergeant Ricks. I alerted headquarters," the radio man responded.

"Okay, listen up. Tell 'em two men down."

"Make it two more," said a voice from the 1st Squad.

"2nd Squad?" Ricks roared.

"I can't find Makowski."

"Gates?"

"Okay, I think. We're all nursing welts and bruises."

"Cut the crap, Gates."

"All accounted for—no, wait. Goddamn it! Pappy is down again."

"Check it out, then get your ass over here."

"I'm on it. Medic!"

Wild Bill rolled Pappy over. "Nothing busted, Pappy. Betty bounced you real good. You have to run faster, old man."

"Shut up, kid, and give me some aspirin," Pappy grumbled.

"Squad leaders, assemble on me!" shouted Lieutenant Grinnell. Grinnell checked his watch. "Hartman is bringing up his crazy bridge. We gotta hold for a half-hour. Dig in and hang tough. This outfit may test us."

Zach moved up to Ricks and Grinnell. "Can we get any mortar fire on 'em?"

"Good suggestion, Gates. You're learning. Mortar squad!"

"Hold it, Russ. I hear heavy vehicles moving up," Ricks shouted.

"Jesus, the cavalry is ahead of schedule. Radioman! What the hell is going on?"

The radioman rushed over. "Sir, there's a small stream a quarter mile north where we are ordered to secure a beachhead for the bridge."

"We know about the damn stream. The krauts have already retreated past the stream. Get me the captain."

Lieutenant Grinnell got off the radio, reporting, "Captain Black is bringing up the rest of the company. We are to move out. Colonel Hartman intends to try out the new portable treadway bridge."

"Russ, we're expecting a counterattack!" Ricks countered.

"I know that. I'm going after our 50-calibers. You and Gates move forward and hold the fort till I get back."

"Give us the machine gun squad," Ricks implored.

"They're back with the tracks."

"Great!" Ricks moaned.

"That's enough, Sergeant Ricks. Move Gates and the 3rd Squad forward now."

"Yes, sir," Ricks snorted.

The 3rd Squad advanced cautiously to within two hundred yards of the stream. The terrain was open with no cover, but still no enemy fire was evident. Zach felt a cold sweat breaking over him as an ominous silence permeated the battlefield. He signaled a halt. "Norm, it's too damn quiet. What do you think?"

Before Ricks could answer, heavy German machine gun fire erupted from across the stream. The squad hit the ground. Loud voices were screaming *"Yankee bastards!"*

"Here they come," Ricks called out as a platoon of bold German 7th Parachute troops charged across the shallow stream in another desperate attempt to buy time for their retreating main body.

"FIRE!" Zachary screamed as he leveled his Garand. The Germans were closing fast with another platoon close behind. "Holy shit, they're coming in force. Where the hell is the machine gun squad when we need them? Bashford! Get that BAR reloaded," he ordered as his eyes locked on the advancing Germans.

Bash resumed firing with deadly effect. Goldman proved he was a deadeye with the Springfield 03, but still the tough Germans kept coming. Rapid, pragmatic thinking raced across Zach's mind. *Damn, where is the rest of the platoon? We're all alone out here. We need more firepower.* The squad went prone on a skirmish line with little cover. To retreat was suicide. "Keep firing," Zach shouted. "Where the hell is Grinnell? We're in trouble!"

Then, above the noise of the small arms fire came the rumble of heavily tracked vehicles. Zach's heart raced and he yelled, "Keep firing, goddamn it—we've got help."

Grinnell had mounted the platoon and was charging to the action. The halftracks formed a line directly behind the embattled 3rd Squad and coordinated their deadly 50-caliber fire.

The lead Germans, now only fifty yards away, took a terrible clubbing from the hard-hitting guns. Those who survived fled in full retreat across the stream, a safety that would be short-lived as Colonel Hartman ordered the engineers to bring up their huge M-32 tank recovery vehicle, on which they had mounted a thirty-six-foot treadway bridge span.

"Good old Colonel George. He's bringing up the whole damn battalion," Zach whooped as he flashed a triumphant smile and a broad salute at his squad and the halftrack gunners. Amazingly, the squad had suffered no casualties, but the men were clearly in an anxiety-ridden state.

John Brenner sat in a tearful stupor as he disconnected his bayonet from his rifle. "I hate these damn things," he choked.

Ken Whedder stood in a state of emotional bewilderment as he put his bayonet back in its scabbard. "I…wonder if I could have used this…this *thing*?"

The squad slowly recovered their shaken élan as they watched the combat engineers struggle with Colonel Hartman's bizarre bridge contraption. The huge tank recovery vehicle stopped at the very edge of the soft, narrow river. The treadway bridge section rolled off the top and was pushed across. It worked! The halftracks rumbled across the makeshift bridge and headed for Roermond.

Some of the hardy German paratroopers survived by swimming across the Roer River or racing to cross the bridge at Roermond. Most were cut down or taken prisoner. Hartman's portable bridge was a success.

*****

When the weary 3rd Squad reached the north end of the river opposite Roermond, all of the permanent Roer bridges had been blown. However, the trailing 35th Infantry had captured one strategic bridge south of Roermond at Hilfarth. The Infantry rushed a bridgehead company across, while the engineers secretly boarded assault boats to establish at least twelve small beachheads, enabling the bridge companies to move up and go to work.

Ten elite German divisions, three of them armored, still threatened the whole operation. They were located further north and west of Roermond. Thanks to the strategic planning of the 9th Army's General Simpson and the heroic, determined action of the Canadian 1st Army, the threat was contained and construction of the twelve large vehicular bridges could continue.

By the next morning, four infantry divisions were stacked up behind the 18th Armored Division. OPERATION GRENADE was ready to roll across the Roer on all thirteen bridges. General Simpson brought up two thousand 9th Army big guns. A monster artillery barrage would precede the crossing. Newly repaired rail lines were already bringing thousands of tons of backup equipment to the crossing area. By the end of the day, the deafening roar of the artillery began. Twenty-five thousand foot soldiers rushed across to secure all of the bridges. The spearhead armored division was ready to roll. Lieutenant Russ Grinnell surveyed the bridge his heavy vehicles would have to cross. "I hope to hell we never have to back up."

Norm Ricks looked to the rear. "There isn't anywhere to back up to.

It must be solid traffic all the way back to Antwerp."

"I guess people have a lot of confidence that we'll break out and keep going," Zach added wryly.

"Recon says the Germans have two broken infantry divisions and the crack 116th Panzer Division which they will use to delay us while they move their main line of defense to the Rhine," Lieutenant Grinnell reported.

The artillery stopped. There was no return fire. The Germans had withdrawn. When the orders came down, B Company moved out. The Roer bridge crossing went smoothly. Somehow, the rapid movement strategy or perhaps German panic had made it happen. Even the Luftwaffe failed to show up. "They're probably saving them for the Rhine," Zach said, releasing a stressed moan.

GERMANY

Go Get 'Em!

Small groups of cheering Dutch citizens came running out of nowhere and stood on both sides of the Roer River. "What's the big deal?" Stosh asked.

Zach pulled himself down from the command ring as his track left the bridge. "Stosh, we're in Germany now. The five-year occupation of the state of Limburg is finally over."

"That's a big deal and we helped do that, huh?"

"Yes, Stosh, we helped do that, but the krauts still hold northern Holland."

Zach climbed up and put his elbows back on the ring. The infantry beachhead was now two miles deep, and the happy doughboys cheered, "Go get 'em," as the armor rolled past. As the squad approached their first German village, Ken Whedder grumbled, "Now comes the hard part."

*****

Whedder was wrong. The Germans were in full retreat and cities and towns with names like Vosch, Alderkirk, Richelrath, Duken, Boisheim, Flothend, and Lobberich were quickly overrun with minimal casualties. However, the heady, mad dash toward the Rhine came to a screeching halt at the city of Saelhuysen when two hard-hitting 88 rounds stopped the two lead tanks dead in their tracks. Ken Whedder's "hard part" prediction had begun.

German tank and artillery fire commenced raising hell with OPERA-TION GRENADE. The halftracks, caught in the middle of open fields, offered only minimal cover underneath their tracks. For one squad just one hundred yards from Babe, there was no cover when a high explosive (HE) artillery round scored a direct hit.

Moments later, a screeching shell landed close to Babe. The squad hunkered down between the tracks and front wheels. Zach felt his body lift off the ground. He could feel the blast angrily roaring through the spaces between the bogie wheels.

"Naylor, off your ass! We gotta get outta here! Mount up!" Naylor spun Babe around with the squad skulking down behind the one-quarter-inch armor. Naylor floored the big vehicle as artillery chased the overheated track until it was out of range. The rest of the operational halftracks followed.

B Company regrouped south of town. The battered 2nd Platoon was in an unhappy mood. Lieutenant Grinnell called for a meeting of the squad sergeants. "Assemble on me, goddamn it. Casualties?"

The reports came back. "Three missing." "Two wounded." "One KIA." "Two missing."

"Not a good day," muttered Platoon Sergeant Ricks.

"Better than A Company!"

"At least most of our tanks survived," Bruno Nitchke mumbled.

"We'll need a lot more troops and tanks to even budge 'em," grumbled Lieutenant Grinnell.

Zach was looking toward the town with his field glasses. "That's for sure, and how do we get our tracks and tanks past all the obstacles they're resetting?"

Before anyone could answer, an angry Captain Black rushed over, followed by his radioman. "Here's the plan," Blackie said. "At dark, the engineers will clear the tank obstacles. At dawn, the 939th Field Artillery will plaster them. Then the 85th will mount tanks and go in with marching fire. A battalion of infantry from the 83rd Division will follow and hold the town after we push them out."

"Then what?" Grinnell asked.

"Then we give chase, but only after our 939th's M-7s hit them again with our new proximity artillery shells. That's it," Captain Black snapped.

Zach looked over his shoulder as he heard tanks moving up. "More of our big brothers are arriving. That's good news."

Bruno scratched his very large head. "I knew this was not going to be easy."

"We'll get them tomorrow, Bruno. How's the squad doing?"

"Goldman got hit, and Bash and Pappy are missing. I think they're hiding in town."

"How bad is Goldman?"

"A couple of grazing rounds in the arm. Wild Bill says he'll be back in a couple of weeks."

"We were lucky…Bash and Pappy know how to survive."

"Yeah, not like our 71st Battalion over at Schraphysen."

"What have you heard?"

"Bad. Company C had twenty-four casualties. Lost two halftracks and their company commander."

"What about our sister B Company?"

"I heard that a lot of guys are missing."

Zach hung his head. "A lot of ASTP men are in that company."

"Sorry, Zach."

"Yeah."

*****

In the evening, combat engineers from the 35th Battalion were called upon to clear the way for the 18th Armored tanks. The M-7s from the armored field artillery battalion moved up to give them covering fire and some relief from the German multiple-barrel rocket mortars, the Screaming Meemies. The experienced engineers worked through the night marking tank traps and tipping obstacles. They reported few tank mines but plenty of Schu antipersonnel mines. The word went out to the troops: "Ride or follow in the tank tracks."

At dawn, the artillery battalion again laid down a devastating barrage of high explosives followed by smoke rounds to give the task force some cover. The heavily armed tank force moved out with a curtain of marching fire. The Germans held on tenaciously. When the smoke cleared, the Germans had blasted three M-4 tanks and four tracks, but were clearly taking a beating. The terrifying Screaming Meemies and deadly, screeching 88-mm artillery finally came to a halt under withering American firepower. The Germans were slowly forced to withdraw.

The tough Panzer Grenadiers paid a heavy price. Five retreating Mark IV tanks were on fire, seventy-two prisoners were taken, and an untold number were killed. A following battalion from the 83rd Infantry Division stormed through town, released Bash and Pappy, who were found safe in a deep wine cellar, feeling no pain.

*****

B Company remounted tanks and shot through the 83rd in hot pursuit of the now-mangled regiment of the 116th Panzers. At the far edge of town, the lead Sherman struck a Teller antitank mine. A call went out to the engineers, who cleared the field in less than an hour, leaving the mines in piles as a kind of monument to their work. That well-planned delay allowed the retreating Panzers to negotiate two thousand yards of open fields and disappear into the woods beyond.

Lieutenant Grinnell and Ricks ran some fifty yards from the town's end house to a four-foot rock wall surrounding most of the southern edge of the town. "The krauts got their tanks over and through this wall. I guess we can too," Grinnell said.

"Right, but we'll be exposing our tank bottoms—great targets."

"Yeah, Norm, but a long one. It must be fifteen hundred to two thousand yards to the woods."

Zach joined them. "Sir, that big Jagd Panther we met earlier has a range of three thousand yards."

"Jeez, you bookworms know more shit! Is that the turretless?"

"Yes, sir, all forty-six tons of it." *Thank you, Captain Fred.*

"Here comes Colonel Hartman. Let's see what's up."

The colonel leaned on the wall. "The corps commander has left our next move up to General Devane, our division CO. I'm waiting on a radio message now. Where is Captain Black?"

"Two tanks over, sir, with the rest of my platoon."

"I'll brief him. Hold until further orders."

"Yes, sir."

John Brenner came running over. "What's the word? Are we moving out or not?"

"We're on hold," Ricks replied.

"Good. We'd be dead out there in the open," John said.

"Right, Brenner. Gates says their S.Ps (self-propelled guns) have a range of three thousand yards." The threesome moved to a clump of small trees and shrubs growing close to the wall.

"Unless it's a Jagd Tiger…that's even bigger."

Ken Whedder joined them and handed Zach his field glasses. "Thought you'd need these."

The foursome debated what their orders would be and what the Germans would do next. "I can't believe they will counterattack," Lieutenant Grinnell mumbled.

"Yeah, they're hurting…but you never know," Zach muttered.

A runner joined them. "Captain Black wants to see you, Lieutenant."

"Right."

"I'll go with you, Russ," Sergeant Ricks said.

"Good idea," replied Grinnell as the two hotfooted it over to Captain Black.

Zach, Brenner, and Whedder resumed their survey of the distant woods. Zach refocused his binoculars. "I think if we move out there in the open, they'll lay down artillery and then counterattack in force. They did it before."

"Christ, Zach, you're a real optimist."

"No, just a realist."

Brigadier General

Staring intently at the woods, the men paid little attention to the small-ish soldier who fell in behind them. A mature voice responded. "Your sergeant may be right." The three bookworms spun around and found themselves face-to-face with a brigadier general. "As you were, men. I'm just trying to get a firsthand assessment." The general raised his field glasses. "Well, Sergeant, what would you advise?" Before a startled Zach could respond, Captain Black, Lieutenant Grinnell, and Colonel Hartman rushed up, having just heard of the general's presence on the front line. "At ease, men," General Devane said casually. "The sergeant here has some ideas."

The three battalion officers glowered. *What the hell has this kid sergeant done now?*

"Well, speak up, Sergeant. The General hasn't got all day," Colonel Hartman ordered.

Zach screwed up his courage and sputtered, "Stay hidden…bring up the heavy artillery…create a diversion several thousand yards on the flank, sir." *Thanks again, Captain Fred.*

"So, Sergeant, you're pretty sure they will counterattack?"

Zach felt trapped. He took a deep breath and looked at his battalion commander, then at General Devane. "Yes, General, I think so."

Everyone turned to the general, who was stroking his chin. "So do I, son. The 116th Panzer Division is the best and boldest tank outfit in the German Army, and they're buying time."

Colonel Hartman shook his head in disbelief at the patience of his diminutive divisional commander. The general called up his radioman while Colonel Hartman narrowed his eyes and approached Zach. General Devane interrupted. "The artillery will be in place shortly, and the 71st Battalion is already causing a distraction down the line. If they go for it, that should give our tanks some side shots."

Colonel Hartman backed off and secretly rolled his eyes. "What is our next move, General Devane?"

"I agree with the sergeant. We hide and we wait."

"And if they don't attack, General?" Captain Black asked in a tentative voice.

General Devane smiled. "Then we demote the sergeant here. What's your name, Sergeant?"

In one of life's ridiculous moments, Zach gulped and blurted out, "Sergeant John J. Jones, sir."

Lieutenant Grinnell removed his helmet and slapped the top of his head, barking, "It's *Private* Zachary Gates, sir."

Zach suffered a moment of terror before the general broke into loud laughter. The rest joined in the outburst. A flood of combat anxiety was released by everyone, especially Private Gates. Their laughter halted when the general's aide came running. "General, the 71st Tank Battalion reports movement in the woods."

The general raised his field glasses. "Goddamn, here they come, tanks and infantry. Hold your fire until they're one thousand yards away."

"Here comes their long range artillery. Take cover," ordered Captain Black.

The group crouched behind the wall as the general talked into his radio. "Hold the artillery till they're halfway across the field and be prepared to move it up one thousand yards when we move out." The general turned to the group. "Did you get that?"

"Yes, sir," Colonel Hartman replied. "When do we move?"

"When you attack is a battalion decision, George."

"Yes, sir."

"Good luck, men. I must get back to headquarters."

When the general was out of earshot, Russ Grinnell groaned. "You asshole, Gates—Sergeant John J. Jones!"

The colonel intervened. "Easy, Lieutenant. We have an attack to mount."

"Yes, sir. When do we go?"

"When half of their tanks are down or turned around," the BC replied. The colonel turned to Captain Black. "Blackie, what do you think?"

"I think General John J. Jones is right, sir."

"So do I, Captain. Stay alive, Sergeant Jones. Good hunting, men."

"Something's up. They're shifting their artillery." Captain Black raised his glasses. "They're moving toward the 71st. Carry on. I'm going back to company headquarters."

Brenner slapped his good friend on the back. "Can I come to your court-martial?"

"Very funny."

"Does he know your name?"

"Yeah, Sergeant John J. Jones."

*****

The German armored infantry and tanks, concentrating on the diversion group, were now halfway across the open field. "Fire!" was shouted up and down the line of hidden American tanks. The German Mark IVs took some direct hits and then the American artillery battalion opened up. Zach raised his binoculars as his squad assembled. "My God, our new proximity fuses are deadly!"

"How do they work?" Stosh Kosinski asked.

"They explode before impact. A built-in radio signal sets them off."

"You mean above the ground, like a tree burst?"

"Yup. They spread shrapnel and blast over a much wider area. These must be new to the Germans." Zach paused. "We fooled them. Their counterattack is shot to hell. Get ready to move out. We're following the tanks."

The tanks marched out on a skirmish line, stopping only for a better shot at the retreating Mark IVs. What was left of the Panzer Grenadiers were now running back to the woods, which proved to be poor cover as the 399th Field Artillery moved up and poured it on.

Zach surveyed the battlefield from his perch on top of an M-4 Sherman. "My God, what a massacre!" Dead and wounded Grenadiers were scattered among the burning tanks and halftracks. A lone German Jagd Panther, however, was still firing with deadly accuracy from the woods, taking down two M-4s. The big German tank retreated when the Shermans entered the woods. The 399th lifted its artillery and the infantry dismounted and moved up in front of the tanks to protect them from Panzerfausts.

The Germans were now in full retreat. The two German regiments involved had lost 50 percent of their personnel.

"It's What I Do."

As the battlefield grew silent, ambulances of the division's 78th Medical Unit ventured out into the chaos to pick up the wounded. Almost all were Germans. Medic Wild Bill came running alongside Zach's now-stopped M-4 tank. "Anybody hurt?"

Zach jumped down, along with Private John Bashford who took Zach's order to "stay close" very seriously. "Not that I know of, Bill, just Germans."

At that moment a German unterofficer struggled to his feet using his rifle as a crutch. "*Hander hoch* (hands high)," ordered Zachary. The German did not comply. Sergeant Nitchke, seeing the rifle, raised his M-1. "Hold your fire, Bruno. The guy has shrapnel in both arms." The German soldier fell back to the ground.

Wild Bill dashed to help the wounded German sergeant with Zach following behind. A burning Mark IV tank stood a few yards away. Shrapnel from the new American artillery shells had torn through the flesh of both of his arms. One exposed ulna bone was broken, causing severe pain and profuse bleeding.

Wild Bill knelt over the moaning Grenadier. "Zach, I need help here."

Zach knelt down and moved closer. His steel helmet banged against Bill's. "Sorry."

First a shot of morphine, followed by tourniquets applied to both arms. Zach closed his eyes and gingerly held the soldier's bleeding arms off the ground while Anders calmly carried on, stopping the bleeding as best he could. "Okay, Zach, let him go."

Zach's knees trembled as he wiped his bloodstained hands on his pants and started to rise. He was up on one knee when he heard the *click* of a clip going into a weapon. He looked up just in time to see a solitary SS soldier emerge from behind the burning Mark IV with his Schmeisser submachine gun aimed directly at him.

Zach had no chance to draw his holstered Luger. Wild Bill looked up from the wounded soldier, his eyes as big as saucers. Both men ducked as they heard a chatter of gunfire. Zach felt his body—no hits, no blood, no holes. When he looked up, the SS soldier was lying in a crumpled heap. Seconds later, John Bashford stepped out from behind the tank, slung his BAR over his shoulder, leaned on the still smoldering tank, and calmly lit a cigarette.

Wild Bill murmured, "Thanks," and went on attending to the wounded German.

Zach, trembling and breathing hard, struggled to his feet and threw a salute to Bashford. Bash took a long drag on his cigarette. "It's what I do. How's the good kraut?"

"This kraut will bleed to death if he doesn't get more help," Bill said, waving frantically at one of the ambulances.

The German started to speak. "*Danke, danke, der SS ist Verucht* (crazy)." He looked at the three American soldiers and closed his eyes. The ambulance crew rolled him on a stretcher and took him away.

"Will he make it, Bill?"

"I don't think so. Gates—"

"Yeah?"

"Get that new guy a medal. He saved our asses."

Zach looked at the sky. *Thank you, God.* The battlefield was quiet now except for the medics moving about. He stared at the ambulance carrying the German feldwebel. *He was an armored infantry squad sergeant just like me...I hope he makes it.*

The squad came running and Zach slowly recovered. "Assemble on me, goddamn it."

Fight One More Round

Despite all of their casualties, the German strategy to delay was working. Large numbers of German troops and material were escaping east toward the Rhine River. The 116th Panzers fought a fierce, well-executed, two-week delaying action all the way to the city of Grefrath, Germany, five miles west of the Rhine River. The American troops that made it to the Moers bridge found it demolished.

Battle-weary and bruised, B Company soldiers were told they could stand down once they captured Grefrath. OPERATION GRENADE had been stalled.

"I'm so tired I can't see," John Brenner said.

"Roger that. The whole squad is out on their feet," griped now-bearded Bruno Nitchke.

"Amen. One more step and the whole platoon falls on its face," a sleepy voice grumbled.

Sergeant Ricks called the squad sergeants together. "Look alive. One more mission and we get to shave, sleep, and try eating a meal without being shot at." He turned to the still-shaken Zachary Gates. "Bookworm, are you awake?"

"Yeah, Norm."

"What's that motto of yours?" he snorted.

Zach groaned. "What?"

"That boxer guy, James J. something-or-other."

Zach yawned. "Corbett—Fight one more round."

"Yeah. Now let's get this platoon off its ass. We're gonna fight one more frickin' round."

Bruno Nitchke rolled his eyes. "Jesus Christ, a pep talk on the battlefield. What shit!"

Lieutenant Grinnell returned from his meeting with the company commander. "We're going in mounted. S-2 says they've pulled their tanks out. Sergeant Ricks, button up your lead track and move out—come on, wake up."

The five halftracks moved out in single file. Five hundred yards from the first houses, the column stopped and the 2nd Squad track lined up next to the 3rd Squad's track. No enemy fire had been encountered.

Lieutenant Grinnell joined Sergeants Ricks and Gates up front. "They must be as tired as we are. Let's wake 'em up. FIRE!"

Both tracks fired three long bursts of 50-calibers into the town and waited. They were about to fire again when a white flag appeared on the roof of the nearest building. "Hold your fire," Russ Grinnell shouted.

Suddenly a procession of exhausted Wehrmacht troops exited the city with hands on their heads. An entire battalion of thirteen hundred men had had enough. They had done their delaying job. Theirs was a wise decision, for they had neither armor nor artillery. Their main force had gone to Rhineberg to form the next main line of defense five miles away. Grefrath was taken without a single American casualty.

Even Sergeant Nitchke was impressed. "Goddamn, it worked. Fight one more fuckin' round."

The people of Grefrath were the first German citizens who finally seemed resigned to losing the war.

*****

The experienced American 2nd Armored Division had also been stopped at the river. They, like the 18th Armored, were ordered to stand down for rest, refueling, and rearmament. Hunting had been good for the 85th Battalion since the tough battle at Saelhuysen. Another five fair-sized cities had been taken.

The real wonder in this heavy action was the performance of the reorganized company. Sergeant Gates had proven himself and was now fully accepted and respected. He trudged wearily over to where Grinnell and Ricks were talking. "Maybe all the krauts will give it up."

"Not a chance. They have all their heavy stuff just across the river," Grinnell replied.

"Or at Rhineberg on this side," Ricks added.

"I hope not. That's our next objective," Russ Grinnell griped.

Zach walked away. "This time I am too tired to fight one more round."

COMBAT PERSONNEL COMPLICATIONS

Replacement Problems

Good news! Stan Goldman was on his way back from the evacuation hospital and the more seriously wounded Bob White was only a few days behind. Pappy returned from the aid station, carrying a bottle of liniment for his backside and advice on where to stick his premonitions.

The attack on Rhineberg, the German city hard on the west bank of the wide Rhine River, was put on hold. The 85th Battalion was standing down in Grefrath just five miles from the river.

Colonel Hartman believed in training and more training, especially if the next battles would, in his opinion, be monumental. "Crossing the Rhine is a second D-day!" he roared. All of his companies were required to train with a bridge company to learn from experienced combat engineers. Coordinated training became a part of each day of the short stand-down.

The B Company platoons were billeted in four adjacent German houses, all facing a four-acre square common which was surrounded by still more houses, enough to house the entire battalion. The common became a training and assembly area as well as a parking lot for halftracks, trucks, jeeps, and other vehicles. Lieutenant Grinnell ordered Sergeant Ricks to have the 2nd Platoon fall out. Captain Black was going to orient the company.

"At ease," shouted 1st Sergeant Bob Klein as Captain Black stepped up on a small bench.

"I want to welcome the new replacements to the best damn armored infantry company in the European Theater," he called out, his voice echoing across the common.

Among the replacements stood a thirty-five-year-old, dour-looking private named Ludolph Kolchak. During the time replacements were being assigned, Tom Sander caught up with fellow bookworms John Brenner and Ken Whedder. "Is that who I think it is?"

"He looks like that sick Neanderthal from Camp Polk who hated the bookworms," replied Whedder.

"Kolchak? Was his name Kolchak?" Brenner asked.

"Yeah, Ludolph Kolchak. It's him. What's that son of a bitch doing here?"

"Beats the hell out of me, but it's Ludolph Kolchak all right," choked Tom Sander.

Stosh Kosinski's blood ran cold. "Ludolph? Isn't that a Nazi name?" Stosh grumbled.

"In his case it is. We'd better alert Zach. Kolchak really hates his guts."

Brenner's muscles tightened and his voice turned gutteral. "Yeah. Ricks and Grinnell were also on his hit list."

A new replacement sensing the tension asked, "How'd a shithead like him get in the army?"

Bookworm Tom Sander tried to explain. "Before the war, when he was still in the CCC (civilian conservation corps), he damn near killed a guy in a fight. He was arrested and, the way I heard it, the judge told him to join the army or go to jail."

"Can a judge do that?"

"The old guys say it happened all the time."

Tech Sergeant Ricks joined the group wearing a worried look. "Watch your backs. That's Kolchak all right," he said.

"Norm, how could this happen? Wasn't he court-martialed?" Zach asked.

Ricks sighed and explained through an expression of disbelief. "Right, but he volunteered for overseas duty and got off."

"How in the hell did we get him?" Sander griped.

"He *asked* for Company B," Ricks replied.

"In God's name why?"

Ricks gathered his thoughts. "I guess he thought his sadistic army buddies Stillvert and Furk were still running the company."

"Is he nuts? Everybody knows they were kicked out," Sander said with disgust.

"Thank God we got rid of them," grunted Whedder.

Brenner, his mind filled with dark memories, speculated, "I can't believe he wasn't drummed out of service. He's a section eight (mentally disturbed)."

Stan Goldman was fuming. "I heard the bastard beat a recruit so badly he had to be given a medical discharge!"

Stosh was listening wide-eyed and shaken. "I guess I was pretty lucky, huh!"

"Yeah, you were. I hope to hell he's not in our squad. Zach, you're unusually quiet"

Zach mustered a calm expression. "Perhaps we're all overreacting…where are we, Norm?"

Taking a cue from Zach, Ricks said stiffly, "Grinnell put him in the 1st Squad…I alerted the squad leader." No reaction came from the squad. "Okay, party's over."

Bruno caught up with Zach. "We'll watch the bastard—keep your head down."

"Yeah, I know. Thanks," Zach replied as he became aware that his right hand was resting on his holstered Luger.

*****

"Attention!" shouted Sergeant Ricks as Colonel Hartman, Captain Black, and Lieutenant Grinnell entered the company assembly. Colonel Hartman paused for a long moment. "At ease, men. The stand-down is over. Find your seats. I have new orders for the battalion. General Montgomery has ordered the 2nd Armored to assist the British Army in taking the city of Wesel about ten miles north of Rhineberg. It, like Rhineberg, is on the MLD (main line of defense) and also has a bridge. As part of the plan, our battalion is to lead the 18th Armored in an attack on Rhineberg where we are to capture the vital bridge. If G-2 and British intelligence are correct, the heavy stuff has already moved to Wesel or crossed the bridge to set up a new MLD west of the Rhine and…" The colonel cleared his throat, indicating distrust of the information to follow. "That Rhineberg is defended by three hundred demoralized troops supported by a few self-propelled weapons and anti-aircraft guns."

"You don't sound convinced, Colonel," Captain Black said.

"No. I get suspicious when the crafty 116th Panzers and the tough paratroopers we met in Holland are involved."

"Are we going it alone?"

"No. The good news is we will have the help of a regiment from the 35th Infantry Division, our 81st Tank Battalion, and an attached company—as you were—two companies of tank destroyers from the 908th TD Battalion."

"Why all the support if it's such an easy objective?" Captain Black persisted.

The colonel's eyes riveted on Captain Black as he spoke slowly and clearly. "That's why I've asked the 88th Recon to make an early morning probe." He paused. "I was wrong about Grefrath…"

After a long silence, an A Company captain ventured a question. "Sir, when do we move?"

An apprehensive hush spread over the group as the colonel hesitated and then replied in a level voice, "We are to be on the line outside of Rhineberg at 0700, day after tomorrow." The battle-weary group stirred and vented a clearly audible groan.

The colonel waited for the group to settle down. "Any more questions?"

A concerned staff officer asked, "Sir, what if they blow the bridge?"

The BC smiled for the first time. "Then we wait for the bridge companies, the combat engineers, and the 30th Infantry to secure a beachhead."

Encouraged, a lieutenant inquired, "Sir, how wide is the river at the bridge?"

The BC glanced at his map. "I'd guess a half-mile or more. Anything else?"

An S-2 major was upset. "Sir, where the hell is TAC (tactical air command)?"

"Fair question, Major. The planes are all up in northern Holland on the North Sea coast trying to eliminate the V-1 and V-2 launch sites that are wreaking havoc in England. I have asked for emergency air support if we run into any tanks. That's all." The group came to attention.

*****

A company briefing for officers and noncoms was held that afternoon. Lieutenant Grinnell sought out Ricks and Gates. "I'm sorry Kolchak is in our platoon. Just don't take any shit from him. He's already been sounding off."

"Haven't we got enough with the krauts?" grumbled Ricks.

"Keep an eye on him," Grinnell said flatly, and walked away. Ricks groaned and looked at Zach. "Bookworm, I have another problem for you."

"Not another Kolchak?"

"No, but this comes down from Battalion S-2."

"Now what?"

"Private Henry Franier, a replacement with a problem."

"Has he got the clap or something?"

"It's not that easy. He's been accused of cowardice and may be facing a court-martial."

"Norm, I don't need that. Send him to A Company."

Russ Grinnell responded, "He came from A Company!"

"Why me?"

Norm Ricks shrugged. "You're the only bookworm squad leader."

"Oh for Christ's sake!" Zach snorted.

Grinnell frowned. "Zach, S-2 wants to give this soldier another chance. It was his first action—your name came up."

Zach shot Grinnell a knowing look. "Yes, sir, I get it. So what happened?"

"It's not pretty." The lieutenant took a breath and exhaled. "He was running alongside a Sherman when a Tiger Royal spotted the tank. The Tiger fired, and the round went right through the guy next to him before hitting the tank. The guy was literally blown apart."

Zach felt his stomach turn sour. "Good God."

Ricks sliced the air with his hand. "Zach, the tank crew was burned alive."

Zach gasped and choked out, "Some initiation of fire."

"The problem is…" Grinnell looked away. "When ordered to get up, he ran."

Zach shook his head. "We've all felt like that," he mumbled sympathetically.

"See, that's why you got him," Grinnell grinned.

"That's an order?"

"Colonel Hartman's recommendation—it's not an order, but it will be done."

*****

Zach called the 3rd Squad together and briefed them on the Rhineberg mission. The word on the Private Henry Franier problem apparently had not reached the squad. Zach thought it better that way. Questions regarding Rhineberg were many.

"What's this about some sad-sack troops holding Rhineberg?"

"If it's such a piece of cake, why didn't Montgomery take it himself?"

"Jesus, if it's the 116th Panzers, they'll have tanks, both Tigers and Panthers."

"British G-2 says the heavy stuff has withdrawn," Zach replied stiffly.

"You don't believe that, do you, Zach?" Tony Holter asked.

Zach stared at the floor. "No, I don't, and neither do Hartman and Black. That's why our recon people are on their way now to check it out."

"I hear we have plenty of fire power to move these three hundred sad sacks," Sergeant Nitchke declared.

"True, Bruno. Even the 908th Tank Destroyers are being attached."

Bruno put on a toothy grin. "Why all the firepower if they don't have any heavy stuff?"

"Training? Insurance? Hell, I don't know, Bruno."

John Brenner intervened. "The 908th I saw is full of surprises, Zach. You better check 'em out."

"Why? Aren't they M-10s like Hood?"

"No. They're light tanks and they have some other big experimental models."

"Thanks, John. Bruno, you and I will give them the once-over. Anything else?"

"Yeah, Gates. What's to the rumor about this new guy that runs?"

"He's recovering from shock, that's all."

"Shock?"

Zach looked away and then back into the eyes of his squad. "Okay, on his first action, the guy next to him was blown apart by a 128-mm round from a Jagd Panther. The same round took out a tank and burned the crew alive. He'll join us tomorrow," Zach said flatly. There was no response. "We move out at 0600 day after tomorrow. That's all."

Bruno cornered Zach. "I hope you didn't screw up, taking this Private Henry Franier."

"I've talked to him, Bruno. He's handling it. He's a good kid—and I didn't have much choice."

"Yeah, I get the picture," Bruno grumbled.

Brenner had been listening. "I say give him another chance."

Bruno raised his eyebrows. "Okay, bookworm psychologists—I give up."

"Bruno, sometimes it's a thin line between running and holding it together," Brenner scowled.

"If you say so."

"General Patton also says so," Zach added. "Remember Colonel Crane? He said, 'Courage is fear holding on a minute longer.'"

"Yeah, I also read that shit in *Stars and Stripes*," Bruno grunted.

Independent Tankers

The next day, Zach, Bruno, and Brenner walked to the large common where the tank destroyers were located. A buck sergeant dismounted and removed his leather headgear. "Thought you guys had your own tanks. We usually work with foot infantry."

Zach noticed that all of the men were sporting beards. He smiled. "Is that why you guys all need shaves?"

With that, a fully bearded head popped out of the tank's open turret. "Cut the jokes, Sergeant. It's our badge of honor."

Zach saw his gold bars as he stepped off the tank. "Sorry, Lieutenant. We come in peace."

The bearded lieutenant laughed and came over to shake hands. "Looks like we're going to cover your asses tomorrow."

"I hope so. Is this the new M-18 Hellcat we heard about?"

"Right. They're brand new. We've only had them for a month."

Zach looked down the open hatch. "Brenner and I trained with M-10s. Is this their replacement?"

"Not entirely. Our B Company has the brand new, thirty-six-ton M-36s. Jacksons, they call 'em. It's built on an M-10 frame, open turret, and a 90-mm gun."

"Will it take out the Tigers?"

"We'll see."

Zach shrugged. "We need something like the Panther to hold our own."

"Our C Company has the first really big American tanks, the T-26, or maybe it's M-26. They're brand new."

"How big are they?" John asked.

"I heard forty-six tons with either 90-mm or 120-mm guns. The ones I saw had wide, twenty-four-inch tracks, huge rifles with big muzzle brakers, and heavy armor up front."

"They should shake up the Germans," John reflected.

"What do you call them?" Zach asked.

"Pershings. They have a low profile and a cast hull and turret. The really different thing is the Christie-type suspension."

"The what?"

"All the wheels are the same size, like the German tanks."

"No more bogie wheels?"

"Nope. They look a little like the Panthers and Tigers and should compete."

"Are they fast?" Zach asked.

"Oh yes. They have a 470-horsepower Ford V-8, and they have more firepower. They fire a monster twenty-four-pound AP round."

"We may surprise some German tankers," Zach said. "Now what about this M-18 Hellcat? It isn't very big."

The tank lieutenant frowned. "Nineteen tons is all, but she's quiet and she's fast. We've had her over fifty miles per hour."

"Is this a 76-mm?" Bruno asked.

"Right. It's the same as a three-inch naval gun, a real blaster, but that's not the best part. Johnston, show 'em the gyroscope."

The sergeant climbed aboard the tank and motioned for the others to follow. The group peered down into the open turret. "That gizmo down there allows us to fire on the move and still hit a target."

"You mean it operates independent of the rise and fall of the tank."

"Right, Sergeant. It kind of floats."

"Looks like you have a continental engine and what's this, an automatic transmission?"

"Right again, Sergeant. You know your engines."

"I studied some engineering."

The sergeant continued. "This nine-cylinder baby generates four hundred horsepower, and the automatic transmission is new. It's called 'torgmatic.'"

"Sounds great, Sergeant, but I wish you could tell us how that big M-26 competes," Zach said.

"So do I, but C Company just got 'em."

The conversation was interrupted when the tanker officer called for an assembly of his other four tank commanders. "Got to leave you, doughboys. You'll get a demonstration tomorrow if we see any German tanks. Good luck."

"Yeah, you too."

Bruno, Zach, and John climbed down from the tank. "Bruno, let's bed check the troops now; we have an early call."

"Good idea. One thing more, Gates."

"Yeah?"

"How did our platoon get stuck with that asshole bully, Ludolph Kolchak?"

"They had to assign him someplace."

The big buck sergeant frowned. "That son of a bitch is stupid. He's already bitching about you, Grinnell, and of course, Ricks, who replaced him at Polk."

"What have you heard?"

"The ugly bastard says it was Grinnell who had his asshole buddies court-martialed after the bookworms lied."

"That's a crock!"

"I know. The BC himself relieved them of command."

"Just don't take any shit, Bruno. That's what Grinnell told me."

Bruno pawed the ground. "Gates, this jerk has threatened to get even with anyone who was in the ASTP. I say again, watch your back!"

Zach tried to calm the big, concerned sergeant. "It's all smoke, Bruno."

"I'm not so sure. The guy is an animal, and he was sighting a rifle when he said it."

"He's not that crazy, Bruno."

"Be careful out there, Gates."

"Yeah. Thanks again."

Zach looked at the darkening sky and headed for his billet. *That damn Ludolph Kolchak. He is one ranting idiot...he could screw up the whole damn platoon...he could hurt somebody.* Zach glanced at his four stripes. Thoughts of responsibility were mixed with fear and anger.

B-17 Nightmare

The "night off" before the attack on Rhineburg turned into a long and tragic nightmare for Zach's 3rd Squad. A flight of B-17 bombers returning from a mission over Berlin found themselves in trouble. One plane went down behind enemy lines. The lead plane sputtered overhead, trailing smoke. Parachutes were seen drifting into the Allied-held territory. Then the last chute caught a wind, carrying it into no man's land, a problem for the flyer, since that area was a stronghold for renegade SS and Hitler Jungend.

Hurry-up orders reached the 3rd Squad to retrieve the airman before the Germans captured him. Medic Wild Bill Anders was attached and Zach assembled the group. "Should be a piece of cake. I doubt the Germans are that close. Let's go get that flyboy."

Zach assigned just-returned veteran Bob White and replacement Henry Franier as lead scouts. *Where I can keep an eye on him,* Zach said to himself. They reported nothing for almost a mile, when suddenly Franier came running back. "Sarge, we spotted a chute."

"You did good, Henry. Lead us to it."

The squad found the chute partially hung up in a tree. On the ground below lay an unconscious, bleeding airman. Zach turned him face up. The airman's eyes opened and he stuttered, "Wheeler, Buchanan, Major, 10724905," the only required information if taken prisoner.

"Relax, Major. I'm an American sergeant. You're in enemy territory but we're going to get you out of here."

"Thank God. Bless you, Sergeant, but I may be a problem. I've pulled all the muscles in my back and my legs aren't working right."

Wild Bill took a long look. "I don't think anything's broken, but back injuries are tricky."

"What do you need, Bill?"

"Some kind of conveyor or cart we can load this guy on—I can stop the bleeding."

Zach nodded. "Franier, Whedder! Check out that barn."

"Understood. We're on it."

In minutes they were back with a small farm cart loaded with hay. "Brenner, Sander, you're on the cart," ordered Zach.

"Got it."

"Okay, Major, we're going to load you up and get the hell out of here before the Germans arrive."

"Thanks, Sergeant. I owe you one."

"We're not out of here yet, Major."

"Let's go," shouted Bruno Nitchke.

"Okay, move out. Brenner, Whedder, keep a sharp eye. If the Germans spotted the chute, they may be trailing us. White, Franier, take the point. Stosh, you're our rear guard."

The squad had covered two hundred yards when White, the lead scout, raised his hand. Franier, a few paces behind, passed the signal on.

"What do you think, Bruno?" Zach whispered.

Sergeant Nitchke peered into the dark. "Maybe it's one of our patrols from A Company."

"I hope so. We're running out of time."

Nitchke checked his compass. "It's the shortest way back—let's find out."

Zach signaled to move forward and ordered Bashford to bring up his BAR. Bob White had gone only a few more steps when a burst from a hidden Schmeisser machine gun blew him off his feet.

Bashford instinctively returned fire. During the few seconds of Bashford's covering fire, new replacement Henry Franier bravely dashed forward, grenade in one hand, rifle in the other. He released the grenade just as Bashford was reloading. Franier went down as the grenade went off. All went strangely silent—then suddenly the Schmeisser resumed firing. Franier, wounded, struggled to his feet. He ran forward and threw his second grenade. He staggered another step and emptied a clip from his M-1 into the fleeing survivors. The firefight was over. Henry Franier was wounded, clutching his face and neck.

"Hold your fire," Zach shouted as he rushed forward, his heart pounding, to check on White and Franier. "Medic! Bill, get over here."

The first burst of machine gun fire had stitched across White's chest and neck. He was bleeding profusely. Zach looked at his face. There was no sign of life. One bullet had exploded in his throat. Zach had seen that face of death before and he knew White was gone. White's eyes were wide open as if he were still looking for the guns that had killed him. Zach rose up as the medic arrived. One look and Bill knew too. There is something about a dead man's face that combat veterans recognize without understanding why. "He's gone, Zach," Bill said in an almost inaudible voice.

Zach's adrenaline spiked as he slowly scanned the area. *Are there more renegades out there?* He stood stiff-legged, his mouth dry as he felt the weight of decision.

"Zach?"

"Yeah, I know." He walked over to Franier's crumpled body. "How is he, Bill?" he asked uneasily.

"Not good, Zach, but he's alive. He's asking for you."

Zach fought his retching gut as he viewed the horrific scene. Henry Franier had been shot in the face, neck, and right arm, all of which were bleeding profusely. Part of his left cheek was laid open but his eye was intact. Small facial bones were exposed. Blood dripped over the corner of his mouth. He recognized his squad leader and with great effort mumbled, "I got 'em, Sergeant Gates…I got 'em."

Overcoming his heartache, Zach rallied. "You're a hero, Henry. Hang on. We're going to get you out of here."

Bill Anders administered morphine and sulfa. He was able to stop most of the bleeding. "This is bad, Zach. We need to get him back real quick."

Dulled by morphine and shock, Franier closed his eyes and slipped into unconsciousness. Pappy came over to help. He stared at Franier's bloody, ripped face and could not speak. His body trembled and it appeared he might fall down. Zach had seen and experienced shock many, many times before. He steadied Pappy and turned him around. "Franier will make it, Pappy. Now get your act together and bring that damn cart up here. It has to hold two—go!"

Pappy blinked, nodded, and went after the cart. Funny thing about shock. Some guys freeze and lose it completely. Others snap out of it somehow and are able to function. Zach was able to do that. Apparently so could Pappy Becker.

Brenner, Becker, and Whedder rushed forward with the cart and quickly loaded Henry Franier alongside the air corps major. Whedder looked at the badly wounded Franier. "No coward here. He saved our asses."

"Get 'em moving, Bruno, or Franier is dead," Zach shouted.

"What about White?" Bruno asked.

Zach paused. "It's almost dawn. How far to our lines?"

"At least a thousand yards. Zach, we'll never drag him that far," Bruno replied.

Medic Wild Bill came forward. "Let's move, guys, or Franier has had it."

The tough combat decision was made easier when another German patrol was spotted in the light of a flare. "Mark the spot. We'll come back for him in force. Move out, double time!" Zach ordered.

The Germans stopped their pursuit when they saw the American frontline. Finally, Zach's tired squad was out of danger. Sergeant Ricks and most of the 2nd Platoon met them. "You're late, Zach! What was all the shooting?"

"A shitload of irregulars. Norm, I had to leave Bob White," Zach said with a note of guilt.

"Is he dead?"

Zach's throat became tight and dry. "Yeah. We had all we could handle with Franier and the pilot."

"What a bitch. Wasn't he wounded twice earlier?"

"Yeah…" Zach stammered as he paced back and forth.

"Stay with your squad. I'll go get him," Ricks said, patting him on the shoulder.

Zach rallied as he had so many times before. "Take Bruno and Bash. They know the route back."

Wild Bill wouldn't wait on an ambulance. He loaded Franier on a jeep and roared off to the aid station. Major Buchanan, held until the ambulance arrived, insisted on seeing Sergeant Gates. "Sergeant, you saved my life. I owe all of you. I won't forget this."

Zach nodded and spoke in a voice just short of rage. "Neither will I, Major…I lost two men out there."

Sergeant Ricks rounded up the 2nd Platoon bystanders and struck out boldly into the now-rising sun to retrieve Bob White's body. The startled German irregulars fell back.

Wild Bill returned and reported that Henry Franier had a fifty-fifty chance of making it. Tom Sander, still shaken, reflected on Franier's bravery. "Patton was right. 'Courage is only fear holding on a minute longer.'"

Henry Franier was recommended for the Bronze Star medal for gallantry in action.

*****

The squad had just returned to their house on the Grefrath common when a concerned Stosh entered Zach's room. "Zach, can I ask you something?"

"Is it important, Stosh? It's been a long night."

"I think so, honest."

"Okay, shoot."

"Why does this Ludolph Kolchak hate the lieutenant, Sergeant Ricks, and you so much?"

"That's a big question, Stosh. What brought it up?"

"Well, Sergeant Palmeri, you know, the old guy in the mortar squad—"

"Yeah, a good soldier, been in since 1940—so what happened?"

"Palmeri and Kolchak got in a fight. Sergeant Klein broke it up."

"That's all we need. What was the fight about?"

"I guess because Kolchak has been sounding off about me and you guys."

Zach's voice dropped. "Maybe it's authority, Stosh."

"Authority?"

"He resents power unless it's from the two bullies he knew at Polk."

Stosh fought through his thoughts. "Tom says Kolchak doesn't like bookworms because he feels inferior when they're around. I think Kolchak's jealous. He only got as far as the sixth grade…I'm going to finish high school when I get home."

Zach smiled. "I know you will, Stosh. Do you think the bookworms are hard on you?"

"No. I like the bookworms. Okay, they tease me sometimes but they're all good guys. So are Grinnell and Ricks. Brenner says Ludolph is a sick, angry dumbass."

Zach laughed. "Maybe John is right."

Stosh turned serious. "Maybe you should talk to Ludolph."

"Stosh, Russ, Norm, and I already tried that. He just glowered at us. He'll back off once he gets used to the platoon."

"I hope so. Some of the guys are really angry."

"Stosh, if he doesn't calm down, I'm sure Captain Black will have him removed."

"Bruno says he threatened to shoot you guys."

Zach straightened up. "Did he say it just like that? That's grounds for a court-martial."

Stosh gathered his thoughts and revised them. "I think it was, 'Those guys better watch their backs.'"

Zach thought for a moment and shrugged. "I think he's just blowing smoke…let's hope so. Thanks for your concern, Stosh. Go get some rest."

Zach did not sleep well. *Is everyone overreacting? Am I in real danger here? Is the crazy bastard capable of carrying out these veiled threats? Maybe I'm just battle-weary…Hell, when your number's up, it's up—one day at a time.*

12

RHINEBERG HANGS TOUGH

Dawn Surprise

"2nd Platoon, mount up and prepare to move out." Driver John Naylor, who had not been on patrol, was the only man in the squad not out on his feet. At 0600, the heavily armed battalion moved out toward Rhineberg, arriving at the assembly area west of the city at 0700. Reconnaissance elements reported no tanks and only sporadic small arms fire met them. They were, however, concerned, since no recon had yet reached Lintfort.

Zach and the other squad leaders were ordered to report for a final briefing. Still tired from the trials of the previous night, Zach wearily studied the detailed maps showing the small, suburb-like towns outside of Rhineberg. Pitgen, Lintfort, Ratschendorf, and Ossenberg were prominent, especially Lintfort. The open land between Lintfort and Rhineberg was flat and crisscrossed by canals—not a happy place for armored vehicles.

There were to be three attacking elements, one from the south, another from the northwest, and the 85th from the west right in the middle. B Company would lead in its sector. Montgomery had ordered a heavy RAF bombardment of Wesel, but not of Rhineberg, much to the consternation of Colonel Hartman and General Devane.

Colonel Hartman insisted on more recon before committing B Company and its support company of tanks to any assault across the canal country. Recon had already scouted the area, but agreed to send one M-8 six-wheeler to look again, knowing that the Germans were excellent camouflagers. B Company halftracks, the assigned M-4 tracks, and the independent M-18 Hellcat tank destroyers remained hidden in the woods edging the flatlands.

Zach was traversing the three thousand yards of flatlands in front of him with his binoculars when Lieutenant Grinnell and Captain Black joined him. "Well, General Jones, what do you think? Have they all pulled out?" Blackie asked with a straight face.

Zach continued his observation. "I don't think so, Captain. I see movement on the edge of the city."

"Anything else?"

"Just recon's six-wheeler, sir."

"That six-wheeler has guts. Why didn't we wait for aerial reconnaissance?" Grinnell asked.

"There isn't any. Colonel Hartman has been screaming for airplanes for two days," Blackie replied.

"The M-8 is within range of small arms fire now—nothing," Zach observed. Suddenly a bright muzzle flash was followed by a horrific explosion as a large HE round hit the recon's small armored car. The observers stood open-mouthed as the disintegrating parts of the car shot skyward. The larger parts reached their apex and then appeared to just hang there until they slowly tilted and came crashing to the ground. Captain Black was fuming. "Those bastards. That was no AP (armor piercing) round. They deliberately blew those guys to oblivion."

"That flash was from a 120-mm or larger gun. We're vulnerable," Zach exclaimed. "Incoming!" someone shouted, and the transfixed men regained their senses and ran for cover behind and under the tracks and tanks to escape the increasing fire.

"Withdraw! Withdraw!" Captain Black ordered. "No three hundred worn-out troops are doing this," he snarled.

Zach, breathing hard, ran to his track and ordered Naylor to turn the halftrack around. "Go! Go! Get us out of range."

Once out of range of the German guns, Colonel Hartman collected his scattered battalion and ordered a long end-around maneuver to take advantage of more hilly and wooded terrain. A fortuitous two-track road allowed the battalion to advance in narrow tank/halftrack, tank/halftrack formation right to the edge of a woods only one thousand yards from the outskirts of Rhineberg.

Captain Black looked through his field glasses. Still fuming, he sputtered, "We can run that gap if they're not alert."

"Easy, Captain," Colonel Hartman asserted, jogging up behind him. "They have tanks and artillery and they know we're here. We hold till we see if they show."

Minutes later they did show. And in force with Mark IV tanks leading the way.

"Prepare to fire," shouted the rushed colonel. "Get that TD outfit up here!"

The tank destroyers clanked forward, their drivers shouting for clearance as they rushed the German tanks, firing as they went. The five small M-18 Hellcats with their gyroscopic firing and their speed caught the German Panzers by surprise. Thirteen of the twenty slower Mark IVs were knocked out in short order, but a price was paid. Two Hellcats went down hard. Only one crew was able to escape their burning tank.

Zach turned away from the horrific scene and gasped, "We met some of those Hellcat guys…" John stole another look. "What a bitch."

Their torment was broken when they heard the BC shouting, "Now we go! Blackie, get your company moving."

B Company mounted tanks. Their four lead tanks covered eight hundred yards before they met dug-in Germans. The lead tank was disabled by Panzerfausts, knocking Zach and Whedder off its top. The second tank was stopped by a Teller mine and then took a hit from the same Panzerfaust team.

Zach struggled to his feet and checked his body parts—all intact, but bruised and sore. *Get your act together, squad leader.* He checked Whedder, who was on his feet rubbing his neck. The tankers were in trouble. Zach grabbed his rifle, adjusted his helmet, and shouted, "Bash, follow me! We're nailing the goddamn Panzerfausts."

Whedder waved and yelled, "Over there, Zach—foxholes!"

Combat-proven John Bashford came running forward. Zach waved and pointed toward the foxholes. "Cover us, Bash. We're going after those guys." Bashford dropped the bipod on his BAR and started firing from the prone position. Zach and Ken rushed forward under his covering fire and hit the ground when Bashford changed clips.

Zach caught his breath. "How's your arm, Ken?"

"Like Bob Feller's. Give me your two grenades," he replied brusquely.

"Wait till Bash starts firing. Okay, now! Throw!"

Whedder stood up for maximum range and threw all four grenades in rapid succession. He ducked down, waiting for the explosions. The few seconds seemed like minutes. And then *blam, blam, blam, blam* came the explosions which drove out four Germans who started running toward Rhineberg.

"Stay down!" barked Zach as Bashford stood up and fired from the hip, the bullets screeching over the two prone men. Zach felt a hard bump on his right hip. A bullet hit his binoculars. Another round struck Whedder's rifle. "Are you okay, Ken?"

"Yeah, how about you?"

"My glasses are shot to hell. Damn! Is Bashford losing his touch?"

The firing stopped and Bashford yelled, "Got 'em all."

"Where the hell are you?"

"Over here, Zach."

"What the hell kind of shooting was that? You almost killed us!"

"Not me—no way!"

"Yeah—look at my glasses and Whedder's rifle."

Bashford nervously pulled out a cigarette. "That's single shot damage. I was firing on automatic."

"Later! Bash, where the hell is Bruno?"

"Over here, Gates."

"Were you giving us covering fire?"

"Yeah. So were the 1st and 2nd Squads," Bruno said uneasily.

"I'll talk to you later, Nitchke. Move your sharpshooters forward."

Whedder looked at his damaged rifle. "Zach, this shot came from the rear. You don't think Kolchak…"

"No, I don't, but I'm going to talk to that crazy bastard."

Zach's inner voice was reproving—*If that madman killed Ricks, Grinnell, or any of your men…you…you, Sergeant Gates, are responsible.*

The mind-numbing screech of an 88 whistled over them. Ken Whedder was shouting, "Zach, look alive. Incoming fire! Where's our tank support?"

Zach's inner voice stopped and his blood started to pound. "Where the hell is the radioman?" he called out.

A winded voice responded, "Over here, sir. The captain sent me."

"Call for a goddamn tank!" Zach shouted.

The radioman, huffing under his heavy backpack, answered, "I called for the tanks, sir."

"Good. Now you stay with me."

In short order, a platoon of M-4 Sherman tanks which had been following came grinding through the debris to take the heat off of the 2nd Platoon. They clanked forward to a small group of houses outside of Rhineberg where the Germans were holed up, desperately continuing their delaying action. A half-day of pounding from the American tanks followed by bitter house-fighting in the small enclave finally forced their withdrawal.

The company now faced another three hundred yards of open space. The Shermans were moving smartly across when a hidden Panther tank showed itself and fired two quick shots from its 88-mm gun. Two M-4s were stopped dead in their tracks and the battle changed. The 3rd Squad following the tanks was in peril.

"Oh shit! Now we're in big trouble," Zach said to anyone listening. "Take cover back in the houses." Two more Shermans were hit! The struggling radioman caught up with Zach. "What now, sir?"

"We need the tank destroyers *right now!*"

The radioman raised the aerial. "Captain Black says to *hold.* They're on the way."

"They'd better be or we're history."

Bruno Nitchke worked his way over. "We're in trouble, bookworm. What happened to the last Sherman?"

"He made it to the houses. Blackie says help is on the way."

"I hope so. Christ, four tanks down." Bruno stood up for a better look. "Shit, the krauts are bringing up a Tiger!"

"That's all we need," Zach said glumly.

Bruno, breathing rapidly, called, "Zach, the squad is scattered all over the place—"

Zach raised his hand. "Listen. I hear tanks, heavy tanks."

"Jesus, are there Tigers behind us?" Bruno moaned.

"Can't be. Wait, here come Ricks and Grinnell. They're yelling something."

"They're yelling, 'Friendly. They're ours,'" Bruno said with relief in his voice.

One of the new forty-six-ton M-26 tank destroyers came cautiously around the corner of a house, its huge gun with its German-looking muzzle brake leading the way.

"What the hell is that?" a voice cried out.

"Friendly!" was again shouted up and down the houses.

"It's a company of the new Jacksons or Pershings or whatever the hell they're called," Zach yelled. "They must be C Company from the 908th."

"They are some big bastards," Bruno cheered.

"Yeah, and mean. Where the hell is that Tiger?" Zach asked.

Norm Ricks peered around the building. "He's just sitting there, the arrogant son of a bitch."

Bruno, atypically analytical, was seeking revenge. "He's probably reloading. I hope the 908th sees him. This is a good time to nail him."

"They see him, Bruno. Here they come. Go get 'em, General Pershing!" Zach screamed, feeling a rare moment of combat exhilaration.

Two of the Panther-sized M-26s cleared the houses, stopped, and simultaneously fired their heavy twenty-four-pound AP rounds at the Tiger. The Tiger rocked violently but did not go down. Zach watched as the wounded Tiger swung his deadly 88 around. "He's going to fire. Get down!"

There was a deafening screech and an AP round went through the second floor of the house next door. A third Pershing tank appeared and immediately fired, this time engulfing the Tiger in smoke.

"They blinded him. Now they'll pour it on." A whole platoon of five M-26 Pershings came out into the open and fired into the smoke. After ten or twelve rounds, a thin column of black smoke emerged from the cloud of white smoke.

"They got 'em!" Grinnell shouted. The accompanying Panthers had seen enough and were retreating. "Assemble on me," shouted Grinnell. "We're moving out."

The new M-26s moved forward in company strength with the hurried 85th Battalion following. Only one Pershing had been hit and the 88 ricocheted off the new cast hull.

Monster Barrage

The first few blocks into Rhineberg drew no enemy fire. "What the hell is going on?"

"Where the hell are they? I can see the central city."

"I don't like this. We're almost downtown."

BLAM! BLAM! BLAM! Without warning an enemy barrage unlike any the division had ever seen erupted. 88-mm guns supported by 20-mm and 40-mm antitank guns ringed the entire central city. The stubborn members of the 2nd Para Regiment were determined to hold this last escape route at all costs.

Shells exploded everywhere—there was no place to hide—and the noise level was unbearable! Zach looked at his panic-stricken men. *There is a time to fight and a time to run. This is run time!*

Zach's judgment was confirmed when Sergeant Ricks came running through the heavy fire shouting, "Withdraw! Captain's orders—run, goddamn it!"

Zach signaled to the 3rd Squad who ran pell-mell back to their half-track who bravely met them halfway. The hurried withdrawal was successful thanks mostly to the American mobile artillery. The fast moving M-7s rained 105 and 155 shells on what the men named "88 Lane" and "Suicide Corner."

Once reassembled out of range, the battered battalion received new orders. Two companies would attack on the south flank to take heat off of a critical frontal attack to be led by Company B assisted by a company of the new, big M-26 tank destroyers.

At the corner of the ringed city stood a church with its huge steeple—an obvious observation post for the German guns. Colonel Hartman met with the TD battalion commander. Their plan was to have the big tanks run the gauntlet to get within range of the observation post and take it out. They would then turn their guns on the ring of 88s. B Company would follow.

Meanwhile, the entire division supported by the rest of the TD battalion and a regiment of the 35th Infantry were to make an all-out third assault on the central city. Both of the armored artillery battalions were now on line with their new proximity shells starting to take a toll on the ring of 88s. None too soon, for the Germans had just brought their hidden, long-range, giant 150-mm and 170-mm artillery into action. Clearly, the Germans intended to make a real fight of it. The American assault was stopped dead in its tracks by the monstrous bombardment, the worst anyone had ever seen.

"Where the hell did they get those big guns?" Grinnell sputtered.

"We'd do a lot better if we knew where those giant artillery batteries were located," grumbled Captain Black.

"Yeah, they can hurt us," Grinnell said, scanning the city with his binoculars.

"See anything?"

"I don't believe it. Looks like a lost Piper Cub spotter plane coming toward us."

"Yeah, I see him. He's circling."

"Here he comes. I hope he's on the radio—he could help us with those big guns."

"Jesus, there's a big dog flying that Grasshopper."

"What?"

"Look, here he comes again."

"I'll be damned!"

The dog and the Grasshopper climbed to five thousand feet and headed for the German lines.

"That dog has guts—he's going after the guns."

Within minutes, the American artillery battalions moved up and accurately redirected their fire with devastating effect on the hidden artillery. The heavy German guns slowed their barrage and then went silent. The Grasshopper came speeding back amidst a hail of tracers swooping low over Company B and waving its wings. The entire battalion waved and offered a salute.

"That's one lucky dog. One tracer would have brought that flying cotton jeep down."

"Yeah, he saved our asses."

Captain Black returned from his meeting with Colonel Hartman and reported. "Thanks to that crazy pilot we also know that the Germans are streaming east across the Rhineberg Bridge."

"Who was that crazy dog?" Stan Goldman chuckled.

Stosh, listening to all of the chatter, put on a radio announcer's voice. "That dog was the Lone Ranger." The group laughed therapeutically. It had been a long, difficult day.

*****

Thanks to an errant Piper Cub recon pilot, accurate American artillery, and the big Pershing tanks, the large American force now moved unstoppably into the city. The cost was high: forty-one tanks lost, over two hundred men killed or wounded. None, this time, from the 3rd Squad. The halftracks brought up the rear and were all intact. German casualties were unclear, since many were evacuated across the bridge.

Bridge Theater

Now five days into this "easy" objective, the Americans finally viewed the bridge several thousand yards away. A ring of tanks fiercely defended it while other tanks, trucks, and troops raced across it.

"Why don't we blow the damn bridge?" Zach demanded.

"Our orders are to *take* the damn bridge," Ricks grumbled with obvious frustration.

Before Zach could reply, a large, noisy group of B-17 bombers flew overhead, returning from a run into Germany. Two escorting P-51 Mustangs dropped out of formation and buzzed the bridge.

"Two hot dogs looking for a target of opportunity," Ricks said.

"They know they're kraut tanks. They just took some flak," Zach said.

Nitchke ran over. "If they have bombs, the bridge is gone."

"No bombs, just rockets," Ricks said while trying to adjust his binoculars.

"Won't the rockets blow the bridge?" Bruno asked.

Former air corps cadet Ricks thought for a moment and then speculated, "I don't think so. They're powerful but too small a charge. They are tank killers, not bridge killers."

The two Mustangs wheeled around, coming at the bridge only fifty feet off the water, flying under the flak. Their first salvo of rockets took out two of the tanks and brought traffic to a halt as the Germans tried desperately to push the disabled tanks off the bridge.

"You're right, Norm. The rockets didn't injure the bridge. Judas, maybe we can still take it," Grinnell argued.

Zach shook his head. "Not a chance. They'll blow it."

"Don't be so sure. I just heard the 9th Armored took the bridge at Remagen twenty-five or thirty kilometers south of here," Grinnell debated.

"Really? The kraut engineers must really have screwed up. Hitler will have 'em shot," Zach declared.

"Here they come again!" Stosh Kosinski yelled. Another salvo of rockets hit their tank targets and the bridge traffic was stopped once and for all. Six tanks were wrecked. Three of them were on fire. Their rockets expended, the P-51s banked sharply and made one last pass directly down the length of the bridge, strafing with what ammo they had left in their wing-mounted 50s. Now the chaos on the bridge was complete. The Mustangs climbed sharply, waved their wings, and rejoined their air group, not realizing they had intruded on General Montgomery's grand battle plan.

The enemy guns guarding the bridge suddenly went silent. A cease-fire order was passed along the heavily armed but weary and ticked-off American forces. Officers and noncoms of Company B collected around Captain Black. The group stared down at the bridge. Blackie stared at his watch. "Whoever is in charge down there has only a few minutes to make up his mind before our generals give us the green light to fire."

Russ Grinnell looked at the German troops stranded on the west side of the tangled, burning bridge. "Jerry can't move anybody across anymore. He has to blow it."

"We should blow it while they're making up their minds," growled Bruno Nitchke.

"The decision probably has to go to General Simpson," Captain Black said with a note of frustration.

"Yeah, or Monty," said Colonel Hartman, arriving to get a better look at the bridge.

"Colonel, what do you think?" Captain Black asked.

"They'll blow it as soon as all survivors are off the bridge. We'll honor that. Those on this side will have to surrender. They have no purpose anymore and no way out."

"Yes, sir, nine hundred feet is a long swim even if you're not under fire," Captain Black replied.

The last surviving Germans were still exiting the bridge when the west side started to collapse amid a series of well-planned, sequential explosions. The collapsing rolled on across the bridge, taking dozens of vehicles with it as it fell slowly into the river.

The battalion commander was right. The Germans on the west side of the river were trapped. White flags appeared. The elite 116th Panzer units proudly lined up to make formal surrenders.

Zach thought for a long moment. Then he remarked softly, "What a waste. Look at the proud bastards. I wonder if we could do that."

Stosh Kosinski had been listening in on the bridge discussion. "Sarge, ain't we as good as them?"

Zach wasn't sure anyone had heard his comment. Nor was he quite sure how to respond. He turned and studied his now-seasoned squad—they had developed an esprit de corps, what Captain Fred had said was traditional in elite German squads—a *kameradshaft*. He forced a crooked smile. "We are now, Stosh, we are now."

Grefrath Revisited

With the Rhineberg bridges down, the war across the Rhine was put on hold. The radios crackled and passed on the next set of orders. The 35th Infantry was to occupy Rhineberg; the 79th Infantry and the 809th Tank Destroyers were to move on to Wesel; the 18th Armored Division would stand down in reserve with headquarters in and around Venlo, Holland, now a liberated city twenty-five or thirty kilometers behind the front lines.

B Company, along with most of the 85th Battalion, was reassigned to Grefrath, Germany, only a few miles from the Rhine River. This was the same city they had taken with weary ease some two weeks earlier. The stand-down was a much deserved one. Rhineberg had been some of the bloodiest fighting the division had yet seen.

On the march back to Grefrath, the company passed many badly beaten, hungry, and demoralized German units who, knowing escape was impossible, were happy to surrender.

"These guys are hungry. I think they're giving it up to get our K rations," cracked Tony Holter.

"They fulfilled their mission We are delayed," Zach observed.

*****

The people of Grefrath, especially those living around the big common, were not thrilled at the unit's return but they now seemed resigned to occupation.

An assessment of casualties became the first order of business. Hardheaded Ludolph Kolchak was among the missing. Zach, with some misgivings, sought out Sergeant Nitchke. Bruno, anticipating the question, spoke first. "The krauts got him."

"Oh yeah! Where the hell is he now?" Zach asked with a skeptical squint.

Locking eyes, Bruno said quietly, "Out there. Wild Bill said he was dead…shot full of holes."

Zach hung his head. "Bruno…"

Sergeant Nitchke raised the palm of his big hand for silence and lit a cigarette. "Gates, the krauts got the son of a bitch. Ask any man in the platoon. Leave it alone."

Zach's inner voice was more hesitant and apocryphal than ever before. *Yeah, leave it alone. Maybe the krauts did get him!*

*****

Colonel Hartman's battalion worked hard at honoring civilian status, too hard some thought. Shortly after arriving again in Grefrath, an irate, heavyset German hausfrau stood berating a squad of men who were using her house. Her screaming, all in German, found the GIs standing openmouthed, wondering, "What did we do?"

A weary Captain Black arrived on the scene and shouted, "Get me somebody who speaks German."

Stosh Kosinski, like most of the GIs, had learned a few words of German—*hander hoch, aufgabe, fraulein,* and *danke.* He rushed to the confrontation and offered his services. The woman quieted down.

"Okay, soldier, ask her what she wants," Blackie said, running out of patience.

Stosh cleared his throat, looked directly at the red-faced woman, and said in slow, deliberate tones, "Vot do you vahnt?"

The hausfrau looked bewildered; the captain lost it, and screamed, "Kosinski, get the hell out of here! Where the hell is Sergeant Gates?"

Zach came running over. "Yes, sir?"

Before Blackie could respond, the woman once again started her tirade. The captain threw up his hands. "Handle it, Gates. That's an order; I'm out of here."

The problem, Zach determined, was that the GIs ate off of her best Dresden china, and then, instead of saving the dishes, sailed them off into the bushes. Zach faced the guilty men.

"What'd we do, Sarge?"

"You guys don't know shit about Dresden china."

"What the hell is Dresden china?"

"Expensive stuff. Go pick it up, and next time use kitchen dishes. Captain's orders!"

The stout hausfrau folded her arms, glowering at the men picking up her dishes. One young soldier handed her a broken plate. "Sorry, Mother." The hausfrau stormed off without a *danke.*

The whole company, hearing about the episode, confronted Zach with howls of laughter and good-natured teasing. "Vot do you really vahnt?" bantered Tom Sander.

"I vahnt to be alone," Zach retorted.

"Zach, you should be a psychologist," teased John Brenner.

"Yeah, or a half-assed linguist," Zach replied.

Stosh returned and sheepishly approached his squad sergeant friend. "I'm sorry, Zach. I was just trying to help."

"Not to worry, Stosh, but…"

"Yeah, Sergeant Gates?"

"Stay out of the captain's way for the next few days."

"Right—I can do that."

Stosh did not have many days to duck the captain—D-day on the Rhine was just ahead.

13

ACROSS THE RHINE

Grunt Commission

Grefrath: During the last hectic days before crossing the Rhine, Zach received an urgent call from Company B headquarters. 1st Sergeant Bob Klein and Corporal Jim Wing met him there.

"What now, Bob?" Zach asked.

Sergeant Klein gave him a dour look and spoke in measured tones. "You're being transferred to the foot infantry."

"Not funny, Klein. What's this all about?"

"We just received a new pronouncement from the War Department. They're running out of shavetails in the grunt infantry. The new ones from the states lack combat experience and are the first to die."

"So?"

"So, they have a deal for any ASTP guys who are combat sergeants."

"What kind of deal?"

"You're not going to believe this."

"For Christ's sake, Bob, get to it."

"You go to Paris for two weeks, get a new uniform, an officer's guide…and a commission to 2nd lieutenant. You must, however, become a grunt."

"What is this, Klein, a joke? Where are the brass on this?"

"The brass are ordered *hands off*—and they're not very happy about it."

Zach was incredulous. "I don't believe this crap, Bob."

"Believe it! You can guess how Blackie and Russ Grinnell feel about this coming just three days before the Rhine crossing."

"I can imagine!"

Klein smiled through his teeth. "Oh yes, I'm not allowed to influence you either."

Corporal Jim Wing, know-it-all company clerk, cleared his throat. "Nobody said I couldn't influence you. This should make you pause—"

"Jim, let's hear it for Christ's sake."

"Your platoon has been selected to be first across. I mean the whole damn 9th Army."

Zach was dumbstruck. "Which means my squad leads…"

The 1st sergeant broke the tense moment of silence. "You got it, Gates. You have until 0800 tomorrow to make up your mind. You'd leave us at 1300 hours tomorrow. That's it, Sergeant. Let me know."

Zach turned, said nothing, and walked out. This time his inner voice was unequivocal. *Three days before the Rhine? You'd be branded a coward. You'd have to start all over with men you've never met. Don't do it. If the army wants to commission you, let it be in B Company. Turn it down!*

When he arrived at the house where the 3rd Squad was billeted, the whole squad plus Platoon Sergeant Norm Ricks were waiting for him. Jim Wing had passed the word. Ricks spoke first. "Well, bookworm, what ya gonna do?"

A hush came over the squad. Zach stared at the floor and took a deep, audible breath. "I'm going to learn how to salute." He paused. "And become a platoon leader." He paused again. "In the 116th Panzer Division."

For a moment, confusion reigned before the message took hold. Ken Whedder rushed up and hugged his old friend. The rest gathered around, slapping him on the back and expressing their relief.

Lieutenant Russ Grinnell had been listening just outside the room. He walked in. "Attention," Ricks called out. "At ease," Grinnell replied nonchalantly, and turned to Zach. "Sergeant Gates, I'm ordering you to get this goddamn squad of panzergrenadiers ready to cross the Rhine."

"*Ja Herr, Leutnant,*" Zach retorted.

As the group dispersed, Ken Whedder caught up with Zach. "You could have ducked this ugly fight ahead of us."

"Yeah, I know."

The River's Edge

Only five miles separated B Company from the bustling bank of the nine hundred-feet-wide Rhine River. Division artillery was already at the river's edge. Their mission—support the beachhead attempts by the 30th and 79th Infantry Divisions.

There stood the largest collection of Allied artillery anyone had ever seen. Not only had this artillery been organized and moved during the last 117 days, but also 245,000 tons came with it, including one-hundred-foot-long bridge sections and LCMs fourteen feet wide. By the third week in March, the Americans alone had stockpiled 124 landing craft, eleven thousand assault boats, and enough lumber, pontoons, and structural sections to build sixty-two bridges across the Rhine.

This was traffic the likes of which the men had never seen, not at the Roer, nor even in the days of the first D-day in France. Unending lines of semi trucks poured in, loaded with buoys, anchors, cable, boats, pontoons, ammunition, even outboard motors. Everything moved in only one direction—east to the Rhine. Westbound traffic was nonexistent.

By March 22, the division's three mobile artillery battalions were joined by fifty-one other battalions on the west bank of the Rhine. At the same time, elements of the 30th and 79th Infantry Divisions were preparing their assault boats for the initial attack scheduled for 0400 on March 24. Their mission—establish beachheads which would allow the combat engineers to get their bridges in place.

At 0300 hours the entire 9th Army front erupted in one tremendous roar. The massive barrage was the heaviest concentration of such firepower staged during the entire war. This barrage made it possible for the infantry assault boats to race across the wide river with a minimum of casualties. Establishing and holding the small beachheads became a larger problem. The main body of the German forces had pulled back five miles to escape the murderous artillery barrage, but the rear guard Germans were dug-in and putting relentless pressure on all of the beachheads. The American infantry hung on with great tenacity; they were determined to give the bridge companies and combat engineers two or three days to bridge the huge river. Incredibly, the bridge companies completed nine bridges in two days.

On March 26, B Company received orders to cross the Rhine at bridge site H near Rhineberg. B Company was to have the honor of being the point of the lead armored division across the Rhine in the 9th Army sector. Again, this would be a married procession, tank/track, tank/track. Horrendous traffic at and behind the bridge site caused rampant confusion. Part of the 2nd Platoon was hung up a quarter of a mile behind the three rifle squads, leaving Captain Black up front with the 3rd Squad. He, like the men, stared wide-eyed at the awesome show of American firepower. Hundreds of steel cables, all restraining huge barrage balloons, laced the bridge area. Searchlights crisscrossed the night sky, interrupted by intersections with the barrage balloons. An unending stream of red and white tracer bullets chased the German aircraft attempting to destroy the bridge. The deafening roar and rumble of the unremitting artillery fire made speaking almost impossible.

The heavily burdened company commander looked up at the chaotic sky and then at the empty, undulating pontoon bridge. He started to speak just as a German airplane flew low, its guns chattering. Ear-splitting antiaircraft fire followed. He finally muttered, "What an honor."

The 1st sergeant yelled, "What's that, Captain?"

Blackie shouted above the thunder of the monstrous artillery barrage. "I said, what an honor!"

The 1st sergeant nodded just as another low-strafing German plane blinded by the searchlights clipped a cable on one of the barrage balloons and crashed into the river, missing the bridge by less than three hundred yards. "Close call," Captain Black shouted, and added, "We're okay. They're clearing traffic for us. Get your ducks in a row. 2nd Platoon, up front. Lieutenant Grinnell, front and center," he yelled.

No response.

"Where the hell is Russ Grinnell?"

Bruno Nitchke rushed forward. "He's caught in traffic, sir."

"What?"

"He and Sergeant Ricks are stuck near the end of the column, sir."

"What a time for a snafu!" The captain cupped his hands to his mouth and shouted, "Sergeant Gates, front and center."

"Here, sir."

Frustrated, Blackie was speaking in rapid bursts. "Gates, you're lead track when we roll. I'll be two tracks behind you. Keep in touch if you can make that damn radio work." He rushed off to meet Colonel Hartman, who had fought his way through traffic just in time to meet a flight of three German planes making a desperate run at the bridge. A wall of antiaircraft fire met them at close range and two crashed into the water. The bridge was still intact but a barrage balloon came down, tangling its cables in the bridge access area. During the delay to clear the cables, Blackie and Colonel Hartman were summoned to a small, tight group of men standing at the river's edge.

"Colonel, is your battalion ready to lead us across?" asked a tall man with three stars on his helmet.

"Yes, General Simpson, ready and eager."

The general then turned to the division CO, Brigadier General Devane. "John, is there anything else your division needs?"

"No, sir. We're loaded for bear."

"Good. How about our lead platoon commander?"

Colonel Hartman glowered at Captain Black. "Where the hell is Lieutenant Grinnell?"

Blackie threw up his hands in frustration. "I've been trying to tell you, sir. He and Sergeant Ricks are caught up in a nightmare of traffic."

"We need a point leader *now*, Captain, and I don't want you up front."

The stressed captain signaled to Sergeant Gates, who came running. *Hell, why not…he could have been an officer in another two weeks.* He turned to his BC. "Sir, Sergeant Gates is our point leader."

Heavily burdened General Simpson faced Zach. "Very well. We're counting on you, son. Anything we can do for you?"

Still stunned at this sudden and unexpected responsibility, Zach did not respond.

"Sergeant, I say again, anything we can do for you?"

Zach cleared his throat, attempting to find his voice. *Get your act together. This is why you stayed in this damn outfit.* He took a hurried look at the navy lieutenant who was consulting on the operation. "Yes, sir. My field glasses were shot up at Rhineberg."

General Simpson looked at the seven-by-fifty Bausch and Lomb glasses hanging around the navy officer's neck. "Commander, the sergeant is going to need those a lot more than you will." The general took the glasses and handed them to Zach. "Son, if you break out of that beachhead and get us five or six miles of geography, these glasses are yours. The navy will never miss them."

"Thank you, General."

"Any questions, Sergeant?"

Zach looked up at the curtain of fire, some of it hitting the distant riverbank. *Yeah, like, how do I get out of this?*

"Sergeant!" the general said impatiently.

"Ah…yes, sir. When will you lift the covering fire?"

"When you reach the bank. We'll halt the artillery when you've secured one mile of beachhead."

"Understood, General."

"Very well. Move out and across."

"Good luck, Sergeant," said the navy commander.

Zach tossed an awkward salute and headed for his squad's halftrack. The lieutenant in the tank ahead of him popped his head out of the turret. "Where is your officer, Sergeant?"

"He's lost. My company commander is two or three vehicles back," Zach replied, just loud enough to be heard.

In infantry/tank operations in an armored division, the infantry leader is usually in command. "You mean I have to take orders from a sergeant?" the lieutenant hooted in an effort to relieve the building pressure.

Zach stiffened his back and rallied. "Only if you screw up, Lieutenant."

The tanker laughed and, given the staggering burden of the mission, opted for cathartic battlefield humor. "Try not to get lost."

"Don't back up," Zach cracked, slapped the tank, and shouted, "Good luck, Lieutenant."

"All clear," the combat engineers shouted.

One Thousand Feet of Terror

With that, the heavy vehicles started out across the rolling bridge. Covering fire intensified, making talk impossible. A slow, terror-ridden march across a narrow, moving bridge began. The night sky remained alive with bright-red tracers and the omnipresent searchlights. Deafening noise continued from the relentless artillery barrage. Overhead, more German planes screamed past, barely clearing the barrage balloons. At the halfway mark, panic overcame driver John Naylor as he watched the tank ahead of him struggling to keep its tracks aligned with the narrow runways that swayed with each weight change. Some of the undulating pontoons were leaking badly from the strafing, adding to the rocking of the heavy vehicles. The lead tank came to a near halt as it realigned itself.

Zach pushed his steel helmet back and shouted, "We're too damn close, Naylor!" The track skidded on the wet bridge when Naylor hit the brakes. "Jesus, Naylor, straighten her out or we're going over the edge!"

"I've got it, Zach—I've got it!"

Zach's heart raced as he muttered, "Close call," and chanced a tentative glance to the rear. The men were untangling after being rocked off their bench seats. "Anybody hurt?" Zach shouted.

Bruno answered in an uneasy voice. "No, I don't think so…"

"What?"

Bruno assessed the disarranged men and yelled, "*No*, but we're all seasick. How much more of this *shit*?"

"We're about halfway—hang on," Zach shouted as he faced forward.

The squad hunkered down, bracing their feet against the other bench across the floor. The track moved forward a few rocky yards. Zach scanned the river ahead and choked, "Oh my God."

"Jesus, what now?" screamed a voice from the rear as the men peered over the side of the swaying halftrack.

Zach pointed to the water, where several bodies were floating down the river from the bridges upstream. "Combat engineers…poor bastards.

Move it, Naylor. Let's get off this goddamn bridge."

"I hear ya—we gotta be halfway."

"Good. Keep her centered. I hope they lift the artillery when we climb the bank."

The noise increased.

"Can't hear you."

"I said, keep her centered," Zach screamed.

The bombardment lessened as the opposite shore drew near. Zach saw an object just ahead of the tank. "Watch it, John! Trouble ahead."

"What is it?"

"Jesus, it's an assault boat hung up in the bridge."

"The tank is going to hit the damn thing," Naylor yelled.

"He's bumped him clear! We can get by," Zach exclaimed.

"We ain't gonna turn around!" Naylor yelled.

Audible groans came from the rear seats.

"We're clear, John—good job."

As the halftrack cleared the listing assault boat, Zach could see the slumped bodies of six or seven GIs inside. His eyes widened and his stomach churned. "Move it, John. Let's get off this damn bridge," Zach murmured inaudibly.

The lead tank finally cleared the bridge and picked up speed. The overhead tracers stopped but the longer-ranged artillery continued as the bruised and shaken squad reached the river's bank. The crossing had been one thousand feet of sheer terror and torment. Once over the bank and into the hard-won beachhead, Zach could see and hear the men of the 30th Infantry standing up and cheering.

"What's Old Hickory saying?" Naylor shouted above the noise.

"God bless you, 18th Armored."

"The poor bastards. What a lousy mission."

"Yeah. Their captain just gave us a salute."

Zach forced a slow-motion inhalation as his heartbeat finally pulsated normally. *We made it. Thank you, God. We made it.*

Once out of the beachhead, the single column split into several columns and pressed the fight against the rapidly retreating rearguard Germans. B Company and the other lead elements quickly gained the four miles necessary to assemble the whole battalion plus the tankers. The Germans had fallen back to a new main line of defense out of range of the American artillery. With light fading, Colonel Hartman elected to wait for dawn before aggressively probing the 116th Panzers' new main line of defense. The exhausted troops crawled into any deserted house they could find.

14

TROUBLE AT KIRCHELLEN

Zachary's overly dramatic commencement speech was still echoing in his troubled sleep when he was rudely awakened by Platoon Sergeant Norm Ricks. "Up and at 'em, Sergeant Bookworm."

Zach closed his eyes for one last nostalgic but trying moment and repeated silently, *Fellow graduates, parents, and friends. Somewhere on a distant battlefield a boy is dying, young in years, ageless in the experience of war…we are looking forward with eagerness and enthusiasm…* "What crap."

"Off your ass, Gates! And quit talking to yourself. There's a war on."

"I hear you. What's up?"

"Piece of cake. We follow the tanks this time."

"Are we leading the platoon as usual?"

"Of course, but ya got a platoon of tanks ahead of ya."

"Thanks, Norm. Do we have time for coffee?"

"Yeah, the mess truck caught up to us."

*****

The mission sounded simple enough—aggressively probe the new MLD. It was thought to be five miles due east near the town of Kirchellen.

An intrepid six-wheeled armored car from recon led off. A platoon of tanks followed close behind. The 2nd Platoon's five halftracks came next. The probe group started rolling down a tree-lined road leading to the town, now just four kilometers ahead. The recon vehicle entered the village and signaled it abandoned. When the armored car and the lead tank poked their noses out of the other side of town, all hell broke loose.

The Germans had deployed an unusually large number of Panther tanks plus one or two Jagd Tigers or Hunting Tigers, the largest tank destroyers in the German arsenal.

The little recon vehicle and the lead tank went down first. The German gun then trained on the other four tanks. Three more tanks went down hard. The last tank just ahead of Zach's Babe was hit and disabled only fifty yards from the town's first building. Grinnell spun his jeep around to race down the column, wisely ordering a retreat.

Zach looked to the rear. The tracks, strung out in 50-yard intervals, were turning around—all but the one directly behind. The nearest building offering cover stood only seventy-five yards away. His eyes locked on the disabled tank fifty yards ahead with the buildings only twenty-five yards beyond. His pulse thundered as he considered a difficult decision. *We're the next target—they expect us to retreat.* A tightness gripped his throat. "Naylor, we're next. Head for cover in those buildings."

There was no turning back now—the tough combat decision had been made.

Naylor floored the big track and skillfully dodged the burning tank in the roadway. The track behind made the same decision and followed. Just a few yards from cover, the 3rd Squad's luck ran out. A huge, 128-mm, armor-piercing round tore through the star on the vehicle's left side. The doomed halftrack coasted to the relative safety of the buildings as the following track roared past. Two men were blown out of the now burning track. The rest of the 3rd Squad were jumping over the sides. Panicked, Naylor tumbled out of the left door. Zach, shaken and bruised from the horrendous impact, exhaled deeply, climbed over the ring, and stood on the hood. His muscles turned rigid as he fought off an emotional overload—*Get with it, Sergeant Gates!* He jumped to the ground and surveyed the burning track—all the men were out! Miraculously, the land mines, racked in holders on the track's side racks, had not yet exploded.

The Germans, now out of visible armored targets, switched to high explosive shells, causing more smoke, fire, and casualties among the dismounting infantry. Through the smoke, Zach saw a sturdy building across the road. The crew from the surviving halftrack were running toward it, carrying their wounded leader and driver.

Fighting off panic and running out of options, he started screaming, "Everybody across the road. Stay in the basement till this fire lets up!" Calling upon what courage he had left, he turned to assess his mangled, burning vehicle and its casualties. Tony Holter, in a tearful stupor, a wicked gash in his shoulder, was leaning over a fallen soldier who was partly covered by parts from the halftrack. Tony spoke in rapid bursts through a constricted throat. "It's the new guy, Zach—Bob Paxton. He was blown out of the track…I don't know what to do," he cried.

Zach took a deep breath and ground his teeth. "I'll take care of Paxton. You find a medic—now go!"

His shoulder bleeding profusely, Holter dashed to the basement across the street just as the German guns resumed firing. Clouds of red dust erupted from the exploding brick buildings as the withering German fire hit them.

Zach removed the steel pieces from the track and turned Paxton over. He was alive and semiconscious. Ugly red dirt covered part of him. Zach's stomach sank when he saw blood oozing through the heavy coat of dirt. He retched when he saw that Paxton's leg was almost blown off. Only skin and flesh kept it attached to his body. "Medic," Zach choked as his throat went dry and his pulse quickened, but no medic could hear him. *God, help me do this,* he said silently.

"Hang on, Bob. I can do this, I can do this," Zach repeated over and over as he reflexively applied a tourniquet to Paxton's leg, tore open his aid kit and shook sulfa powder on the ghastly wound. Then he administered a shot of morphine from his belt kit. A close blast caused Zach to look up from his gut-wrenching efforts—burning vehicles appeared ghostlike through the clouds of red dust filtered by black smoke. Zach's panic turned to simmering rage. He waved his fist and yelled defiantly at the exploding artillery. Then, miraculously, as if his outburst had made a difference—the barrage lifted.

Tom Sander bravely rushed over with tears streaming down his face. "Ken is missing…he was seated in front of the star."

Zach's heartbeat was finally slowing and his head started to clear. He grabbed Tom's arm. "Easy, Tom. Anybody else?"

"Brenner and Holter are in the basement, both wounded," Sander stammered.

"I saw Tony. How bad is John?" Tom just stood shaking and wide-eyed. "Tom, hear me! How bad is John?"

Tom tugged nervously at his loose hanging helmet strap. "Sorry, Zach. About like Tony. He's mobile."

"Good. Tom, get Wild Bill over here before this damn artillery starts up again, and find a door or something to put Paxton on. We're taking him back."

"Zach, Wild Bill knows about Paxton but he's swamped. Several recon and tank guys were also hit."

"Damn. Tell him to hurry. Now go."

"Yeah. I'll look for a door too." Tom hesitated. "What about Ken Whedder?"

"I'll find him. Go!"

Zach turned back to Paxton. Again his stomach retched as he readjusted the tourniquet on Bob's bleeding, mangled stump of a leg, avoiding the loosely attached knee and lower leg. Paxton lay partially conscious with the morphine seemingly working. "I've got to leave you, soldier, but I'll be back."

He scanned the area for the missing Ken Whedder. Nothing. Then, only fifteen feet away, he saw a helmet protruding from a pile of brick and debris. He rushed over to find a soldier torn almost in half and covered with the same ugly red dust. A knot closed in his stomach. *Please God, not Ken.* He brushed the dirt from the man's face—it was Ken Whedder. Zach clutched. He had seen that grotesque death mask so many times before. Whedder was nothing more than a broken, crumpled pile of ugly red dust. The sheer impact of the giant 128-mm round had blown him out of the track, instantly driving the life out of him.

Tom and Wild Bill came running over. "How is he, Zach?"

Zach closed his eyes and called on every bit of energy he had left. "He's dead, Tom. He's dead."

Tom forced himself to look at Whedder's blown-apart, half-buried body, then at Paxton's horrendous wounds. Paralyzing shock enveloped him. Zach spun him around. "Tom, listen to me." Zach's body stiffened and anger possessed his voice and demeanor. "Get Wild Bill and take care of Paxton. I'm up to my ass in decisions."

Tom hesitated and Zach went nose to nose. "Damn it, Tom, get off your ass. We're getting out of here."

"Yes, sir," Tom said, taking a deep breath as the incoming fire resumed.

Zach dashed across the street and tumbled into the basement, where the surviving infantry, two tankers, and two very lucky recon team members were hunkered down. The tanker lieutenant was badly wounded. The tank driver and the recon men were mobile. The wounded lieutenant, looking exhausted and beaten, assessed the young sergeant.

"What's our status?" he asked weakly.

"Twenty-five or thirty men standing, four or five more wounded...I don't know how many we lost. We have one operational halftrack."

"I left three tankers and one or two of my recon men," the lieutenant said unsteadily.

Zach nodded and turned to the wounded recon sergeant. "What did you see out there?"

"They're loaded for a counterattack. We just interrupted their timetable."

"Do we have time to get out of here?"

"Who knows? I called for air power before we were hit."

"What the hell are they hitting us with?"

"Eighty-eights and I think 128-mm guns from one or two of those giant Jagd Tigers."

The sobbing lieutenant rallied, his eyes urgent. "You'll have to leave the dead behind, Sergeant. You're in command. Get us the hell out of here." His voice trailed off as he closed his eyes.

Zach, unprepared for the sudden change in command, needed a moment to process the horrendous responsibility. His legs stiffened. "Yes, sir, I'm on it."

Once again the heavy pounding let up. Zach looked out of the basement window. *They're probably reloading or moving up—it's now or never.* "We're moving out," he shouted. "Everybody in the track. Get the wounded on board—move, damn it."

After a wild scramble, everyone was in or at the remaining track. Wild Bill and Tom Sander arrived with Paxton on a makeshift stretcher made from a door. His leg lay alongside his body.

"I had to sever it," Wild Bill said, with torment and guilt in his voice.

Tom was crying. "I had to leave Ken."

"I know, Tom, I know." Then, looking directly at Wild Bill, "Is Paxton still alive?"

"Barely," the medic mumbled.

Zach took a deep breath, squared his shoulders, and commanded, "Get Paxton on the hood where we can stretch him out and tie him down." The men froze in a moment of panic. "NOW! Do it now. That's an order!"

He climbed into the ring as Pfc. Robert Paxton was tied to the hood. He surveyed the overloaded halftrack and looked down at John Naylor, who had replaced the wounded driver. "Start this son-of-a-bitch, Naylor, before they resume fire."

Naylor started the engine as Bruno limped over shouting, "We're loaded—I count twenty-seven—get us the hell out of here, Gates."

Naylor punched the accelerator and the heavily loaded track jerked forward, leaving the cover of the building just as the enemy fire resumed. Zach ducked down and shouted above the exploding artillery, "John, if they bracket us, one kick means stop. Two kicks mean go like hell. Got it?"

"Got it."

Zach stared at the artillery rounds crashing in front of him and then looked down at the body of Bob Paxton, his bloody, severed leg tied eerily to the windshield support. In the smothering heat of battle, he looked away and felt sick. For a brief moment, he froze and was somewhere else—anywhere else. Naylor was shouting, "Gates, wake up! Give an order. Any order!"

Zach reached back for one last measure of calm. *Get your head on, Sergeant! Study the fire pattern—make a decision,* he told himself. An 88 round screeched overhead. The track came to a near halt. Zach gritted his teeth and gave Naylor two quick kicks. "Go, damn it, go!"

A wild ride ensued with Zach and Naylor trying desperately to outguess the German gunners. With less than a kilometer to go, the giant Jagd Tiger appeared to have a bracket on the struggling halftrack. Zach's single kick missed when the halftrack lurched.

Zach dropped out of the ring and shouted, "Stop, damn it, I said stop!"

Naylor slammed the brakes. Too late! An ear-splitting screech and a frightening clang hit some part of the track. "Shit! Okay, go!"

Naylor floored the still straining track as Zach looked up through the ring where he had been standing seconds earlier and saw an ominous, gray-blue flickering haze. An eerie, hideous, whirring sound accompanied the blue haze.

"Jesus, an AP (armor piercing round) hit the barrel of the machine gun," Zach shouted.

"Stay down, Gates," Naylor screamed. "That fan will cut your head off."

Naylor knew he was on his own as he roared out of range and finally entered friendly lines. The aid station had been moved up when it became clear there would be many casualties. The overloaded, overheated halftrack screeched to a halt and the medics rushed to attend the wounded. A young replacement medic stared at Paxton stretched out on the hood of the track with his bloody, severed leg tied to a windshield stanchion. He leaned on the track crying and throwing up. Veteran combat medic Wild Bill Anders had recovered and rushed to the hood. "Get this man off of there and to the aid station."

Zach observed the drama as he gingerly slipped out from under the still spinning 50-caliber machine gun.

The medics placed Paxton on the ground. Wild Bill took one last look and shook his head. "I'm sorry, Zach. He didn't make it."

Zach leaned heavily on the halftrack. His head drooped to his chest. Lieutenant Russ Grinnell and Norm Ricks rushed over and gagged at the carnage. Lieutenant Grinnell put his hand on Zach's shoulder but was unable to speak.

"I left Ken Whedder out there," Zach mumbled over and over.

Grinnell stared aimlessly at the wounded men and finally found his voice. "The 95th will find him. They're relieving us," he said quietly.

"Russ!" Zach shouted as his inner voice overcame the emotional fallout.

"Yeah, Gates, what is it?"

"The 116th is planning a counterattack. We ran right into their lead elements."

"A counterattack? Are you sure? When, for Christ's sake?"

"I don't know, Russ. I don't know."

Colonel Hartman's jeep roared over. "Well done, Sergeant. G-2 confirms that your men broke up a major counterattack." The colonel checked on all the casualties, swallowed hard, and turned to Zach. "You made all the right decisions, son."

The colonel tapped his driver and sped off, swearing at the weather and Montgomery for tying up all available tactical aircraft. His complaining must have paid off, as a squadron of Thunderbolts roared overhead. The men cheered and yelled, "Go get those bastards!" And that they did. Not with rockets this time but with five-hundred-pound bombs. A pillar of black smoke confirmed their success on the Jagdpanzers as the now lighter aircraft took off after the retreating tanks.

Norm Ricks put his hand on Zach's shoulder and looked at the casualties being hustled away. "It's not your fault. Like the BC said, you made all the right combat decisions."

Tom Sander listened with tears rolling down his face. "Norm, we're all still in shock. Give him a minute. It was a nightmare out there. He got us back by sheer guts."

Ricks looked at the big 50-caliber gun still spinning ominously. "I know, Tom, I know."

Zach wiped the tears from his face as Grinnell returned and looked again at the battered halftrack and the wounded being evacuated. He cleared his throat. "Gates, I'm...sorry about Paxton and Whedder." Zach just stared at the ground, saying nothing. Grinnell drew very close. "Damn it, soldier, I need you. You will continue."

Zach raised his head and responded reflexively. "Yes, sir."

The lieutenant patted him on the back. "Good."

Zach looked down. *I'm not sure I can do this anymore...all these men lost...Paxton was with me only five days...now Whedder is gone and Brenner and Holter wounded.*

Bruno Nitchke limped over with what was left of the 3rd Squad. Norm Ricks, Russ Grinnell, and Captain Black joined them. Blackie spoke quietly. "Sergeant Gates, you did good." The captain withdrew as the squad offered a soft "hear, hear."

Sergeant Nitchke broke the awkward moment. "Off your ass, Gates. We have to fight one more fucking round."

Drained and weary, Zach stood up and tossed the men a soft salute.

15

COMBAT DEPRESSION

The German plans for a counterattack at Kirchellen were now totally disrupted by the 85th Armored Infantry Battalion and the Tactical Air Command. The 95th Infantry Division marched boldly into the city without incident. It was they who recovered Ken Whedder's body and the bodies of the other battle casualties.

Company B was pulled off line for two or three days of rest. The scruffy, emotionally drained 3rd Squad located a small, shot-up farmhouse a few hundred yards away from the billets of the rest of the 2nd Platoon.

Unheralded driver John Naylor was anxiety-haunted and bitching. "Damn halftracks draw fire, but they beat the hell out of hoofing it."

Stosh's voice reflected the deadly chain of events. "Damn, no water, no nothing," he moaned.

Stan replaced his depression with anger. "I gotta get out of these clothes. They can stand alone!" he screamed at no one in particular.

"Knock it off, Stan," Bruno shouted in a gutteral roar. "Look at Gates and Sander. They're soaked in dry blood!"

Remorse gripped Stan. "Yeah, sorry," he replied in a voice laced with guilt. "They gotta be hurting. What an ugly sight."

"Enough of that crap," snapped tired, battle-weary Bashford. "When do we eat?"

In a voice still thick with anguish, Pappy grumbled, "I heard the mess truck is already here."

Downhearted and subdued, Zach finally looked up and spoke tiredly, "I'll believe it when I see it."

Before the dejected squad could respond, Ricks roared up in the company jeep. "Look alive, you miserable looking sad-sacks. I've got good news."

Zach exhaled heavily. "Yeah, let's hear it."

"Perk up, bookworm. You have two more days in reserve to get cleaned up."

"Yeah, what about chow?"

"Mess call in ten minutes, so get off your asses—and look alive for Christ's sake!" Zach nodded and turned away despondently. Ricks hit the horn. "Zach! Goddamn it, come with me. We need to talk."

*****

After devouring their first hot meal in many weeks, the blood-stained, weary squad stretched out in front of the house, which gave them their first real opportunity to bitch and moan about their near-death experience. Zach had remained with Norm Ricks.

Stan spoke first in a tearful stupor. "I'm worried about Gates. He carried a heavy load out there."

Bruno replied bluntly, "We all need a break! Thank God we're in reserve."

Remorse gripped Tom's speech. "The real cross was losing Whedder and Paxton."

Sounding down in the mouth, Pappy added, "Leaving Ken out there had to be tough."

"Zach didn't have a choice," Tom Sander retorted in a level voice.

"We know that, Tom! Everybody knows that," Pappy declared.

A dispirited moment of truth enveloped the troubled squad. Bash broke the quiet, but added to the depressed mood. "Poor Bob Paxton…seemed like a nice guy."

Naylor's voice caught. "How long was he with us?"

"Four or five days, I guess."

Tom shook his head and shuddered. "Some initiation of fire."

While the squad commiserated, Bash summed it up. "Yeah, what a lousy break."

A tightness gripped Naylor's throat. "Don't forget, the tankers also took a real hit. They gotta be hurting."

Stosh paced the floor and spoke uneasily. "Amen. One of the tanks had the turret blown clean off."

In a rare expression of emotion, Bruno grunted, "Yeah, with body parts attached."

Tom turned philosophical. "We owe Gates plenty. He got us the hell out of there."

Bash, secretly recalling his tragic days at Omaha Beach, quietly replied, "Yeah. I'm glad it wasn't my call."

A long, subdued pause followed. "We're lucky we only lost our track and four guys," Naylor mumbled.

Goldman's voice quavered. "Whedder and Gates were buddies since basic training…that has to hurt really bad."

Sandy felt himself bristling but restrained his thoughts. "So were Brenner and I. Thank God John's wounds are minor."

Bash patted Tom's shoulder. "I hope they're minor…what about Tony Holter?"

A recovering Tom forced a slow smile. "Wild Bill told me both guys will return to duty—soon, he thinks."

A look of defiance enveloped Goldman's face as he stood up. "We've got to get past all this damn depression," he spouted.

John Naylor scowled. "What the hell is this depression shit anyway?"

The men shrugged and looked to bookworm Tom Sander. "John, depression means you're feeling down, like from an overload—too many bad things all happening at the same time. Sometimes you act sad, sometimes mad, sometimes you just want to quit or give up."

"Not Sergeant Gates!" Stosh declared.

"Right, Stosh, but everybody can lose it temporarily. You know, for a short time," Tom explained.

"Kinda like Henry Franier, huh?"

"Yeah, like Henry. The nightmare of fear he faced on his first day under fire caused him to freeze, then lose it and run. He felt guilty which led to depression."

"But Henry got over it and he became a hero," Stosh asserted.

"Right, Stosh."

Jim Wing arrived in the company jeep looking upset. "Is Gates here?"

Bruno was apprehensive. "No. What kind of shit now?"

"News about one of your ASTP guys."

"We don't want to hear it!" Bruno snarled.

Wing persisted. "Remember Jack Franks? A Company?"

Goldman frowned. "Yeah, he finished second or third behind Ricks in the Polk race."

"Right. Tom, you should know him."

"A good guy, he aced every course at Illinois. So what's the news?"

"He took that grunt commission—the one Gates turned down."

"Yeah, he went to the 83rd Infantry—so what?"

"He got the silver star…"

"Good for him," Stan mumbled.

Wing paused ominously, then replied quietly, "...posthumously."

There was a shocked pause. Bash recovered first. "Shit, he couldn't have been with them more than a month."

Wing shook his head. "Two weeks."

The squad groaned and Bruno asked with a voice full of strain, "Jim, does Gates know about this?"

Jim locked eyes with the concerned squad and forced a quiet, "No."

Tom threw up his hands. "That's all Gates needs!"

Stosh was near tears. "That could have been Sergeant Gates."

Bruno stomped the floor. "Enough bullshit. Squad, keep your mouth shut about this—you too, Wing. Where the hell is Gates now?"

"I think he's with Norm Ricks," Pappy Becker said, looking away.

Goldman, trying to pick up the mood, said, "That should help. The platoon sergeant and Zach are good friends."

Pappy forced a slow but beneficial moan. "Good. I'll feel better when he's yelling at us."

John Naylor picked up the beat and cracked, "You should know!"

Nitchke pounded his fist. "I think we should cut this crap and think about something else."

"A bath and new clothes would help," Goldman griped.

"Come on. Help me here..."

Stosh raised his hand. "Pappy found a couple bottles of Calvados."

"Now you're talking. Elmo, go get your stuff," ordered Sergeant Nitchke.

Pappy returned in a flash carrying the Calvados and one liberated glass. The squad brought out their canteen cups. A jeep screeched to a halt and Zach and Norm Ricks joined the squad.

Pappy filled the glass with the volatile Calvados and handed it to Zachary. "What are we drinking to?" Zach asked quietly.

Sergeant Ricks raised his cup. "To the best damn squad leader in the battalion."

"To the best 2nd lieutenant in the 116th Panzers," Wing joked.

"What brought that up?" Zach mumbled.

"Bottoms up, bottoms up," the squad yelled before Gates could ask any more questions.

The party lasted long into the night. Wild stories of better times were peppered by some really raunchy jokes. Even the Germans must have heard the soulful wailing—*And as I strolled away I heard that pale moon say, "It gets lonesome way ou' chere."*

*****

The next morning Jim Wing returned, hung over but shouting, "Listen up, fellow drinkers. The divisional chaplain has caught up to us, so shape up and clean up. For Christ's sake, at least shave. You look like shit."

"Up your ass, Wing, we lost all our gear when the track burned up," Bruno hollered.

"Relax, Bruno, the chaplain brought along two six-by-sixes full of such shit—even clothes and hot water for you bums."

Zach staggered over to the jeep. "Thanks, Jim. Where is this shit?"

"The quartermaster is next to the mess truck, and Zach…"

"Yeah?"

"I have news." The squad eyed Jim nervously. "The medics released Holter and Brenner. You should have 'em back in a few days."

"Thank God. Thank you, Jim," replied Zach as his spirits lifted and the squad cheered.

Wing smiled and waited for the emotional release to wane. He called out, "Gates, you still look God-awful—ya got thirty minutes to the chaplain's assembly."

Zach studied his dirty, torn clothes. Both his blouse and pants were heavily stained with Paxton's blood and caked with ugly red dust. He felt another moment of depression mixed with elation and rage as he frantically tore off his clothes. "Take 'em off, guys. I don't want to see any more blood," he barked.

The men happily stripped. "Do we get new toilet articles?"

"Of course, shithead, even underwear."

"You wear underwear?"

"Only on dates."

Jim Wing spun the jeep around and stopped. "Jeez, you guys look worse naked."

*****

The bathed and reuniformed 3rd Squad men were late joining the assembled 2nd Platoon. The chaplain stood waiting on them. Zach called out, "Sorry, Chaplain MacArthur."

The chaplain nodded. "Let us pray."

Chaplain MacArthur concluded with requiem-sounding words eulogizing Robert Paxton and Kenneth Whedder. He ended with prayers for all those killed or wounded at Kirchellen, for deliverance, and for a rapid end to the war. He dismissed the platoon but asked the 3rd Squad to remain.

"Men, your battalion commander informed me of your courage at

Kirchellen. I wish to congratulate all of you on your bravery under horrendous combat conditions. Your faith in our great cause and in yourselves will provide the strength to carry on. Your comrades who died would want it that way. Let us pray."

After a silent prayer for the lost men of the 3rd Squad, the chaplain took Zach aside. "Zachary, it was on your shoulders that the greatest burden fell. I shall pray for an end to your understandable depression and wish you Godspeed in helping win this terrible war."

"Thank you, Father MacArthur, for your kind words and for bringing us baths and new clothes."

"It was the least I could do. Godspeed, my son."

"All the men thank you, Father MacArthur."

*****

That evening, a worried Stosh Kosinski approached his squad leader. "You're okay, aren't you? You're not all depressed or anything?"

"Except for the Calvados, I'm feeling much better, Stosh. Where did you hear about depression?"

"Tom and the guys were talking about it."

"That's good, I guess, after that mess at Kirchellen…"

"I liked what the chaplain said about Ken and Bob."

"Yeah. Chaplain MacArthur was a big help."

Stosh shuffled his feet. "Sarge…"

"What's on your mind, Stosh?"

"I was really scared…I didn't think we were going to make it back. How come you weren't afraid?"

"Stosh, I was afraid. Everybody was afraid. The trick is to act as if you're not afraid."

"Act? How do I do that?"

"Have you ever whistled while walking through a dark alley?"

"I get it—whistling in the dark."

"Right. Some people tell jokes. I sometimes substitute anger for fear. Depression is a little more complicated."

Stosh gathered his thoughts. "That's what Tom said. I feel sad about Ken and Bob and the others. Really sad…but I think they would want us to carry on, as Captain Black would say."

Zach's mouth dried and he felt emotionally drained at Kosinski's simple but intelligent analysis. He forced a smile and lowered his eyes. "That's very good, Stosh…I, too, am very sad…heartbroken about my close friend Ken. I'm going to act as if he's with us in spirit and telling us to carry on."

"Thanks, Zach. I'm acting 'as if' from now on."

Zach exhaled heavily and lowered his voice. "Good, Kosinski. Now go get some sleep."

"Zach…just one other thing."

"Yeah."

"I'm really glad you didn't take that grunt commission."

Stunned, Zach pondered, *What the hell brought that up?* Then he frowned. "Yeah, yeah, now get the hell out of here."

*****

The next morning, the battalion was ordered to the city of Dorsten. The trackless squad found rides wherever they could. B Company brought up the rear of the battalion. Lead A Company met only sporadic small arms fire and pushed through to the outskirts of the city. There they found the British hung up at Dorsten's main canal. Because the canal had strategic importance, the Germans were determined to make the British pay dearly for it.

While the American 9th Army was trying to figure out how best to help the British, B Company stood down and waited just outside of the battle zone for mess call and another welcome night off. The trackless but cleaned up 3rd Squad had last choice of a group of houses near a large wood. Before they were settled in, Sergeant Gates was called to headquarters for a meeting of all officers and noncoms. There, the 3rd Squad was singled out for their exemplary performance of duty. Zach returned to the squad with his shoulders back and a forced take-charge attitude. "Okay, assholes, assemble on me and listen up. Headquarters reports movement around our perimeter."

Goldman whispered, "He's back."

"Thank you, God," Tom sighed.

"Tonight I want two men posted in that outbuilding facing Dorsten, just in case. Bruno, post the guards," Zach commanded.

"Got it, Mein Herr," Bruno cracked. "Bashford, Sander, follow me!"

"Yo," came the quick response.

Zach commandeered a bedroom off of the kitchen, found a feather tick, and stretched out. John Naylor joined him. "Welcome back to the war, Gates. Room in here for me?"

"Sure, but no snoring."

"Good night, *Feldwebel* (staff sergeant)."

"Shut up."

SENEGALESE

At 0200 hours, Zach woke up to see Naylor drumming his fingers on the windowsill while staring out of the window of the farmhouse. "What's up, John?"

"Probably nothing…I thought I saw movement."

Zach looked out. "I don't see anything, but we'd better check the barn. See if Sander and Bashford are awake."

"Yeah, maybe they've seen something."

Zach pulled on his boots. "Go. I'll check with Bruno."

Within twenty minutes, Naylor returned, ashen-faced, trembling, and unable to speak. Bruno and the rest of the now wide-awake squad gathered in the large farm kitchen and stared apprehensively at Naylor. "For Christ's sake, John, what happened? Are our guys okay?" Zach asked.

Naylor's voice slowly returned and he spoke in a strained pitch. "Yeah, they're okay, just scared shitless like me."

"So what happened?" Zach demanded.

"I was almost to the barn. I called to Sander and Bash. Then, from out of nowhere, I felt a knife at my back and a vice grip on my throat. I couldn't move. I thought I'd had it."

"Then what?" Stosh sputtered.

"This big hand reached under my blouse, found my dog tags, fingered them, spun me around, tossed my rifle into the field—"

"Damn it! What next, for God's sake?" Bruno barked.

"…Then he released me and just disappeared."

"Who was this guy?" Stosh Kosinski asked in a trembling voice.

"Beats the hell out of me, Stosh. He looked like he was wearing some kind of British uniform and he had a turban on his head."

"*Senegalese!*" shouted Stan Goldman. "I saw them in England."

"What's Senegalese?" Stosh asked.

"Big tough guys from Africa, I think," replied Goldman, looking toward Zach for help.

"Right, from Senegal, West Africa, I think, which is either a British or French colony. The British and French both use them as commandoes. The limeys we met in Holland said they let them operate pretty much on their own."

Still shaking and upset, John Naylor choked, "What's with the dog tags?"

"Identification. You're lucky you had yours on or you'd be a dead man," Zach answered.

Naylor frowned. "It took him long enough to decide."

"German tags are round," Zach replied quietly.

The squad, to the man, reached for their dog tags. Bruno Nitchke pulled his out of his blouse and fingered them. "I'm glad these spooky bastards are on our side. They must give the krauts nightmares."

"John, how big was this guy?" Stosh asked nervously.

"Like King Kong, Stosh," Naylor said, starting to calm down. "He eats Polish guys."

Stosh made a wry face. "Polacks wear their tags outside their shirts."

Nervous laughter followed. Zach held up his hand. "Enough bullshit. Bruno, check again on Sander and Bashford. Then alert the platoon and make sure all replacements are wearing their tags."

"Inside or outside their shirts?" cracked Bruno.

Zach frowned. "Go, Bruno. Now!"

"Yeah, I'm on it."

The word spread rapidly among all troops. Most slept poorly that night with one hand checking their dog tags.

*****

The next day, the 9th Army Corps commander ordered fifteen battalions of artillery into the Dorsten battle zone. B Company watched as the American artillery pumped one hundred rounds per minute for a fifteen-minute duration into the beleaguered city. A and C Companies dismounted and moved out. Within the hour, their infantry was on the city streets. Two hours later, Colonel Hartman announced that all resistance had been overcome. American artillery had really come of age. The British were delighted.

THE RUHR POCKET

Encircle the Ruhr

B Company was abruptly ordered to the fortress city of Recklinghausen, ten miles due east. The crack 116th Panzer Division under the command of shrewd General Von Waldenburg controlled very favorable terrain flanked by the Lippe Canal on the left and the Rheine-Herne Canal on the right.

"This is a fight I could do without," Grinnell said, peering through his field glasses.

"I read about Von Waldenburg," Zach mumbled.

"I should have known. Okay, bookworm, so tell us," said Norm Ricks.

"He asked his men to take an oath to die rather than surrender."

"Oh, that makes my day."

"We should bypass this Nazi and head for Berlin," grumbled Bruno.

Colonel Hartman's jeep arrived. "We have a new letter of instructions from XVI Corps. We are relieved by the 75th Infantry, who will hold while we go around the canal and race one hundred kilometers east to Hamm, Lippstadt, and Paderborn. We are to meet the 1st Army at Lippstadt on April 1 and completely encircle the industrial Ruhr Valley. Any questions?"

"How many German troops are in this big pocket?" Grinnell asked.

"We're not sure, Lieutenant, probably twenty or more divisions, including part of the 116th Panzers."

The colonel left and an audible sigh of relief went up from the officers and noncoms. "Corps must have heard you, Russ," said Sergeant Ricks, clearly relieved at escaping the attack on heavily defended Recklinghausen.

"Oh we'll meet the 116th Panzers down the road. They are probably withdrawing some units as we speak."

"Sir, do we have any help?" Zach asked.

Grinnell looked at the letter of instructions given him by Colonel Hartman. "Good question—yes, we do. The 2nd Armored, good old 'Hell on Wheels,' is on our left flank, followed by our friends in the 30th Infantry. The 83rd Infantry will be mopping up behind us. The 3rd Armored will now be leading the 1st Army."

Except for a skirmish at Delbruck, the forced march to close the Ruhr pocket at Lippstadt proceeded on schedule. On April 1, 1945, armored divisions of the 9th Army, now back under American control, linked up with the American 1st Army. No one was quite sure "what was in the bag," as Sander put it.

"That run was way too easy," Ricks said, a note of foreboding in his voice.

"Too many divisions not accounted for," Zach speculated. "Thirty divisions is my guess."

"Hartman guessed twenty."

"I'll bet he's revised that number."

"I hope they don't all try to break out at the same time."

*****

The 18th Armored headed east toward Paderborn and Berlin as soon as the war correspondents finished taking pictures of the two-army linkup. The division proceeded east to an assembly area 185 miles from Berlin. The 9th Army had been pinched out by the British 2nd Army on the north flank and the American 1st Army on the south. A two-day stand-down was ordered to sort things out.

After the scary Senegalese encounter at Dorsten, Zach decided to clear the new area himself. He, Sandy, and Wild Bill casually inspected two nearby houses as Bashford tagged along, looking out for his squad sergeant. As they approached a third house, two uniformed teenage Hitler Jungend appeared. Zach raised his hand and shouted, "*Du muss aufgeben* (You must give up.)"

A sharp crack of rifle fire was the response. Zach felt a stinging pain in his raised hand as Sandy hit the ground. The rifle fire stopped quickly as Bashford's BAR went fully automatic. Tom got up and felt his body. *Nothing.* "Zach, are you okay?"

"Yeah, thanks to Bashford, but my hand hurts like hell."

"Jeez, looks like a wooden bullet," Tom observed.

Wild Bill came running. "Let me see it, Zach. What the…? It's a piece of wood." Bill extracted the object. "What the hell happened?"

"I'm not sure. They were shooting at me. You better check on 'em."

Wild Bill ran over to check the young Germans. Bashford was already there. He shook his head. "They're dead, Bill."

"Yeah. What did they hit Zach with?" Bashford picked up a clip from the dead Germans. "I'll be damned—wooden bullets. They must be used in training." Wild Bill shook his head and went back to bandage Zach's hand. "Let me know if this gives you trouble."

Tom Sander joined Bash and his eyes moistened. "Brainless kids, must be fifteen or sixteen. What a waste."

Bashford grunted and picked up a second clip. "This one's for real."

*****

Thanks to the short stand-down, the mail caught up to the fast moving troops. Only one letter reached Zach. Sander had none. "Damn! So, Zach, what's new back home?"

"Nothing. This letter is from the air force major we pulled out of a tree the night before Rhineberg."

"The B-17 guy?"

"Yeah, Buck Wheeler. He wants to thank us for saving his ass."

"Is he flying again?"

"Yeah. He says he'll give me a ride when the war is over."

"Another B-17?"

"Yeah. He changed the name from *Tahoe Lady* to *Tahoe Revenge.*"

"I hope he appreciates White and Franier."

"He asked about them. I'll write and fill him in. He lost some guys too, Tom."

"Yeah, I know. Any news on Henry Franier?"

"He's in England. I guess it's still fifty-fifty."

"He'll make it, Zach. Thanks to you, he'll go home a hero."

"I hope so. I still feel guilty."

"That's bull, Zach. That was no more your fault than Kirchellen."

"I know, Tom. I'm working on it."

"Good. I'm sure Brenner and Holter will be back soon."

Zach perked up. "Wing said maybe today."

"Great. We need 'em."

Zach turned away and sighed. "Poor Ken. I've just finished writing to his family."

Sander put his hand on Zach's shoulder. "Don't be so hard on yourself, Zach."

"Yeah," Zach muttered dejectedly.

Tom struggled to change the subject. "Zach, *vot do you really vant?*" Zach offered a weak smile and mumbled, "Grefrath."

"Yeah, the hausfrau with the Dresden china. Did Stosh ever get off of KP?" Tom howled.

Zach perked up. "That was after the mess at Rhineberg."

"Right, Zach. How about that crazy dog flying a Grasshopper?" Tom laughed.

Zach chuckled and said in a monotone voice, "That was the Lone Ranger."

Tom patted him on the back. "Hang in there, bookworm. None of us knows when our number's—"

"Up!" said John Brenner as he entered the room.

Zach jumped up and gave him a bear hug. "Thank God you're okay. How is Tony Holter?"

"Good as new," shouted Holter, who was only a step behind.

Brenner paused. "Zach, we're really devastated about Ken."

"Yeah...you know, we also lost Paxton and Bob White...and Franier is fifty-fifty."

"I heard," John said softly.

The whole squad joined in welcoming Tony and John, their return celebration dampened only by reminders of the squad soldiers lost.

*****

Zach's speculations back at Lippstadt were correct—the breakouts from the pocket had started. The surrounded, powerful German divisions under the command of tough Field Marshal Walther Model were attacking the 9th Army from the rear, a dangerous development. A forced march was ordered to the city of Soest, where the breakout was already underway.

The 18th Armored and the 95th Infantry arrived just in time to meet the breakout head-on. Both divisions attacked abreast on a wide front. The German breakout divisions, led by part of the 116th Panzers, were forced to retreat and seek another escape route. The grunts from the 95th Infantry blocked the hole. Armored B Company hit the road back to once-bypassed Recklinghausen. Repeated attacks by the 75th Infantry Division had not budged the stubborn Germans.

Grinnell was scowling. "Damn, not this diehard Von Waldenburg again."

"Courage, Lieutenant," Captain Black remarked as he scanned the city from the top of a tank. "The city is too quiet...but I don't see or hear any tanks."

Lieutenant Grinnell raised his glasses. "Yeah, the city is way too quiet. It could be a trap."

Colonel Hartman joined the observers, took one look, and slapped his helmet. "Good God, here comes an American jeep across the battle zone."

Grinnell took a close look. "I think it's Colonel Hallace, our regimental commander, sir."

Colonel Hartman borrowed a pair of glasses. "He must think we've already taken the damn place."

"Or that they withdrew," Lieutenant Grinnell added.

The jeep was following a road along the bank of the Ruhr River on B Company's right flank. Suddenly, a squad of German infantry rushed out, surrounded the jeep, and took the colonel and his driver prisoner.

Blackie adjusted his binoculars. "Well, at least the colonel exposed an ambush. I can see tanks coming out of hiding across the river."

"Get that forward observer over here," ordered Colonel Hartman.

"The artillery officer rushed over with his radioman. "I'm on it, Colonel. Our M-7s are within range."

"Blast those treadway bridges."

"Yes, sir, can do."

Grinnell swallowed hard. "Sir, what about Colonel Hallace?"

"He'd make the same call," Hartman replied flatly.

The first artillery shells rumbled overhead. "Just in time, Colonel. I count seventeen tanks advancing to the river," Grinnell reported.

"Thank God we didn't move out in front of them. What now, Colonel?" Captain Black asked.

Always the patient tactician, the colonel replied calmly, "We'll see if they get across the river."

Zach moved up behind the observers, holding his big navy field glasses to his eyes. "The artillery is on target. They hit all three bridges," he shouted.

"Good. They'll have to pull back," said Captain Black. A relieved-looking Colonel Hartman said, "Hallace is a tough old bird. He'll make it. The Greyhounds are an honorable division."

"Greyhounds, sir?"

"That's what the 116th Panzers are called."

"Good name; they are fast," Captain Black replied.

The colonel borrowed Zach's navy field glasses. "Well, Sergeant Jones, should we go after them?"

Zach gulped and smiled at the colonel's reference to his pseudonym. "No, sir, my BC says exposed tanks are great targets for the Tactical Air Command."

The BC laughed. "Good call, son." In short order the colonel diverted a whole wing of P-47s from an unspecified mission. They wreaked devastation on the retreating tanks, waved their wings, and were gone. The crack division artillery then turned their guns on Recklinghausen. The garrison there, unnerved after losing most of their tank support, now found themselves facing a deadly accurate artillery barrage.

B Company and the 85th Battalion proceeded to the river and then into Recklinghausen, taking many shaken, weary prisoners. John Brenner nudged Zach. "Thanks to Colonel Hallace's screw up, we avoided a well-planned ambush."

"Yeah. I hope he ducked when all that new artillery hit," Zach mumbled.

Reduce the Ruhr

"Here comes Grinnell. Let's see what kind of shit he has for us now," said Tom.

Grinnell shrugged. "Our orders are simple. Reduce the Ruhr."

"That's *it*?" Ricks exclaimed.

"Yup. We go as soon as the patrol out looking for Colonel Hallace reports in."

"Hey, they're back already. I'll go check," said Ricks. He returned in a few minutes. "They are fairly sure he's a POW."

"Okay, let's mount up."

"Russ, where do we start? The Ruhr pocket is thirty miles wide and God knows how deep," Ricks asked.

"We enter the pocket near Unna. If we're successful, we proceed and hit targets of opportunity. That's all I know. Ask Sander about the Ruhr. He studied geography," Grinnell retorted and left.

Ricks looked at Tom, who thought for a moment. "This valley is one big collection of cities, one after another—places like Dortmund, Essen, Duisberg, Wuppertal…even Dusseldorf and Cologne way back at the Rhine."

"Okay, but what do you know about Unna?" asked Zachary.

"Nothing, Zach. Sorry."

A few yards away, the captain and Russ Grinnell were studying a sector map. "There's a ridge on the south side of town above the road that we have to use to get there. Maybe our Grasshopper pilots can scout the ridge. Once that's cleared, we'll probably ride our tracks in," Blackie said.

"I'm still missing two tracks," Grinnell remarked. Zach was listening. "Any idea when we'll get 'em?"

"Yes, Sergeant Gates. We have one reassembled vehicle. Your driver is picking it up now."

"Thanks, Captain."

"Don't thank me till you've seen it. Naylor says it's a piece of junk."

Two Hours Later—Into the Ruhr Pocket

B Company arrived at the outskirts of Unna where a recon unit was assessing the formidable-looking ridge off to one side of the city. A Grasshopper observer made a specific report. "Eleven enemy tanks and eight motor transports on the ridge." TAC was notified while the 939th Artillery marked the area with a concentration of violet smoke. Twenty minutes later, four P-47 Thunderbolts arrived and had a field day. Soon the whole ridge erupted in flames from the burning vehicles.

"Poor bastards."

"Yeah, they never knew what hit 'em."

B Company silently mounted up and headed closer to the city. Naylor, fighting the replacement halftrack, finally caught up to the company. The 3rd Squad members bailed out of their temporary rides as Naylor stopped to pick them up. Zach climbed on board. "How does she look?"

"It's a piece of junk. Only the 50-caliber is new."

"Yeah, Blackie warned me. See if we can move up. Blackie wants us to be lead track."

"With this pile of bad welds?"

Zach laughed. "I guess he doesn't want to lose any good tracks."

"Move out!" was shouted down the column.

Naylor prodded the replacement track jerkily to the front of the line. He drove erratically, then cautiously as the first building came into view. They could hear small arms fire up ahead. The column stopped and the tracks dropped their windshield armor. Once within range, Zach fired the 50-caliber in the direction of the small arms firing. The squad hunkered down on the floor as Zach fired another burst. The small arms fire ceased. Zach raised his hand and shouted, "Cease fire! I see a white flag."

The weary Germans had enough. A platoon of soldiers emerged with their hands in the air. "Move it, Naylor. The MPs will get these guys."

Naylor jumped the track ahead another hundred yards and stopped. "What about that T in the road?"

"Hang a right, but easy," shouted Zach above the din of small arms fire.

"I can't see through all the smoke," yelled Naylor.

"What?"

"I can't see," Naylor yelled.

"Lift the damn windshield armor."

Naylor stopped and Zach helped him prop up the armor plate. "Okay, let's go."

Ahead stood a half-destroyed building spewing clouds of black smoke. Naylor headed slowly into the smoke-filled intersection and cautiously turned the corner of the burning building. There the calamity of all calamities awaited. Silhouetted in the smoke stood a giant Tiger Royal tank. Naylor slammed on the brakes as the eight-ton halftrack went nose-to-nose with the seventy-ton tank. Zach froze and stared through the smoke at an open-mouthed German officer in the tank's turret. The silence was deafening as the huge 88 muzzle swung around and down, stopping directly in front of Naylor's face.

Naylor's murmuring of "Hail Mary, Mother of Jesus, Hail Mary, Mother of Jesus," broke Zach's trance-like state. Panic-stricken, Gates shouted reflexively in German, *"Commen sie heraus! Hander hoch! Das Krieg is fertig! Schnell! Schnell!* (Come out with your hands high! The war is over! Fast! Fast!)"

The wide-eyed, open-mouthed officer considered his rapidly diminishing options. Zach felt sweat trickling down the sides of his body. He nervously thumbed the triggers on the 50 caliber. *This is it…my number's up.* After what seemed like an eternity, the stressed officer shouted down to his tank crew, put his pistol on the tank, and called out, *"Ja, wir aufgaben, alles ist kaput."* He resignedly climbed out of the turret followed by the rest of his tired-looking crew. They slowly lined up in a straight line outside of the tank staring blankly at the halftrack.

Zach breathed deeply and struggled to find his voice. He pointed to the rear. Then, in a moment of relief, or perhaps redemption, he threw a salute at the German officer. *"Guten gluck, Leutnant.* (Good luck, Lieutenant.) " The combat-exhausted German returned the salute and marched off, turning only to stammer, *"Ja."*

The moment of peril and shock slowly subsided. Zach recovered his sense of duty and his voice. "Okay, dogfaces. The show is over. Dismount."

The men quietly climbed out the back door and over the side, except for Naylor, whose eyes were still fixed on the big gun's muzzle not eighteen inches from the windshield, his hands clenching the wheel in a death grip. Zach kicked Naylor's shoulder from his position up in the gun ring. "Naylor! Your 'Hail Marys' worked. Now back up, dismount, and guard this goddamn track."

Naylor looked skyward. "Jesus, thank you, Jesus."

The dismounted, shaken squad stopped and stared through the smoke at the huge tank while Naylor extricated the halftrack from under the long gun barrel. "Okay, there is a God! Now look alive and follow me."

Stosh caught up with his squad leader. "Sarge, Pappy Becker fainted. He's still in the track."

Bruno Nitchke, normally loud and active, was listening quietly. "Jesus Christ, what next?"

*****

Now dismounted, B Company pushed further into the war-wracked streets of Unna. The platoon of Grenadiers following the big Tiger gave it up after seeing the tank officer surrender. Further into the pocket, the fighting stiffened. Combat became house-to-house and factory-to-factory. Streams of DPs (displaced persons) poured out of the buildings, all intent on returning to their country of origin. The danger of hitting them with friendly fire slowed the American advance. However, the trapped Germans had no such compunction. An 88 screeched into the house in front of the 3rd Squad. DPs ran out of the burning building as the squad, trying to get out of the way, moved forward. Zach stayed behind. His knowledge of German was needed to direct the DPs to the rear.

Wild Bill was administering aid to some of the less fortunate people. "Zach, this lady says there are two girls trapped upstairs in that burning building."

"Shit, where the hell is everybody? Bill, get to my squad. I'll go check inside."

"Be careful, Zach."

Zach stormed up the steps, pushed through a jammed door, and found one girl overcome by smoke, the other crying hysterically. He picked up the fallen girl and carried her to the street. The other young woman followed. Bill was still there. "Bill, look after these girls. I've got to find my squad."

"Yeah, go."

Zach caught up with Bruno as the squad was honoring more white flags. "Where the hell have you been?" Bruno shouted.

"No place—it's a long story. Anybody hit?"

"No, we're held up here by a shitload of POWs."

Brenner ran over. "Where ya been? We've been worried."

"Later, John. What did you see up ahead?"

"I haven't seen any more tanks, but I can hear 'em."

Lead scout Holter trotted over. "They seem to be heading southeast."

"They're trying to slip out around Marburg. We're thin there," Zach observed.

The file of POWs finally passed. Grinnell worked his way up to the stalled group. "I saw the Tiger. Are you guys okay?"

Zach forced a smile. "Yeah. I out-talked the krauts."

"That figures. Now what's holding us up?"

"A big, exposed intersection with tanks moving southeast."

"Damn. A Company is thin over there. The krauts may escape," the lieutenant groaned.

"Doesn't A Company have tank support?" Zach asked.

"No, only halftracks. Are we ready to run this intersection, Gates?"

"Soon as Bashford is in place to cover the scouts. I don't like that two-story building that survived the bombing."

"Okay, you call it when ready."

"Scouts out," Zach yelled.

Three 3rd Squad members stepped gingerly into the intersection, rifles at port arms. They made it to the other side, checked the building, and signaled the all clear. Russ Grinnell was about to step out in front of the building when the rattle of Bashford's BAR erupted. Two soldiers with Schmeisser machine guns fell directly in front of him.

"They're on the right flank," Bashford shouted as he turned his weapon around. Ricks came running and barking commands. "2nd Squad, take the rear, machine gun squad, base of fire. Zach, wait for orders."

Grinnell was still recovering from his close call. "Remind me to put Bashford in for a medal," he stammered. "Good call, Gates."

The platoon routed the Germans, sustaining only two casualties, and continued deeper into the pocket. Grinnell returned after checking with battalion headquarters. "We're relieved by the foot infantry. Our armor is needed elsewhere."

"Suits me," said Norm Ricks. "I hate this house-to-house stuff. What happened to A Company, Russ?"

"They got out of the way, but they lost two tracks and the krauts took two of our guys prisoner."

Zach looked at the sky and then the ground. "So what now?"

"East. The krauts who escaped have reassembled in the Harz, Mountains. That's where these panzers are headed."

"Not another pocket?"

"Yup, but not for us. We're going around the south side of the Harz, hopefully all the way to Magdeburg on the Elbe River."

Zach peered over Grinnell's larger map. "Through Gottingen, Duderstadt, and Nordhausen."

"Right, and Halberstadt on the northeast side. That seals 'em off."

"Haven't we taken some of these places?"

"Yup. The 2nd Armored is already on its way to Magdeburg, but I think they bypassed Nordhausen."

18

A SERIES OF CALAMITIES

New orders called for a two-day, two-hundred-kilometer forced march to Nordhausen on the southeastern edge of the Harz Mountains. The seemingly never-ending column of tanks and tracks was slowed only by the thousands of DPs, mostly slave laborers from camps in the industrial Ruhr Valley. They were wearily trudging east toward Poland and Czechoslovakia. Some came from prison camps titled internment or concentration camps.

B Company first heard of death camps when one of their sergeants returned from an evacuation hospital where he had met a soldier from the 4th Armored Division. They had overrun a camp at Ohrdurf on April 4, 1945. It was a chilling, mind-numbing report. "Many victims were lying where they had been shot by the retreating Nazis. General Patton vomited when he saw the wretched inmates more dead than alive and corpses stacked one on top of the other." The soldier reported that Patton ordered the bürgermeister and his wife be brought to the camp. When they returned home, they hung themselves. Stan Goldman was furious. "I knew it! Nobody would listen to the reports."

Zach exhaled heavily. "Now we know."

Tom Sander was dumbstruck. "This is unthinkable," he sobbed.

Taylor shook his head and let out a slow moan. "Could this guy be wrong?"

Zach checked his map. "We'll soon find out. That's Nordhausen ahead. The Brits report a similar scene."

Four visibly shaken MPs from the 9th Infantry met B Company. "Are you sure you want to see this?"

"Is it that bad?" Naylor asked from the driver's seat.

"It's unbelievable! Take your armor and go kill the Nazi bastards."

Corporal King and the radioman caught up with Zach and the 3rd Squad. "The place is clear. The SS men in charge of this death hole are being chased by the 3rd Armored."

Their rush was understandable, for they were the psychopathic cadre of the Nordhausen extermination and concentration camp. Revulsion overcame the hardened 3rd Squad Armored Infantry soldiers when they too discovered thousands of emaciated inmates. In one corner of the camp, corpses were stacked one on top of the other, just as the 4th Armored soldier had said.

"The dirty bastards," Sergeant Bruno Nitchke exclaimed.

Stan Goldman fell to his knees crying openly. A shaken Captain Black put his hand on Stan's shoulder. "I'm sorry, Stan. We are ordered to move out. The rear echelon will have to take care of this."

Zach put his arm around Stan but found himself struck dumb—silenced by stark disbelief, rage, and sadness. Finally, as he helped Goldman to his feet, they heard shouting. "Captain Black, Captain Black!" There stood Tom Sander in front of a small building serving as an entrance to a huge underground slave-labor rocket factory and laboratory. Blackie took a step inside, where he saw more pitiful, tortured people. After an unnerving pause, he choked, "I'm sorry, men…we're ordered to move out. Let's get this war over and hang these bastards."

The men moved silently back to their vehicles, a sickening bewilderment haunting their faces. Bruno Nitchke, his visage ice-cold, growled, "Let's go kill somebody."

Stosh was feeling sick. "Who are these people?" he implored.

Tom Sander wiped his eyes and spit out the word, "Psychopaths."

Stosh furrowed his brow. "What's that?"

"Sick, intolerant bastards," Zach called out in a truculent voice.

Stosh shot him a knowing look. "Like Ludolph, huh?"

Goldman, still badly shaken, wiped his tears and bawled, "Yeah, Stosh, like Ludolph…or Adolph, or Himmler, or Eichmann."

"Move out!" was, for once, almost a welcome call. The war ground relentlessly onward.

*****

The march, now under new orders to go to the west side of the Harz Mountains, was a long, looping one. The troops, still shaken and somber from their experience at Nordhausen, suffered another paralyzing shock when word passed down the column that President Roosevelt, their commander in chief, had died unexpectedly. It was April 12, 1945. No one spoke for a long, long time as morale sank to a dangerously low level.

Zach broke the silence with a fearful thought. "I wonder how the Germans will use this," he mumbled.

John Brenner shook his head and groaned, "Now they'll never give up."

Goldman sliced the air with his hand. "I can hear Axis Sally's radio propaganda to our troops—another Jew is dead."

Tom patted Stan on the back and observed, "Roosevelt was an Episcopalian like our chaplain."

"Yeah, I know," Stan choked.

"I don't remember any other president," Tony Holter sobbed.

The group looked to the bookworms. Brenner shrugged. "I was only seven or eight when he was elected."

"Me too," said Sandy. "This was his fourth term, wasn't it?"

"Who was the guy before FDR?" Tony Holter asked.

Thirty-seven-year-old Pappy Becker snorted, "It was Herbert Hoover, for Christ's sake."

"Do we know how FDR died?" Naylor asked.

"Probably polio," Tom offered.

"No. Grinnell said he heard it was a cerebral hemorrhage," Zach replied.

"What's that?" Tony asked.

"Zach, is that like apoplexy?" Stosh asked.

"I'm not sure, Stosh. It's some kind of blood clot that screws up your brain. I think the lieutenant was talking about a stroke."

"I think stroke and apoplexy are the same," Tom said.

"Ok, bookworm, enough medicine. What happens now?" Bruno snorted.

"The Vice President takes over," Brenner replied.

"Who is the Vice President?" Stosh asked.

"Harry Truman, you dogface," replied Tony Holter.

"Mr. Truman is a good man, Stosh. He'll make a fine President. He was an artillery captain in World War I," Brenner explained.

Tom Sander was shaking his head. "No warning…I wonder how the people back home are taking this."

Tony Holter spoke softly. "They didn't know any more than we did—this has to be a terrible shock."

"Why didn't we know?" asked a perplexed Stosh Kosinski.

The squad turned to Zach, who shrugged. "I guess because…because we didn't want the enemy to know."

*****

Morale continued to sag. Zach thought about all the men he had lost and his own mortality. His thoughts were interrupted when the convoy slowed and word came down for a midday break. Zach climbed up from the front seat to the command ring. "A farmhouse is just off the road, John. Let's see if we can get there before all these tankers do."

"Wilco, Zach, if this wreck hangs together."

At the farmhouse, the solemn squad quickly dismounted and checked the place out. Naylor stayed with the replacement track, nervously revving the engine as Zach toyed with the 50-caliber just in case.

"All clear. Nobody home, but you gotta see this. It should help morale," Bruno said.

Zach left Naylor looking under the track. "I'll be right back, Naylor. I want to check out this sad box of bolts too." He followed Bruno into the house.

The dining room table was set as if a final banquet were being held. Cooling on a kitchen counter stood three homemade pies, or at least what was left of them. The men were happily devouring the delicious desserts.

"Beats K rations," Stosh said, wolfing down a big bite.

"Save a piece for Naylor and me. I have to check out this screwed up track."

Back outside, Zach looked at Naylor and the tired halftrack. "So what's wrong with this thing?"

"Everything. It's all welded with spare and broken parts. Notice the front bumper and roller?"

"Is it from the track we lost at Kirchellen?"

"Sure is. I guess that's all they could salvage."

"Clever people, these ordinance guys."

"Yeah, but not too careful. The tracks aren't evenly matched, and the brakes are almost shot."

"Can we make it to Magdeburg?"

Naylor shrugged. "The nearest spare parts are in Braunschweig and that's seventy-five kilometers through the Harz Mountains and what's left of the German Army."

Still overwrought and dismayed over the loss of FDR, Zach asked caustically, "Naylor, if we don't go off-road, can we make it or not?"

"Maybe, if it's not too hilly. I can brake by shifting down, and so far I've been able to correct for the mismatched tracks. Just don't ask for speed."

Bruno emerged from the house carrying two small pieces of pie. "I hope you guys aren't too hungry. This is all I could protect."

Naylor looked at the plate in his hand. "How am I supposed to eat this?"

"Sorry, guys. I'll get you some sterling silver forks."

While Naylor and Zach were waiting for their forks, a jeep came speeding up to the house. A medic lieutenant wearing a helmet marked with a red cross inside a big white circle insignia dismounted. "Sergeant, I'm working the convoy to alert you to a new problem."

"What now, Lieutenant? Is it worse than the news on the President?"

"Might be! We just received word that some men in the 95th Infantry were poisoned by booby-trapped food." The lieutenant looked at the pie. "My God, what are you eating?"

Zach's heart sank. Naylor sailed his pie plate into the field. "Pie, sir, and there are ten men inside who ate a ton of it."

Nitchke returned with the forks. "Who's been hit?"

"Nobody's been hit, but the lieutenant says there's been a poisoning in the column."

Bruno felt his stomach. "I feel fine."

Zach looked at the lieutenant. "What kind of food? What kind of poison?"

"Desserts like you had in your hand, and it's strychnine or rat poison."

Unperturbable Sergeant Nitchke scowled. "Shit! So what do we look for?"

The harried medic handed Zach a card of things to do and then ticked off the symptoms: "Convulsions, then twitching, then arching of the back, followed by rigidity of the facial muscles."

Zach swallowed hard. "And how long have they got?"

"Depends, but probably another ten or twenty minutes should bring on the first sign of convulsions. I'm sorry, Sergeant…I have to go. Good luck."

Zach stared at the ground. *Come on, God. This is no way to die.* His watch read 1400 hours as he followed big Bruno into the farmhouse. Bruno, as if he were in combat, put on his hardest face and elected to shout and pass the buck. "Look alive and listen up. You're all gonna die. Sergeant Gates went to college. He'll explain."

The snoozing squad sat up quickly. Zach stalled. "We have a broken halftrack, but Naylor thinks we can make it." He looked at his watch—1405 hours.

John Brenner jumped up. "What's this crap about dying? I just got a Purple Heart!"

Zach could stall no longer—he measured his words. "There's been some booby-trapped food up the column and the medics were concerned about our pies." He paused and his voice softened. "Does anyone have a sick stomach or any new aches or pains?"

A very quiet group looked at one another and felt their stomachs. Only Pappy Becker offered, "My bowels are tied up and my leg aches." The soldiers groaned. Pappy often said that, and he was always limping.

Zach paced the floor looking at his watch. It was now 1410. He palmed the first aid "flush and vomit" card he had been given. *Thank you, God.* "False alarm, guys."

"What's a false alarm?" Goldman shouted.

"Case closed," Zach shot back, just as "Mount up" echoed up and down the line. The relieved squad dashed for the halftrack. However, after such a trial, Zach was morbidly curious. *Why were we spared? I really thought it was a trap.* He walked slowly back to the kitchen for a last look. He stared at the cupboard above the counter where the men had found the pies. He felt an overwhelming compulsion to open the cupboard door. His eyes wandered to the top shelf. There, near the back, he discerned a small, yellow box. His hand reached out as if strangely guided. The unopened box had a picture on it—a rat inside of a red circle. Zach felt a sinking feeling in the pit of his stomach tempered by gratitude. "Rat poison!" he stammered. His stupor was broken by a shout from outside. "Come on, Gates, or Bruno says we'll leave you behind."

"Yeah, I hear you." Zach took a deep breath, covered the box with his hand, and moved it to another shelf. Stosh entered the kitchen. "Orders to move out, Sarge."

"Yeah, thanks, Stosh. Go. I'll be right there."

Zach took one last, unsettling look at the yellow box. *They'll know I know when they see the box is moved.* He pondered the close call. *Thank God some good German family broke ranks with the crazies.*

"Gates, come on!"

"Yeah, I'm coming!" Zach closed the cupboard door, glanced around the kitchen, and in a voice filled with emotion, choked, "*Dankeschoen, gute leute.* (Thank you, good people.)"

19

WEREWOLVES AND SNIPERS

"*Dankeschoen noch einmal.* (Thank you again)," Zach muttered as he climbed into the front seat of the halftrack. The squad sat strangely silent. Bruno had moved up to the center seat while Naylor jerked the tired, patched-up vehicle forward.

"What's up, Bruno? What's the rush?" asked Zach.

Bruno looked up from his map. "We're going off-road to attack some crazies."

"What? Where did you hear that?"

"Jim Wing."

"Why didn't you call me?"

"Jim was in a big rush and you were busy looting the kitchen."

"When and where is this action?"

"A few miles up the road. We go as soon as we're lined up."

"Did Jim describe the mission?"

"Yeah, real simple: clear out all broken or irregular German units harassing the movement east to Berlin."

"No wonder the guys are so quiet," Zach grumbled.

*****

The griping continued as the battalion assembled.

"I hate this kind of action."

"Yeah, you can't predict what these psychos will do."

"No Panzers. That's the good news."

"Don't count on it—these guys are tricky."

"Yeah, and scary. Some call themselves Werewolves."

Fear swept across Stosh's face. "What's a werewolf?"

"Beats the shit out of me. Ask one of the bookworms," Bruno replied nervously.

Brenner thought for a moment and opted for simplicity. "Stosh, it's a guy who is able to transform or change himself into a wolf."

Stosh's eyes widened, registering panic. "John, nobody can do that... can they?"

"No, of course not, but they can *act* vicious, like wolves."

"They're real bad guys, huh?"

"Yeah, anything goes."

"Like those wild krauts who pulled that fake surrender on A Company."

"Right, Stosh. They'll do anything to kill you."

"Jeez, I'm sorry I asked."

*****

Colonel Hartman's strategy was straightforward: "A, B, and C Companies abreast. Shoot anybody in the way."

One under-strength tank platoon was assigned to the battalion to support B Company in the center of the skirmish line. A and C Companies had only their halftracks.

A few hours into the well-coordinated advance, C Company fell behind. All visual contact had disappeared. Radio communication became garbled. B Company was ordered to initiate reconnaissance and find out what was happening. The 2nd Platoon drew the mission and Norm Ricks sought out Zach. "One squad should be enough. Piece of cake, Zach. They're probably boozing it up in town."

"I've heard that before," Zach grunted as he prepared his squad. "Okay, scouts out. That's you, Holter and Brenner. Bruno, bring up the rear. Move out and spread out."

Soon a small village appeared in the distance. Zach checked his map. "Must be right in front of C Company." He looked up. One of the scouts signaled a halt. He waved Zach forward. "Zach, we've seen men out there, but we can't make them out."

Zach signaled the squad down and took out his navy field glasses. "They're in American uniforms, probably a patrol from C Company."

Always wary, Holter argued, "Or some nuts in our uniforms."

"I don't think so, Tony. I'm going to stand up and wave."

"Looks like a group of five or six. Be careful, Zach. Give me your glasses," said Brenner. Zach stood up and waved. The small group froze. John focused on the man with the glasses. "The leader is looking you over." John's voice sounded optimistic. "Show him your patch." A tense moment ensued before a quiet smile crossed John's face. "He's waving—now he's moving forward. All clear!"

The two patrols met some one thousand yards from the nearest buildings. A young lieutenant, his eyes urgent, stuck out his hand. "Boy, am I glad to see you, Sergeant. C Company needs help."

"What do you need, Lieutenant? What's holding you up?"

"Snipers, a bunch of 'em. They shot up our communications—" His voice caught. "And five of my men…all head shots."

"I'm sorry, Lieutenant. Do you know where these snipers are located?"

"They gotta be in the houses out there in front of us."

"We need a tank, Lieutenant," Zach replied.

"We don't have any tanks, and these guys aren't afraid of halftracks," he replied pessimistically.

"Hang in there, Lieutenant; we do!" Zach waved Bruno over. "Sergeant Nitchke, get the lieutenant two tanks. Take two men with you."

"Got it. Two tanks coming up. I'll try the walkie-talkie when I get close enough."

"Yeah, tell 'em ASAP."

The lieutenant hyperventilated, still feeling the pangs of losing five men. He locked eyes. "Thanks, Sergeant. Let's kill those bastards!"

The two patrols compared notes while waiting on the tanks. "Are we safe here?" Zach asked.

"Yeah, one thousand yards is out of their range. At five hundred yards, you're dead. We tried moving up our best sniper in a buttoned-up track, but they got him at three hundred yards."

Zach shook his head and scowled. "Lieutenant, how do you want the tanks to get these bastards?"

"Not from this side. C Company is in the line of fire."

"Okay, we'll have 'em race around. Did you see any antitank weapons or mines?"

"No, but you never know."

"Here come the Shermans."

Zach and the lieutenant approached the lead tank. "Snipers, Sergeant. Shoot everything from the second floor up. You'll have to circle around."

"Can do, Lieutenant. Describe and locate the buildings you think they're in."

Zach, the lieutenant, and the tankers studied the map. "All of these on this side of town," the lieutenant said.

The tanker nodded. "We'll burn 'em. Stay out of our line of fire."

"Understood. One other thing. Button up at six hundred yards, or these guys will pick you off."

"Wilco. We'll hurt 'em. We have a ton of incendiaries and HE on board. We'll unstick you guys."

The two patrols moved several hundred yards away from the field of fire and set up a skirmish line to intercept any retreating snipers. The tanks circled around and commenced firing. Unchallenged, they ground forward, blasting away at point-blank range. In short order, the whole village seemed to be exploding and burning. The tanks' new incendiary shells, followed by high explosives, left seemingly little chance for the snipers to survive. Zach studied the buildings with his powerful glasses. "Damn, two got out—Goldman!"

"Here, Sarge."

"Take a look."

"That's a really long shot."

"They're coming this way. Everybody down. They don't see us," Zach ordered.

Stan Goldman, the seldom-used sniper in the 3rd Squad, polished the scope on his Springfield 03. "At five hundred yards, they're dead."

"Your call," Zach replied.

The lieutenant crawled over to Stan. "Nail 'em, soldier, right in the head!"

The two squads lay prone and deathly quiet. Then the tanks started to return. They could give Goldman's position away. Zach tapped Stan on the shoulder. "It's now or never."

"If they'd stop running…"

Zach raised his glasses. "They heard the tanks. They stopped—"

The Springfield barked with two quick detonations. "You got 'em, Stan—they're down."

"I'm pretty sure, but it was close to six hundred yards."

The lieutenant had his patrol on their feet. "We'll make sure. Thanks, guys, we owe you one."

*****

The squad had just returned to its own skirmish line when the whole battalion was abruptly pulled off line and put on hold. A new, urgent problem had arisen. In the 2nd Armored Division's rush to the Elbe, they had bypassed a large force of German regulars who could now be a threat to the whole operation.

Colonel Hartman assembled his company commanders. "Men, the situation is fluid. We're awaiting recon and new orders."

"Colonel, where is the 2nd Armored now?"

"Past Hanover, the main obstacle. If they swing north of Braunschweig, it's a straight, sixty-five-mile shot to Magdeburg on the Elbe River."

"Colonel, what do we know about this force they bypassed?"

"G-2 reports sizable units from the 5th Para Division, the 26th Grenadiers, the 9th Panzers, and a few of our old friends from the 116th Panzers. The mixed force is commanded by Hitler's friend, General Walther Lucht, another real hardhead."

"I thought we trapped all those guys in the Ruhr."

"These are the troops who escaped from the Ruhr and lower Rhine pockets. They now operate out of the Harz Mountains."

"Are they nuts? What the hell is their objective?"

"Top brass thinks they're trying to get organized and head west to release their troops trapped in the Ruhr or..." The colonel paused. "They'll run east, cross the Elbe, and help defend Berlin."

"Do we have to go after them?" Captain Black asked.

"Depends on Magdeburg. If the 2nd Armored Division beats us to the Elbe, which looks likely, we may get that dirty job."

A disgruntled A Company commander asked, "Isn't that a job for the foot infantry?"

The colonel nodded. "Our 1st Army has elements from the 104th and 1st Divisions headed into the Harz sector. Let's hope they disrupt them long enough for us to continue east."

Captain Black checked his map. "Colonel, if they go east, we must be squarely in their exit route. They have to break out between Nordhausen and Halberstadt."

"In my judgment, the 1st and 104th Divisions will contain them. I'd like to catch up to the 2nd Armored," the colonel replied.

"Colonel, any word on how the Russians are doing?" ventured the A Company commander.

"I'm guessing they are thirty or forty kilometers east of Berlin. G-2 says some forward elements have bypassed Berlin and may get to the Elbe before we do. That's it for now. I'll alert you when our orders come down. Dismissed."

Deadeye Stan Goldman heard mostly kidding. "Shouldn't I get a medal or something?" he griped.

"You got an *Expert* medal at Polk!" Bruno bellowed.

COUNT TO THREE!

Good news. The Germans in the Harz were being contained by the veteran 1st and 104th Infantry Divisions. The battalion headed east, but once again was given mop-up orders. Another German force of unknown size had been bypassed at Hammersleben only thirty miles from the Elbe. Orders were terse. "Divert to Hammersleben and neutralize the German threat."

No one was quite sure what kind of force was at Hammersleben. Were they a delaying force or were they headed toward the Elbe? "Can't be more than a broken battalion of Wehrmacht," said Russ Grinnell to his 2nd Platoon.

"Or some crazy Werewolves," groused Norm Ricks.

"Let's just hope they don't have any heavy artillery," Zach added.

"Here comes Blackie with the word from G-2."

"Men, G-2 tells me there are no tanks, but two or three companies of Wehrmacht are holed up in a small factory area."

"How are they so damn sure about the tanks?" a 1st Platoon officer asked.

"Well," the captain said, forcing a smile, "it was confirmed by aerial recon."

A tired officer shook his head and groused, "Yeah, and they are frequently wrong."

Lieutenant Grinnell questioned the tactical problems. "Captain, do we go in on foot?"

Blackie paused. "Yes, but we may have to swim."

There was a stir in the group. "What?" Grinnell asked.

"Recon reports a canal or small river in front of them. Nobody knows how deep it is."

"Can't we get some close recon on that?"

Blackie's expression was uncertain. "A Company is on it. That's all I have." He frowned and walked out.

Norm Ricks caught up to Lieutenant Grinnell and grinned. "Russ, do you Iowa guys know how to swim?"

"No. That's why you and your buddy Gates can lead this one."

*****

At 0100 the dog-tired company came to a halt two miles from where the Germans were holding. "Dismount," shouted a weary looking Captain Black. "We go on foot from here."

"That's it?" Russ Grinnell queried.

"That's it, Lieutenant. I'm tired, the company is tired, we have no tank support, no artillery. Be creative, Lieutenant, or let the sergeants on line figure it out. We rendezvous at 0300."

"What's his problem?" Ricks whispered.

A sympathetic Zach replied, "Even captains suffer battle fatigue."

A shit-eating grin crossed Norm's face. "Bull! Blackie doesn't know how to swim," he howled.

*****

0315. Grinnell met with Ricks and the 2nd Platoon squad sergeants. Groans and gripes were audible. "At ease. Recon says the river is less than waist deep in most places." More groans followed. "At ease, damn it! Now listen up. A Company is on our left flank. C Company is in reserve. Sergeant Ricks, prepare Gates and the 3rd Squad. They'll lead."

"Yes, sir."

"Dismissed."

*****

"Guess I shouldn't have teased Russ about his swimming ability," Ricks chuckled.

"Yeah, thanks for nothing," Gates replied.

"Anyway, he said you can call your own shots."

"Good. Tell him to get me some water wings for Pappy and Bruno. They can't swim either."

Nervous laughter followed. Ricks sighed. "I'm sorry, Zach. We're all tired. How do you want to do this?"

"Well, at dawn we should be close enough to get a better look at what we're up against. I'll check it out while Bruno sets up a base of fire with half the squad and, Norm, get me some help from the machine gun squad."

"You got it."

Nitchke grumbled, "How do I know when to fire?"

Zach looked at Norm Ricks. "0400?" Ricks nodded. "Okay."

"Bruno, my group will jump off a few minutes later. Lift your fire when you see us go."

"I keep firing?"

"Yeah, over our heads, please. Any questions?"

"Yeah, when do I bring my group forward?" Bruno asked.

"As soon as we get across the water or close to the buildings...or whenever you think it's propitious."

"*Propitious*? For Christ's sake, speak English."

"Okay, advantageous." Bruno looked perplexed. Zach paused. "Bruno, whenever you say so—when it looks good to you."

Bruno grunted and Ricks nodded agreement. "Good plan, bookworm. Coordinate your advance with A Company on your left flank. We'll move up on your signal."

"Understood, Norm. Brenner, you're in charge of checking on A Company."

"Got it. I'm on it right now."

*****

At 0330, the squad gathered quietly at the jump-off point fifty yards from the river and three hundred yards from the buildings. John Brenner returned. "Sergeant Banzai Bill Ferrow has A Company's lead squad on our left—he's all steamed up."

"What his plan?"

"Charge at 0400!"

"That's it?"

"That's all he'd tell me."

"Some coordination that is! How this guy has survived three campaigns beats the hell out of me."

At 0400, Bruno and the machine gun squad laid down a blistering base of fire. Five minutes later, Zach's group headed for the canal. Bruno's covering fire was working. Zach met little incoming fire. His men quickly reached the canal, which was war damaged and, luckily, only knee-deep. The group waded across and sprinted to a small hedge just seventy-five yards from the factory. Zach signaled a halt and scanned the factory and his flanks. Most of the fire was directed at

Sergeant Ferrow's squad. Zach raised his field glasses. "They're pinned down. The crazy bastard didn't set up any covering fire."

"So what do we do now?" Stosh asked.

"We go it alone, Stosh." Zach focused on the buildings. All of the heavy doors were buttoned down. "We hold here. Holter, get over here!"

"Yeah."

"Do you have your rifle grenades?"

"Yeah, two."

"I want you to hit one of those big doors."

"That's a long shot."

"Figure the range. I'll signal Bruno to move up. We'll need a closer base of fire once they know we're here."

"No need, Gates. Bruno is on the way with part of the machine gun squad."

Bruno rushed up and hit the dirt next to Zach. "Thought you'd need some help. It was *propitious*."

Zach grinned. "Well done, Bruno. You came with alacrity."

"Who's he?" Bruno grunted.

Zach slapped him on the back and turned to Holter. "Okay, Tony, open a door for us. Bruno, give us all the fire you've got when we head for the door."

"Got it. I'll have Ricks bring up the rest of the platoon on your signal."

Tony Holter fastened the grenade to his rifle, aimed, and fired. A window above the door blew open. Tony fastened a second round, his last. He fired, scored a direct hit, and the door blew into the room.

"Now we go!" shouted Zach as the machine gunners commenced firing. They met little incoming fire from the startled Germans. Zach signaled and Bruno brought up the rest of the squad. The platoon followed. The 3rd Squad double-timed it to the door and were quickly inside.

"They're gone," Bashford yelled. A fusillade of bullets singing up the basement stairway belied his assessment. Zach ducked as the bullets whizzed past his head. Shaken, he hit the floor, loosened a grenade from his harness, pulled the pin, and rolled it down the steps. The firing from below stopped. The squad waited for the explosion. Instead, the grenade came hurtling back up the stairs, its five-second fuse not expended. It rolled over to Stosh. In one quick motion, he picked up the grenade and tossed it back down the stairs. The five-second fuse ran out near the bottom of the staircase. The detonation echoed throughout the stairwell, and several grenade fragments ricocheted up the steps. One nicked the top of Zach's thumb, another bounced off of Stosh's helmet. Sergeant Nitchke charged down the stairs into the smoke, his .45 blasting. Then silence.

"All clear," Bruno shouted as he bounced up the steps. He slapped Stosh on the back. "You saved our asses." Then he turned to Zach, who was nursing his laid-open thumb. "Count to three after pulling the pin in a building, bookworm."

"We were under fire, Bruno…it didn't seem propitious," Zach replied with a note of discomfort.

"Next time leave it to Al Lacrity," Bruno cracked.

Zach rethought his fast action. *With three seconds, it could have been a potato masher…who knows?*

Tom Sander and John Brenner came running back from scouting the other sides of the buildings. "They've withdrawn. The whole company is in pursuit. Blackie says to hold here and clear the area."

Russ Grinnell rushed into the building. "Anybody hit?"

"Just Gates. A nick in the hand," said Bruno.

Wild Bill took a look. "Should have a stitch."

"I don't have time for a stitch. Tape it up."

"How's the wooden bullet? Jeez, the same hand."

Stosh showed his helmet to the medic. "I got hit in the head," he reported as a drop of sweat rolled off his forehead.

Wild Bill looked at the crease in the helmet and smiled. "You were lucky, Stosh." In his most professional manner, he put a piece of tape on Stosh's helmet and wordlessly handed it back.

The squad was laughing nervously when a runner arrived. "Action's over. Return to your tracks. Captain's orders."

"What about the krauts?" Bruno asked.

"We're taking a shitload of prisoners."

The squad worked their way back through the stalled A Company sector to see what went wrong. The medics were attending to several wounded men. Zach and Brenner found Sergeant Banzai Bill Ferrow's body. A single bullet had entered just under his left eye, tearing his eyeball loose. Blood covered the whole left side of his face. His right eye was wide open. Brenner shook his head. "The guy didn't know fear. Even in the States he was fearless."

A medic joined them. "Sorry about Ferrow. He's being recommended for the Silver Star."

John gave Zach a rueful yet agitated look. Zach forced a last view of Staff Sergeant Ferrow's broken, bloody face. "He should have set up a base of fire," Zach mumbled through a voice laced with pity and dismay.

John's mouth turned down. "It was just a matter of time."

"Easy, John. He drew most of the fire…he made our job easier."

John's voice hardened. "Yeah, so did Stosh."

21

RECON PATROL

Tactical Plan

Still short-handed, the dog-tired squad finally heard some good news. "The whole 85th Armored Infantry Battalion is going into reserve."

A cheer went up. "About time. Where are we going?"

"Neuhaus. We're promised rest, hot food, and maybe some replacements."

"How far, Sarge?"

"Just up the road a few kilometers. We'll join all of B Company plus a company from the 81st Tank Battalion."

The squad had just dismounted in Neuhaus, Germany, when a runner from the 2nd Platoon rushed over to Sergeant Gates. "Lieutenant Grinnell wants all squad leaders on the double."

"What's the big rush, Corporal? We're in reserve," Gates shot back.

"Krauts, what else?"

The squad groaned and griped. "At ease. It's probably a false alarm," Gates grumbled.

Weary Sergeant Nitchke was adamant. "Tell 'em to go to hell."

"Hang loose, everybody. I'll find out what this crap is all about," Zach said.

The squad leaders assembled on the east edge of Neuhaus. Lieutenant Russ Grinnell met them there. "Bad news, guys. G-2 intelligence says an enemy regiment from the 116th Panzers with as many as twenty tanks may be in the woods a thousand yards east of where we're standing."

Tired Platoon Sergeant Norm Ricks frowned. "Damn it, Russ, we were told the area was clear. Who screwed up?"

Grinnell raised his hand. "Peace, Norm. I don't know. The Germans must have moved up during the night."

"Some reserve duty," one of the squad leaders griped quietly.

"At ease," Ricks called out.

Lieutenant Grinnell cleared his throat. "Men, that's all I have. Stay with your squads and await orders. Sergeant Gates, Sergeant Ricks, follow me."

The trio of friends moved up to the wall at the edge of town. Norm Ricks turned to Zachary Gates. "What do you think, bookworm? It's all open fields except for the farmhouse and barns about seven hundred yards down the road from here."

"Yeah, and another two hundred yards to the woods. Looks too quiet. We need—"

"I know—reconnaissance," Grinnell said, anticipating Zach's message.

"Right, Lieutenant."

The harried platoon leader spoke briskly. "Norm, you and Gates sort this recon out and come up with a plan. I'll work out some back-up support from the tankers. That's all," Grinnell announced as he hurried off.

Zach turned to his platoon sergeant, a look of complaint on his face. "Norm, I'm two men short; two guys are green; why always your old 3rd Squad?"

Ricks frowned. "Because you're good at it. Because Grinnell likes you, bookworm."

"What a crock. Norm, my squad's worn out."

Ricks's mouth turned down. "Suck it up, Zach. We're all tired."

Grinnell returned. "The tankers won't move without reconnaissance."

"Where is our recon squadron? Can't they handle this?" Ricks asked.

"Blackie says they are in reserve twenty miles back."

"Where the hell did Division G-2 get their information?" Ricks grumbled.

"An artillery L-4 Piper Cub spotted 'em."

Zach gathered his thoughts. "Didn't he check the farmyard?" Zach asked.

"Too many trees and buildings to be sure but the spotter said it looked quiet."

"So what's the rush?" Norm Ricks asked.

"Colonel Hartman worries about counterattacks and ambushes."

"Are we going from reserve to a frontal attack?" Ricks said, with a touch of sarcasm.

"Not until we find out for sure what's behind those farm buildings.

Okay, enough! Sergeant Gates, how do you want to do this?" Zach stalled. "Come on, Gates. I'm counting on you," the lieutenant barked.

Zach exhaled and lowered his eyes. "I'll send Sergeant Nitchke down the left culvert with five—no, four—men, and I'll take—" Zach hesitated. "I guess it's also four men down the right culvert for cover."

"What? You have only eight men?" the lieutenant snapped.

Zach answered tiredly, "No, I have ten, but Naylor is doing track maintenance and Bashford is on sick call."

"What's wrong with Bashford? You may need his BAR."

Zach hesitated. "He's not well, sir."

"What's wrong with him?"

Zach looked away and sputtered, "The GIs—a real bad case."

The lieutenant's eyes looked skyward. "Crap," he grunted.

Ricks interceded. "Russ, two of Zach's men are new replacements."

Grinnell frowned. "Look, I've already worked out a base of fire with the tankers and the rest of B Company. It's too late for any changes. What's the goddamn plan, Gates?"

Zach stared at the distant farm while formulating a plan. "One, we check out the farmhouse. Two, if it's clear we check out the yard and barns. Three, Nitchke covers us and we scout out the woods beyond."

"What if the farm complex is occupied?"

Zach paused. "Then...I guess we'll evaluate their strength...and get the hell out of there."

"Okay. Use the radio if you can. We'll fire only if you're in trouble. Got it?"

Zach's voice dropped. "Understood, sir."

Grinnell moved closer. "Zach, be careful out there."

"Yes, sir."

Zach double-timed it back to his squad. Norm Ricks turned to Lieutenant Grinnell. "It's a load, Russ; the 3rd Squad is hurting."

"I know that, Sergeant, but Gates and Nitchke are still the best team we've got."

"Yes, sir. Gates and his bookworms can think, and Bruno doesn't give a shit."

The lieutenant smiled. "That's about right."

*****

Zachary called his squad together. "So Gates, what's the bad news?" grumbled Bruno Nitchke.

"Bad news is we're tapped for recon duty again."

"Why us, Sarge?" asked one of the new replacements.

This time Zach's voice echoed across the room. "Because we're good at it. Now suck it up and follow me to the wall."

"Shit—always the 3rd Squad," grumbled Stan Goldman.

"I'll guard the halftrack," said track driver Naylor with a note of relief in his voice.

Bruno was resigned to the mission but a little testy. "Stuff it, Naylor, or you'll be lead scout. Now the rest of you move it," Sergeant Nitchke commanded.

The squad arrived at the wall. Zach pointed toward the distant farmhouse complex and passed his field glasses around. "Take a good look and listen up."

The distant farmyard included two large barns, a silo, and several smaller buildings enveloped by dozens of pine and elm trees. "You could hide a whole battalion behind that mess. What does G-2 say?" John Brenner asked.

"Who cares? They never know shit," grumbled Tom Sander.

Zach handed his field glasses to John and scowled at his uptight squad. "Guys, all I know is G-2 isn't sure about the farm, but they do think there may be twenty tanks and a regiment from the 116th Panzers out there someplace."

"And they are frequently wrong," Tom added dryly.

"I hope you're right, Tom. Either way our objective is simple: see if krauts are setting up a counterattack or an ambush behind the farm buildings."

Bruno snorted. "Okay, Gates, how we gonna do this? Let's get it over with."

Zach pointed to the road and the culverts lining it. "Okay, here it is. Everybody listen up. I'll take Brenner, Sander, and Kosinski down the right culvert. Bruno, you take the leftovers with you down the left culvert."

"Yeah, then what?"

"Stay behind us to make sure you don't give us away. Wait until we're sure the krauts have pulled out and we give an all-clear from the complex. Then cover us from the farmyard as my group heads for the woods."

Bruno nodded. "Okay, I got it."

Zach turned to Brenner. "John, you have the glasses. You're lead scout on my team."

John smiled drearily. "Gee, thanks. I always wanted another Purple Heart."

"You're welcome," Zach replied briskly. "Any questions?"

Stosh Kosinski waved a nervous hand. "Sarge, what do I do?"

"Stosh, you're our rear guard. Stay alert."

"I can do that."

"Fine. Any more questions?"

Bruno Nitchke faced Zach. "Gates, what about communications?"

"Hand signals; walkie-talkie only if we're fired upon. And stay behind us; watch for our helmets."

A shout came from Russ Grinnell. "Gates, get ready to move out. I'll coordinate with the tanks."

Move Out!

Zach took a last anxious look down the culvert. "Move it," he shouted. The split 3rd Squad entered the ditches. The road was straight but the culvert wandered. He could see the end but not the farm complex. The unusually wide ditch sloped downward a few degrees and was just deep enough to cover all but a man's head. The patrol moved head down and bent over. After two hundred yards, Zach signaled a halt and peered over the edge. He could see the farmhouse clearly now—there was no movement. After another three hundred yards, Gates's team had now gone as far as it could without being seen. Brenner, scouting ahead, was only fifty yards from the large, stone farmhouse. He took cover behind a pine tree bordering the edge of the culvert and waved Zach forward.

Zach signaled Tom and Stosh to hold up, then ducked down and joined Brenner. "I don't see a damn thing," Brenner whispered.

"Good, then we can go home," Zach joked nervously as he steadied his field glasses. He scanned the farmyard area and then the big farmhouse. A driveway one hundred yards to the left crossed the culvert over a gravel bridge covering a large drainpipe. A fieldstone wall stood halfway between the house and the culvert. The wall had two gates that were flattened. One gate was close to the drive. A second gate opening was right in front of him. "John, if we can get to the wall, we can get a better look."

"If you say so," John answered as tightness gripped his throat.

Zach silently signaled Tom and Stosh to move up for covering fire while he and John crawled out from under the pine tree and slowly crept to the wall. Zach looked at John, who was breathing hard. Zach put his finger to his lips, inhaled deeply, took off his helmet, and crawled to the wall opening. He lay as close to the ground as he could and cautiously peered around the edge. He raised his head to see better above the uncut grass. Beyond the house stood a huge barn, a silo, several outbuildings, and many large trees—*no wonder the L-4 couldn't be sure.* The house appeared to be deserted and run-down. Zach's eyes roamed the surrounding—nothing. He raised his head still higher. His stomach sank when he saw tank tracks in the flattened grass a few feet past the wall. He slid back to Brenner. "Tank tracks. They've been here."

"Any movement?"

"No, nothing, but I can't see behind the damn house."

"Maybe they've pulled out," John sputtered hopefully.

"We'll see. Signal Tom and Stosh to move up."

Tom crawled up and peeked around the wall. "Someone is in that spooky house. I know it."

"All the windows are open. They probably have a sniper in every window," Brenner grumbled.

Zach trained his glasses on all of the windows. "Not just open—all the frames are gone. No, wait, not in the gable windows."

"What's that all about?" Tom asked uneasily.

"That's for clearview firing and observation. Someone's been there recently," Zach whispered.

"Yeah, but how recently?" John shuddered.

Zach continued to search the windows. "I really think the house is empty. I don't see a damn thing. Where's Stosh?"

"He's back there covering our asses."

Zach waved him forward. Stosh came running in a half crouch. "What's up?"

"We're going to the house."

"Now?"

"Yeah, now," Zach answered. "We have to chance it or Bruno will get ahead of us. John, you and Tom head for the house. Stosh and I will cover you."

"Do we get flight pay or something?" Tom groaned as tension mounted.

"Why not! Just don't run in straight lines and keep five yards apart."

"Got it," Tom replied as nervous perspiration appeared on his forehead.

"And John!"

"Yeah?" he responded apprehensively.

"Look for booby traps when you get in the house."

"Yeah, yeah."

"Okay, go."

John and Tom went through the gate and made a zigzag dash for the house. Zach peered over the wall and held his breath. They drew no fire. Brenner reached the first-floor window. Tom huddled close to the foundation. Brenner removed his helmet, handed his rifle to Tom, and peeked over the window ledge. Zach watched through his field glasses as Brenner climbed through the open window. After what seemed like an eternity, his head appeared in the window. Even without the field glasses, Zach could see Brenner put his finger to his lips and wave for them to come forward.

Zach and Stosh moved to the house quickly and silently. Tom and Stosh pushed Zach through the window. John, his finger still to his lips, motioned Zach to follow him through the big house to a room on the far side. He signaled down, and Zach crawled to the window across the room. A quick peek said it all—two Panther tanks and a broken squad of infantry hidden under the spreading trees. One tank stood just thirty feet from the window. Zach dropped to the floor and crawled back to Brenner. His stomach churned as he fought off a numbing fear. His mouth went dry. *Damn, I know I can get through this...I've done it before.* He looked at John. Panic was written all over his face. "Easy, John. They don't know we're here," he whispered.

The sound of his own voice helped Zach regain his sense of duty. "We're overmatched, we're really overmatched. Hang tough. We're going to get out of here before they find us." John just nodded. Zach's stomach still churned, but his combat cool returned as it had so many times before. "John, listen up. Were they SS?"

Brenner was unable to speak. "Damn it, John," Zach muttered as he crawled over to the window and risked another look. There was no movement—soldiers were stretched out on the grass looking exhausted. Zach studied the sleeping tankers and infantry. Their SS insignia clearly showed on their helmets. He waved his hand, making two jagged lightning bolts. John started to get up. Zach crawled over and whispered, "Stay with me, John—these guys are so worn out they haven't posted guards. We're getting out of here."

"What about Bruno?" John asked fearfully.

"I'll have to chance the walkie-talkie."

Before John could respond, loud German voices and the sound of men moving about broke the silence.

"Shit! What woke 'em up?" Zach grunted. He drew his holstered, hard-earned Luger and released the safety. Would they send their missing lookout back into the house?

The noise outside grew louder, followed by the sound of a tank hatch being opened. Taking a calculated risk, Zach took still another look out of the window. "Two SS headed for the front of the house carrying Schmeisser machine guns," he whispered. German voices grew louder. "Damn! They must have spotted Bruno across the road."

Bruno's two green replacements had moved too far forward. One SS trooper rushed across the road firing his submachine gun on the run.

Several wild shots hit the scouts. Bruno bravely moved forward. He arrived just in time to get flattened by a burst of fire in his chest. The several bandoliers he carried absorbed most of the shock and deflected the bullets. The German, thinking Bruno was dead, started changing clips. Tough Sergeant Nitchke somehow regained his footing, picked up his rifle, and shot the shocked SS trooper at point blank range.

Bruno's two inexperienced men were bloody but mobile. Bruno directed them back to the culvert where Stan and Pappy were already running up the ditch. Bruno and the two wounded replacements took off running for their lives. The rest of the unnerved SS had turned their attention to manning and protecting their tanks.

Bail Out!

Back in the house, Brenner was on his feet. "Time to bail out!" Zach cried as he ran through the house and followed John out of the window. Tom and Stosh, still outside of the house, stood wide-eyed in near panic. The jumpy, nerve-wracked soldiers looked to their squad leader for an order, any order. They collected in a tight circle, their helmets almost touching. The frightened young soldiers listened to the tank engines behind the house and waited for the word. Utilizing the calmest face he could muster, Zach spoke quietly and deliberately. "They still don't know we're here. We are going to run our asses out of here."

"Who leads?" Tom asked.

"Brenner, you lead. Brenner, look at me. You're lead runner followed by Sander and Stosh. I'll cover you in case their lookout comes back in the house." John nodded. "Okay, John, take off."

The three made a frantic dash from the house to the opening in the wall. Stosh Kosinski held up and returned to his squad leader. "You said I was rear guard."

"Your orders are changed. Go, Stosh, run!"

"Good luck, Sergeant Gates."

"Yeah, go."

Zach's pulse pounded as he watched Stosh clear the big pine tree hanging over the ditch. The gunfire directed at Bruno's group had stopped. Only the roar of the 50-ton Panthers' engines filled the air. He dashed to the wall, stopped, turned around, and scanned the windows—nothing. It was time to unload some gear. He dropped the radio, leaned his rifle against a wall, and proceeded to pull the heavy bandolier of M1 clips over his head. When the bandolier dropped, it knocked down his rifle. As he was about to retrieve it, a sixth sense, the kind one learns with combat experience, prompted him to take one last, hurried look

before taking off. His heart sank and his blood went cold. An SS trooper stood in the window, shouldering his Mauser. Zach looked helpless-
ly at his rifle lying on the ground. A bullet whizzed past his head.
Reflexively, he drew his Luger from its shoulder holster and fired four
quick rounds, then dropped behind the wall. There was no return fire, no
voice calling out, so Zach cautiously raised up and peered over the wall.
One or more of his hurried shots had found their mark. The German was
slumped over the window ledge, his helmet askew, his rifle dangling
from one hand. He never got off a second round. Zach stood up and
froze in place, expecting another man to appear. The house remained
quiet. The commotion and loud engines on the other side of the house
must have masked the gunfire. He studied the slumped German to make
sure he didn't recover. He watched transfixed as the man slowly lost his
grip on the rifle and it fell to the ground.

Zach's heart jumped as he holstered his Luger and ran terror-stricken
for the culvert. His legs went into overdrive—he dashed past the pine
tree and slid into the ditch. He could see Stosh some 100 yards ahead of
him. He ran at top speed for seventy-five yards and then slowed to catch
his breath. Then he panicked—a louder roar from a Panther engine
flooded his senses as it clanked forward and straddled the culvert. Zach
chanced a backward glance. Only a few pine branches obstructed the
tank's field of fire. The turret turned ninety degrees, and its machine
guns started their rapid chatter. Zach's combat instincts to hit the dirt
were vetoed by the same sixth sense he had heeded before—*Run, run,
there is no cover… get out of effective range… run like you've never
run before.*

What looked and sounded like loud, hard, driving rain pelted the
ground around his feet. Bullets whistled past his ears. *Run, run,* the
inner voice pleaded. *Faster, faster.*

The earsplitting screech of an 88 soared a few feet over his helmet.
The armor-piercing, heavy round buried itself in the right side of the
culvert fifty yards ahead of him. Deafened by the horrendous screech,
Zach experienced an eerie sensation of silently running some three feet
above the ground on an unearthly battlefield. The now-silent bullets
continued to pelt the ground around his feet. Then the raindrops took on
a soft, popping sound as his hearing started to return. The popping
sounds from the rear grew intermittent, and he could hear the slower rattle of the American 30-caliber machine guns. Then he heard the friendly crack of heavy 76-mm American tank fire. Now Zach could feel his
feet hitting the ground as his ears and head cleared. He saw the friendly wall, the blessed wall. *If I can make the wall, I'm safe. I've got to*

make it to the wall, he repeated to himself over and over. He scrambled out of the culvert—men were cheering him on as if he were the anchor leg of a relay team. He jumped high in the air at full stride and tumbled over the wall, the heavenly wall. He dropped to his knees and kissed the ground. He felt all of his extremities. All seemed to be in working order. Wild Bill Anders was checking him out as most of the 2nd Platoon looked on. Wild Bill always followed the heaviest action and, since the 3rd Squad always seemed to be in the thick of it, he was like a thirteenth member of the squad. "Zach, you're clean, not a scratch. Your ears will stop ringing in a few hours." Bill moved over to check Brenner and the others.

Still stupefied by his close call with death, Zach began roll calling old names from his 3rd Squad. "Cooper, White—"

"Sarge, Cooper and White were killed a month ago," John Naylor replied quietly.

"Well, damn it, answer for them!" Zach shouted as tears streamed down his face. It was then he noticed John Brenner holding his head in his hands. He heard a sob from this brave young soldier who rarely showed emotion under fire. Months on the front line had finally caught up with him. He was crying openly when Wild Bill whispered, "He's not hit, Zach, just overloaded."

Zach nodded as his own head began to clear. "John, you're okay. You did good."

Brenner, not responding, just stared at the ground. Corporal Naylor tapped his squad leader. "Zach, I'll stay with him. Sergeant Ricks is looking for you."

"Thanks, Naylor. Look in on Sander and Kosinski too."

Norm Ricks came running over, a look of concern on his face. "Zach, are you okay?"

"No, but I've stopped shaking and my ears have almost stopped ringing."

"Close call, old buddy. How is Brenner?"

"Shook up. He led the group out of that nightmare."

Casualties

Ricks locked eyes with Zach and spoke slowly. "Zach, you better check the rest of your squad. Your two new replacements and Bruno got hit."

Zach threw his hands in the air. "Christ, I'm still not with it. Did they all get back?"

Ricks thought for a moment. "Yeah, more or less."

"Shit," Zach mumbled as he rushed over to check on Nitchke's group.

The two wounded men had already been evacuated. One, wounded in the hand, would probably lose two fingers. The other lost part of his right ear. Bruno Nitchke returned from the aid station, still carrying his mangled bandoliers. Zach, shaken, cautiously approached the big, rugged sergeant. "Bruno, are you okay?"

His tone rough, Bruno answered, "Hell, no, I'm not okay. I have a gorilla sitting on my chest. These bandoliers saved my ass. I'm taking 'em home."

Zach raised his hand. "Bruno, what did they say at the aid station?"

Still up tight, Bruno replied in a forced voice, "They taped me up just in case I cracked a rib. Oh yeah, they gave me a couple aspirins for my headache."

Zach gave a sigh of relief and then saw Bruno's damaged helmet still strapped to his chin. He moved closer. A collective gasp came from all present when they saw a small, single bullet hole just above the rim of Nitchke's helmet. Zach shook his head in disbelief. "Bruno, nobody is that tough! Let me see your helmet."

Bruno removed his helmet and the whole 2nd Platoon held their breath. When Zach pulled out the helmet liner, two pairs of mangled socks fell out, revealing a crease that followed the curve of the helmet and liner. A bullet had taken the same route and exited out the back of the helmet. Bruno's insistence on putting two pairs of socks in his helmet had jacked it up and insulated his head, saving his life.

Zach closed his eyes, shook his head in disbelief, and then declared, "This helmet is an even better souvenir, Bruno. Can you explain this?"

Bruno slowly examined his helmet. "I remember my helmet being banged. That's all." Then he looked down and grinned. "Shit, look at my socks." Nervous laughter turned into bedlam as Nitchke rubbed his large head and then untangled his socks. Bruno grunted. "Gates, how come you always get us the easy shit?"

Zach gave him a bear hug. "Just lucky, you hardhead." *From now on, I believe in miracles,* he said to himself.

Sergeant Bruno Nitchke was recommended for a Bronze Star for having saved the lives of the two young soldiers.

*****

Zach, after gathering his wits, returned to check on John Brenner, who was now standing up and talking to Stosh. "How now, old buddy?" Zach asked.

"I'll be okay. I'm sorry I lost it."

"John, we all lost it. Stosh, how are you holding up?"

He held up his rifle. A bullet had shattered the stock. "Okay…okay, I guess."

Feeling drained, Zach sighed. "We all better go to church."

Tom was still vibrating but slowly getting his act together. "How's Bruno's group? I heard they got hit."

"They all made it back, thank God, but the two new kids were hit…I don't think we'll get 'em back. Pappy and Stan are okay. Bruno is okay, but that's a long story."

Ricks interrupted. "Stow it, we have new orders."

"What? We're attacking Berlin?"

"No, good news. Company A is relieving us. Rest time. For real this time."

"Thank God," Stosh choked.

"Yeah, thanks, Norm," Zach mumbled as he reviewed the deadly chain of events that his squad had survived.

"What about Nitchke?" Tom asked.

Zach raised his hand and noticed that it was still trembling. "Stay with me, guys. I'll fill you in on Bruno when we're behind the front."

The recon patrol was a success, the enemy soldiers had revealed themselves, an ambush was avoided, and the Germans were not apt to counterattack.

*****

The ailing M-3 halftrack stopped in front of a huge, deserted hay barn and the eight men still left in the 3rd Squad dismounted. Medic Wild Bill Anders had joined them. "I'm studying shell shock," he said with a grin.

"Thanks for looking in on us. Bill, you should go to premed when you get home," Brenner replied.

"Yeah, as soon as I finish my last year in high school," Wild Bill laughed.

The weary group slumped down on the hay-strewn floor. A few headed for the hayloft.

As night fell, Zachary Gates struggled to the open door and looked toward the now-more-distant front line. He watched the eerie, disquieting flares and cringed at the sporadic gunfire. He imagined he heard German voices. He looked away from the doorway and shuddered.

Tom Sander stirred from a hard sleep. "So…what happened to Bruno?"

"I sent him back to the aid station just to be sure."

"All I heard was that he got shot in his hard head and is still alive,"

Tom laughed.

Zach was just finishing the incredible story when a figure appeared on the loft stairway. Zach reached for his Luger.

"It's me—Stosh. Just checkin' on you, Sarge. Are you guys okay?"

"We're fine, Stosh. Where are you sleeping?"

"In the loft with Bruno and the guys."

"Bruno is back from the aid station?" Zach said with surprise.

"He didn't go. He said once was enough."

Zach rolled his eyes. "That sounds like Nitchke."

"Yeah, he's tough. I'm very sorry about the two new guys. I didn't really get to know them."

"Yeah, that's a sad story. The good news is Bash is feeling better."

"That's great," Stosh said and shuffled his feet.

"Is something wrong, Stosh?"

Stosh took a deep breath. "Back at the farmhouse?"

"Yeah?"

"You were way behind us coming back from the farmhouse…and I was wondering…did you have trouble back there? I saw you putting rounds in the clip for your Luger when we got back."

Zach paused. He hated this kind of battle talk. Stosh persisted. "The SS came back in the house, didn't they?"

Zach hesitated and looked toward Tom, who had fallen asleep. "Go get some sleep, Stosh…you'll wake Tom."

"I'm sorry I asked…but…I was sure we all owed you big time."

"Beat it, Kosinski."

Stosh Kosinski flashed a knowing smile and headed for the loft. Zach reached for his nearby Luger, checked the clip, then the chamber and safety. He stared at it for a long time and mused: *I have a license to kill…does anyone really understand?…life seems so cheap…will it ever end?…how the hell did I ever get into this never-ending shooting and killing?*

Zach sought solace in reflecting back on better times before the army. He started to doze off—then he revisited his less-than-happy high school graduation. Half the boys were already gone or on furlough like Zach. Six pictures of Gold Star alumni—all killed in action—were displayed on stage; the parents were in tears at the close. The speeches, including Zach's, were either overly dramatic or depressing—he finally drifted off into a troubled sleep.

STAND-DOWN AT THE ELBE

The race east to the Elbe and Berlin resumed, this time with three armored divisions abreast: the 2nd on the left, the 5th on the far right, and the 18th in the more mountainous center.

The 2nd Armored followed by the 83rd Infantry bowled over roadblocks and roared forward, covering forty miles in one day, easily winning the race to the river. At the Elbe, they met heavy German fire and endured the frustration of watching the Germans destroy all of the crucial bridges. The trailing 83rd Infantry was desperately trying to catch up to the fast-moving 2nd Armored Division.

When B Company of the delayed 18th Armored finally reached the small city of Seehausen near Magdeburg on the river, confusion reigned. Seventeen hundred German prisoners guarded by a handful of MPs were marching west and perhaps deliberately snarling traffic.

Zach, Ricks, and Grinnell were looking west when they saw a bus raising dust clouds a mile down the road. Grinnell raised his glasses. "It's some kind of German school bus with a lot of other strange looking vehicles following at high speed. We'd better stop them. It could be krauts trying to cross the river."

Ricks quickly ordered two squads to park their tracks across the road and the machine gun squad to set up. The lead bus screeched to a stop and an American bird colonel jumped out. "Hold your fire," shouted Lieutenant Grinnell. The column leader was irate. "Move your goddamn tracks. You're holding up a combat command of the 83rd Infantry."

Ricks signaled the track drivers to clear the road. The colonel jumped back in his bus carrying forty or fifty GIs and roared off, followed by the most unusual collection of personnel carriers the American army had ever seen: German trucks, fire engines, more buses, even horse-drawn wagons, all loaded with GIs, some hanging on for dear life. The lines of POWs scattered to save their lives.

A dumbstruck look crossed Zachary's face. "What the hell kind of a wacky regiment is that?"

Before anyone could respond, a war correspondent came speeding up alongside the convoy. Russ Grinnell recognized the reporter and flagged down his jeep. "Hold it right there, Ernie Pyle."

"I'm following the 83rd, Lieutenant."

"Far as you go. We have a fire fight up ahead."

The reporter stepped out of his jeep. "Damn! I wanted to follow this crazy colonel right to the river."

"What is this cockamamie posse all about?" Grinnell demanded.

"And *why* is it?" Sergeant Ricks added, watching the bizarre collection of vehicles.

The reporter laughed. "I'm reporting it as the Ragtag Circus. These guys have been breaking ass trying to keep up with you armored guys, and the colonel ran out of trucks."

Zach repressed his laughter and asked, "What happened to his trucks?"

"You armored guys are loaded with vehicles. Foot infantry regiments have only enough trucks to transport one battalion at a time. Colonel Buckshot, I call him, wanted all three battalions on line."

Zach chuckled. "I like this Buckshot. He's damn creative."

"He sure is, Sergeant. He's the same guy who tried the old Trojan horse trick back at the Roer."

Ricks's jaw dropped. "Trojan horse trick?"

"Yeah. Back at Oberkassel bridge, he led a task force disguised as Germans right up to the bridge before he was discovered. The Germans blew it up, of course."

Ricks's voice hardened. "I'll bet General Simpson was pissed off."

Ernie waved his hand in the air. "Hell no, he was in on it. Simpson is one of the most audacious, unheralded generals we have."

Grinnell shook his head and shrugged. "Okay, Ernie. Go follow the Ragtag Circus."

*****

B Company's next orders were to move up to Barly, a small town on the river five miles south of Magdeburg, to assist the Ragtag Circus. The bridges at Barly, like those at Magdeburg, were all blown. Two miles north of Barly, the battle-tested 2nd Armored engineers were furiously building a bridge while their infantry was boarding boats. At the same time, fifty miles southeast, the 5th Armored had captured the town of Tangermunde only fifty-two miles from Berlin, but again, no bridges.

Barly seemed quiet except for an occasional mortar round coming from the other side of the river. A mile or two on either side of Barly, however, heavy German artillery fire erupted. A group of high-ranking officers stood near the broken Barly bridge. Among them were General Simpson, General Devane, and three full colonels, including Colonel Edwin "Buckshot" Crabel. Field decisions were being made. General Devane signaled Colonel Hartman to join them.

General Simpson announced the game plan. "Gentlemen, we are going to secure our bridge beachheads, cross this damn river, and run our two best armored divisions abreast right into Berlin." He turned to the colonel from the 2nd Armored. "How are we coming with the bridge building?"

"We are within seventy-five feet of the other shore, sir. The German artillery has been off target."

"How are the boat people doing?"

"General Hinds reports one battalion across just south of Magdeburg. Two battalions are in the boats."

"Very good. It's important we get tanks across soon. Those brave men are naked if the Germans counterattack."

"Are the Germans in strength?" General Devane asked.

"John, they have three veteran divisions and twenty or thirty thousand home guards and nobody knows how many tanks."

"Do we know who is in charge?"

"Yes, General Walter Wenck, an experienced soldier who gave us the slip from the Harz, and he intends to fight."

General Simpson's aide called him to the radio. In a few minutes he returned to the group. "General Hinds reports that his bridge just south of Magdeburg has suffered several direct hits. His second bridge to our south at Schoenbeck is half-completed. The two battalions already across at Olagdeburg are working their way south to stiffen the beachhead at Schoenbeck."

General Devane looked at the river and stroked his chin. "What can the 18th Armored do, General Simpson?"

"I want you to get a fresh battalion of armored infantry and a fresh battalion of tanks ready to roll across that bridge as soon as it's completed. The 2nd Armored has worn itself out. We need heavy firepower across the river or those troops already there are in trouble. Damn! We need bridges," General Simpson exclaimed.

General Devane looked at Colonel Hartman. "You heard him, George. Let's get on it."

"Yes, sir. I'll send A and B Companies to Schoenbeck right now."

"Very good. Even halftracks will help. I'll alert the tankers."

Colonel Hartman returned to Captain Black and the frustrated Ragtag Circus. "Blackie, prepare B Company to be first across. Get to the 2nd Armored bridge. I'll bring the rest of the battalion ASAP."

B Company mounted up and marched a few miles south, reaching the half-completed bridge just before daybreak. The American foot troops on the east side of the river had made it to the new beachhead. There was nothing to do now but wait for the combat engineers to complete the treadway bridge.

Captain Black called the platoon officers and noncoms together. "All we can do now is hope the Germans don't counterattack the beachhead before we can get some heavy stuff across."

"What are we up against now, Captain?"

"Another determined general and about fifty thousand diehards ordered to keep us out of Berlin."

Corporal Wing came running and shouting, "Captain, here comes the press corps." Jim flashed a toothy smile. "Maybe they'll take our pictures for a change." The press did take pictures and did ask questions, mostly of the 2nd Armored, who had troops across the river.

The reporter who had been following Buckshot and the Ragtag Circus spotted Sergeant Gates. "Hey, Sarge, what are you doing here? I thought you were rear echelon."

"Right, Ernie, that's why I'm first across if we ever get the damn bridge completed and my shot-up track holds together."

"Heh, sounds like a story. Can I tag along?"

"Suits me if my CO agrees."

"Don't tell him."

Zach put on a bargaining smile. "Okay, but can I pick your brain?"

"Sure. I'm not going anywhere."

Seeing Zach talking to a news correspondent, Tom and John walked over, followed by most of the 3rd Squad. "Can we get in on this?" Tom asked.

"Sure," the reporter replied. "What can I do for you?"

"What's going on with Montgomery up north?"

"British progress has been spotty. He slowed down when he lost your 9th Army. The VII Corps moved ahead only after you guys broke it wide open in the center."

"What was he up against?" John asked.

"Nazi General Walter Wenck and what's left of the German 12th Army. You get him next. He's just across the river."

"What about the seaports on the North Sea? How are the British and Canadians doing up there?" Zach asked.

"I think they are approaching Bremen, where the SS are hanging real tough. They also have canals, dikes, dams, and the kind of shit that held you up at the Roer River."

"Has Holland been completely liberated?" Tom asked.

"Hell, no. I think the Germans are still holding Arnhem. This war ain't over yet, guys." Then, turning to Zach, "Such big questions. Where did you get all the Ph.D.s?"

"Bookworms," mumbled Sergeant Bruno Nitchke.

The reporter was curious. "What did you say?"

"Bookworms," Bruno repeated.

"What the hell is a bookworm?"

The men looked at one another, not knowing how to respond. Stosh stepped forward. "Real smart guys—like professors."

The reporter looked confused but interested. "Hey, I may have a story. You guys aren't part of that ASTP bunch of savants, are you?"

Before Stosh could ask, "What's a savant?" a sudden volley of 88s abruptly ended all talk, scoring a direct hit on the nearly completed bridge. Air erupted from the pontoons, immediately causing whole sections of the bridge to sink or drift down the river. The 3rd Squad headed for their track on the double. "Jesus, now there's no way to help those poor bastards across the river," Zach choked.

The foreboding rumble of heavy vehicles echoed in the air as Nazi General Wenck started his counterattack on the beachheads across the river. The lightly-armed 2nd Armored Infantry stood in great peril while the heavily-armed rescue troops on the west side were left frustrated and helpless. After two hours of fanatical assault, the beleaguered American troops called for artillery fire on their own positions. Their call for air support went unanswered, because the Elbe River was just beyond TAC range.

By 1100 hours it was every man for himself and the proud 2nd Armored men were forced to get back across the river any way they could. The toll was 330 dead with many others wounded, missing, or taken prisoner. Survivors later related horror stories of becoming prisoners and then being forced to walk in front of the German tanks as they moved to attack the rest of the dug-in defenders, the tanks killing GIs at point blank range.

More American artillery moved up while the bridge companies prepared to start over. The American armored divisions waited in frustration.

As the reporter had said, "This war ain't over yet, guys."

*****

The whole war took a critical and unexpected turn when General Simpson received a direct order from General Omar Bradley. The message was brutally clear—stand down at the Elbe River. A political decision had been made. The Russians were to take Berlin. General Simpson was stunned. General Hinds and General Devane were incredulous, but there was no mistake. The orders had come down from Ike himself.

It was another about-face for the 85th Battalion and B Company. Their casualties on the wild ride to the Elbe had been light compared to the beating the 2nd Armored had taken across the Elbe. The 18th counted only 178 KIA or wounded. The race to Berlin was over.

"That's one race I'm glad we lost," Zach muttered.

OUT OF CONTROL

The new orders called for B Company to march west to the city of Braunschweig for much needed repairs. The 83rd Infantry Division and the Ragtag Circus were sent back to the Harz Mountains to face stubborn German General Walther Lucht and his escapees from the Ruhr pocket.

All of the short routes to Braunschweig were jammed with trucks carrying tons of material, fuel, and ammunition for the anticipated crossing of the Elbe and the battle for Berlin. The only available roads wove around the southern edge of the Harz, the same ones used by the 18th going east, a distance double that of the northern route.

Zach checked out his squad and inspected his beat-up track. He shook his head and mounted up. Ricks signaled for him to dismount. "Zach, I don't trust your pile of spare parts. Bring up the rear so you won't be in the way if she quits."

"What happens if we get stuck?"

"Park it and hitch rides like you did at Kirchellen."

Zach shot him a startled look. "Jesus, Norm, not like Kirchellen."

"Sorry, Zach…"

T/5 Naylor, already behind the wheel, shouted, "How about a new goddamn track?"

"Grinnell says it's waiting for you in Braunschweig. Try to hold this piece of junk together."

Naylor growled, "No big hills or we're screwed."

"That's a promise, John," Ricks retorted. "Now move out."

"Yeah, promises, promises," Naylor snorted.

Zach looked at his map and said ruefully, "John…there is one real steep grade at the city of Seesen just west of the Harz Mountains."

John frowned and grumbled, "Great! I hope we don't burn out the transmission and what's left of the brakes."

*****

Captain Black stood up swinging his arms from his lead jeep. "Let's get this show on the road."

Bruno mounted up, carrying a walkie-talkie. Zach eyed him wearily. "What's that for? They never work."

Bruno shrugged. "Blackie gave it to me. He says the batteries are fresh."

"Okay, better than nothing."

In a rare effort at humor, Bruno responded, "I asked supply for one of those Dick Tracy wrist radios."

"Very funny, Bruno. Okay, Naylor, see if this wreck will run."

The ailing halftrack rattled but held together as Naylor expertly nursed it up, down, and over the rolling hills. Then, a few miles south of Seesen, came the real challenge for the now-steaming halftrack: a one-thousand-foot-high ridge.

"I'm not worried about going up," Naylor declared, "but what's on the other side?" he asked sullenly.

Naylor's tone accelerated Zach's anxiety. "I'll check with Grinnell; he's with Blackie."

"How far ahead of us is he?"

"Less than a half-mile. I can see the jeep most of the time."

Zach extended the aerial on the walkie-talkie and was surprised to get through to Grinnell.

"What's the problem, Gates?"

"We're still moving, but Naylor's concerned about going down the other side."

"Hold on, I'm at the crest now." Grinnell paused. "Zach?"

"Yeah, I'm here."

"It's pretty much a straight shot into town, about four thousand yards I'd guess."

"Any curves?"

"Two that I can see, but they don't look too sharp."

"Ask him how wide the road is," Naylor shouted.

Grinnell heard him. "About like what you're on now."

"Can we pass if I lose the brakes?" Naylor asked ominously.

"You can pass if we move right and nobody is coming toward us," Grinnell shouted. Naylor grunted and squeezed the wheel.

"Is Seesen clear?" Zach asked. No response. Zach shouted, "Russ!"

"Yeah, wait till I get my glasses focused. Shit, there's a ton of military traffic. The MPs have a traffic platform in the intersection. It's a mess. I'll try to radio them."

Zach's mouth dried. "Thanks, Russ, over and holding."

The track labored over the crest of the hill and then started to gain speed at an alarming rate on the steep, downward slope. "Goddamn it, Naylor, slow this son-of-a-bitch down!" Zach yelled above the noise of the squealing brakes.

"No brakes, Zach. Shit!"

"Now what?" Zach angrily shot back.

"We can't gear down! We just lost all of our hydraulics!" Naylor screamed.

Zach stared wide-eyed as the interval ahead was closing at a horrific pace. He tilted the swinging 50-caliber down and struggled to grasp the ring while reaching for the radio. "Russ, we're in big trouble and can't brake. Alert all vehicles and the traffic cop that we're going to need the left lane."

"Got it, Zach. For Christ's sake, be careful. Over and out."

The tank sirens started wailing as Zach shouted, "Left, John, swing left—we're out of interval!"

Naylor fought the big wheel as the track shot into the narrow left lane, gaining speed at a fearsome rate. The column slowed and moved as far right as possible. The first curve came into view. Zach paled as he saw the steep drop-off on the left side. Suddenly, the hard-charging halftrack lurched left and shook violently as the mismatched left rubber track soared off into space. It gave another violent lurch and the right track flew over the column into the mountain, barely missing some startled tankers. The "no-track" was now streaking along on its bogie wheels.

"Good!" yelled Naylor, as the track became easier to control with both treads gone.

The busy Seesen intersection now stood less than five hundred yards ahead. The MPs, madly trying to open a hole for the out-of-control vehicle, cleared the road just in the nick of time. Parts from the disintegrating vehicle spewed left and right as it rocketed through town at eighty miles an hour. The shaken, nerve-wracked men inside peered wide-eyed over the side while a stressed, grim-faced Naylor repeated over and over, "Hail Mary, Mother of Jesus, Hail Mary, Mother of Jesus."

After what seemed like an eternity of bumping, clanking, and bouncing, the overheated, smoking "no-track" coasted up the hill on the other side of town, coming to a stop at the crest. His heart still racing, Zach jumped over the ring onto the hood and then to the ground where he frantically blocked a front wheel with his helmet. As the frazzled, ashen-faced troops slowly and silently dismounted, they could hear the cheering and horn-tooting from the observers back in town. Zach ran to the driver's side where T/5 Naylor, his hands welded to the wheel, was still mumbling his Hail Marys. "Let it go, John. You just won the Indy 500!"

"Thank you, Mother Mary," Naylor murmured.

Zach picked up the radio still within range of Grinnell and shouted, "We just parked this son of a bitch. We all need new underwear!"

"Goddamn it, Gates. That's government property you're hot-rodding. Your whole squad is under arrest. Over."

Sweat was wandering down Zach's forehead. He exhaled in relief and shouted, "Thanks, Russ. I love you too. Over."

"Shut up. Over and out." Zach was slow to hit his switch. "Thank God," was all he heard as Grinnell signed off.

*****

When the 2nd Platoon caught up with the "no-track," Zach ordered Sergeant Nitchke to have the 3rd Squad find rides in the remaining four halftracks. T/5 John Naylor rode with 1st Sergeant Bob Klein. Horns tooted and the men cheered when he drove by. Zach, riding in the jeep with Captain Black, Russ Grinnell, and Jim Wing, gave a weary thumbs up to the men of Company B.

Driver Jim Wing slapped Zach on the back. "You guys were great—what a show."

Zach frowned. "Yeah. How far to Braunschweig?"

"About 50 kilometers."

Zach growled, "Drive carefully. I'm still a nervous wreck."

"Hey, I'm an excellent driver. All flat land ahead. Get ready to party when we get to Braunschweig. Right, Captain Black?"

"We'll see, Corporal. Three German divisions are still fighting in the Harz, and the road ahead comes very close to the action."

"A Company is ahead of us—right, Captain?"

"Right, Corporal. Let's hope they solve any problems between here and Braunschweig."

The A Company, weary of delays, assaulted the few enemy renegades with a vengeance, clearing the road to Braunschweig once and for all. Jim Wing put on a happy face. "I'm still thinking party time." Emotionally drained, Zach had fallen sound asleep and did not respond.

BRAUNSCHWEIG: PERILOUS PARTY

A vigorous intensity encompassed the city of Braunschweig. Several divisions had summarily moved their headquarters there. Parking was at a premium—trucks, tanks, tracks, mobile artillery, and assorted vehicles were everywhere. Norm Ricks finally located the platoon's designated stand-down area, a wide boulevard lined with small apartments. Smaller streets divided by grassy strips ran parallel to it. These multiple lanes made for easy parking of the large armored vehicles.

"Gates, if you can find your squad, put them in that empty corner apartment building next to that company of tank destroyers."

"Thanks, Norm. Looks good. How long will we stay here?"

"We've been put in 9th Army reserve. I'd guess eight or ten days."

"Norm, one more thing."

"Yeah?"

"What about my new halftrack?"

"It's here in Braunschweig. I'll get back to you."

Sergeant Bruno Nitchke and Tom Sander caught up to Zach. "Found everyone but Pappy. What's the word on our new halftrack?"

"It's here someplace."

Bruno perused the large collection of tanks, tracks, and other vehicles and frowned. "Gates, I don't trust these damn German kids who are eye-balling our vehicles."

"Right, Bruno, take Tom and get 'em out of here."

The two Americans chased after the youths who moved across the median and hid behind a row of new M-36 Jackson tanks. "We better warn these green tankers," Bruno shouted.

"Yeah. They're all wearing clean uniforms," Tom replied while running across the grass strip. Zach followed to the spot where Tom was trying to warn a young buck sergeant.

"Relax," said the tanker. "These kids are just curious. Hell, the war is almost over."

Zach bristled. "Get off the tank, soldier. I want to talk to you." Zach's four stripes and combat badge carried some weight and the tanker climbed down. "Now hear me, soldier. These kids have been in the Hitler Jungend since they were twelve. The fifteen- and sixteen-year-olds have more military time than you do, and they are fearless and fanatical. Don't play games with them."

"I'm sorry, sir. We just arrived overseas, but you should be talking to our officers."

"I will. Now get these kids away from your tank before they hurt somebody."

Tom and Bruno were spreading the word among the tankers but not soon enough. Across the boulevard, two of the Hitler Jungend found an open turret and dropped grenades on the crew members inside the tank. Screams of agony followed the muffled explosion.

"There they are," Zach yelled, pointing at the pair.

Bruno dashed across the street, his Colt 45 barking as the two defiant teenagers were stopped cold by the big slugs. One of the two carried an American hand grenade, the other an American 45, the same kind of gun that had just killed him.

Zach climbed the smoking tank and looked down the turret. The bloodied driver and tank commander were dead, killed by an American fragmentation grenade. Fortunately, the three other crew members were outside of the tank.

A newly arrived tank officer, tears streaming down his face, cautiously approached Bruno and Zach as the medics arrived. "Thanks for trying to warn us. Those men are our first casualties."

"Welcome to the war, Lieutenant," Zach said dryly.

The word spread quickly and there were no more lapses in security.

*****

On day two in Braunschweig, a happy John Naylor was dry-running a brand new M-3 halftrack while the rest of the squad was out exploring the subdued city. It was then they made the find of the war—deep, cavern-like cellars under the central city stacked with thousands of bottles of French wine looted by the Germans. Better yet, there were enormous wooden vats of brandy, schnapps, and several unknown demons. Lines formed almost immediately and the 3rd Squad found itself in the liquor business. Cups, canteens, even Jerry cans were pressed into service and filled with every variety of alcohol. An officer's small liquor ration could not compete with some of the vintage red wines, and soon they too visited the liquor store.

"What the hell, we're in reserve," was the shout as a war-weary group of young men started to party.

Sergeant Gates was about to try his first sip of something called kümmel when Grinnell and Ricks arrived. "What the hell is going on here?" Grinnell demanded.

Zach finished his sip and grimaced. "Sir, the USO is distributing some new kinds of Coca-Cola."

Norm Ricks chuckled. "Come on, Russ, you like Coca-Cola, don't you?"

Russ Grinnell frowned and pushed his way past Ricks into the cellar entrance. A few minutes later he emerged carrying two bottles of wine. A false grin accompanied his explanation. "These are for the battalion commander."

"Hartman prefers champagne," Zach kidded.

"Watch it, Gates, or I'll hide your new track."

"Too late, Lieutenant. Naylor already found it."

"Try not to blow it up."

"You can count on it. Try a hit of this kümmel."

"Ugh, bad stuff. Now here's a fine wine."

Zach agreed and the three old friends lit cigarettes and drained the two bottles. Norm Ricks stood up with a slight lean. "I'm going after a fine white wine this time…if I could only find a swordfish steak."

"Bring a couple extra bottles," Grinnell bellowed.

Several bottles later, Zach had trouble standing up and his lips seemed unusually slack. "I think I'm over my limit…I feel a little woozy…I have to hit the sack."

"Stick around, Zach. We haven't hit the champagne yet."

"Good night, party boys…maybe tomorrow."

The party raged on for one more day and night before the MPs arrived and closed down the free liquor store. The monster party was over and all the troops in Braunschweig had one colossal hangover.

*****

The sun was already up when Zach opened his bleary eyes, struggled to his feet, splashed water on his tired face, and looked in the mirror. "Oh, you are beautiful, Zachary Gates."

Tom Sander laughed. "I'm in better shape than you are, booze guzzler.

I'm going to check out the mail. I'll get yours."

"Don't shout," Zach grumbled.

Tom returned with a copy of *Stars and Stripes* plus a letter for Zach. "I ran into Russ Grinnell."

"He's gotta be hurting," Zach said with a wry smile.

"I'll say. He looks awful and he just barfed."

Zach managed a weak laugh while opening his letter. Tom moved closer. "What's in the letter?"

"Read your own," Zach groaned.

"I didn't get any."

"Tough stuff."

"Come on, Zach."

"Okay…it's from a girl I'd die for."

"Joy? The one with all the boyfriends?"

Zach felt his aching head. "Yeah. I must be number twenty."

"Let me see that," retorted Tom.

"Okay, okay, she says I'm number one."

"Why are you playing so hard to get?"

Zach paused, cleared his head, and mumbled, "Because I'm a jerk…I don't know…after Ken was killed, I wondered if I, or any of us, would ever get home. It didn't seem fair."

Tom faced him directly. "Zach, that's a crock and you are a jerk. You're the one who's unfair."

Zach held his head and groaned, "You're a big help—and don't shout."

"I'm not shouting. Damn it, Zach, the war is almost over. Hell, it's still party time."

Zach painfully reflected on the pre-party troubles and grumbled, "Some party. Bruno shoots two teenagers, two tankers are dead, a stupid binge, and now this colossal hangover. It can't get much worse."

"Oh yes it can, Sergeant Gates," announced 1st Sergeant Bob Klein, entering the room.

Zach covered his ears. "Bob, I don't want to hear it."

"You'll hear it, party boy. The whole drunken division is needed in the Harz. You have twenty minutes to get ready for a forced march to Blankenburg."

Zach squinted in disbelief. "Judas Priest, Klein, this outfit isn't ready to fight."

"We won't have to. It's just a show of strength to get some Nazi general to surrender. Now get your drunken squad off its ass."

Zach stood up. "This is crazy, Bob. Get those green independent tank companies to show off."

"They moved out, except those who are falling down drunk."

"How come you're so damn chipper?" Zach asked wearily.

"I know how to drink, school boy. Move it!"

"Thanks a lot," Zach groaned and looked at Tom Sander. "Sandy, get Bruno and the squad on their feet. I have to check with Norm Ricks."

"Yes, sir. Jesus, I hope Naylor can see to drive."

"Go! And don't shout."

"Okay, okay."

Zach ran to headquarters where the briefing had already started. The CO was speaking. "The Nazi calling for this show is one Lieutenant General Walther Lucht, a bigger egoist than his cousin, Heinrich Himmler, who we met back in the Saar."

"What kind of show?" asked red-eyed Russ Grinnell.

Blackie looked at the lieutenant and frowned. "A show of strength and professional soldiering. He wants two hundred tanks lined up outside of town for his dramatic surrender."

"Oh for Christ's sake," grumbled a hungover lieutenant.

"Captain, the whole division can't field two hundred tanks," sputtered another officer.

"A garrison review? Today? Not a chance," griped a third.

Blackie bristled. "Enough crap. Suck it up and get ready to move out. Corps thinks if we scrounge up fifty tanks, fifty halftracks, some M-7s, and some trucks we can satisfy this asshole."

"Captain, my whole platoon is hungover," pleaded a bleary-eyed platoon sergeant.

"Sorry, Sergeant. The men will have to sober up on the march. Use substitute drivers if you have to. That's all."

*****

A call went out to the 2nd Platoon squad sergeants. Russ Grinnell dragged himself to the meeting. "Sergeant Ricks, take over. I don't know what this crazy maneuver is all about, and my frickin head is about to explode."

Sergeant Ricks found only four tired drivers; two of those were substitutes. One track and fifteen men had to be left behind. The other platoons had similar problems. After an agonizingly slow assembly and vehicle lineup, the tired, griping, sad-sack soldiers mounted up and moved out on the fifty-kilometer march to the Harz Mountains.

Blankenburg, a picturesque city nestled at the foot of the mountains, was defended by a half-ring of outer defenses up in the hills and an inner ring within the town itself—a tough nut to crack if the Germans chose to fight. The show of strength was put in motion. All vehicles were ordered onto the ridge where they could be seen by the town's defenders. This stand-for-show exercise became a hysterical circus of huge bumper cars. With hung over, substitute, sick, and tired drivers, the heavy vehicles weaved, spun, reversed, and clanked together in an almost comic way.

"Boy, I'll bet the Germans are impressed," Sergeant Ricks said in disgust as the odd assortment of vehicles finally achieved some kind of order.

"I hope it's enough," Zach said pessimistically.

"We look like shit," Ricks griped while holding his head.

"Hell, Norm, this is a tough show cold sober."

"Shut up, Gates. You're not helping me."

*****

A truce team marched out to midfield to accept the German general's surrender. A few minutes later, they turned around.

"Hold it. The truce team is back and the corps colonel looks mad as hell," Grinnell grumbled.

The full colonel had strongly demanded an immediate surrender since he had demonstrated overwhelming strength. The German officer reported that General Lucht was insulted by the demonstration put on either by inept or drunken troops. German military tradition prevented him from surrendering without a fight.

Another meeting was called at midfield. This time the American colonel spelled out in no uncertain terms what lay in store for the general and the lovely city of Blankenburg. General Lucht's reply was a real slap in the face. He wanted one hundred tanks, not the mixed vehicles driven by drunks. "Chutzpah," Goldman called it.

The American corps commander was rapidly losing his patience. He ordered a platoon of tanks to fire five rounds each at non-strategic targets.

Still no surrender response.

Next, an impressive volley from the mobile artillery. Again, no response.

The corps commander, reluctant to commit his hung-over troops, tried another show of strength. He ordered a squadron of P-47s to do a fly-over. During the wait on the Tactical Air Command, K rations were delivered. With the help of food, the bleary-eyed soldiers began to regain their composure.

"I thought 1st Army had two divisions chasing this clown,"

Lieutenant Grinnell said.

"They do, the 104th Timberwolves and the veteran Big Red One, but they are bogged down in the steep hills. It's a great place for defense and a lousy place for attack," Captain Black growled.

"What kind of strength does this general have?" Lieutenant Grinnell asked.

"Colonel Hartman says he has what's left of the 11th Panzer Army plus escapees from the Ruhr pocket—about seventy thousand men," Captain Black replied.

"What about the regiment from the 116th Panzers that got past us?"

"They're a problem if they saved their tanks."

"Yeah, they could hurt somebody," Lieutenant Grinnell groaned, peering through his field glasses.

During the wait on the Thunderbolts, the 9th Army Psychological Warfare Section decided to get into the act. They set up a public address system and loudly demanded that the city surrender. Still no white flags of surrender appeared, nor even a flag of truce. The tension and confusion rose to an even higher level with their next stratagem. They brought the bürgormeister from the nearby captured town of Westerhausen to plead the Allied case. At last another flag of truce showed and the bürgormeister and his assistant were dispatched to midfield.

The two politicians did not return, but two representatives of groups wishing to surrender did. The first group represented a service company of the proud 116th Panzers. They asked only to see an *ehrlick nuchtern* (respectably sober) show of strength. The second, a lone sergeant major, wanted the same plus a halfway meeting with his commander and the American officer in charge.

The livid corps commander did not wait for a translation. "If that son-of-a-bitch wants a show of strength, he's going to get it!"

The P-47s were now overhead doing an impressive flyover. They were summarily ordered to bomb and strafe an open area just past midfield.

The display elicited no response! The German general was still not impressed.

ATTACK!

The American commander went ballistic. "Clear the area. We attack this son-of-a-bitch NOW!"

Orders came down swiftly. Two battalions of mobile artillery were ordered to fire directly into the city. The 85th and B Company would maintain positions on the ridge while the 94th Armored Infantry Battalion, supported by a tank battalion, attacked from the south.

Difficult terrain and unexpected heavy resistance further slowed the rushed, understrengthed and hungover 94th Battalion. The frustrated American commander called for Hartman's 85th Battalion to attack in force from the northeast. The P-47s had not reported any enemy tanks, so Colonel Hartman ordered his now-famous marching fire tactic. Companies A and B divided up the access streets on the northeast side of the city. C Company stood in reserve. The lead tracks poured a steady stream of hard-hitting 50-caliber rounds down the streets. The Germans clearly were not expecting such a bold and aggressive action. White flags appeared after only a few blocks of advance. However, the prisoners cleverly blocked any rapid advance by filling the streets, thereby allowing many of their units time to withdraw into the Harz.

"Bastards, even when they give up, they beat you," Sergeant Nitchke snorted.

Once past the prisoners, B Company roared through the city to the foothills of the Harz Mountains. There they were forced to dismount and push forward on foot.

"Poor tank country, Norm. Where are we headed?" Zach asked.

"Mt. Brocken, the highest peak, about thirty seven hundred feet tall Grinnell says."

"Oh, happy day. How far?"

"Ask Russ, here he comes."

Lieutenant Grinnell pulled himself together and stretched out his map. "Looks like fifteen kilometers from Blankenburg. From here I'd guess two or three kilometers."

Ricks looked over his shoulder. "Really rotten terrain. What's our mission?"

His sense of duty wearing thin, Grinnell shot back, "To take the heat off a company from the 1st Infantry Division and then climb Mt. Brocken."

*****

Meanwhile, the 83rd Infantry Division of Ragtag Circus fame had plunged further into the pocket from the north. The 104th Ozarks and the 1st Infantry Divisions, deep in the pocket, were now surrounded by the Germans, the American 83rd Infantry Division, and the 18th Armored Division. B Company headed out toward the mountain and the embattled company from the 1st Infantry.

"I hear shooting. We must be getting close," said Norm Ricks.

"Here come our scouts. Wave 'em over here, Zach. They're your guys," ordered Grinnell.

Tony came running. "What's up, Tony?" Zach asked.

"Two dead German tracks. Bazookas got 'em."

"Where are the krauts?"

Tony took a deep breath. "Everywhere."

Zach frowned. "Come on."

Tony exhaled and replied, "It looks like they've surrounded these infantry guys. Ask Brenner. He was farther forward."

Brenner rushed over, breathing hard. "Tony's right. I think the Big Red One is low on ammunition. Most of the shooting is coming from the Germans."

"Do the krauts know we're here?" Zach asked.

John caught his breath. "I don't think so. They're looking the other way."

"How do you know that?"

"That's what my gut says."

"What do you think, Gates?" Norm Ricks asked.

"Well, Tony and John are experienced point scouts."

Ricks turned to his lieutenant. Grinnell made a quick assessment. "Let's go get 'em from the rear, but let 'em withdraw so we don't shoot up the 1st Infantry grunts."

"Bring the machine gun squad up here," Ricks ordered. The base of fire was quietly established without alerting the Germans. "Rifle squads on line. We go when the machine guns lift their fire. I want everybody shooting. Zach, get your BAR man up front."

"I'm on it, Norm."

"Okay, commence firing."

After a few minutes of 30-caliber machine gun fire, the surprised Germans were totally confused. Some ran toward Mt. Brocken, directly into the rest of the 1st Infantry who used up their last rounds with telling effect. A few diehards returned fire, but were met with another blast from the American machine gun squad. The rifle squads moved forward, firing as they went. The Germans had finally had enough. The ones who had not been hit quickly surrendered.

Despite their difficult and dangerous mission, the trapped company from the 1st Division somehow managed to knock out two small armored cars. The men of the Big Red One warned B Company about the hellish German tactic of offering to surrender and then disappearing into the gorges and ravines. Later, they would double back and attack from the rear. B Company took note and pushed through to within one thousand yards of the big mountain where General Lucht and his stubborn German defenders had now retreated.

"They sure have the high ground," Grinnell observed. "How many do you think?"

"Two broken companies at best," Ricks guessed.

"Do they have artillery up there?"

Zach arrived and raised his glasses. "I'd guess mortars, Lieutenant. They're firing right now at our guys on the left flank."

Grinnell, now feeling better, joked, "I thought the noise was in my head."

Zach forced a smile. "That was very good wine, Lieutenant."

"Very funny, smartass bookworm!" Grinnell replied coldly.

Norm Ricks interceded and said sullenly, "So what do we tell Blackie?"

Grinnell groaned and responded wearily, "Ask General John J. Jones."

Zach grimaced and said uneasily, "Well, they're within range of our mortar squad. Let them shake 'em up till we see if our BC can reach TAC. They're sitting ducks for Thunderbolts."

Lieutenant Grinnell grumbled, "Yeah, yeah," as he radioed the C.O. and said just that. Captain Black replied, "Good call, Russ. Hartman was holding 'em off until he heard we were clear." Zach overheard

Blackie's response. Grinnell groaned and raised his hand. "Gates, just shut up." Zach saluted and walked away.

The IX Tactical Air Command plastered the top of the mountain in a dramatic show of air power. The shaken German survivors now became an easy mission. General Lucht and his senior officers had nowhere to turn and were forced to surrender, not to a general, but to an armored company captain. The arrogant, duty-bound general and successor to Field Marshall Kesserling remarked with pride at his formal internment that he was the last of his 11th Panzer Army to be captured and "that was as it should be."

The battle for the Harz was over. For once, B Company had zero casualties. A very tired, bleary-eyed group of young soldiers returned to the battered city of Blankenburg for some much needed sleep. The party boys who had missed the show rejoined B Company and were promptly put on guard duty. "It's an honor, you drunks."

FREE GUNS

The following morning, B Company mounted up and headed for Halberstadt, Germany, thirty kilometers northeast. The men were billeted in a recreation area near an intact, picturesque estate. A palatial log lodge stood surrounded by several elegant cottages. Obviously, the war had missed this place.

"Some big shots hung out here," Bruno proclaimed.

Bashford entered the lodge through a window and unlocked the huge entrance door. The walls inside were covered with dramatically posed pictures. "These people look like stage and screen stars," Tom remarked.

"Yeah, probably came from Berlin," Zach replied.

"This must have been their retreat," John said.

"Sarge, can you read what it says on these artsy pictures?" Stosh asked.

"Well, let's see." Zach was reading and translating some of the citations when a shout came from another room in the immense lodge.

"Sergeant Gates, get a look at this!" A gun room holding rack after rack of mint-condition hunting rifles and fowling guns had been discovered.

"Make damn sure they're not booby trapped," Gates commanded. He pulled a 7.7-mm Mauser off the wall and carefully tested the bolt action.

"Looks like a keeper to me, Zach," said Bash, an avid sportsman for all of his life in Virginia.

"Yeah, Bash, but how will we ever get 'em home?"

"If the army post office ever catches up to us, maybe," Bash said, pulling an 8-mm Mauser off the wall. Zach slung his Mauser over his shoulder. "All these guns have slings," Bash observed.

By now, the platoon was shouldering guns like drunks in a free liquor store. "Two to a customer," Zach shouted, fearing he would otherwise have a free-for-all. He found an engraved, double-barreled Mueller action shotgun. "What do you think of this baby, Bash?"

Bash examined the piece. "Christ, every screw and bolt head is engraved and look at the ebony inlays." Zach slung the 16-gauge over his shoulder and eyed another Mauser.

"Hey, you said two to a customer," Bruno grumbled.

The ranking man in the room, Zach shot back, "*RHIP*."

The gun party came to a screeching halt when Colonel Hartman and Captain Black entered the lodge. Zach motioned to gun-fancier Bashford. "Put these guns in the track," he whispered. Bash slipped out a back door as the two officers inspected the gun room.

"I'm sorry, men. Corps orders are to destroy all military and sporting small arms. The Werewolves and Hitler Jungend are collecting these guns and using them to prolong the war."

A sub-audible groan echoed throughout the lodge. "At ease," Captain Black ordered. "Sergeant Gates, I want all of the guns in this room, I mean all of them, out on the road in fifteen minutes."

"Yes, sir. You mean all of the guns in this room?"

"That's what I said, Sergeant! Now hop to."

The disgruntled men hauled out the guns and rifles, laying them in two parallel lines on the road. Then came the crushing rumble of a thirty-two-ton Sherman tank. "I can't look at this," said another gun lover, Tony Holter.

The troops moaned as they watched a fortune in hand-tooled sporting weapons cracking and groaning as they became metal scrap and wooden splinters, crushed and ground up by the thirty-two-ton steel tank treads. Pfc. Bashford walked silently past Sergeant Gates and simply blinked his eyes. Holter smiled at Zach. "He's one good soldier."

"Who?"

"Bash, you crook."

"What? My guns were *not* in this room."

"You should go into law."

LANGSAMO

On to the village of Wernigerode, Germany, where gas trucks were to meet B Company just outside of town. Naylor wheeled the smooth-running, new halftrack into an open field. Three hundred yards down the road stood six houses, all appearing to be abandoned. Zach ordered a close inspection of the area, since refueling was an especially dangerous time. Gas trucks were favorite targets, easily blown up by a single German incendiary. The squad found the first five houses empty. Zach and Stosh casually approached the last house. Stosh looked in the open kitchen door and quickly retreated. Wide-eyed, he reported, "Sarge, there's two old kraut soldiers in there drinking schnapps or something."

"Cover me, Stosh. I'll check 'em out."

Zach slung his rifle, drew his Luger from its shoulder holster, and entered the kitchen. One hard look showed that the Germans were in no condition to fight. They were slumped in their chairs with their weapons stacked in a corner of the room. They stared expressionless at two half-empty bottles on the table between them, paying little attention to Zach. Zach pointed his Luger at the floor and took a step closer. *"Guten tag, mein herr."* The two *feldwebels* (staff sergeants) smiled ever so slightly while each took another sip of schnapps.

Zach assessed them more carefully: about thirty-five, veteran *panzer-grenadiers* (armored infantry) from the 116th Panzer Division. They were hopelessly drunk and thoroughly defeated. For a brief moment, Zach saw himself. *Poor bastards...they just don't give a shit anymore.*

Stosh gingerly entered the kitchen. "Are you okay, Sarge?"

"Everything's fine, Stosh." Zach pointed to the weapons in the corner. "Get their weapons, move quietly, and withdraw."

One of the weary veterans crumpled an empty cigarette pack as Stosh left the kitchen. "*Scheiss,*" he muttered. Zach holstered his Luger, reached in his pocket, and pulled out a fresh pack of Lucky Strikes. He stepped forward and dropped the pack on the table. "*Gute Gluck.* (Good luck.)" The closer soldier fondled the pack and mumbled, "*Ja.*"

Zach backed toward the door. He was about to turn and step out when he heard a quiet, "*Danke, sehr.*" Zach paused, took a last look at his older counterparts, and replied, "*Langsamo* (take it easy)," turned, and left the two old soldiers to their quietude.

MUNCHOFF: REST AREA?

After the final surrender of General Lucht and the rest of the 11th Panzer Army, the 18th Armored headed east. Weary B Company arrived at Munchoff, Germany on April 24 with a promised ten-day stand-down. The Berlin battle was now left to the Russians and, hopefully, the fanatical Werewolves would give it up, seeing that the last of the 11th Panzer Army had surrendered. The American troops were optimistic that the war would end soon. "In the next two or three weeks," Tom announced confidently.

Munchoff was a pleasant small town with a central park, woods, and rolling hills. "Good place to wait out the end of this wretched war," Brenner said.

"Kind of like the Kettle Moraine back in southern Wisconsin," Zach mused.

Many small hotels covered this once-popular tourist town and Zach moved his squad into one of them. He took over the small lobby and the best first floor room. Rank has its privileges. His room overlooked a tranquil meadow and hedgerows leading to a railroad siding some five hundred or six hundred yards beyond. The company had barely settled in for its vacation when area reconnaissance was ordered.

"No mail or chow until the area is secure," came the word from Captain Black. Griping was minimal, since the mess and mail trucks had not yet appeared.

The 1st and 3rd Squads were given responsibility for the east side of town plus the two dozen boxcars on the rail siding. The patrol became more of a stroll in the park as men chatted and smoked with their rifles comfortably slung over their shoulders. Even the German citizens, most of whom elected to remain in town, seemed hospitable. They felt the war, for them at least, was over. Army special services had distributed volleyballs and nets, a good sign for sure.

Zach's 3rd Squad began leisurely inspecting the train cars on the left while the 1st Rifle Squad inspected cars on the right. The rest of the platoon strolled around town. A shout came from one of the cars on the left and Zach walked over.

"What the hell is all this stuff?" Stosh Kosinski asked.

Zach climbed into the car, read some labels, and sniffed the contents. "The smoking light is out!" he shouted. "This is black powder!" Everyone scrambled out and quickly snuffed their cigarettes when another shout came from a car far down the lines where a similar load had been found.

"How bad is this stuff, Gates?" Sergeant Nitchke asked.

"I'm not sure, but it's tons of gunpowder. No smoking, Bruno."

Zach alerted headquarters and asked for an ordinance evaluation and/or disposal team on the double. Other than the two dangerous boxcars, the patrols found nothing to raise concern.

"A shit job for ordinance," snorted Bruno.

*****

Back in town, Zach located Babe 3. There lay his three sporting weapons. "Good old Bash." A window box became a crate. Two tablecloths from the hotel provided the wrap. Zach carried the box to headquarters, addressed it, and handed it to Corporal Wing. "See that this gets to Milwaukee."

"I'll give it to the mail guy, but it's a crapshoot. What ya got in there?"

"Tablecloths for my mother."

Jim looked skeptical. "Damn heavy tablecloths. You wouldn't have guns in there, would you?"

"None of your business," Zach replied with a guilty smile.

Jim flashed an Irish grin and said with a lilt, "Okay, Gates. I'll see that your *tablecloths* get on the truck."

"Thanks, Jim. Where's my mail?"

"Tom took yours."

"Where?"

"Try the church."

Zach found his squad waiting impatiently for a hot meal as they watched the mess sergeant happily setting up his kitchen in the church guildhall. It was party and relaxation time again but this time without the alcohol. Zach found Naylor, Bash, Brenner, and Sander sitting in soft chairs in a corner of the church lobby.

"Where you been, Zach?" Tom asked.

"Mailing souvenirs."

"You dirty dog. You shipped those rifles, didn't you?"

Zach raised his eyebrows and replied briskly, "What rifles? Where's my mail?"

Tom reached under his chair. "You got a bunch." He studied the envelopes.

Zach scowled. "Damn it, Tom, give me my mail."

"Okay, okay, but tell me what Joy says."

"You mean you didn't read it?"

"No, you got here too soon."

Zach took Joy's letter and started to read. "Well, it's none of your business, but she does say she's anxious for me to come home."

"That's a good sign."

"Yeah."

Bash picked up his *Stars and Stripes* newspaper. "According to this article, Berlin is now totally encircled by the Russians under Marshal Zukov."

"How close are they?"

"On this little map I'd guess the circle is ten or twelve miles one way and eight or ten the other. One hell of a battle is going on. The Russians are taking heavy casualties."

"Will they get Hitler?"

"He's probably on his way to South America."

"I doubt it. He'll never get out."

"He'd better commit suicide. The Russians will cut him up for souvenirs. It says here the battle may be the biggest bloodbath of the war," Bash added.

Zach's mind filled with disaster images. He choked, "I'm glad we're sitting this one out."

"Yeah. We were scheduled to lead the attack with the 2nd Armored," Bruno grunted.

"Dinner is served," someone called from the church dining hall.

"My God, tables and chairs and church china. What's for dinner?"

"SOS and Army Swiss steak. Even the mat-gray gravy looks good."

After the first sit-down dinner since England, a lively discussion ensued. John Naylor started it. "The hell with Berlin. I'm thinking about going home."

"You mean, on your way to the Pacific Theater," cracked Corporal

Jim Wing.

"Hell, let the marines win that one," Bash replied.

"What do you bookworms think?" Stosh asked.

Zach hesitated. "We still haven't met the bulk of the Japanese Army. They're in China and Japan."

Brenner nodded. "I'm with Zach. The Japanese are not caving in. It's going to be another year or two of war."

"Boy, I'm sorry I asked," Stosh groaned.

"So what are you going to do, Zach?" Goldman asked.

Zach thought for a moment and said half-seriously, "I'm putting in for a transfer to the air corps."

"You're all nuts. This war over here is almost over, and the Japs will fold when they hear about it," Naylor said, hoping for the final word.

Zach shrugged. "I hope you're right, John."

"Maybe Naylor is right," Tom said, pointing to the *Stars and Stripes*. "It says here, 'The British are almost to Hamburg and Mussolini has been strung up by the heels by his own people.'"

Brenner yawned out loud. "It's getting late, guys. Go get some sleep. We got a volleyball game tomorrow."

*****

The next morning, Zach was called to company headquarters about three blocks away. A fourteen-year-old German soldier accompanied by his mother had arrived to surrender. Anticipating language problems, Captain Black had invited Zach to the unusual occasion. A major from Battalion S-2 was in charge. Zach, it turned out, was not needed—the boy and his mother had lived in England before the war and both spoke English.

The young boy, in a uniform two sizes too big, not only looked ridiculous but was also scared to death. His mother was carrying his rifle. "How long have you been in the army?" the major from S-2 asked.

"One week, Herr Major. I've never fired my rifle," he replied as tears streamed down his cheeks. Before anyone could respond, the boy's mother intervened. In perfect English she pleaded her son's case. She pointed to their home less than a block away. "I will not let him out of the house until the war is over."

The mellow, war-weary Americans came to a quick decision. "Hell, the war is almost over. Let the poor kid go," the major pronounced.

"Yes, sir," Captain Black responded.

The major pointed his finger at the boy. "Carl, dump the uniform. Go home and stay there." Only Sergeant Gates, the unnecessary translator, had any second thoughts. Both the Braunschweig teenagers and the episode with the wooden bullets still haunted him.

The boy and his mother rushed out of the room as Sergeant Norm Ricks entered. "Bad news, gentlemen. One of Lieutenant Grinnell's patrols reports Werewolves in the area. He's on your phone line, Captain Black."

Blackie headed for his field phone while the others hurried back to their units. He looked up, phone in hand. "Gates, squad leaders' meeting. Grinnell wants you right now."

"Yes, sir. Where?"

"Your place."

IRREGULARS

"At ease; stop your griping," Ricks barked as the squad leaders assembled.

Grinnell waited for quiet. "It may not be serious. A displaced Pole reported three German soldiers sleeping in a barn about five or six kilometers from here."

"That's a relief. We don't need these roving gangs of fifty or more."

Grinnell looked toward Norm Ricks. "Norm, at 0530 tomorrow I want you to take the 1st and 2nd Squads over there and check these out. Oh, and take this new replacement, Staff Sergeant Ron Hutten, with you."

"Is he the guy from Ft. Knox?"

"Right. He's been training cadre for almost five years and has been asking for overseas duty most of that time."

"Is he nuts?"

"No, he's a good soldier and wants to make the army his career. He's even applied for West Point."

"He's gotta be nuts," Ricks snorted.

"Whatever. Let him shoot a round in the air and try to get back by lunch time."

"Yes, sir, no problem."

*****

At 0530, Ricks found the barn, dismounted the two squads, and followed the Polish DP to the building. He signaled replacement Sergeant Hutten to come forward. They were about to enter the barn when an SS officer showed himself just fifty yards away. The Werewolf distraction worked. Small arms fire erupted from the opposite direction. A sniper's bullet caught newly arrived Sergeant Hutten squarely in the chest. He went down as if he had been clubbed. The rest of the men hit the dirt and returned fire. A track driver, standing in the ring of his track, had a clear view of the woods from where the firing was coming. He quickly manned the 50-caliber and opened fire, forcing the Werewolves to withdraw.

Ricks rolled Hutten over and he simmered with rage. A sniper's mushroom bullet had exploded in Sergeant Hutten's heart, soaking his uniform with blood. He had died instantly. Norm Ricks looked to the other flank. "Son of a bitch! I'll kill those bastards!" Calling on his speed as a track star, he took off after the German officer while the radioman put in a call for assistance, since the size of the irregular force was unknown.

Within minutes, Ricks caught up with the renegade officer and two other irregulars. At ten yards, he fired his Colt 45 at the slowest man. The heavy round caught him in the shoulder, spinning him around. He raised his weapon to fire—Ricks fired a second round which plowed through the soldier's chest. The shocking power of the heavy slug knocked the runner off his feet and rammed him to the ground, the life pounded out of him.

Ricks took up the chase. When he was within fifty feet of the second man, he fired two quick rounds while still running. Both missed. He closed to within twenty feet, stopped, and fired. This round slammed the runner to the ground with the bullet entering through his neck and coming out of his mouth. Ricks slowed. The man was dead. He was about to take up the chase again when he saw that the renegade SS officer had stopped and was aiming a handgun at him. Ricks dropped behind the body of the dead man, the only cover available. Two rounds whistled over his head. He looked up and returned fire. Both shots were wild. The renegade was running again. Ricks continued the chase. The gap closed quickly—the exhausted, outmatched Werewolf slowed, turned, and raised his weapon.

Ricks stopped, held his breath, and leveled his Colt 45. *Have I fired seven rounds? Eight? Did I have one in the chamber? No time to change clips....* He pressed the trigger and was rewarded by a blast. Praise God, one round had been left. The massive bullet entered the man's mouth, killing him instantly. The extra bullet in the chamber had saved Sergeant Norman Ricks's life.

*****

Back in Munchoff, Zach received an urgent call to get his 3rd Squad on line. Lieutenant Grinnell had wisely requested two ambulances from the aid station. When Sergeant Gates and Babe 3 arrived on line, the fight was already over. Norm Ricks, still breathing hard, was sitting on a boulder toying with a Luger pistol. "The bastards set us up, Zach. These assholes killed two of our men…one is poor, eager Sergeant Hutten."

Zach walked over to Hutten's body. The medics had covered his exploded chest with a large bandage which was now also soaked in blood. He looked at Hutten's contorted face and felt sick. "I'm sorry, Ron…you never had a chance. What rotten luck."

Norm Ricks came over, his breathing still labored and his body shaking. Zach put his arm around his good friend. "You did good, Norm. Are you okay?"

"Yeah. I just need a few minutes. I outran that butcher and two of his Nazi friends. They're all history."

The medics picked up two more dead Germans and one seriously wounded American. Russ Grinnell checked out the casualties and then joined Ricks and Gates. "Well done, Ricks. I'm putting you in for the Silver Star."

"Put Hutten in for something. He took the hit."

"Should we be pursuing these guys?" Zach asked.

"No, we'll never find them in this terrain," Ricks replied as he put a fresh clip in his 45.

"Any idea how many there were?"

Ricks stood up. "From the fire power, it had to be thirty or forty, but who knows?"

Grinnell signaled for the men to mount up after the medics had completed their unhappy task. "Let's shake up the people in any buildings between here and Munchoff. Somebody is feeding and supplying these nuts."

Zach's squad mounted up and took a longer route back to Munchoff to cover more ground. They came upon a platoon of unarmed, war-weary Wehrmacht who were carrying a white flag, eager to surrender. Zach steered them toward the MPs in Munchoff. The squad dismounted and proceeded up the small logging trail where the Germans had emerged.

"No SS or Werewolves in that group," Sergeant Nitchke observed as he directed two new replacements to take the point.

Zach caught up with Bruno. "Send somebody to baby-sit those green kids."

"Good idea. Pappy, keep an eye on our scouts."

Within minutes, Pappy hurried back. "Looks like twelve or more krauts want to surrender." Zach and Bruno followed Pappy back up the trail. Pappy raised his hand. "About one hundred yards ahead."

Zach raised his field glasses. "Bruno, what do you think?" He handed him the glasses.

"I have a bad feeling about these irregulars. Pappy, go get our scouts out of there."

"I can't see any weapons and the officer out front has a white flag, but their formation looks suspicious," Zach warned.

"Yeah, remember France when they faked a surrender?"

"Let's move up, Bruno. Get the squad off the trail and in firing position. I don't like this."

Bruno gave the signals silently and quickly returned. "We're set."

"Good. Bruno, where the hell are our two scouts?"

Bruno borrowed Zach's glasses. "Damn, they didn't wait on Pappy. Oh Christ."

"Now what?"

"They're moving up to take them prisoner."

"Hit the dirt!" Zach shouted as the Werewolf fanatics on either side of the officer fell prone, exposing machine guns attached to their backs, which were instantly manned. The heavy concentration of fire at close range tore through the bodies of the two scouts, knocking them to the ground in an ugly, bloody mess. Using the machine guns as cover, the remaining Werewolves charged ahead brandishing hidden handguns. They assumed the squad was still centered on the trail.

"*FIRE! FIRE! BASHFORD! GOLDMAN! Get on 'em!*" Zach screamed. Before his shout ended, the deadly BAR was rattling and the Springfield was cracking. Goldman got the prone machine gunners with two quick head shots. Deployed rifle fire then took its toll. Within minutes, half of the Werewolves were cut down and the rest had their hands in the air.

Pappy was in tears. "They didn't listen to me."

Zach was furious. "Not your fault, Pappy—get out of my way!" He sprinted to the still defiant SS officer. Anger erupted as he looked at the two mangled, bloody, dead Americans, kicked the fallen white flag, and faced the arrogant fanatic. "*Verruckta Arshlock!* (Crazy asshole!)" screamed Zach. In a rage, he crashed the butt of his M-1 to the Werewolf's jaw, knocking him to the ground. His jaw was broken; blood spurted from his mouth. Zach screamed, "*He killed two of my men for no reason, no reason at all!*" He faced his equally incensed squad. "*Get this asshole out of my sight before I kill him!*" he shrieked.

A new war correspondent, anxious to write a story on the Werewolves, sped up in a jeep and rushed over to the stormy scene. "Jesus, Sergeant, what have you done? They have a white flag."

Zach went manic. He slung his M-1, jerked his Luger from its holster, and jammed it under the reporter's chin. "Look at the two krauts with the machine guns on their backs, shithead. Then check those two dead Americans—and don't breathe or you'll be as dead as they are."

The shaken reporter looked at the scouts, their shattered bodies lost in pools of blood. Ashen-faced, he sank to his knees, tears streaming down his cheeks. The tragic, emotional scene was interrupted when Colonel Hartman and the medics arrived. Hartman ignored the sobbing reporter. "Sergeant—situation report."

Zach hyperventilated and struggled to regain his senses. In a distressed voice, he replied, "Sir, two of ours down after a phony surrender. I'm helping this asshole reporter with his story on brutal Americans."

"Very well, Sergeant Gates. Carry on."

The angry squad jerked the now-terrified surviving irregulars to their feet, put guns to their heads, and double-timed them up the trail. Minutes later, shots were heard. The colonel gave Zach a circumspect look, then turned his attention to the panic-stricken reporter, his voice ominous. "You better get the story right!"

The trembling, unstrung novice correspondent wiped his eyes and struggled to regain his voice. "I didn't understand...I can't believe all this violence. I'm sorry...so sorry."

"Did you hear me?" Colonel Hartman snapped.

The nerve-wracked reporter stood up shaking his head. "How do they do this day after day after day?"

"I think you have your title, son. Now do one thing more when you write about these brave young Americans."

"Yes, sir?"

"Use the word 'magnificent.'"

*****

Zach watched the medics attending to the two dead replacements. Both had been shot with multiple bullets, one in the chest, the other in the stomach. It appeared that most of the bullets had gone clear through their bodies. Bloody entrails were strewn on both sides of one soldier's body. Wild Bill stopped Zach from coming any closer. "Zach, you don't want to see this."

Zach felt weak and nauseous for the second time on this long day. He leaned against the ambulance, his head drooping. *I don't even remember their names. What kind of a cold monster have I become? I've put the dead out of my head...even Ken Whedder. When will this nightmare end?* He stood back as the two bodies were loaded into the ambulance. His back and legs stiffened. *Goddamn it, I'm not giving in to these sons of bitches! Don't anybody push me.*

*****

A very quiet group arrived late at the Company B mess call. One of the men killed had been with the division since it was activated in 1942, the two green replacements for less than a week. Eager Sergeant Ron Hutten was killed in this, his first combat action. His planned military career was over.

The whole company had heard of the tragic encounter. They gave Platoon Sergeant Ricks and the steaming Sergeant Gates a wide berth. The chaplain patted Zach on the back but said nothing. He turned to the other soldiers saying quietly, "Beware the wrath of a patient man. Give him some space."

Lieutenant Colonel George Hartman asked the divisional chaplain to hold an immediate memorial service in the church sanctuary. Captain Black opened the impromptu service with an announcement. "If it's any consolation, intelligence reports the German citizens are much relieved that these *ermordener verbrechener* thugs are *kaput*. The bürgormeister is especially happy to see them go, since they also had a gun to his head."

Chaplain MacArthur's sermon helped calm down some very angry GIs. Zachary swallowed hard and hyperventilated. It had been a very, very long day. AMEN.

Booby Trap

The next morning broke bright and quiet, a mismatch for the happenings of the day before. The heartsick 2nd Platoon had been allowed to sleep in. They were finishing a late breakfast when Corporal Wing, leading two new men, caught up with Zach. "Got you two replacements. They just arrived."

Still shaken from yesterday's torment and heartache, Zach was not expecting replacements so soon—he was barely able to greet the frightened new soldiers. "Don't salute officers in combat areas—snipers love that. If you want to survive, find an old soldier and do what he does."

"How do we find them, sir?"

"Look for a tired guy with a combat infantry badge…" His voice trailed off as he walked away.

"He didn't even ask our names," one replacement choked.

Brenner had been listening. "Sergeant Gates just lost two men. We're all a little down. He'll get you fully oriented before we see our next action. Come on, I'll introduce you to Sergeant Nitchke and the rest of the guys."

An uneasy Corporal Wing came running after Zach. "One more thing, Sergeant Gates," he called out.

"Yeah, what?"

"The captain wants to see you. It's important."

"It's probably about that damn black powder." Sullenly, Zach followed Jim to headquarters.

"Sergeant Gates, I have some good news. You, Ron Hutten, and Sergeant Ricks are to be given medals for this last action. Well done," the captain announced.

"Thank you, Captain Black," Zach said softly as his mind wandered. *A medal? Bruno and I should be sent to the stockade for letting those green kids play scouts. Thank God Pappy survived. I wonder if I've been at this too long...maybe it's time to let somebody else make life-and-death decisions.*

"Gates, hear me!"

"Yes, sir."

"Colonel Hartman wants to make it official at 1300 hours today. A week from now there will be a formal presentation by General Devane at a review in Halberstadt."

"Yes, sir."

Captain Black smiled. "I know it's been tough. Now go shave or Hartman will have you gigged instead."

Zach walked outside where a grinning Corporal Wing offered a sharp salute.

"Knock if off, Wing. I don't have the medal yet, and I'm not sure I deserve it."

At that moment, a command car rolled up and dropped off a demolitions officer and a sergeant. Captain Black rushed outside. "You're late, Lieutenant. That stuff should have been inspected yesterday afternoon."

"Sorry, Captain. We're short-handed. A lot of guys were granted passes."

"Well, get on it."

"We'll need a jeep and a driver, sir."

"Okay. Wing, get the jeep."

"Yes, sir."

Blackie turned to the demolitions officer. "Lieutenant, Sergeant Gates here discovered the stuff and can take you to it." Zach looked at his watch—1230. "Yes, sir. I should still have time to shave."

Blackie nodded and turned to leave.

Jim Wing returned with the jeep. "Zach, I know where those cars are. I was out there yesterday. I'll show them."

"That would help. I'm running late."

"No problem. Can we give you a lift to your hotel?"

"Yeah, thanks." Zach jumped in the jeep and waved a salute at Captain Black, who was about to enter his front door. A few minutes later, Zach jumped out at his hotel where he was greeted by Stosh Kosinski. "Congratulations, Sergeant Gates."

"Yeah. How'd you hear?"

"I had a call from Sergeant Klein when I got stuck with guard duty."

"I'll keep you company for a while, Stosh. Where is everybody?"

"In the park playing volleyball."

"Stosh, I have to shave and change clothes."

"Yeah, you should look good for a medal."

Zach took out his shaving gear, emptied his pockets, and stripped off his shirt. "Damn," he griped as the chain on his dog tags snapped. He put his tags in the shirt pocket of his blouse hanging over a chair. He was about to lather up when Stosh shouted from the lobby window.

"Zach, there's a jeep with three guys heading out to the train."

Zach moved over to the window. "Yeah. Wing is showing the demolition team what we found. They should have been here yesterday."

"They're through the holes in the hedgerows. They're at the first car," Stosh reported.

Zach was just about to check the window when suddenly a huge, silent flash of blinding light followed by an enormous cloud of black smoke caused the entire sky to turn a dull gray. A thundering sound that grew louder and louder followed. In the few seconds of brilliant light, the two shocked soldiers saw a jeep rise eerily into the darkening sky where it then literally evaporated.

When the enormous blast of energy reached the hotel, the building shook violently. The windows blew out and part of the roof caved in. An acrid smell permeated the air. Zach felt stinging pains in his neck and right hand. His back, neck, and arms were covered with glass cuts and bruises.

"*STOSH!*" screamed Zach.

Then he saw Stosh's body blown clear across the room. He rushed over. Stosh was still breathing and partially conscious. Except for a wicked bruise on his forehead, he appeared to be unhurt. "You're okay, Stosh. Stay put and wait for the medics. I have to get some firepower out there. The krauts booby trapped the train."

Stosh felt his bruised head, nodded, and mumbled, "Go."

Zach grabbed his Luger and climbed out of the shattered building half-dressed, convinced that a roving band of Werewolves would use this planned distraction to attack, create havoc, and capture equipment needed to continue their fight.

He saw a group of volleyball players running for their weapons. All of the halftracks were in a central motor pool except for one brought up by the machine gun squad to clean their guns. Zach waved and shouted, "Get that 50 on line!" There was no response. Zach moved forward. As the smoke cleared, he could see small groups of irregulars moving across the tracks. Zach ran to the first hedgerow for a better look. The lead group of four or five Werewolves was getting closer. Zach paled and his mouth went dry as they approached the other side of the hedgerow. No place to run, no place to hide. He released the safety on his Luger.

Meanwhile, the machine gun squad had its halftrack on line and quickly opened fire. Zach and the Werewolves hit the dirt. Then something happened for which the renegades were unprepared. The long-range, blue goose exploding rounds from the 50-caliber struck the second boxcar of black powder, causing another horrendous explosion. The blast was followed by a river of fire rolling toward the hedgerows, searing and burning everything in its path. The intense heat enveloped all of the area as far as the hotel. The Werewolf forces closest to the second boxcar were incinerated or burned beyond recognition. Those approaching Zach's hedgerow also paid dearly. Only one or two reached the rise of the hedgerow. They, with Zach, were lifted into the air and slammed to the ground.

The threat of attack was over. The smoking battlefield went deathly quiet for a very long time before the American battalion medics could venture out.

MIA AND PRESUMED DEAD

Captain Black and 1st Sergeant Klein were assessing American casualties. "Klein, any more news on the men in the jeep?"

"Yes, sir…just burned body parts. They're all dead, sir."

"Then it's four KIA: the two ordinance men and Wing and Gates?"

"Yes, sir."

"Damn, I'll miss Sergeant Gates. Zach knew something about everything…and a cool man under fire," Captain Black declared.

"Yes, sir, and Jim Wing was the best company clerk in the battalion."

The captain spoke in a halting voice. "Poor Gates. What a rotten way to go."

"Yes, sir…without a trace."

"If he'd taken that grunt commission, he'd probably still be alive," Captain Black mumbled.

Klein grunted and changed the subject. "Captain, except for the men in the jeep, we were lucky. The machine gun squad saved our asses when they got their track on line."

"Yeah…"

"And the krauts screwed up when they missed that second boxcar," Klein added.

"Right, Sergeant…thanks. What about our men on guard duty?"

"Just minor wounds. Most have already returned to duty."

"Were any evacuated?"

"I think just two. Four or five are still at the aid station."

"We'll need exact figures, Klein."

"Yes, sir."

"Who were the two men evacuated?"

Sergeant Klein checked his notes. "Pfc. Kosinski, a nasty head wound, and Pfc. Johnson, a new man. I don't know the extent of his injuries."

Captain Black looked out of the window and spoke slowly. "Klein, what about the Germans?"

"Most were burned up or blown to pieces."

"That's *it*?"

"The few we found in one piece died before we got them to the aid station. As you were…two krauts were evacuated."

Norm Ricks and Bruno Nitchke burst into the room. "What about Gates? Was he in the jeep or not?"

Blackie shook his head. "Sorry, men, last time I saw him he was in the jeep."

"The machine gun squad thought they saw someone signaling," Bruno implored.

Again Blackie shook his head. "Nitchke, all I know is I saw him get in the jeep and I told him to show the black powder to the demolitions officer."

"Maybe he got out. Didn't Wing know where the cars were?" Bruno pleaded.

"I don't know, Bruno," Captain Black replied.

"Wing knew everything!" Ricks insisted.

"The machine gun squad saw *somebody*," Bruno asserted.

"Look, facts are we can't find him. At best he's missing in action," declared the 1st sergeant.

The group became very quiet. The captain cleared his throat. "List the two men from ordinance and Corporal Wing—the men we're absolutely sure were in the jeep—as KIA, and Sergeant Gates as MIA."

Sergeant Klein hesitated. "Yes, sir…and presumed dead?"

Captain Black exhaled heavily. "I guess so…we can't find him and nobody saw him get out of the jeep."

"What about the machine gunners?" Bruno pleaded once more.

"If they're right, where is he?" Klein asked.

"I just can't believe he's gone," Ricks lamented.

Ricks and Nitchke were near tears when Russ Grinnell rushed in. "*What?* Is Gates dead or alive?" he demanded.

The 1st sergeant responded quietly, "I'm sorry, Lieutenant. We think he was killed with the others in the jeep."

"Do we know for sure that he was in the jeep?" Grinnell debated.

"Nothing is for sure, Russ. The machine gun squad may have seen somebody," Black reported.

Grinnell huffed, "So how are you listing him?"

"MIA and presumed dead."

"Why not just MIA?" Grinnell argued.

Blackie exhaled and explained, "Russ, nobody saw him get out of the jeep and we can't find him."

Sergeant Klein interceded. "Lieutenant, if Gates wasn't in the jeep, he was in the field with the Germans who were burned up."

Lieutenant Grinnell hung his head and sighed. "I can't believe he's gone...after all we've been through together."

Norm Ricks patted him on the shoulder. "Russ, we're all devastated. Where do we go from here?" Ricks looked toward Sergeant Klein and Captain Black.

Klein paced the floor and replied darkly, "Whatever we do, we better get telegrams out before that dumbass reporter puts it in the newspapers."

After an unnerving pause, the captain concluded, "The presumption is he's dead. I think we must call Gates MIA...and presumed dead."

There was no response. After a painful silence, Lieutenant Grinnell intoned with obvious emotion, "Norm, Bruno, follow me. We have to tell his squad the bad news."

The War Department was notified the next day.

*****

Milwaukee, Wisconsin

It was early May and spring had finally started in this Midwestern homefront. The news improved daily. Berlin had fallen, Hitler was a presumed suicide, the United States armies in Italy had advanced to the Brenner Pass, Mussolini had been strung up by his heels, and the Germans had surrendered in Italy.

On May 7, 1945 came the jubilant news that Eisenhower was in a Reims schoolhouse accepting the unconditional surrender of all German forces. On May 8, the official proclamation was made. After five years, eight months, and six days of bloodshed and destruction, the war in Europe was over. President Truman rejoiced, but he reminded the nation that the war in the Pacific was far from being over.

The people of Milwaukee reacted to the news in two sharply contrasting ways. A noisy minority greeted it with the turbulent enthusiasm of a New Year's Eve celebration. However, the bulk of the city's population responded, like the Gates family, with quiet thankfulness that the war in Europe was won, tempered by the realization that a grim and bitter struggle was still ahead in the Pacific.

A happy family celebration was planned for Wednesday, the ninth of

May. Joy Ricky was included. She arrived absolutely buoyant. Her feet seemed three feet off the ground. At last Zachary was safe, and she was sure he would be home soon.

"Thank God it's over. Zach had the worst job in the army," declared Zach's father.

The group sat down at the dining room table. Sam Gates offered a silent prayer of thanksgiving. The mood picked up quickly as they reviewed the war news and the good times they had with Zach in the past.

"Sam, when can we expect him to write again?" Zach's mother asked.

"Well, if his company is on the road, it may be a while. Maybe he's just too busy celebrating," Sam said with a smile.

"He'd better be doing it with just the guys," said Joy.

An ice cream dessert saved for this kind of special occasion had just been served when they heard a knock at the front door. Sam excused himself and went to the door. He returned with a telegram in his hand. Tears streamed down his face. "It's the worst possible news." In a shaken, broken voice he read the War Department telegram.

THE SECRETARY OF WAR CALLS UPON ME TO EXPRESS HIS DEEP REGRET THAT YOUR SON SSG ZACHARY GATES HAS BEEN MISSING IN ACTION AND NOW PRESUMED DEAD AS OF 01 MAY 45. A VIOLENT EXPLOSION HAS MADE THE RECOVERY OF THOSE INVOLVED IMPOSSIBLE. WITH DEEPEST SYMPATHY

J. A. ULIO THE ADJUTANT GENERAL

The grieving became intense and uncontrollable.

32

MIA AT BEST

Munchoff, Germany

Four days had passed since the explosions. The shaken troops of Company B were still trying to get their lives in order. New billets were found for those unhoused by the explosions. Men who were only slightly wounded and bruised returned from the battalion aid station. The grave detail grimly went about their business of trying to retrieve and identify the German dead, including the Volkssturn, Waffen SS, and Hitler Jungend who were all part of this Werewolf gang. There were still no identifiable body parts of Sergeant Gates, Corporal Jim Wing, the demolitions officer, or the jeep driver.

On the fifth day, Private Stanley Kosinski was released from the evacuation hospital and returned to duty. Sergeant Nitchke rushed him over to company headquarters. "Captain! Stosh says Sergeant Gates was not in the jeep."

"Kosinski, how do you know that?" Captain Black demanded.

"I saw him dropped off at the house. I was on guard duty. We both saw the jeep fly in the air and just disappear."

"You're sure of all this, Private Kosinski?"

"Yes, sir. I talked to Sergeant Gates. He's my close friend."

"Do you have any idea where he went? Or what happened to him? Did he say anything?"

"I remember him bending over me. He said I'd be okay and then said something about firepower."

"Anything else, Stosh?"

"No...I guess I passed out."

"You're damn sure he wasn't in that jeep?"

"Yes, sir."

Sergeant Klein put his hand on Kosinski's shoulder. "How's your head, Stosh?"

"Okay, Sarge. They said I had a concussion and they want to check me later."

"Stosh, can you think of anything else, any little thing that might help us?" Klein asked.

"Nothing, except he was getting ready to shave."

Captain Black shook the private's hand. "You've been a big help, Kosinski. Now get some rest."

Stosh fought back his tears. "Yes, sir…please find him, Captain Black."

After walking Stosh to the door, the captain turned to his 1st sergeant. "I was so damn sure he was in the jeep. See if you can stop that telegram to Gates's family. We now know he wasn't in the jeep… that's something."

"Sorry, sir; the telegram has already been sent."

"Crap! Then we need an instant follow-up explaining that the first message was in error. It should read… what the hell should it read?"

"He's still missing in action, sir."

"I guess. Jesus! Colonel Hartman is going to ream us new assholes."

"Sir, he is still…probably…also KIA."

"We said he was in the jeep."

"No, sir, we said he was in a violent explosion."

"Same thing. We should have checked on Kosinski."

"We did, sir. Kosinski was unconscious or under sedation for three days."

"Damn. Klein, prepare a new telegram. Say that he was not at the center of the explosion…and only that he's missing in action."

"You're sure, sir?"

"No, I'm not sure, but that's the point. Send the damn telegram."

"Yes, sir. What about Grinnell, Ricks, and Nitchke? They've been riding me on this."

"I'll talk to them. Kosinski has probably already informed the 3rd Squad."

"Yes, sir, but you might want to talk to Sander and Brenner too. All the bookworms in the company have taken this very hard."

"Thanks, Klein. I'll do it. One of 'em might be president some day."

"That does it then, Captain. I'll get on the paperwork. Lord, I miss Corporal Wing."

*****

Milwaukee, Wisconsin, May 14, 1945

The grieving Gates family received a second telegram from the War Department. Sam Gates read it with trepidation, but as he turned to his wife, his voice held a note of hope. "The secretary of war says that new evidence suggests Zach was not at the center of the explosion and that he is now officially listed only as MIA."

"Oh, Sam, he may be alive!"

"Oh God, I hope so. Apparently the men closest to the explosion were completely annihilated and will never be identified."

"Zachary is a survivor, Sam. He will show up. I feel it."

In another part of town, Joy was commiserating with her father when her mother burst into the room. "Sam and Clara Gates just called. There is now reason to believe Zachary may be alive."

Joy gasped while struggling to absorb this hopeful news. "Thank God…but…is he still among the missing?"

"Yes, Joy, but he's no longer presumed dead, and that's the important message."

"I know, but it's been three weeks since the explosions. If he's alive, why doesn't he write? Why?"

"He could be in a hospital incapable of writing. We have men like that at Wood Wisconsin Hospital," her father answered.

"Or a prisoner of war," her mother suggested.

"I suppose, but the war is over. He should have been released on May 8."

"I know he's alive and will be found very soon," Joy said softly through her tears.

*****

Munchoff, Germany, May 1, 1945

The horrendous second boxcar explosion ended the Werewolf attack in Munchoff as it roared over the hedgerow where Zach had taken cover. The first wave of the explosion's heat and fire was mostly deflected by the hedgerow. Smoke and flying debris started to clear— Zach got up to run—and a second wave of explosive energy followed. He felt a sharp pain in the back of his head. He grasped his Luger like a bulldog with a bone. Large, concentric gold rings flashed in his brain as he slipped into unconsciousness and was slammed violently to the ground.

The smoke and heat finally subsided enough for the medical corps to venture out and assist the wounded. The closer Americans were attended to first. Most suffered only minor injuries. For the small group of lead Germans, it was a different story. It appeared that only one had survived. Their uniforms were badly burned. Only their dog tags and weapons identified them as German. On the sheltered side of the hedgerow, the medics found another, less beat up, alive but unconscious survivor. One medic's voice hardened. "This kraut made it over the hedgerow."

The man had no helmet, no blouse, no dog tags. His pants were shredded and he was clutching a German Luger. The medics bandaged his bleeding neck, head, and right hand and earmarked Zachary Gates as the second German soldier to be sent to the evacuation hospital.

"This fanatic is wearing our combat boots," one medic observed.

"So is the whole damn German Army. Bastards! Get his Luger."

The two unconscious men were loaded on stretchers and delivered to a late-arriving ambulance which rushed them to an evacuation hospital. The German died en route.

Zach's first moment of conscious awareness came after he was carried into a surgical tent where two medics were extracting metal from the back of his neck at the base of his skull. "This kraut is real lucky. A little deeper and it would have hit the spinal cord."

"Yeah. What about the other Nazi?"

"He was DOA. Must have died in the ambulance."

"Did you get it all, Sarge?"

"Close enough. The real docs can check him out when they get through with our guys. Orderly, get this Nazi over to the POW ward."

*****

Three days later, the sedation wore off and Zach regained consciousness. He checked his body parts: cuts and bruises, a bandaged hand, a stiff neck, and a huge bandage on his head. *Except for a headache the size of Germany, I'm alive. I'm okay, I'm okay,* he repeated to himself. Then he struggled once again to relive that violent action and somehow put it together in a meaningful way: *the krauts had to take a beating…Oh, my God, poor Wing and the guys in the jeep…Stosh was injured…the squad must be okay.* With mixed emotions, he turned a weary look toward the other wounded soldiers in the ward tent. "Where the hell am I? What outfit are you guys from?" His ward mates stared at him in amused disbelief. "What?" Zach shouted.

"*Du bist ein Amerikaner,*" one said.

A stunned and confused Zach replied in German, "*Javohl, und du bist Deutchers. Was is los hier?*" The group talked excitedly to one another in German. Near panic enveloped him and a knot tightened in his stomach. "Ye Gods, I must be in a German hospital," he exclaimed in stark disbelief. At that moment, an American MP and an army nurse entered the tent.

The MP pointed at Zach. "This one speaks English."

Zach rallied. Rage crawled up his throat. "You bet I do. I'm an American combat sergeant. Get me out of this goddamn POW ward!"

"Sure you are, Adolph. I heard you speaking German to your buddies here."

Zach shrieked, "They are not my buddies! Ask them!"

The Germans became expressionless and stone silent, thoroughly enjoying the confusion. The lieutenant frowned and demanded, "Let me see your dog tags, *soldat*."

Zach reached for his neck chain. He froze and sputtered, "It broke when I was shaving." He knew his answer was a dumb one almost before it left his mouth. He stood up and yelled at the MP, "I'm 36824905! Look it up."

The nurse's expression tightened and she commanded, "Lay down, *soldat*. Your act is over." With that, she administered a shot that knocked Zach out in seconds. Turning to the MP, she said through tight lips, "Keep an eye on him, but he shouldn't be any trouble for a long time."

"Wilco, Lieutenant. There are a couple more krauts in here who speak some English. They won't bamboozle me."

Zach's steady diet of sedatives kept him in a fog most of the time, but his wounds were steadily improving. Even his head seemed to ache less. On May 8, the orderly failed to medicate Zach and everyone else in the ward. Zach's head cleared and he walked out the open tent flap to confront the MP. To his surprise, the MP was not at his post. Indeed, the entire evacuation hospital staff was nowhere in sight. Zach looked toward the main surgical and administrative tents. The staff and all mobile patients were congregated around four radios, oblivious to the rest of the world.

Suddenly loud screaming, yelling, and clapping erupted. "The war is over! It's over! It's over!" All hell broke loose as people broke out their liquor rations, dancing and jumping like children at a gigantic birthday party.

THE GREAT ESCAPE

May 8, 1945, Victory in Europe Day

The enthusiastic cheering outside grew louder and wilder. The dozen mobile Germans in the hospital POW ward stood up and peered out of the tent. No MP, no nurse—no one was minding the store. Time to escape! The group studied Zach in a menacing manner. He could blow the whistle on them.

Zach reacted quickly. *"Das kreig is fertig! Gehen sie heim.* (The war is over! Go home.)"

The Germans paused and wrestled with their options: "Take him with us?" "Tie him up?" "Kill him?"

A narrow-eyed, veteran *stabsfeldwebel* (1st sergeant) raised his hand for silence, then abruptly snapped off a chair leg and pointed it at Zach. Zach froze. His heart raced and his mouth and throat went dry. The German limped closer. His teeth were clenched and the scar on his face reddened. It was panicked decision time for Zachary Gates. *Do I fight or is this the time to run?*

The cold German lifted his arm to raise the club. Icy sweat trickled down Zach's cheeks, and then he saw the 116th Panzer insignia on the sergeant's POW-marked tanker blouse. He shouted in panic, *"Feldwebel, Achtezehn Panzers.* (Sergeant, 18th Armored.)" The German hesitated and processed the words. Hard battles had been fought between the Greyhounds and the Herders, but always there was respect. In desperation Zach searched for a way out. An old German proverb emerged. *"Zu schmerz ist stumm,"* Zach called out—*too smart is dumb.* The other Germans watched intently, waiting for a cue from their 1st sergeant, who held his swing and stared at Zach for one long, anxious moment. His eyes blinked and he exhaled heavily. Zach, feeling like a caged animal, seized the moment to plead his case. "*Ich werden hier bleiben. Gehen sie heim. Fahren schnell!* (I will stay here. Go home. Travel fast.)"

The war-weary German sergeant slowly put the club down and limped toward the tent opening. "*Ja, alles is fertig.*" His voice caught. "*Wir gehen.*"

The ambulatory Germans gathered their few belongings, gave Zach a cold look, and followed the stabsfeldwebel out of the tent. Zach's respect for a proud German Panzer division, his high school German classes, and an old German proverb—*too smart is dumb*—had turned an uncertain, threatening situation around.

Zach watched the German soldiers quickly clear the area, cross the highway, and disappear into the woods beyond. He hyperventilated and wiped his brow. Once again it seemed as if he were in combat, where any decision was often better than none at all. Feeling emotionally drained and still shaking, he made another hurried decision. *I'm out of here. I have to find my squad.* He stared at the silent Germans still in the ward, all too badly wounded to escape. "*Es tut mir leid, meine drehen zu fluchten.* (I'm sorry, my turn to escape.)"

Zach frantically undid his POW-marked shirt and sorted through the assortment of German and American boots. He was buckling a pair in his size when one badly wounded young German raised up on one elbow and said in near-perfect English, "*Ja*, too smart is dumb. Good luck, Yankee." He, too, wore a Greyhound insignia. Zach surveyed the ward and gave a half-salute. "*Danke,* good luck to you, *soldat.*"

Taking advantage of the chaotic victory celebration, Zach nervously ambled half-dressed toward the laundry tent, trying to act like any other wounded GI. He glanced back at the POW ward—all was quiet. He picked up his pace and then slowed at the tent. He peered inside. Praise God, it was deserted. He feverishly sorted through the clothes. He pulled on a blouse with an undesignated armored patch and four stripes, forced his booted feet through an oversized pair of fatigue pants, and headed quietly out of the tent. He smiled and attempted to look casual as he walked through the crowd of happy celebrants. Once on the highway, he checked the sun for directions and waited for the Red Ball Express, the hard-driving truckers who were legendary in their ability to carry supplies and ammunition to the front lines. *Lord, I feel like I'm escaping from a German POW camp.*

The first truck stopped and a huge black man hollered out of the window, "Where you going, Sergeant? The war's over."

"Out of here," Zach replied, jumping in the front seat. "I'm trying to return to my outfit at Munchoff. Are you headed that way?"

"Nope. What outfit are you looking for?"

"The 18th Armored."

"Then you don't want to go there. They pulled out last week sometime."

"Crap! Do you know where?"

The big six-by-six started to roll. "Not exactly, but my log says they were headed toward Czechoslovakia. I can take you part way."

"I really appreciate the lift."

"Hey, I like the company. Yours was a heavy combat outfit, wasn't it?"

"So I'm told. I was fine until the last ten days of the war."

"Boy, that's really lousy luck. Some head you've got. Are you okay?"

"Just a headache and a sore hand. Our division medics will check me out when I catch up. Have you got any aspirin?"

"There's a first aid kit under your seat."

Zach chewed several aspirins. "I'm Zachary Gates, Corporal."

"I'm Jefferson Jones. Call me Jeff."

Anxious to change the subject from the hospital, Zach asked, "This is a big rig, Jeff. What is this thing?"

"It's a four-ton Diamond T. I hauled assault boats to the Roer and to the Rhine with this baby."

"That must have been interesting."

"Oh yeah! What was left of the German Air Force went after the big trucks first."

Zach looked to the rear. The hospital was out of sight. His heartbeat finally slowed as he started to calm down. He exhaled and turned to the driver. "Thanks for taking the heat off of us crossing the river."

"You're welcome." Jeff smiled. "I was real happy to unload and get my ass out of that craziness."

"Yeah, it was a long night. Were you also hauling gas?"

"No, thank God. That was a nightmare job."

"I'll bet. Jeff, I've been out of it while I was in the hospital. What happened to Berlin?"

"You didn't hear?"

"The last I heard the Russians were at the gate."

"Berlin fell on May 2, no, May 3. It was a real ugly battle."

"I'm glad I missed that one. That was supposed to be our next mission."

"You lucked out. I heard the Russians lost three hundred thousand men."

Zach shook his head. "You mean thirty thousand men?"

"No, man, I said three hundred thousand!"

Zach's eyes widened. "My God, that's almost thirty divisions! What happened to Hitler?"

"They think he committed suicide, but nobody has found his body."

"Jesus, the Werewolves will never give up."

"Why is that?"

"They took some kind of an oath not to surrender till they had proof of Hitler's death."

"Well, I heard on the BBC they're still fighting in Czechoslovakia, Austria, and Croatia, wherever that is."

"Yugoslavia, I think."

"That's probably why your combat outfit is headed that way."

Zach felt his head and sighed. "Jesus, I should have stayed in the hospital."

"Naw, Sarge. It will be all over by the time you catch up with 'em."

CZECHOSLOVAKIA

B Company had just ended its long march to Czechoslovakia. The news of the May 8 surrender reached them on the road, but the celebration was restrained. The 3rd Squad, still despondent over the loss of their leader, were grumbling about the shooting still going on in parts of Czechoslovakia and Austria.

"I'll believe it's over when the shooting is over," Sander griped.

"Yeah, we thought it was over in Munchoff," Brenner groused.

"Poor Zach. When the hell are we going to hear something?" Bruno grunted.

"Maybe now that this marathon march is over," Brenner said quietly.

The squad was settling into their new quarters in Klatovy when Norm Ricks and Russ Grinnell found the morose soldiers. Bruno stood up. "Any news, Lieutenant?"

"Headquarters says Gates wasn't among the unidentified German dead as far as they know."

"What does that mean?"

"They can't be absolutely sure—some of the krauts were badly burned up."

"Then we still don't know shit," Bashford grumbled.

After a quiet moment of reflection, John Brenner raised his hand. "Lieutenant, I think all of us may have overlooked another possibility. It's a long shot but…"

"But what?"

Brenner wrinkled his brow. "But…I heard that one or two Germans survived and were sent to the hospital."

"So what?"

John took a breath and forced a slow exhalation. "So maybe—"

"One of them was Zach," Tom gasped.

John shot a look at Grinnell. "Right."

Lieutenant Grinnell scratched his head. "It's a long shot, but it makes sense. If they mistook him for German…"

Sander's eyes riveted on the lieutenant. "He could be unconscious in a POW ward."

Grinnell shrugged. "I guess…"

Excited at the thought, Stosh cried out, "He wasn't in the jeep, honest." Bruno grabbed him by the arm. "We believe you, Stosh."

Goldman waved his hand. "And Zach always carried that damn Luger."

"That would hang him," Bash growled.

Naylor furrowed his brow. "Right, and if his tags were blown off…"

Stosh cleared his throat. "I think maybe…"

"Maybe what?" Bruno snapped.

"Maybe Sergeant Gates's chain broke when he took his shirt off…I'm not real sure."

Russ Grinnell stroked his chin. "Headquarters should have working field phones by now. I'll call the evacuation hospital in Gottingen and have them check their POW wards." The lieutenant returned within the hour. "I got through. They said they'd get back to us."

Ricks was skeptical. "Yeah, but when?"

Grinnell affected a similar note of distrust. "They said ASAP but things sounded pretty confused."

Frustrated, Bruno paced the floor. "Let's get on those shitheads!"

"We will, Sergeant Nitchke, we will."

*****

On May 10, Grinnell, Ricks, and Nitchke were hounding their Klatovy headquarters. Captain Black stood up. "Men, I may have good news."

"May have?" Lieutenant Grinnell responded glumly.

The captain raised his hand. "Let me give you the story as it came down on a long phone call with the nurse in charge of the POW ward."

*****

"Captain Black, it's possible we may have had your missing soldier."

"What do you mean, 'may have had'?"

"An MP remembers, as I do, one man who insisted he was an

American, a sergeant, he claimed."

"Gates was a staff sergeant."

"He came in May 1, which also fits."

"So where is he now?"

"Our security went kaput with the celebration and all mobile Germans escaped. Your man may have gone also."

"Christ almighty, Lieutenant, what kind of a hospital are you people running?"

"I'm sorry, Captain, but the war doesn't end every day."

"How the hell did he get in a POW ward?"

"He was tagged as German."

"Didn't you check his dog tags?"

"He wasn't wearing any, Captain, and he spoke German."

"Zachary Gates could speak German. Can you describe him?"

"Six feet, 170 pounds, a good-looking guy even with bandages. He spoke fluent English."

"That could be our man. What kind of shape is he in?"

"He has a head wound—nothing life-threatening as far as I know, but I'm really not sure."

"What do you mean 'you're really not sure'?"

"He was a bit unruly…we sedated him."

"You mean you drugged him?"

"It's SOP (standard operating procedure) for difficult POWs."

"Oh great! Do you have any idea where he is now?"

"No. He could be on the road following you or he may be with the POWs."

"I hope to hell they didn't kill him."

"I doubt the Germans did him in. I think they would have left him here."

"I hope you're right, Lieutenant. His family must be losing their minds."

"I'm sorry, Captain. There is one other disturbing thing I've discovered."

"What?"

"There were two men tagged as German on May 1. One died in the ambulance."

"Did he fit our man's description?"

"I don't know."

"Anything else?"

"Captain, I really think he's on the road someplace. See that he gets medical attention if…when he shows up. Good luck."

"Yeah."

*****

The group wasn't quite sure how to react to the captain's report. 1st Sergeant Bob Klein broke the silence. "Should we notify his family?"

"Christ, not another telegram! His family will go nuts," Blackie sputtered.

"You're right, Captain. We're not absolutely sure it's Gates," Klein replied.

"It's gotta be him. The nurse thinks it's him. We should tell his family," Ricks implored.

Russ Grinnell put his hand on Ricks's shoulder. "Norm, we have to be sure...and another thing..."

"Yeah, what?"

"I'm told that German POWs who speak English often try to pass themselves off as Americans."

"That's a stretch, Russ," Ricks argued.

"Okay, but why didn't he stay in the hospital?" Grinnell asked.

"Hell, I don't know," Ricks grunted.

"Maybe, just maybe, Sergeant, the krauts forced him to go with them," Blackie speculated.

"Why would they do that?"

"To keep him from sounding an alarm."

Conversation stopped momentarily. Then the 1st sergeant mumbled, "In which case they probably killed him."

"Knock it off, Klein. That's bullshit," Ricks shouted.

Grinnell raised his hand. "At ease, guys. Captain, it's your call."

The captain's face hardened. "No telegrams until we know for sure. Let's not screw this thing up anymore than we have already."

Bruno was in a rare, tearful stupor. "Should I tell the squad?" he asked warily.

The captain locked eyes with the burly sergeant. "Your call, Sergeant Nitchke."

Ricks shook his head. "You have to tell them, Bruno; the POW idea was Brenner's."

Captain Black stood up. "That's it, men. We wait until we have solid proof that he's alive...or dead."

35

RED BALL EXPRESS

Zach's Red Ball Express roared into Mulhausen, Germany, where Jeff Jones had to switch roads to get to his destination at Eisennach. Zach said good-bye and looked at his watch—1630. Time to find chow and a billet at a quartermaster company stationed up the street.

He spent a wearying night receiving mostly good-natured ribbing about the armored troops getting all of the glory while the rear echelon held the fort during the Bulge. He elected not to tell them about his hospital POW drama. His bandaged head ached and he wasn't sure if it was the company or his injuries. He excused himself, chewed more aspirins, and fell exhausted onto an army cot. The next morning, the quartermaster company medic redressed Zach's wounds and recommended he see a doctor soon. After a hearty breakfast and some aspirin, Zach was back on the road.

His next driver, a really inquisitive type, wanted to know exactly how he was wounded. Zach related the entire bizarre story and felt better for the telling of it. The incredulous driver widened his eyes. "Hey, man, does your family know all this?"

Zach pondered the question and felt sick. "My God, it's been nine days. I thought…what the hell did I think? I guess I was thinking…" Zach, laced with guilt and growing pain, sighed heavily. "The less they know the better."

"That's crap!" the driver exclaimed. "You better do something, soldier. God knows what kind of shit they got from the army."

Zach held his head. "I should have written something…but when? I was in a POW ward till yesterday."

"You better set the family straight, Sergeant—like right now!"

"You're right, Corporal. Three guys evaporated in that jeep but one guy knows I got out of the jeep."

The driver took one hand off the wheel and pointed a finger at Zach. "They probably still have to list you as MIA."

Zach pondered the worst-case scenario, held his aching head, and choked, "Or KIA. Judas, if Stosh was sent to the hospital, they may still think I was in the jeep."

"Listen to me, Sergeant! There's V-mail paper under the seat. Write to your family while you can. Bayreuth has an army post office and a hospital."

Zach attempted to rotate his bandaged head while reaching under the seat. "Thanks. Maybe I can call my unit if the signal corps has the phone lines working."

"The phones may not help you if your battalion is still on the road high, balling it toward Czechoslovakia."

Zach drummed his pencil nervously and mumbled, "God, my folks, and poor Joy."

One hour later, the Redballer bypassed a traffic jam in Gotha about halfway to Bayreuth. "I'm glad to go around this place," he said in a quiet voice.

Zach, while pressing his hand to his head in a futile attempt to relieve some of the increasing torturous pain, groaned, "Why is that?"

"It was a slave labor camp. Wretched bodies were everywhere. Ike himself ordered the townspeople to work night and day until all of the bodies were buried."

"I saw a similar thing at Nordhausen," Zach said quietly through his mounting discomfort.

The driver shook his head. "I thought all that atrocity stuff was propaganda shit but not anymore."

The two drove quietly until the driver switched on the BBC. The big news was the surrender of the last Germans in Czechoslovakia. "That's a break for my outfit," Zach mumbled. "The war may finally be over for those poor guys." The news went on. Himmler had been captured by the British and had committed suicide. "Ran into him in the Saar-Moselle Triangle. Good riddance," Zach muttered.

Norway was also in the news. The commander in chief of their army, one Major General Otto Ruge, had been rescued from a POW camp by the Russians in Treuenbrietzen, Germany, just fifteen miles east of the Elbe. Zach attempted to clear his throbbing head. "That must have been about the time we were at the Elbe." The news continued, saying Crown Prince Olav and part of the government were back in Norway. "That's a surprise," Zach rasped.

"Why is that?"

Zach once again tried to pull himself together for a response. "Because the German Army was there in force and in good shape."

"They probably gave up. All the Germans can't be crazy," the driver scowled.

Zach fell into a troubled sleep as the announcer was exalting over the capture of William Joice, the British traitor who called himself Lord Haw Haw on the German radio. He awoke an hour later when the six-by-six rumbled into Bayreuth, 150 miles from the Czech border. "My head feels like it's going to explode." The worried driver dropped him off at the German hospital in Bayreuth, now manned by both German and American personnel. The driver told the American floor nurse the incredible story of Zach's injuries and headed back onto the road.

Zach awakened the next morning in a hospital ward. For a moment he thought he was reliving a nightmare when he heard his nurse speaking German. "*Was gibts, Fraulein?*" Zach asked uneasily. The nurse gave him a cold look and responded in near-perfect English. "Your medical corps is in charge of this German hospital. We are cooperating."

Zach gave a sigh of relief, proffered his V-mail letter, and mumbled, "That has to be a first." The nurse frowned and pocketed the V-mail. "We're not all Nazis," she asserted as she left the room. "*Danke.* I mean, thank you," Zach called after her.

Shortly afterward, an American doctor, a major, came into the ward. "How are you feeling, soldier?"

"Okay, I guess. What happened? Did I pass out? All I remember is a very large headache."

Dr. Mudgett took Zach's pulse, looked up, and said, "We gave you some painkillers." He paused. "Your driver told us a somewhat inconceivable story."

"Crazy, but true, Dr. Mudgett."

"Uh huh. The nurse tells me you have no dog tags."

"My chain broke seconds before a train car of black powder exploded."

"We have been informed that most of a POW ward escaped from the hospital in Gottingen," the doctor said in a flat voice, while examining Zach's arms.

"You're looking for a tattooed blood type, aren't you?" Zach asked wryly.

The doctor grumbled, "You know about the SS, I gather?"

"Yes, sir. I saw a lot of them dead and alive."

"We take care of all soldiers here, but I have to check, especially since you have no tags and no medical records."

"I doubt there are any, Doctor. They thought I was an unidentified German."

"Well, you're not SS."

"Boy, that's a relief," Zach chided.

"Very funny. Now shut up and let me look at the back of your head."

Zach rolled over. "I think it's weeping a little."

"Oh for heaven's sake!" the doctor exclaimed.

"What?"

"Bad stitches and too few. No wonder you were in such pain. Who did this to you?"

"The real docs were all busy. I remember two enlisted guys working on me."

"Now I believe you. Soldier, I don't like this weeping. I'd like to keep you here for a few days and watch it."

"I should get back to my unit."

"In good time. I want to talk to the medics at the evacuation hospital first."

"Doc, will you keep trying to reach my company? They may not know I'm alive."

"Of course. I'll let you know as soon as I hear something."

"Thanks for the new bandage; I feel better already."

"Get some rest, soldier."

*****

The next morning, Doctor Mudgett returned to Zach's room. "I finally got through to the right person at the evac hospital. She supports your extraordinary story and is convinced you are who you say you are."

Zach exhaled heavily. "Yeah, finally."

"She talked to your company commander a few days ago."

"Great, then he knows I'm alive."

"No. She had no confirmation when she called. Neither she nor I have been able to reach him today."

Frustrated, Zach muttered, "What's the hang up? The war's over."

"The signal corps. Half their men are being sent to the Pacific Theater. Things are snafued."

"Did the nurse say anything about my head?"

"Nothing helpful, but they want you to see a neurologist before you leave Europe."

"Why? To cover their asses?"

The doctor looked away and replied slowly, "Perhaps. Let me try your company again."

*****

Finally, one hour later, the signal corps cleared the lines and Zach was called to the phone. Captain Black was on the line. "Goddamn it, Gates, why the hell didn't you call sooner? Hello? This is Zachary Gates, isn't it?"

"Yes, sir."

"Your folks in Milwaukee must be going crazy. We told the War Department you were MIA and presumed dead." Zach felt like he had been clubbed; he needed a minute to process the impact of such a message. "Gates, are you there?" the captain shouted.

"Yes, sir...my poor family...I've sent a V-mail," he stuttered.

"Good! Are you in one piece?"

"Yes, sir, and I'm sorry. I was in a POW ward."

"I'm aware of that. Now talk to me. What the hell is wrong with you?"

"I have a head injury, but except for a headache I'm fine. Dr. Mudgett wants me to stay here for a few days to fix some stitches or something—nothing serious."

"Well, make it fast. I'm not sure how long we'll be here. The whole division is being broken up. One tank battalion has already left for the Pacific."

"I'll get back, sir, as soon as the medics release me."

"One other thing, Gates."

"Yes, sir?"

"Write to Colonel Hartman. He reamed us all new assholes for the screw up. He's either going to give you a medal or have you locked up."

"I will, sir."

"Stay alive, Sergeant. I have to fix this mess with the War Department."

"Thank you, Captain. One question..."

"Yeah?"

"How is Stosh Kosinski?"

"He's fine, but because he had a head wound, they want to send him to a general hospital, in England, I think."

"Thanks, Captain. Say hello to my guys."

"That's not a problem, Sergeant Gates. They're all assembled outside my door. Over and out."

RESOLUTION AND REDEPLOYMENT

Klatovy, Czechoslovakia

Blackie hung up the phone and shouted, "Sergeant Klein, get in here. Gates is alive!"

"Great news, sir."

"Yeah. Get Grinnell, Ricks, and Nitchke over here."

"Yes, sir, and we will have new telegrams to—"

"Hold it, Klein. My phone's ringing."

Blackie paled, covered the phone, stared wide-eyed at his 1st sergeant, and whispered, "Get ready for a court-martial. It's General Devane." He took a deep breath. "Yes, General."

"Captain, what the hell is going on with one Sergeant Zachary Gates?"

"General, he is alive. It's a very long story."

"I just heard most of it, Captain. Now damn it, I want appropriate telegrams sent immediately. You've screwed this up enough for one war!"

"Yes, General."

"Am I clear?"

"Understood, General."

"Good. That's all."

Captain Black hung up and stared wide-eyed at 1st Sergeant Klein. "I'm glad that's over," he sputtered.

Klein exhaled in relief. "Yes, sir, I could hear him."

"Try to reach Gates again. We need more information."

"Yes, sir, but we better alert the War Department that he's alive, like, right now."

"Right, or the general will have us both shot."

"Jesus, I could sure use Jim Wing," the 1st sergeant lamented.

*****

Milwaukee, Wisconsin: May 23, 1945

A third telegram from the War Department announced tersely that Zachary Gates, 36824905, had been wounded in Munchoff, Germany, on May 1, 1945, and would be returned to duty shortly. Zach's family was overjoyed, flabbergasted, angry, and confused. His dad shook his head in disbelief; his mother stood crying. "It's good news, Agnes, but what a ridiculous, heart-wrenching experience. First our son is killed in action, then missing in action—and now, only slightly wounded. What are we to believe?"

"Sam, if he's going to be returned to duty, he must be fine."

"I hope so. I'll believe it when we hear from Zachary. Damn this ugly war!"

One day later, Zachary's V-mail arrived in Milwaukee.

> *Dear family,*
>
> *I am fine! I am so sorry about the misinformation. The confusion started when I was mistaken for a German soldier and put in an American POW hospital ward. That explains the MIA. The KIA was a case of misidentification. I'm spending a few days in a Bayreuth hospital for a minor stitch adjustment or something, nothing serious. I'll write a complete account when I can. My next destination is Czechoslovakia.*
>
> *Love you, you too, Joy.*
> *Zachary*

Agnes, still in tears, questioned, "What kind of wound, Sam? He didn't tell us. We still don't know."

Sam looked up from the V-mail. His throat tightened. "We'll have to wait for his next letter. The good news is we heard from him and he is still alive. I think it's time we all said a prayer of thanksgiving."

*****

Klatovy, Czechoslovakia, Late May

Captain Black sat at his desk holding his head. The recent orders had been a real shocker. The older, long-service men were already transferred to occupation-duty divisions: the 94th, 26th, 83rd Infantry Divisions, and the 6th Armored Division. Most of the rear echelon units and their longtime personnel remained in the 18th Armored and were to be sent to Reims, France. The tank battalions were being readied for action in China. Zach's group of younger combat men were being redeployed with the 35th Infantry Division, going first to the United States and then on to the Pacific Theater of Operations. It was a busy and confused time.

"What about us, Captain?" Sergeant Klein asked.

Black paged through the stack of orders. "We're going to join Colonel Hartman in Berlin with the 2nd Armored Division."

"What happened to General Devane?"

"He's taken command of the 2nd Armored."

"Who is going to expedite the changing of the guard? We have six thousand SS here!"

"Yeah, hang on. Here it is—a special cadre from all units of the division. Our company is out of it—no, wait. Tech/Sergeant Norman Ricks is part of that group."

"Why Ricks?"

"I guess because he and Russ Grinnell did most of the negotiating with the SS POWs."

"Why did they let Lieutenant Grinnell go?" Sergeant Klein asked.

"Service time. He left a week ago for occupation duty with the 6th Armored Division."

"Too bad he had to miss Gates. They were close."

"Christ, what about Gates? What's the latest on his case?"

"X-rays and something about weeping and infection. Nothing serious, I guess. He should be out in two or three days."

"Damn, we may miss him. He's three or four hundred kilometers from here. Let me check our orders. Good Lord, Klein, we're out of here the day after tomorrow."

"Yes, sir, the orders were just revised today."

Blackie sighed. "Well, at least Gates's buddy, Norm Ricks, will be here to greet him."

"It's a shame the 3rd Squad won't be here to welcome him," Klein lamented.

Blackie hesitated for a long moment before responding. "War is hell, Sergeant. Pack your duffel."

Klatovy, Czechoslovakia, A Few Days Later

Zach staggered into the SS camp headquarters building. He sported a smaller, neater bandage and carried medical orders to see a neurologist before he left Europe. Sergeant Norm Ricks was waiting. "You're late, Goddamn it!"

Zach felt a weakness overcome his entire body at the sound of his old friend's voice. He forced a slow inhalation and struggled to find an oral response. Norm gave him a rushed bear hug while patting his back with both hands. "What the hell took you so long?"

Zach cleared his dry throat. "Traffic was heavy in all directions. My deuce-and-a-half ride bumped along for 360 stop-and-go kilometers."

"You look like shit. How are you feeling?"

"I'm fine. When did everybody go?"

"The last guys left a couple of days ago. I'm really sorry, Zach. Your squad truly wanted to see you."

A flood of images and squad memories crossed his mind and his muscles tightened. He spoke in a near moan. "I'm…I'm so sorry I had to miss them."

"I understand, Zach…I'm still recovering from seeing the whole platoon march away from me."

Zach exhaled and struggled to change the subject. "I talked to Blackie. I'm not sure why I got all the attention."

"Embarrassment, for openers."

"What?"

"Zach, everybody screwed up. They put you in a POW ward and told your family you were dead, for God's sake."

"Snafus happen. I hope I'm clear now."

"Not completely, but it's not all bad."

"Now what?"

Norm brought out a letter of instructions. "You're assigned to the 35th Infantry Division if you ever catch up to the others."

"Where are they headed?"

"France and then the US for redeployment. Your squad and most of the platoon are probably in France by now."

"All of 'em?"

"Yeah, I think so. No, an old guy…"

"Elmo 'Pappy' Becker?"

"Yeah, thirty-seven with six kids. He goes home."

"Norm, what about Russ Grinnell?"

"6th Armored, occupation duty. He cried for the first time in his life when he heard you were blown up. He left you a note."

"A great guy. What happened to Stosh Kosinski?"

"He's en route to England for a final look at his head."

"Is he okay?"

"Yeah, it's just that the army is wary of any head wounds and a little embarrassed again. You know, the telegrams..."

"That wasn't his fault."

"No, it was ours. We didn't check with him about the jeep snafu."

"Thank God for Stosh," Zach sighed.

"Yeah. He shook everybody up when he came back and insisted that you weren't in the jeep."

"I'll bet."

"The whole damn company felt stupid, embarrassed, relieved, confused—take your pick."

"Uninformed! I couldn't talk my way out of that damned POW ward."

"Zach, when we couldn't find you, we had to list you as MIA. Most of us thought you were dead...even after Stosh got back."

Zach looked away. "What a snafu. I came within inches of being in that jeep. Those guys never had a chance."

"Zach, it was your squad that always said, 'When your number's up, it's up.'"

"Yeah, I know. Norm, tell me about my squad."

"Your guys were absolutely devastated. The first four days were the worst. They were finally convinced that you were either blown to pieces with Wing and the others in the jeep or that you were burned up in the field. On the third day, they divided up your stuff, each taking a memento."

Zach smiled. "I guess the medics got my Luger."

"When they heard you were in a POW ward, they went nuts—you can thank Brenner for figuring that one out."

"I'm glad somebody did. I owe John one."

"He and Sander were really broken up when they had to leave before you got back. They left you notes."

Now Zach was near tears. "I hope I catch up to them," he said softly.

"That may be tough. They're all split up. One other thing, Zach..."

Zach rubbed his eyes and choked, "I'm listening."

"Before Colonel Hartman left for Berlin, he came over and talked to your squad."

Zach nodded. "He was a good guy. A fine officer."

"He was with us long enough to know only that you weren't in the jeep. You should write him," Ricks admonished.

"I will. Blackie said the same thing. I should also write to Jim Wing's family. I just don't know what to say."

"That's a tough one…how did Jim know where those damn train cars were?"

Zach offered a weak smile. "Wing knew everything and everybody."

"That's for sure. The company was never the same after he was gone."

"So many great guys…" Zach sighed

"Everybody promised to stay in touch. You gave all of us an emotional ride, Zach." Norm's voice became unsteady. "First you're dead, then you're MIA, and then you're alive. Bashford and even tough Bruno Nitchke were near tears."

A veil of sadness gripped Zach. "All good soldiers and good friends…and now they're all gone."

Norm Ricks put his arm around his good friend. "Yeah, now it's just you and me."

"How long have I got, Norm? Anything else in your letter of instructions?"

"Yeah, I was afraid you'd ask. You leave tomorrow afternoon."

"What? I just got here."

"You know the army. Hurry up and wait, hurry up and wait. Here's the good news. You get to ride in a special medical forty-and-eight boxcar."

"How come?"

"Orders directly from the War Department."

"From the War Department?"

"I guess they're shook up about their telegrams. Hell, you get bunks, a medic, and loving care."

"I can live with that."

"You bet. It's a long ride across Europe in an empty forty-and-eight."

"What else have I missed, Norm?"

"Well, I have some good news and some bad news."

"What's the good news?"

"Remember Colonel Hallace, the guy who smoked out an ambush near Recklinghausen?"

"Yeah, he drove a jeep right out in front of the 116th Panzers."

"Yeah. He thought we'd already taken Recklinghausen."

"Is he okay?"

"Yeah, the krauts took him prisoner. He was still with the 116th when their commander, Siegfried von Waldenburg, surrendered."

"How did he avoid a POW camp?"

"I guess he talked them into keeping him. The way I heard it, he made friends with their second-in-command, a guy by the name of Guderian."

"What's the bad news?"

Norm's face became expressionless and his voice dropped an octave.

"We lost Father MacArthur."

Zach's jaw dropped, his face registering pain and disbelief. "That's terrible. Wasn't the war over?"

"Sure, but there are still land mines. We think his jeep hit one near Pilsen and blew him off the road."

Zach groped for another explanation. "Could it have been Werewolves?"

Ricks sighed. "Who knows?"

Zach shook his head and lamented, "What an irony—God protects him through all those times he was at the front and now this, after the war is over."

"Zach, it was your guys who said it—"

"Yeah, I know. When your number's up, it's up," Zach mumbled.

"He really was attached to you bookworms. All the ASTP guys were present at the ceremony in his honor."

Zach's voice caught. "I should have been there. He held my hand so many times."

Ricks grunted. "You're just lucky your number wasn't up."

Zach lowered his eyes and then looked away. "Yeah...I know." His voice trailed off. "What other death-rattle news have you got?"

Norm looked away, then back at Zach. "Well...this is mixed."

Zach's expression turned cold. "I'm not sure I want to hear it."

Norm spoke with a reluctant voice. "Your guys were talking about it while you were gone—it was kind of a...a secret."

Bewildered, Zach huffed, "Well, now I have to hear it."

Ricks swallowed hard before speaking. "Remember Jack Franks, A Company?"

"Of course. We were at Illinois together, an all-A student and a track star like you."

Norm bit off his next words. "He took that grunt commission just before we crossed the Rhine."

"Yeah, I heard that, so?"

"He went to the 83rd Infantry—earned the Silver Star during his first two weeks—"

"Franks was a brave, natural leader. So what's the mixed news?"

Ricks lowered his voice and murmured, "He earned the medal posthumously."

A pang of sadness mixed with disbelief crossed Zach's face. "That's terrible news!" he gasped. "My God, he was an officer for only two weeks! What's mixed news about that?"

Ricks tugged nervously at his collar. "The good news, old buddy, is that you turned it down."

Zach shook his head. "Thanks, Norm, but why didn't anybody tell me?"

"Zach, you had just lost Paxton and Whedder. Brenner and Holter had been wounded. The guys thought you had enough on your mind."

Images of Kirchellen raced across the inner recesses of his mind with memories of happier times at Illinois with Jack Franks. He was processing all of these thoughts when Ricks suddenly stood up and slapped him on the back. "Hey, bookworm, I've got some sexy news that should perk you up."

"What?" Zach responded, his head and heart still aching.

"I said *sexy* news!"

Zach forced a smile. "Okay, I'm ready for some sexy news. What kind of orgy did you get into?"

"No, not me—you! Remember the two girls you pulled out of a burning building back in the Ruhr pocket?"

"What the hell are you talking about?"

"Wild Bill filled us in while you were playing like a POW."

"The Ruhr? All I remember was bluffing a Tiger Royal—Unna, I think."

Norm shook his head vigorously. "Yeah, it was Unna."

Zach reflected on those crazy days and that rushed episode finally emerged. "Lord, I'd forgotten. Yeah, one girl was overcome by smoke. Bill took care of them. I was directing a shitload of DPs."

"They're both in love with you," Norm sang out.

"Come on."

"No shit. They followed you to thank you and almost caught you at Bayreuth. They stopped here on their way home to Lodz, Poland."

"That's crazy. How would they even know who I am?"

"Bill told 'em. He said they insisted."

Doubt and the possibility of a joke crossed Zach's mind. "Well, that's very nice, but what's so sexy about that?"

"You should see them," Norm exclaimed.

"I saw them at Unna—well, barely."

"Yeah, when they were all beat up! Zach, these are two real sexy-looking babes! They really broke things up around here for a couple of days." Zach laughed but still thought the story was some kind of a put-on. "Zach, I'm serious. They wanted your body."

"That's me, a day early or a day late. Tell 'em to write," Zach bantered.

"We gave them your Milwaukee address. You'll hear from them."

Zach was still unconvinced. "They were really big, fat, and ugly, weren't they?"

"No, they weren't, bonehead!" Ricks gave up. "Come on, I'll show you around the compound."

"Yeah, sex hound, let's see what kind of goldbrick job you've had."

"It was goldbrick for most of the division but not for our battalion. We really got stuck guarding these six thousand SS troopers here in Klatovy."

"That could be interesting."

"Things were out of hand when we got here. They had totally intimidated the ordinance battalion that was standing guard. They quieted down after we took over—more respect, I guess. After Berlin fell, things really settled down. They weren't as stiff and threatening as before, if you know what I mean."

"Yes, I do. What about all the USO troupes (United Service Organizations) I heard about?"

"Not here. The guys closer to Pilsen were on a picnic. They saw Bob Hope, Jack Benny, Jane Froman, even Billy Rose's dancers."

"So all you have to show me are six thousand tired SS?"

"We have one famous resident, an SS sketch artist we named 'Chicago.'"

"I can't wait. Why Chicago?"

"He lived in Chicago for a couple of years before the war. He's a great artist. You'll see."

Chicago made a fast, very serious-looking sketch of Zach and then shook his hand. Zach shook his head and joined Norm Ricks off base for a quiet dinner and war talk that lasted most of the night.

*****

The next afternoon, after a perfunctory medical stop, Ricks joined Zach at the railroad siding. Good-byes were awkward and emotional for the two combat-hardened young sergeants who had gone through so many battles together. "See you in the Pacific, Zach."

"Good-bye, Norm, keep in touch."

Zach waved and walked toward the train. *Such a good friend...will I ever see him again? Will either of us survive the Pacific war? Will this madness ever end?*

Zach boarded the empty special forty-and-eight train car designed for the more seriously wounded or incapacitated soldiers. A medical corporal checked his list. "Welcome aboard, Sergeant. Head wound and former ASTP, right?"

"Right, thanks—I've been up most of the night. I'm going to hit the sack."

37

To Paris and Place Pigalle

The long train journey across Europe was frequently halted for rest stops, food, even showers. The USO, the Red Cross, the medics, even the quartermaster people went out of their way to make the rest stops comfortable.

As the train rolled through one devastated city after another, Zach had all-encompassing feelings of sadness, unhappiness, remorse, even guilt. How could good people do this to one another? It was a mood of melancholy that followed the anger, the exhilaration, the trauma of frontline combat. Zach's disquieting reverie was intensified whenever another wounded soldier was brought aboard. All seemed very young and very frightened. *Replacements whose luck ran out,* Zach thought. *Poor bastards.* Then, somewhere near Heidelberg, a grizzled infantry staff sergeant climbed aboard the train. He limped badly and held his arm in a temporary sling. A cigarette hung loosely from his mouth. He was shorter and wider than Zachary and the lines in his well-worn face put him at age forty or more.

"What is this, a kindergarten?" he roared as he surveyed the young soldiers. "And who are you, Joe, some kid sergeant from the rear echelon?"

"Armored Infantry, 18th Armored," Zach reported.

The veteran sergeant nodded and said simply, "Good outfit."

Zach chanced a question. "Your patch says 1st Infantry. Were you at D-day?"

"Damn right. Got my second Purple Heart there; first one was in Africa."

"Sergeant, I'm Zach Gates. I know the Big Red One had over 200 percent replacements. We met you in the Harz Mountains."

The veteran sergeant interrupted Zach. "What are you, one of those smartass ASTP types I heard about?"

"Good guess," the medic reported.

The gruff sergeant stuck out his hand. "I'm Ralph Drummond. Any armored guy is a friend of mine. You and the 2nd Armored saved our asses more than once." Then, turning to the wounded eighteen- and nineteen-year-olds, he ordered, "Okay, men. Names and units."

The names and divisions were rattled off as if Ike himself had given the order. All but one were infantry divisions—30th, 35th, 4th, 83rd, and the 12th Armored. All of the wounded had been in Europe fewer than three months. The 12th Armored soldier looked at Zach and spoke up first. "I was an ASTP replacement, sir. Many of the 12th were ASTP."

"Will you go back to school?" Zach asked.

"Yes, sir. Michigan, *if* we get out of Japan alive."

Sergeant Drummond snorted. "Christ, two professors. I may get an education." Then the gritty old soldier forced a quiet smile and turned to Zach. "Gates, call me Drum."

The ice had been broken. Between rest stops, war stories and poker replaced small talk and aftermath reflections. It was hard to top the old sergeant's combat tales. Drum also proved to be a professional gambler. Everyone lost the few dollars they had. "You sad sacks have to learn to count cards," he advised as he stuffed his winnings into a huge wad of bills already in his shoulder bag.

"Jesus, Drum, how much do you have there?" Zach asked.

"Plenty. The last guys were really dumb, and they had *big* money."

The train was now close to the Paris station stop and Sergeant Drummond regaled the small group with war stories of wine, women, and the famous Moulin Rouge nightclub in old Pigalle.

Zach turned to the medic. "Corporal, can we look around Paris?"

"I don't know, Sergeant Gates; we're only there for three or four hours."

Sergeant Drummond went nose to nose with the corporal. "That's plenty of time!" he roared.

The medic stepped back. "I guess it's okay for mobile noncoms," he sputtered.

Drum beamed and turned to the others. "Sorry, boys. You should wait on the docs anyway."

The train stopped in the Gare du Nord station not too far from Place Pigalle and about the same distance from the Folies-Bergere. Zach found himself with a rich and worldly escort whether he wanted one or not. "Drum, are you okay getting around with that bum leg and bad arm? The medics wanted to check us out."

"To hell with the medics. We're going to paint this town. Follow me. You're combat infantry, aren't you?"

Zach felt the small bandage on the back of his head. "I already earned a Purple Heart!"

"Double time, Gates. All this argent is burning a hole in this bag."

"Good, I'm broke." Zach turned to the open-mouthed young soldiers in the forty-and-eight. "Hang in there, guys. You'll be heroes when you get home."

Drum gave them a salute. "Don't wait up for us." Zach followed Drum, who limped over to a far corner of the station. "I know where we can get a voiture."

The voiture was just where Drum said he would be. "*Garcon,* Hotel Ritz." The French driver gave him a cold look. Drum flashed his wad of money and the driver smiled. "*Je vous prie de m'excuser. Noi nom Louie.*"

"That means Louie is apologizing."

"I figured that. What are we doing at the Ritz?"

"La dolce vita, what else?"

"All night? What about the train?"

"The war is over, Sergeant—to hell with the train!"

Zach reflected on what he might be getting into with this rough-and-tumble veteran sergeant with the big voice and the big heart. *Why not...still another lousy war ahead*, he thought to himself.

Louie tapped the horse, turned to his passengers, and said in English, "Anything for Yankee heroes."

Drum howled. "Right, as long as they have the argent."

The ride to the Ritz was longer than Zach expected, but Drum said the driver was on course. The Ritz was just that—ritzy. Drum instructed Louie to *rester.* "Sure, Joe, I stand fast."

No enlisted men or junior officers were visible in the lobby. That mattered little to Ralph Drummond. "*Grande chamber,*" he ordered loudly, putting another pocketful of bills on the counter. And grand it was, the most elegant suite of rooms Zach had ever seen.

"Can we afford this, Drum?"

"Hell, yes. This is what gambling money is for—but first, Pig Alley."

*****

The June night was warm and beautiful. After four years of occupation, the City of Lights was aglow again. What a difference from

London—Paris suffered hardly a scratch during the war. Louie guided his cheval to Place Pigalle and dropped the two combat veterans in front of the Moulin Rouge. Zach looked up at the red windmill on top of the roof and muttered, "What the hell. It's been a long, rotten war."

The club was jammed with a few incognito young officers on the first floor and an army of GIs in various states of exuberance on the low, surrounding balconies, all furnished with tables and chairs. The first show was about to begin. Drum ordered a front row table and invited all of the 1st Division men he saw to join him. "Don't eat too much here," he whispered to Zach. "We'll dine at the Ritz. It's better food."

Zach nodded agreement as the lights dimmed and the once-banned, erotic cancan dance commenced. A dozen or more French girls, scantily clad in short ruffled skirts started a high-kick routine accompanied by the loud, bouncy cancan music. At the start of each routine, they held up and shook their skirts while high-kicking. The crowd of GIs went wild. Zach had never seen anything like this. While staring wide-eyed, he heard the GI next to him singing softly, "Oh they don't wear pants in the southern part of France."

The champagne and beer flowed, and the crowd became noisier. Near the close of the wild first show, two drunken soldiers fell off a lower balcony, totally disrupting the performance. One man staggered to his feet and reached out toward one of the dancers. Drum rushed to her defense, putting a strangle hold on the soldier with his one good arm. The soldier's drunken buddy attacked Drum and that brought on the 1st Division guests. "The Big Red One attacks!" Drum bellowed.

Zach, seeing double and feeling sick from the beer-champagne mix, staggered into the free-for-all to help his friend, who was shouting, "Here comes the armor—ain't this the greatest!"

Sirens wailed and Zach warily looked toward the door. The look-away action turned out to be a major error. A hard, blind-sided punch to the jaw rendered him momentarily insensible. Zach came to on the floor, lying next to Drum. Drum raised up on one elbow. "Gates, get your ass out of here and find Louie. The MPs are coming in force."

"Where are you going?" Zach groaned as he searched for his missing bandage.

"I'm getting the mademoiselles—get the hell out of here!"

Zach shook his aching head, stood up, and headed shakily through the melee and out the door. *Just in time!* The MPs burst into the club looking like they had done this before. He staggered across the street to the public pissoir and threw up. Feeling sick, he hung his head for a long, long time. When he came out, the MPs were rounding up the last of the brawlers. Drum was not among them. Two mostly-sober 1st Division soldiers approached Zach. "He's gone, Sergeant."

"He got out?" Zach asked, not believing.

The second GI grinned. "Oh yeah. He and two cancan babes galloped off with a French guy."

"It gets worse, Sergeant—the MPs were in hot pursuit."

"I'm dead," Zach groaned.

"Naw, we'll save him. We owe you one, 18th Armored. Where's your next show?"

Zach grunted, "The Ritz, if I don't collapse."

"We'll get you there. You armored guys don't drink too good," they hooted.

Zach grimaced and nodded okay. The two doughs trotted Zach to the Ritz where they surreptitiously watched a drama going on in the lobby. A paddy wagon and two MP jeeps were parked close by. Six MPs had corralled Drum, Louie, and the two cancan dancers. Zach painfully straightened up, cleared his head, and moved closer to the action. An MP lieutenant was wagging his finger in Drum's face and shouting, "You're under arrest, soldier. I don't care how many medals you have. You're guilty of brawling and causing a riot. And you ticked off the quartermaster general who lives here."

Drum spotted Zach and his buddies from the Big Red One. He furtively gave the combat run sign.

"Let's move it!" said the private from the 1st Division.

"Where is your next act, Sergeant?" the second cracked as the trio bailed out.

Zach struggled to remember. He yawned and mumbled, "Gare du Nord station. My next act is a court-martial if the train is gone."

The two GIs rushed Zach to the station where, wonder of wonders, the train was waiting. "You lucked out, Sarge. Looks like the whole train went AWOL."

Zach smiled weakly. "Thanks, guys. Try to stay out of trouble."

"Look who's talking," they howled.

*****

Zach held his throbbing head and shakily entered his special car. In the dim light from the station, it seemed as if the car was empty. No, wait, someone was sleeping in the corner bunk. He crawled quietly to his bunk and held his head. Suddenly the train jerked to a start. The whistle awakened the sleeping medic. "Where the hell have you been?" he shouted. Zach melted down into the mattress and pretended to be sleeping. "Answer me! Where the hell have you been?"

Cornered, Zach screamed, "Berlin!"

"You asshole," the medic yelled.

"Don't yell—where are the guys?" Zach retorted.

"What the hell do you care?"

"Come on…"

"They're moved to a Paris hospital," he scowled.

"What about me?" Zach ventured.

"You missed a check up. You're screwed."

"We were delayed, Corporal. I'm sorry."

"Bullshit! What happened to your AWOL friend?"

Zach paused and replied sheepishly, "The MPs have him."

"Oh, that's just great! I'll catch hell for this. He was to stay with the others."

"Knock it off, Corporal. My head is about to explode. Do I stay on the train or what?"

"I don't give a shit. Ask the medics at the redeployment camp if the MPs don't get you first," the corporal snapped.

Wearying of the confrontation, Zach grumbled sarcastically, "Well, Drum is still in Paris." The medic was not amused. "Stay out of my life, Gates," he screamed. Zach dropped wearily back on his bunk and speculated about Drum's fate and the two cancan girls. *Then there were those two Polish babes.* He rolled over. *Oh my aching head. Call me lucky…*

38

CAMP PALL MALL– FLIGHT TRAINING

Finally, after an emotional, heart-rending week on the rolling-and-rocking medical forty-and-eight, the French coast, covered by the huge redeployment camps, came into view. Each camp was named after a brand of cigarettes—Camp Camel, Camp Lucky Strike, Camp Philip Morris, and, finally, Camp Pall Mall.

An endless procession of large circus tents served as a camp. Soldiers lounged on row after row of army cots. Zach searched through crowded tents looking for familiar faces and patches. He found a few 18th patches but spied no one he knew and no one from his battalion. Word was they had already left for England where they were awaiting ships to the States.

The disorganized MPs and medics at Camp Pall Mall could care less about Zach's Paris escapade. "Check into a general hospital when you get to England." Nobody seemed to know or care when that might be. "Wait for orders and the end of the war, Sergeant," was what they happily advised.

For all of its rushed construction, the camp mess hall was a good one, the weather was beautiful, and the mood was upbeat, since the men thought the war in the Pacific would end soon. Best of all, passes to Paris were abundant.

This was a good place to doze in the sun, catch the war news, and goof off until war's end. However, the War Department thought the war in the Pacific was far from over and so the troops were exposed to hours of propaganda tapes trying to convince them that this could be the case. A Yale psychologist, Carl Hovland, also had everyone taking attitude tests. Other than that, free time was available for the asking.

Zach decided he'd really seen enough of Paris. One morning, he hiked over to a temporary grass airstrip where Grasshopper pilots were hanging out and giving free rides. He spotted a pilot wearing an 18th Armored patch and petting a German shepherd. Zach jumped the line of GIs and reporters who were killing time.

"Thought you guys were in England," Zach remarked.

"Not the airplanes. We're going to unload them in Göppingen, near Stuttgart, if the Japs give it up. I'm Ron Crego, division liaison."

"I'm Zach Gates, sergeant, and I know you."

"How's that?"

"I remember your dog riding with you."

"Yeah, Spotter was a better observer than some of the artillery officers. Where did we cross paths?"

"Several places. First was Rhineberg. You saved our asses."

"Oh yeah, those big German guns."

"That was great timing, Crego."

Sergeant Crego rolled his eyes. "Just between us, Gates, I was in the wrong sector."

"Our good fortune. I hope you didn't get reamed."

"Yeah, but I got off the hook when some infantry BC put me in for a Bronze Star."

Zach laughed. "That had to be my BC, Colonel George Hartman. Crego, I thought you guys were officers."

"Nope. We're the only noncommissioned pilots in the army."

"That seems unfair."

"I guess they think this cotton-covered kite is like an underpowered jeep."

"Is it a tough airplane to fly?"

"The tail drags and she's slow, but I like flying her. Want to try her out?"

"Not if you're as wild as I remember."

"You mean when I outmaneuvered that ME-109?"

"Yeah, I still don't know how you pulled that off."

"Sheer genius. Come on, I'll show you some evasive moves in this mean little Grasshopper."

The two young men mounted the tiny Piper L-4B, one behind the other. Zach's rear seat was fixed with dual controls. "Are these things operational?"

"Yup. I'm teaching Spotter to fly. Buckle up."

"Okay. Hey, where are the parachutes?"

"Never had any…too heavy."

Zach's eyes widened. "You're kidding."

"Nope. Hang on."

Crego flipped the switches and signaled a bystander to turn the propeller. The little sixty-five-horsepower engine caught quickly and the plane rolled loudly down the grass runway. With two men, the small plane labored to get in the air, finally lifting off just in time to clear a stand of trees.

"That was close, Crego! What circus did you fly for?"

"Relax, Sergeant. I've only crashed two of these little birds."

"Now you tell me," Zach murmured.

"Hell, even Ike can fly one of these. Want to give it a try?"

Feeling trapped, Zach called out, "I don't think so…Eisenhower took lessons."

"Grab the controls. I'll give you a lesson. Watch how they react when I maneuver and don't force the pedals." Crego did some wide circles followed by soft, easy, banked turns. "Okay, doughboy. She's all yours."

Zach followed the same routine he had observed. After completing a big circle, he was gaining confidence. Suddenly the left wing tip dropped, causing the plane to spin and dive.

"You're overcorrecting. *Wooeee!*" Ron Crego screeched.

"Get me out of this!" Zach screamed as the little plane rapidly lost altitude.

Crego calmly took over the controls, gave it gas, and recovered from the spin just three hundred feet from the ground.

Zach struggled to regain his voice. "You set me up!" he yelled.

"Who, me?" Crego howled.

"Yeah you, Ace."

"Sorry. You really did okay, Gates."

Zach hyperventilated and grumbled, "I hope your radio works if we pile up this kite."

"Don't count on it. This sixty-pound crystal set in front of me has a range of only five miles."

"Five miles?" Zach repeated, wondering if he'd misunderstood.

"Yeah, five miles. That's how I got lost at Rhineberg."

Zach shook his head and wondered what he had gotten into. "Where are we headed, Ace?"

"A small French hotel just off a field near Le Havre. Great wine and la dolce vita."

"Do we have enough gas?"

"Twelve gallons."

"That's all?"

"That's a full tank. Heh, we only burn four gallons an hour."

"Crazy!"

Within the hour, the grass strip came into view. Crego circled to come into the wind and headed down. "Hang on, Gates. These flying jeeps always bounce at least once." Zach stiffened his legs as the landing gear came down hard. The gear supports flexed audibly as the plane went airborne for a short distance and then came down again. Crego skillfully straightened it out and taxied up to within fifty yards of the small French hotel where a party was in full swing.

*****

Zach sipped a glass of Muscadet. "I learned a hell of a lesson in Paris, Ace. I'll nurse this drink."

"Well, I'm celebrating V-E Day again."

Zach frowned. "Great."

"Don't worry, doughboy. I fly better with a little French courage in me," Crego grinned.

"Very funny."

After two hours of partying, Ron Crego was slurring his words and looking a little unsteady. Zach ordered a pot of coffee. "Drink this, Ron. That's an order!"

"Yes, mein herr."

Crego sipped the coffee, stood up, and announced, "I'm fine."

"Good. Time to go. It's getting dark."

"You'll have to fly, Gates. I have two heads and my stomach is doing somersaults."

"No jokes, Ace. Get off your ass."

"I'm up, I'm up, I'm ready to fly."

"You better be," Zach replied, starting to worry.

Crego staggered the short distance to the grass landing strip. Zach threw his gear into the Piper Cub and pulled the wheel blocks. "Come on, Ron. What else has to be done before we can get this bird in the air?"

"Yeah, yeah. You'll have to pull the prop. How the hell are you so bright-eyed?"

"Clean living."

"Bull. Get on board."

Ron taxied slowly to the other end of the field and warmed the engine. After a slow, shaky takeoff, they were in the air heading toward the small strip at Camp Pall Mall. Twenty minutes later, Crego's head dropped to his chest as he fought off sleep. The plane began losing altitude. Zach shook the back of Ron's neck. "We're losing altitude. Wake up!" The plane regained altitude and resumed its heading.

"You take over, Gates. I'm beat."

"What?" Zach shouted in disbelief.

"Take over," Crego groaned. "Keep her on the same heading and altitude. If you have trouble, wake me," he sputtered, and promptly fell sound asleep.

Zach closed his eyes, took a deep breath, and gently tested the controls. *I did it once before...as long as I don't try circling and banking.*

Zach flew nervously for ten minutes before Crego began retching in the front seat. Just north of Pall Mall, Crego became violently ill. He threw up and choked, "I'm really sick, Zach. You'll have to land this son-of-a-bitch."

In near panic, Zach looked over the side. "I have the field, Crego. Sober up, goddamn it, and put her down."

No answer came from the front seat. Crego had totally passed out. Zach looked at the quiet, darkening field below. Apparently everyone had the night off. He struggled to remember the feel of the last landing. First, line up with the runway, slowly decrease speed and altitude, and prepare for a bounce. "Damn, I'm going too fast. Ron, wake up, please wake up. I can't do this."

No response came from the front seat. Zach's adrenaline spiked—his whole body trembled as cold sweat trickled down his face and a sick feeling boiled in his stomach. The plane was coming in too fast and at too steep a glide. Suddenly, he was back in combat. *Keep your cool— do something!* The plane struck the ground hard, cracking the landing gear and taking a mighty bounce as Zach pulled up on the stick, cut the engine, and pushed the stick forward. *So far so good—I've done something.* The next touchdown broke the landing gear completely, and the little plane skidded and careened on its belly. "Hail Mary, Mother of Jesus!" Zach screamed as his head smashed into the back of the front seat and flying glass cut into his cheek. Then came those Munchoff visions of flashing, concentric gold rings again—then a dim awareness that he was being helped out of the plane.

*****

Two ambulances took Zach and Ron Crego to the Pall Mall aid station. A welcoming committee of an MP, a doctor, and an angry army major awaited Zach's arrival. Happy to be alive, Zach felt his bandaged face and then remembered Ron. "How is Sergeant Crego?" he asked, fearing the worst.

"Alive! How do you feel?" the doctor asked.

Zach gave a sigh of relief and slowly inventoried his body parts. "Awful. What did I break?"

"Nothing. You lucked out, just bruises, a mild concussion, and two or three stitches."

"That's why my cheek feels numb?"

"Right. How's your head? You took a nasty bump and you already have stitches in the back of your head."

"I have a very large headache."

The MP drew closer. "You look like shit! You're in trouble, soldier."

The army major was next. "Of all the bird-brained stunts. You destroyed valuable government property. What the hell were you thinking?"

"No excuse, sir. Please—how is Sergeant Crego?"

The doctor interceded. "He has a slight concussion and a large hangover. He will recover." Zach mumbled a weak, "Thank you."

The gravel-voiced MP frowned and barked, "Sergeant Gates, were you flying that airplane?"

"Yes and no," Zach stammered through a numb smile.

"What?" the MP and major screamed in unison.

Zach cleared his head and found his full voice. "Sergeant Crego became sick, sir, and we were both flying the airplane."

The MP was unconvinced. "What kind of crap is that?" he snapped.

Zach replied meekly, "It has dual controls, sir."

The major, his voice turning more charitable, asked, "Sergeant, did you land that aircraft or not?"

Zach fought back a painful chuckle and replied wryly, "Thank you for the compliment." The major's face turned red for a brief moment. Then he stifled a laugh. Even the MP sergeant chuckled. Encouraged, Zach bantered, "I'm weak on landings."

The doctor did not laugh. "You're damn lucky you weren't killed," he grumbled.

"Yes, sir." Zach replied quietly. The doctor nodded and reexamined Zach's stitches. Encouraged, Zach again asked about Crego. The MP answered. "He's staying right here until I see about a court-martial."

Zach pondered the court-martial—*time to be creative!* In the most solicitous voice he could muster, he said, "He's a good man. He simply passed out from the exhaust gas that entered the front seat."

The MP looked perplexed. He paused and grunted, "That's pretty weak, soldier."

"Doctor, were these men drunk?" the major asked sternly.

The doctor hesitated. "Sergeant Crego had been drinking. I'm not sure about Sergeant Gates."

The major scowled. "Tomorrow we'll decide whether we court-martial one or both of these assholes."

Meanwhile, the frustrated press corps waiting on news from the Pacific now had dramatic pictures and a wild human interest story on which to apply their talents. The date was August 6, 1945.

ATOM BOMB

August 7, 1945

A terse announcement came from the BBC. The whole camp was at first stunned, then confused, and lastly numb.

> AT 2:45 A.M. PACIFIC TIME, AUGUST 6, THREE B-29 BOMBERS LEFT TINIAN IN THE MARI-ANAS FOR HIROSHIMA, JAPAN. ONE, THE *ENOLA GAY*, WAS ARMED WITH THE WORLD'S FIRST ATOMIC BOMB. ITS PAYLOAD, THE EQUIVALENT OF TWENTY THOUSAND TONS OF TNT, WAS EXPLODED WITH DEVASTATING RESULTS AT 8:45 A.M. THAT WAS 11:15 P.M. LAST NIGHT, BRITISH TIME.

A giant meeting was called. The camp commander, accompanied by his staff and the press corps, asked for quiet. The commander first restated the announcement and then explained that the three planes were part of the 509th Group of the 20th American Air Force. He went on to say that the grisly race between Germany and the Allies to find a weapon that would ensure absolute victory was over. The bomb, he noted, was the result of pooling British and American scientific knowl-edge beginning in 1940 with two billion American dollars spent on its development. He then reminded everyone of the Allies' Potsdam ultima-tum of July 26, demanding unconditional surrender of the Japanese. He invited questions from the press.

"Colonel, is all of this public knowledge?"

"It will be shortly. Both Winston Churchill and the new British Prime

Minister Clement Attlee are working on their announcements. President Truman will make his announcement at 1200 hours, eastern United States time."

"Will there be another air strike?"

"Not if they unconditionally surrender."

"How long will we wait?"

"Politically, who knows? Militarily, I'd guess one week."

"Sir, what is this A-bomb and how does it work?"

"I've been told only that there are two types, a U-235 plutonium bomb and a uranium 238. I believe the latter was used." He hesitated. "Regarding how it works…a West Point friend who saw it tested described it as follows." The camp commander extracted a card from his pocket and read, "There was a blinding flash many times as brilliant as the midday sun and a massive, multicolored mushroom cloud boiling up to forty thousand feet. The steel tower from which the atomic weapon hung was vaporized and where it stood was a huge, sloping crater. A tremendous, sustained roar followed, plus a heavy-pressure wave which could be felt five miles away."

The group went silent. The adjutant rose. "I think that's a good place to adjourn."

*****

The men stayed glued to the radios. That evening, Winston Churchill reported on the BBC. He was accompanied by an army intelligence officer. Their report was a brief but powerful statement: "By God's mercy, British and American science outpaced all German efforts. The possession of these powers by the Germans at any time might have altered the result of the war." He then turned abruptly to the intelligence officer. "Colonel, how close were the Germans to having this weapon?"

"After the British air raids on Penamunde and our costly but effective attacks on the Norwegian heavy water experiments, we always thought we were ahead of them. However, their delivery systems, that is, their rockets, were way ahead of ours. The next in their series, the V-3, was designed to carry an atomic bomb."

That was the end of the news flash. The GIs at Pall Mall were in shock.

"Oh my God, even at the very end we could have lost this goddamn war."

"Now I know why the last battle for Germany was such a mean son-of-a-bitch."

*****

Two days passed without any news from the Japanese. Observer reports and photos of Hiroshima, however, were now made available. "Sixty percent of the city was wiped out; five major industrial plants disappeared; four miles of the city's 6.9 square miles were obliterated. A flash brighter than sunlight covered the city and the slow-rising smoke cloud reached up to the stratosphere."

"My God, they have to surrender now," Zach said to the doctor who was reexamining him.

"Don't count on it. The Japanese people have been kept in the dark about the severity of the raid and, don't forget, they took an even harder hit in March on Tokyo."

"You mean that raid was more devastating than Hiroshima?"

"Absolutely. That was a fire bomb raid by 334 B-29s dropping 1,665 tons of incendiary bombs."

"But this raid was all done by one bomb."

"Yes, and I know it's difficult to believe, but I heard that some of the Japanese cabinet would rather die than surrender. And the main body of the Jap Army is still ready to fight. Some of their generals still believe they can win this thing."

"You're very well informed, Doctor."

The doctor walked over and turned off his radio. "Sorry, Sergeant. I've been listening to the news day and night."

"I understand. So, am I cleared to go home now?"

The doctor hesitated. "I'm sure you'll heal up just fine…but given all the…ah, problems in your case"—he turned a page on Zach's case report—"and it is a head wound…now aggravated by a second injury."

"Doc, can I sign something saying I'm okay?"

"No, I don't think so, especially with all the attention given to your case in the British press."

"I was afraid of that—so what's next?"

"Sergeant, I have no choice; I am obligated to recommend one more neurological examination. The trauma was close to your spinal nerves."

"Great," Zach replied unhappily.

"I really don't think they'll find anything wrong. It should only take a day or two in a general hospital."

"Here in France?"

"No, England. Probably not till after the question of Japan is settled."

*****

Two days after the atomic bomb was dropped on Hiroshima, the Japanese still had not surrendered. Zach, weary of the inconclusive radio reports, bunked down for the night. Loud shouting at 0500 hours awakened him. A second atomic bomb had exploded on Nagasaki, Japan, on August 9 at 11:02 Japanese time, or about 2:02 A.M. French time, only three days after the first.

"This should shake them up," Zach grumbled.

"They'll never quit," replied a sleepy bunkmate.

*****

At 0800, August 11, 1945, there was still no word of surrender. The men gathered around the radio to hear a bomb specialist report. "The Nagasaki bomb was a Uranium-238, not the U-235, dropped on Hiroshima. It is a simpler bomb to physically process. However, this plutonium bomb is less stable than the U-235 so a technique called implosion is used to avoid a premature chain reaction. Best estimates are that forty thousand Japanese may have died."

A political specialist gave the next report. "I wish I could predict flat out that the Japanese have had enough. However, British intelligence has predicted a divided Japanese Supreme War Direction Council. Of the ten men on the council, they predict three generals will vote for surrender and four will vote against it. Admiral Suzuki, the prime minister, and Shigenori Togo are thought to favor a surrender meeting the Potsdam ultimatum. However, intelligence predicts the minister of war, General Anami, will never surrender."

Another political analyst had a translation of what General Anami had said after Hiroshima. "It is far too early to say that the war is lost. We will inflict severe losses on the enemy when he invades, that is certain. It is by no means impossible that we may be able to reverse the situation in our favor, pulling victory out of defeat. Furthermore, our army will not submit to demobilization, and they know they may not surrender, since that would incur heavy punishment. We have no alternative but to continue the war."

"Any more good news?" the BBC announcer asked.

"Sorry, no good news. The fact is the Japanese have stockpiled tremendous resources. Their people are a determined lot, and of major importance are the size and quality of most of the Japanese Army that remains. For some of these fanatics, it is a disgrace to surrender and an honor to fight to the end."

"What about the kamikaze? Are they still active?"

"Yes. The 'Divine Wind' is very active. We have reports on them as late as yesterday."

"I have a question about a note attached to the atomic bomb called Little Boy regarding the cruiser *Indianapolis*. What was that all about?" a reporter asked.

The analyst cleared his throat. "I'm not sure I should comment on that."

"Sir, British intelligence has already released news of her sinking," another asserted.

"Very well then. The cruiser *Indianapolis* delivered the first atomic bomb to Tinian Island on July 26. On July 29, while leaving Tinian for Guam, she was torpedoed. It is a grisly story—883 men died. Most spent eighty-four hours in shark-infested waters. Over four hundred sailors were eaten by the sharks. It was the last major American warship lost to date and one of the greatest losses in the history of the United States Navy." He paused. "We should thank God for one thing—she was torpedoed right *after* delivering Little Boy and not before."

The commentator's discussion came to an abrupt end when a news bulletin interrupted. "B-29 attacks were to be resumed on four cities and the Honshu airfields. The nine days of impatient stand-down by the Allied naval and air forces finally ended. Despite two atomic attacks and the pounding of their almost one-million-man army in China by Russian heavy tanks, the Japanese still had not agreed to demands for unconditional surrender. Adding arrogant insult was the report that Admiral Ugaki was continuing his kamikaze attacks on Allied naval ships."

"They ain't never gonna quit," a GI lamented.

The late breaking news also stated that two unarmed American naval ships had just been torpedoed by a Japanese submarine. That, coupled with the continuing kamikaze attacks, was enough for the camp commander to act. All military personnel were to be on duty the next day, Sunday, August 12, a grim reminder that the war was not yet over.

*****

With all of the excitement, the L-4 Grasshopper case became less important to the MPs. However, the British press, weary of nine days of Japanese vacillation, continued to report the crash, expanding it as a human interest story about an American infantry sergeant who landed an airplane on his first flight, saving the life of the pilot overcome by exhaust gas. Graphic pictures were in abundance.

Zach visited the recovering Ron Crego. "Well, boozer, you made the newspapers."

"Yeah, but you come off as the hero."

"And you come off as a lucky soldier drunk on gas fumes with a dog. How is Spotter?"

"Spotter is big and fat. The guys know he likes beer. What about me?" Crego griped.

"You? What about me?" Zach retorted.

"I heard all about you…"

"Okay, so how are you feeling?"

"One shot of Calvados and I'll be ready to fly."

"Not if you're in the stockade."

"Not a chance. The press bought your gas fumes story and the war is all but over."

"Yeah, but the MPs know better."

"It's over, I tell you. I'm headed back to law school and then into politics."

"Politics?"

"Yeah. My dad is a ward boss in New York."

"I should have known. I hope you'll run on the prohibition ticket."

"Of course…thanks, Zach, thanks for everything. Just one thing."

"Yeah?"

"You're weak on three-point landings."

Zach and Ron shook hands. "Good-bye, Ron Crego. Thanks for the ride! See you in the States."

"Yeah. Good luck, Gates. And thanks."

*****

All talk of court-martial for Sergeants Crego and Gates was dropped abruptly when at 0430, August 15, 1945, the BBC transmitted a message from the emperor of Japan.

A Japanese announcer had asked all citizens and soldiers to stand respectfully in front of their radio sets. Then came the Japanese national anthem followed by the voice of the emperor. It was the first time in history that he had spoken on the radio. The translation of his message followed.

"The enemy has begun to employ a new and most cruel bomb, the power of which to do damage is indeed incalculable, taking the toll of many innocent lives.

For this reason, we have ordered our government to accept the provisions of surrender demanded by the United States, Great Britain, China, and the Soviet Union."

A heartbreaking footnote to this long-awaited good news was the delayed announcement of the torpedoing of the USN cruiser

Indianapolis.

The long war was finally over! After a moment of silent reflection, all hell broke loose and pandemonium reigned. Hundreds of GIs headed for Paris with or without passes. The MPs gave up and joined in the celebration.

ENGLAND: HOSPITAL REUNION

Zach's orders called for him to report to a general military hospital in Tidworth, England. After a medical evaluation there, he would be redeployed to the US.

Within days, Zach and the troops from Camp Pall Mall were on their way to Le Havre. This French port was just east of the D-day beaches. From Le Havre the troops would board small ships and sail across the English Channel to Southampton and other nearby cities.

On August 14, 1945, Zach detrained at Le Havre and boarded his ship headed for Southampton. As he viewed the peaceful channel, he was haunted by memories of less happy days crossing the then-angry seaway. The gentle roll of the ship underway lulled him into a doze and it was as if he was back in England in the wake of D-day...

*****

In the camp city of Tidworth, the anxiety level was high. Rumors were running rampant. Going off to battle for the first time is something a soldier never forgets. He could still see the frightened looks on the faces of the advanced units as they departed for Southampton. Vehicles moved slowly bumper-to-bumper along the jammed roadways, banishing any possibility of secrecy. It was obvious to all that a heavily armored division was headed "over there." Where they would land over there was secret, at least to the GIs. Zach smiled as he heard once again the voices of frightened young men trying to determine their destination.

"Can't be Le Havre. I think the Germans still hold it."

"One Mulberry is still working, isn't it?"

"Is the port at Cherbourg ours?"

"All the beaches are now clear…aren't they?"

Zach brushed away a tear and then agonized over another memory. He heard Ken Whedder's now tragic words. *"Now this beats D-day by a mile. Those poor bastards took twenty-five hundred casualties doing this on Omaha. We are two lucky guys, Zach."*

*****

Zach's reverie was interrupted when land came into view. Soon the friendly ports of Plymouth, Portsmouth, and Southampton greeted the strangely quiet ship. Tired, war-weary ships were rolling gently against their moorings in every port, each drawing more water as they double loaded their human cargo for their long journey to America. Zach walked to the crowded rail and stared quietly at the ships. He heard the soldier next to him sigh and say, "We're finally going home, Sergeant."

Zach turned to the smiling young private and observed that his empty left sleeve was folded above the elbow. Zach forced a smile, turned away, and stared down at the water below. "Yeah," he replied softly, feeling much older than his twenty-one years.

Southampton, England

The magnificent ship *H.M.S. Queen Mary* towered above all of the others in the harbor. In her role as a troop carrier, she could transport ten thousand personnel at one time.

The men on Zach's much smaller ship were being off-loaded to buses and six-by-six trucks for transport to the many nearby campsites for final processing. Zach showed his orders to the dock officer, who directed him to an ambulance. His destination—Tidworth, England, home of Tidworth Barracks and a general hospital.

As he bounced along the road to nearby Tidworth, many poignant memories flooded his head. It was here that his division was stationed before crossing the channel. Tidworth Barracks encompassed a huge collection of historic, pleasant-looking, two-story brick barracks. The grounds were landscaped and treed unlike so many of the hastily commissioned US Army camps.

Zach laughed out loud as he recalled how impressed the men were — "not bad," "damn fine"—and then the barracks filled up! His flashbacks ended abruptly when the ambulance screeched to a stop. "Look alive, Sergeant, we're here," the driver shouted.

At the busy general hospital located in the heart of comfortable Tidworth Barracks, Zach was assigned a patient number and a bed in a crowded ward. He showed his number to a Brit wearing a Desert Rats patch and leg bandages covering severe burns. "Looks good, Yank. A low one means they want you out of the country fast," he chuckled.

"Yeah, I know. Over here, overpaid, and…that other thing."

The Brit studied Zach's armored patch. "Not really, Yank. We were all damn glad to see you when you relieved us in the Ardennes."

"How did you get burned?" Zach asked.

"Flamethrower."

"Never ran into one," Zach said.

The Brit looked sheepishly out of the window. "It was one of ours."

Zach forced a quiet smile. "That hurts double."

"Right you are, Yank. I got too far ahead of a Churchill tank firing one of those monster flamethrowers. Just one small flare of that bloody stuff caught me in the legs and here I am."

"What a bitch. Where were you when you got hit?"

"Just west of Wesel."

"On the Rhine! Know it well. When will you get out of here?"

"Who knows? It takes forever to patch up third-degree burns. I feel for the poor jerries who got hit with that greasy shit."

"I've never seen tank-fired flamethrowers. Do they have much range?" Zach asked.

"Oh yes, 140 meters or more. They had more range than the bloody Panzerfausts."

Flabbergasted, Zach thought for a moment. "Lord, that's about 150 yards."

"Right, Sergeant, and it was a stream like a fire hose. They were death on pillboxes, bunkers, trenches, basements—the stuff just followed the openings."

"Tommy, you're lucky you caught only a flare."

"Amen to that. What they got you in for?"

Before Zach could respond, an orderly entered. "Sergeant Gates, you have a visitor, another patient."

A young soldier with a smile from ear to ear entered. "Hi, Sergeant Gates. How are you?"

Zach's eyes widened and his heart raced. "Stosh! Stosh Kosinski!" The two men embraced as Zach answered, "I'm going to be fine, Stosh. How are you?"

"Good as new."

"That's great news, Stosh. How long will you be here?"

Stosh frowned. "I leave tomorrow. I thought I'd miss you." He shuffled his feet. "Everybody thought you were killed in the jeep. I set 'em straight."

"You sure did, Stosh. Now tell me what happened to our old outfit. Norm Ricks told me the division went everywhere."

"Yeah, Sergeant Ricks got stuck in Klatovy; most of the low-point guys went to the 35th, 26th or 83rd Infantry."

"None went to armored divisions?" Zach queried.

"No. Tom says these divisions are just for transportation home. He thinks we'll be reassigned or discharged when we get home."

"What about the tankers?"

"They were studying amphibious something or other in Belgium. Then they were supposed to go to China. I think Lieutenant Grinnell went to the 6th Armored. He said he would write you."

"He's a good guy. Are any of the squad still here in England?"

"No. The 35th left on the *Queen Mary* last week. Oh, but this is good news. Henry Franier made it and went home with them."

Zach's mind filled with combat images of that terrible night. "Thank God. That's very good news, Stosh. Was he 100 percent?"

"Yeah. We talked about the patrol. I gave him your address in Milwaukee. He wants to write to you."

"Thank you, Stosh. What about Bruno and Bash?"

"They volunteered for some kind of special forces unit before the war ended in Japan." Zach nodded and smiled knowingly. "They were two tough soldiers."

"They wanted you to go with them, said you'd make a good officer."

"That's a real compliment coming from those two."

"Yeah. I always liked Bash, but I didn't think Sergeant Nitchke liked anybody, but he gave me a hug when I told him you weren't in the jeep with Jim." Stosh hesitated as if he had more to say.

"What is it, Stosh?"

His expression was uncertain. "I guess it's okay now—"

"What's okay, Stosh? You're scaring me."

"We never told you about Lieutenant Franks, your friend from Illinois."

Zach raised his hand. "Relax, Stosh. Norm Ricks told me the whole story—you were right in not telling me."

Stosh looked away and then back at Zach. "We were all real happy when you didn't go for the commission."

"Thank you, Stosh."

Stosh brightened and raised his eyebrows. "Did Ricks tell you about the Unna girls?"

"Oh yes, he kept telling lies, trying to lift my spirits when I missed you guys in Klatovy."

"No lies, Zach. These babes were for real! You should have seen them all cleaned up!"

Zach rolled his eyes and changed the subject. "Stosh, is there any more news on Jim Wing and the other guys in the jeep? Norm didn't have much to say."

Stosh gathered his thoughts and lowered his voice. "I heard they found Jim's dog tags and maybe some body parts."

Zach hung his head and his voice caught. "Judas…there but for the grace of God…"

Stosh hurried to change the subject. He picked up a bag from the floor. "I brought you some stuff. I'm glad I caught you."

Zach opened the bag and named each item as he picked it up. "My God, Stosh, my old Walther P-38 pistol, my navy glasses from the Rhine, my Combat Infantry Badge, and my dog tags. How did you get these?"

"Sander and Brenner pulled these out of your stuff, except for the dog tags. They were in your blouse pocket."

"Yeah, I heard they divided up my things."

Stosh's voice had a tinge of guilt. "That was just before I got back…they really thought you were dead."

"I understand, Stosh. Bless all of you guys. Tell you what, Stosh, you keep the pistol. The navy glasses are more important to me."

Looking relieved, Stosh declared, "I'm going to keep it always. Thanks, Sergeant Gates."

A busy British doctor interrupted. "This will only take a minute, Sergeant. I don't want you to be concerned, but I'm going to have a neurologist look at you just to be on the safe side."

"Good, then I can go home."

"Not for a week or so. Our neurologist is consulting in Liege."

Zach nodded as the doctor left.

"That doesn't sound so good," Stosh said with a look of concern.

"Piece of cake, Stosh. The guy won't find anything. I'll be out in a flash."

"Yeah, like shit on a hot tin roof." Stosh smiled.

Memories of the Beak at Heide Woods struck both of them. Zach spoke first. "McNutt was a fine officer."

"I hope his arm gets better," Stosh lamented.

Zach nodded and searched for another topic. "Stosh, Ricks says you figured out this crazy point system. How does it work?"

Stosh was quick to answer. "You need eighty-five points to be first out, but it gets tricky."

"How's that?"

"Because so many low-point guys are already on the way home."

"So now they won't be needed in the Pacific?"

"Right, so they'll be first out and the high-point guys are still stuck with occupation duty."

"So we're better off if we don't have eighty-five points?"

"That's the way Tom figured it," Stosh said.

"How are the points figured?"

"According to *Yank* magazine, you get one point for each month in service and another for each month in combat."

Zach started adding his up. "What else?"

"Let's see, one for each battle star…"

"What about decorations?"

"Oh yeah, five for the Combat Infantry Badge—"

"That's all?" Zach replied in disbelief.

"Right, the guys really bitched about that. Even the Purple Heart and Bronze Star are worth only five points."

Zach scratched his head and responded ruefully, "I guess it doesn't matter in my case. My records are all hung up in the War Department—probably forever."

Stosh laughed. "That snafu is a good thing. You'd be way over with the Bronze Star and three Purple Hearts—you'd be stuck here with the old guys."

"I think just one Purple Heart, Stosh, but I'd still be over eighty-five points."

"Didn't you get a Purple Heart for the canal?"

"You mean my thumb?"

"Yeah, when the grenade came back up the stairs."

"And you threw it back," Zach laughed.

"Yeah."

"No, Bill just put a compression bandage on it."

"He said you needed a stitch."

"Yeah, I blew five points."

"What about that wooden bullet?"

Zach looked at his hand, which still contained a piece of wood. "I guess they thought it was just a sliver. Nobody believed there were wooden bullets."

"Doesn't seem fair."

"Hey, this is the army, only this time it works for me," Zach chuckled.

"If they straighten out all your decorations, when you get to the States you'll be first out."

"We'll see. How many points do you have?"

"About sixty-five or seventy. The guys with kids, like Pappy, really racked up the points."

"Oh really?"

"Yeah, twelve points for each kid, but I think it's limited to three kids."

"Ricks said Pappy got a special deal."

"Yeah, with six kids he should," Stosh agreed.

Several hours of war stories followed before the two friends said tearful good-byes. Stosh gave a final salute and was gone.

Zach picked up his broken US Navy binoculars from the Rhine crossing. *Now that was a day and a half.* "Good old Stosh," he said aloud.

COMBAT-CRAZED VETERAN THEORY

Zach's medical testing began early the next morning. After a quick set of X-rays, he was returned to the ward.

"Well, Yank, how'd it go?" the British combat veteran asked.

"Beats me. The doc said I still need to see a neurologist."

"That means you're stuck till they find one. Now you're in for it," the Brit laughed.

"How's that?"

"Some wet American psychologist will suck your blood and then interview you to see if it's safe to send you packed-up frontliners home."

Zach's face went blank. "Wet? Packed-up?"

The Brit grinned. "That's limey talk for *screwed up,* as you Yanks say."

Zach's eyes flashed. "That's absurd. Are they afraid we'll go crazy when we get home?"

The Brit turned serious. "Not so funny, Yank. Some bloody psychologist thinks just that."

"Bull!" Zach replied, thinking the Brit was putting him on.

The Englishman locked eyes. "No bull! The latrine rumors call it the Combat-Crazed Veteran Theory."

Zach sighed. "Oh, for Christ's sake—all I want to do is sit on my ass and forget this damn war."

"Brace yourself, Yank. You're in for hugger-mugger blood tests, and then you'll have to be deprogrammed."

"Okay, limey, what's *hugger-mugger*?"

"Get with it, Yank. That's what Brits call classified or top secret."

The language overload got to Zachary. "You're pulling my leg, Tommy—that's American for bullshitting me."

The Brit laughed, but replied with a straight face, "I'm telling you, Yank, they want us to learn to be sweet and loverly so we don't shoot up the place when we get home."

Zach shook his head. "Of all the crap. Where are you getting this baloney?"

"I read a lot. It's no baloney, Yank. You'll see."

*****

Zach's British friend was right. During the seven-day wait for the neurologist, he was visited by sixty-year-old Dr. Craig Ryder, a research psychologist. "Sergeant Gates, I'm studying reentry."

"Reentry?"

"Yes. The War Department is interested in how difficult it will be for combat soldiers to adjust to civilian life."

"I'm sure I'll be fine, Doctor Ryder."

"I hope so, but it's clear from your file that you've seen some harsh frontline combat."

"I didn't know I was different," Zach said matter-of-factly.

Dr. Ryder, affecting an objective, professional face and tone, replied, "Well, you're the special one out of every fifteen soldiers in the army who faced extended combat."

Zach processed Doctor Ryder's words and became concerned. "I didn't know that."

"Most people don't. I presume you know you've also been listed as KIA, MIA, and POW."

"That was a comedy of errors," Zach exclaimed.

"Sergeant, you must admit your case is a bit unusual. For example, only 8.6 men out of every one thousand were KIA. You had almost as many in a twelve-man squad."

Zach thought about his British friend's remarks. "Doc, I'm not going to be some combat-crazed nut case."

"Whoa—where did you get that?" the psychologist exclaimed.

Zach felt a little defensive and replied quietly, "From a Brit in my ward. He's been reading."

"Sergeant, that's not where I'm coming from…but it's true there are a few people who worry that combat-violence experience may transfer to society."

Zach's tone became more urgent. "What's with the blood tests and six months of deprogramming for combat guys?"

The startled psychologist opted for humor. "Zachary, I think I'll have you moved to another ward! However, your British friend is right about the blood tests, but that's not related to reentry…well, for the most part it's not."

"I've had plenty of blood tests, Doc. What's this one for?"

"The psychiatrists want to find out if men who have successfully handled the stress of combat have different levels of a stress-related hormone called cortisol."

Zach looked perplexed. "For what purpose…selection?"

"Very astute, Sergeant Gates."

"So this cortisol knocks out stress?"

"We're pretty sure about physical functions like sickness, pain, even temperature extremes, but we're just learning about things psychological."

Zach's face turned serious. "Interesting. What have you learned?"

Dr. Ryder smiled. "I've learned that ASTP guys ask a lot of questions."

"Sorry."

"No, don't be. It fits the profile we're studying. We're quite sure that cortisol also produces more sensitivity to and more awareness of one's surroundings—a critical asset in combat. We're also studying other hormones that produce calmness and relaxation under stress."

"Sounds complicated, Dr. Ryder."

"True, and unproven. In any event, I am primarily concerned about how heavy combat affects social, emotional, and personal adjustment to reentering society."

"Are you saying that guys like me will have problems?"

"Yes, Zachary, I think you'll have some difficult nights, but I am not worried that you'll shoot up the place as a war-crazed combat veteran."

Feeling better about the discussion, Zach smiled. "I'll tell my limey friend that."

"Please do, by all means, please do."

Zach tested the good doctor one more time. "So I won't need six months of therapy and deprogramming?"

Ryder put on a false frown. "I don't think so, but you should know that we have many men undergoing therapy right now."

Zach paused and reminisced. "I understand—I've seen good soldiers lose it on an unusually tragic day, or sometimes from just too many days on line—I've come close."

"Zachary, I understand. I've seen your file."

Zach nodded and spoke slowly. "Perhaps we leave our men on line too long—longer than the Brits, I've heard."

The psychologist sounded a touch defensive. "That's true about the British…we are looking into the problem."

Zach shrugged. "Good."

"Sergeant, all these problems aside, my goal is simply to find out what, if anything, we should be doing for special guys like you."

"I do understand, Doctor. How can I help?"

"Okay, for starters, how do you react to loud noises?"

"A car backfire puts me on the ground, but I expect to grow out of that."

"How about dreams or nightmares?"

"Sure, but isn't that normal for a while?"

"Of course it is. How about feelings of guilt? Things you might have done differently?"

Zach looked away, then spoke in measured words. "Sometimes, usually at night, I relive decisions—situations where I feel I screwed up, and where men died."

Dr. Ryder stood up, looked out of the window, and sat down again. "Zachary, you are not alone. I'd like your opinion on some of the things we've heard from other veterans. Some saw combat, some did not."

"Sure."

Dr. Ryder proceeded to read. *"For most veterans, the first feeling upon reentry into the world of home is relief or perhaps triumph. For many, life began again as if it had never stopped.*

"However, for those who saw frontline combat, the feeling that followed relief was 'I made it! I'm still alive!' But for many, the next feeling was one of guilt. 'So many of my friends didn't make it. So many came home with broken bodies or tortured minds.'"

Dr. Ryder looked up from his notes. "It seems obvious that for those young men in combat leadership roles, the emotional load was unreasonably heavy. Here are some actual statements: *'My orders or decisions caused men to die.' 'How come I survived?' 'If only I had done more or done it differently.' 'Will I be punished?' 'What will I say?' 'How will I…how can I explain?'"*

Dr. Ryder stood up. "Any comment, Sergeant?"

Zach put one hand to his chin and replied slowly, "I've asked all those questions."

The psychologist sat down. "Okay, let me try some more of this on you. *'For some of these tortured veterans, the escape is simply to lose all motivation, to let go, to deny this goddamn war, to avoid the very thought of it, even to seek isolation, to seek help in alcohol or worse.'"* Dr. Ryder paused and spoke directly. "Zachary, in the cases where extreme terror, shock, or guilt are deeply buried in one's psyche, a near neurotic state may pertain. Some combat veterans we have observed suffer periods of acute panic that may last anywhere from a few seconds to an hour or more. They usually come on suddenly, mount to a high intensity, and then subside. In a full-blown anxiety attack, some report the sensation of impending death—a terrifying experience while it lasts. Sergeant Gates, hear this: 39 percent of our medical discharges to date are for combat neurosis or battle fatigue—how are we psychologists doing so far?"

"First of all, you're scaring the hell out of me!"

Dr. Ryder stood up and exhaled heavily. "I'm sorry, Zachary, but I'm really interested in your thoughts and experiences—you're a special soldier. Will you help me out here?"

Zach hesitated before answering. "Of course I will—I've felt all of the things we've discussed, especially when things weren't going well, like when a friend was killed, or when there were gross injuries."

Dr. Ryder picked up Zach's file. "I'm sure you did. In reviewing your file, I agonized over the stress and anxiety you must have experienced at battles in Rhineberg, Unna, Heide Woods, and, a real neurosis producer, at Kirchellen."

"You've done your homework, Professor. Those are days I hope to forget...add Munchoff to your list."

"Well, Zachary, that's what this research is all about. Let me read what another combat infantry sergeant had to say about this. *"I'm not sure that anyone who hasn't been there can really understand. I still jump at every unusual noise. Some nights I awake on the floor searching for my rifle. Doc tells me this will get better, but I doubt I will ever be completely the same."*

Zach stared out of the window. "Oh, I think in time I'll stop repressing and get past the uglier memories."

"Was it sheer repression that allowed you to cope during combat?"

"At first, but that didn't work for long."

"Go on."

"You really want to hear this?"

"Yes, I do."

"Acting 'as if' helped me, especially after I was promoted."

"As if?"

"As if I were very brave and on top of things, sometimes almost nonchalant, as if I were unafraid of the fire."

"A kind of whistling in the dark?"

"Right. That helped but it wasn't enough."

"How do you mean?"

Zach paused and stared out of the window. "This sounds dumb."

"Please go on."

"Okay. Well, to get over the mind-killing fear and hope to survive, you had to become a fatalist and know that you…" Zach paused, "and others, will die. Among my squad the word was 'when your number's up, it's up, and that's that.' Only then can you function as a combat soldier—you still know fear, but you don't fear death in quite the same way as before. You have made a pact with God. He will take you when your time is up."

The psychologist's eyes moistened. He stared at the floor in deep thought. *These brave young men—what a desperate yet pragmatic way to cope.* He cleared his throat. "One more question, Sergeant Gates, and I'll let you go."

"Shoot." Zach smiled. "I mean, okay."

"What are your for plans after you're discharged?"

"I'm going to smell the roses…escape, as you folks say…and then I'm going to work very hard at trying to forget the pain and heartache."

"Time and new challenges will help, Zachary."

"I'm sure…it's all the men killed in action that are hard to forget."

"You will probably never forget them. But life goes on—it will get easier."

"Yeah. I think they'd want me to get on with my life."

"And you will get on with it. Will you go back to school?"

"If this GI Bill is for real, I probably will."

"I'm pleased to hear that, Zachary. Will you study engineering?"

"I don't think so. Being a combat squad leader has raised all kinds of questions about why people do the things they do and why they vary so much under load. I'm still working on thoughts like that."

"Zach, you'd clearly make a good leader but also a good teacher or therapist. Any interest in these areas?"

"I really don't know. I need to escape this war for a bit longer."

"A wise answer. I would only advise that you go back to school as soon as you're ready. I feel that your reentry into the real world will be much easier if you're involved in things intellectual."

"Thank you, Dr. Ryder."

*****

On day six, Zach had another visitor, Major Buchanan "Buck" Wheeler, the B-17 pilot who had been rescued by Zach's squad somewhere across the Rhine.

Zach did a double take. "Major Wheeler, this is a surprise. How did you find me?"

"I wrote to your unit. I heard your crazy Munchoff story from a Sergeant Ricks who was stuck in Czechoslovakia. How are you feeling?"

"A-okay, Major. A final check by a neurologist and I'll be out of here. Are you all healed up?"

"Oh yeah. I was back in the air in less than a month, thanks to you. Gates, call me Buck. We're a lot less formal in the air corps, and the war is over."

Zach grinned. "Okay, Buck. I'm Zach."

"I promised you a ride in a B-17, and it's all set as soon as the medics say it's okay."

"Great! I don't know what to say."

"I owe you a whole lot more than a ride in a B-17, Zach. There is just one problem."

"Oh?"

Buck expressed a quiet, slow smile. "My crew doesn't want you to handle any landings."

Zach chuckled. "They heard about my L-4 screw-up in France."

"Everybody in England read about it. My crew is still laughing about engine gas."

Zach rolled his eyes. "I'll bet."

"Seriously, Zach, the crew thinks you're a hero. They're all anxious to meet you."

"Well I'm anxious to meet them, and I'm really excited about flying in *Tahoe Revenge.*"

"Great. We'll do it. They'll want to hear more about your L-4 and Munchoff experiences."

"Thanks, Buck."

The men shook hands. Memories of that terrible night flashed across Buck's mind. His voice caught. "I'll be in touch."

*****

On day seven, Zach still had not seen the neurologist, but he was examined by the plastic surgeon. "Your Grasshopper scars will fade. The wood splinter in your hand will eventually work itself out. I'll let the neurologist look at the more serious scar on the back of your head."

Zach did a double take. "You know about the L-4 landing?"

"Yes, Sergeant. I read the papers," the doctor replied impassively.

*****

On day eight, the long wait for the neurologist was over. The busy doctor said nothing and went right to Zach's head. He expertly extracted some minor debris from Zach's wounds and studied the bump on his forehead. Almost as an afterthought, he turned to Zach and said clinically, "I've talked to the psychologist. You seem to be tracking. The scar has stopped weeping. You may want to grow your hair longer to cover it."

"That's it?" Zach exclaimed, surprised at the brevity of the examination.

"That's it, soldier. I have more serious problems to attend to. Good luck."

"Then I have no disability to worry about?" Zach asked with a note of anxiety.

The neurologist thought for a moment. "All head wounds are granted 9 percent disability."

Confused and concerned, Zach echoed, "Nine percent?" The doctor nodded vacantly and left. The orderly smiled. "Not to worry, Sergeant, it's SOP."

Still bewildered, Zach iterated, "Nine percent?"

"They're just covering their asses, Sergeant, especially in your crazy case."

"What am I missing here?" Zach persisted.

A lopsided grin crossed the orderly's face. "At 10 percent, you can draw disability pay for life."

*****

The medical research team met the next day. The doctors found that Sergeant Gates met their hypothesized blood and hormonal profiles. The psychologist concluded that Zachary was adjusting on schedule and should have only normal reentry problems. Dr. Ryder concluded, "These young people heal so fast physically. I hope our assessments are correct about emotional and social adjustment. Lord, what we expected of these young men."

The group cleared Zachary for flying on the weekend.

FLYING FORTRESS – AFTERMATH

Pre-Flight

Air Corps Sergeant John Palmeri arrived early Friday to pick up Zach. He stuck out his hand. "Buck says you're ready to pilot *Tahoe Revenge*," he announced with a straight face.

Zach grinned. "I guess you read the *Times* article."

Sergeant Palmeri chuckled. "Yeah, Buck showed it to everybody."

Zach groaned. "I imagine I'll get a razzing from the crew."

Palmeri chuckled. "Oh sure, but don't let it get to you. They really respect your guts in saving that drunken pilot's ass, and Gates...they know how you rescued Buck."

Zach lowered his eyes. "Thanks, Palmeri. Where are we going?"

"Kimbolton, just west of London, home of the 379th Bomb Group."

"How big is a group?"

"Everything in the air force is in twos, it seems. Two squadrons are a group, two groups are a wing, two wings are a command."

"And how big is a squadron?"

"Ours is two, sometimes three flights, and a flight is usually three aircraft. I was warned you ASTP guys ask a lot of questions," Palmeri answered with a grin.

Zach grimaced. "True, Palmeri, but I'm really dumb about the air corps." Zach paused, "Unless you fly L-4s."

Palmeri laughed out loud. "Listen, that liaison flying is no bargain. I'd rather be armed and up as high as I can get."

"You're right, Palmeri. That little airplane is naked—no guns of any kind."

"Yeah, and Dex says the L-4 has no parachutes and only a crystal set radio."

"Right, John, with a range of about five miles."

"Zach, you should quiz Dex on technical stuff. He's our brain—wants to be a history professor."

"Is that Dex Gallant, the copilot I heard about?"

"Yeah. He's the guy who landed in the British sector when he bailed out. We're picking him up at Busby Park."

"He was lucky. What's at Busby Park?"

"Headquarters 8th Air Force. Here we are."

Lieutenant Gallant was waiting outside. "Welcome, Zachary Gates. Thanks for saving my skipper's ass." Zach nodded. Dex responded quickly, "I'm Dex Gallant—how are you feeling?"

Zach posed his hands in a steering position and smiled broadly. "I'm ready to fly."

"Oh no, not that," Gallant chuckled.

Zach's face folded into a phony scowl. "I'm a little weak on landings."

Gallant laughed. "Yeah, I read that. You won't have to land this big bird, but Buck may let you copilot."

"I'm ready, as long as I don't have to navigate."

Dex smirked. "No, Zach, it's my turn."

Sergeant Palmeri interrupted. "Really? What happened to our navigator, Dex?"

"Tomlinson is on his way home—death in the family," Dex replied, and climbed in the jeep.

"Great. I hope we don't get lost," Palmeri joked.

"Hey, I went to school. Drive, that's an order."

"Yes, sir, mein herr."

"Dex, will we have a full crew?"

"Yes and no, Zach. We'll only have two of our regular crew plus John here and our crew chief from our usual group of ten men."

Zach looked up at the peaceful blue sky. "I guess we won't need a bombardier or a team of machine gunners."

"No, not this trip, but we will have extra people now that we're not burdened with six thousand pounds of bombs."

"What's that all about?"

"Our ground crew guys want to see some of the targets we bombed during the war."

"Where are we going?"

"All over the place, if Buck approves. I'm still trying to find a field in Holland. Buck said you would like to visit Margraten."

"I really would. I have friends buried there."

Dex nodded. "I'll work it out."

"Thanks, Gallant. Have you been with this crew long?"

"I joined Buck right after the Allied raids that destroyed 75 percent of Hamburg. That's where they lost my predecessor when *Tahoe Lady* ran into a shitload of flak."

Zach shook his head sympathetically. "Bad day," he said softly.

"Yup, the copilot was killed, but the plane and the rest of the crew made it back."

"That's some consolation. How many missions are we talking about?"

"Buck did seventy missions before we lost the airplane."

"Yeah, I know about that one. What's normal?"

"Depends on the year. Back in '40 and '41 the British lost 60 percent of their planes over a period of thirty missions. When the 8th got into it in '42 and '43, very few B-17 crews survived twenty-five missions. Buck's record was unusual."

"I heard you were a history buff," Zach grinned.

"Yeah, I was a history major at Ohio State. I'd like to teach some day."

"Well, buckeye, I'm impressed. What's the worst you've seen?"

"Ask Palmeri; he's still scared."

John swallowed hard. "Jet fighters."

"Yeah, ME-262s, six of 'em," Dex groaned.

"Messerschmidts?" Zach asked.

"Right. It was brutal. In less than twenty minutes, they took out fourteen B-17s."

"My God! Didn't you have any fighter cover?"

"No, not really," Dex sighed.

Palmeri nodded and took a deep breath. "They were a few miles ahead and by the time they reached us, the jets were long gone."

Zach shuddered. "Thank God they didn't have very many of them."

"Amen to that."

Palmeri called out, "Here we are! *Tahoe Revenge* is sitting out there with our passengers."

Zach eyed the giant airplane. "Is she ready to fly?" he asked with a tingle of anticipation.

"She'd better be. This time it's their asses if we come down hard," Palmeri cracked.

Zach was pushed up into the big plane and moved forward to the cockpit. Dex and Palmeri checked on the passengers. Buck and the flight engineer had just finished going through their checklist. The engineer shook hands and went outside for a hard look. Zach was clearly impressed. "Quite an airplane, Major," Zach observed.

"Want to hear about her? We're still taking on fuel."

Zach exhaled and looked around. "Everything you know."

Buck grinned. "I should have known."

Zach turned 180 degrees to the rear. "I know it's a Boeing B-17 with a very scary catwalk over the bomb bays and that's about it."

"This model is a seventy-foot, B-17G with a one hundred-foot wing span and four cyclone R-1820 engines which move her at 315 mph at twenty-five thousand feet."

"There are guns aplenty; I can see why it's called a flying fortress," Zach observed.

"It is now! The earlier E and F models weren't as heavily armed. At one time, the air force wanted to eliminate some of the guns to increase bomb capacity but the crews nixed that."

"Interesting. How many guns are there?"

"There are three powered gun turrets, a tail, a ventral, and a dorsal turret."

"The ventral is the heavy rotating steel ball hanging down in the center?"

"Right, and the dorsal is on top."

"How many 50-calibers are we talking about?"

"Thirteen, counting two side-beam guns plus two 30s in the nose."

"That's firepower!"

"Oh yeah—we've hurt some people."

Zach studied the instrument panel. "How far will this big bird go on a tank of gas?"

"Around eight hundred to one thousand miles—depends on the load and the wind."

"Dex says she'll carry six thousand pounds of bombs," Zach said.

"You have to put the weight of the fuel into the equation. Only four thousand on a really long flight; on a short run, maybe up to seventeen thousand pounds."

"Got it. Now, do we know where we're going?"

"I hope so. Dex is both navigator and copilot today."

"Yeah, I heard. I thought I'd help out as bombardier," Zach joked.

"Very well. Then you better study that Norden Bomb Sight," Buck quipped.

Zach stood up and looked at the scary bombardier's seat. He shook his head and kidded, "It's more technical than an L-4 system."

Buck was laughing as Dex climbed aboard. "We're loaded—what's so funny?"

"Gates is our bombardier," Buck said with a straight face.

Dex forced a serious face and replied briskly, "They dropped hand grenades from L-4s, didn't they?"

D-day Review

The B-17 was loaded. Buck turned to his part-time navigator. "Dex, are we cleared to go?"

"I am if you and the tower are, Skipper."

"Let's turn 'em over. I assume you have a flight plan?"

"Pretty much. Just head east across the North Sea," Dex said nonchalantly.

"What? We're not bombing Berlin!"

"Oops. Sorry, Buck. I haven't done this for awhile. How about south across the channel?"

"Boy, I'm glad the war's over," chortled upfront passenger Zachary Gates.

Buck coaxed the big plane up into the air and leveled off. "Yeah, things are pretty loose. All flights are milk runs now."

"Is *Tahoe Revenge* named after your hometown?" Zach inquired.

"Right, Zach. Tahoe City, California, right on the lake."

"What does your family do there, Buck?"

"They run a ski lodge at a place called Squaw Valley. It's not much now, but if skiing ever catches on in America, it could be big."

Zach reflected on his leather-loop skis back home. "Yeah, someday I'd like to learn to ski for real."

Buck processed Zach's words for a moment. Then he said quietly, "Sergeant Gates, after what I owe you, you can ski free for life."

With a note of embarrassment, Zach replied, "Someday I'll take you up on that. So, where are we now?"

"A few minutes from the D-day beaches."

Zach stared at the approaching land. "Dex, is that Caen coming up?"

Dex checked his charts. "Right, Zach, and that's Sword Beach now just below us."

"Then that must be Juno and Gold looking west."

"Yes, those are the beaches used by the British and Canadians."

Buck banked and got on the radio. "Gentlemen, we're now flying along the D-day beaches. That's Omaha coming up ahead of us. Our 29th and 1st Infantry Divisions caught hell here. Zach, didn't you know some of those guys?"

Bashford and his BAR flashed across Zach's mind. His voice caught for a moment. "I had a replacement from the 29th. His company had 102 KIA on D-day...twenty from his hometown."

"I hope he survived," Dex pleaded.

"Yes, Bash made it without a scratch, and saved my life two or three times."

The airplane remained very silent until Dex reported, "Buck, here comes one of the two artificial harbors."

"Okay, crew. That mess down below is a Mulberry. It was floated across the channel." He paused. "Just ahead is Pointe du Hoc. See the big cliff? I'll let Lieutenant Gallant, our budding historian, explain that."

Dex turned for a better view. "That's where the heroic 2nd Rangers landed and climbed straight up after the shore batteries. They took a pasting from the Germans shooting straight down. I guess the idea was surprise. Now look about twelve miles ahead and you'll see Utah where the 4th Division had a much easier time than the boys at Omaha."

Buck made a slow left bank and headed toward Ste-Mere-Eglise, five miles inland. "This is where the American 82nd Airborne came down, some of them right on top of that big church below." After another left bank, the B-17 was over Carentan, twelve miles away.

Dex looked at his notes and spoke to the crew. "The 101st Airborne landed just north of there. The British 64th Airborne landed near Caen where we first saw the beaches."

"Gates, wasn't there an airborne operation when you crossed the Rhine?" Palmeri asked.

"Yes, the biggest of the war and a controversial one. General Montgomery ordered his 6th Airborne and our American 17th to drop just north of Wesel, a city on the Rhine. It made my life just south of Wesel a lot easier, but the price was very high."

Dex interrupted. "I have the statistics. The two Allied airborne divisions lost over eleven hundred men on that drop—I mean KIA! In comparison, on D-day the 82nd and the 101st together had 340 KIA."

Zach's heart raced as he recalled those desperate days on the Rhine. "Right, Dex. The critical drops by the British 6th and the American 17th Airborne Divisions never got the credit they deserved."

"I guess the press was hung up on the Remagen bridge," Dex replied.

"Well, Remagen was a big event also. The 9th Armored had guts," Zach replied.

"You armored guys stick together," Dex kidded.

"Damn right. So give us the scoop on D-day."

"Okay. Ike had a total of eight divisions. The Germans had fifty-five including eleven Panzer divisions. Moving our men and equipment across the channel was a gigantic effort. Hang on—I have the statistics: 175,000 men, five thousand ships, one thousand transport planes, six thousand fighters and bombers, plus trucks, tanks, ammunition, and two Mulberry harbors."

"Dex, looking at your notes, I figured out that it would be like moving half of my hometown of Milwaukee across Lake Michigan in one day."

"That's very good, Zach, but then you'd also have to drag two Milwaukee harbors across the lake! We got away with this gigantic operation in part because of some great deception."

Buck was looking at the shoreline. "How far are we from Calais?"

Dex studied his chart. "Across the water, two hundred miles; a bit farther if we follow the shore and include Dieppe and Dunkirk."

"Okay, I'm on course. So tell us about that deception, professor."

"Okay. Remember the Dunkirk story where the small, private boats saved the troops? Well, Dunkirk, like Calais, is only twenty miles to Dover across the channel."

Buck interrupted. "That's Dieppe just ahead."

"Right, Buck. Dieppe was one of the places the German brass thought was a possible invasion point, but Hitler was convinced it would be Calais and the Allies went to great pains to convince the German high command that Hitler was right."

"Excuse me, Dex, but didn't the OSS have a lot to do with that?"

"Right, Buck. That's still classified, but I met a guy in a pub from the Office of Strategic Services who told me the plan was called 'Operation Fortitude' with both the British and Hollywood film industries involved."

Palmeri interrupted. "Dex, is OSS our spy agency?"

"Yeah, spies, propaganda, intelligence, all that kind of stuff. The idea here was to convince the Germans that a huge invasion force under the direction of General Patton was gathering at Dover for an attack on the Pas de Calais. Patton had to be seen in the area and was, of course, furious at being used as a decoy. That's why he missed D-day."

A voice from the rear of the plane broke in. "How did Hollywood play into this?"

"They built cardboard and inflatable tanks, phony airplanes, and ersatz landing craft. They even used electronic noises and loud motor launches to simulate a hidden convoy. Just before the real invasion, they dropped small dummy parachutists all over the place. The deception fooled even Rommel, who kept nine of his eleven Panzer divisions around Calais, far from Normandy."

Buck announced the plane's position. "If you're following on a map, we're at Berck-Plage, about sixty to seventy miles from Calais and then

Dunkirk. Thanks for all the information, Dex."

"What did you bomber guys do during the invasion?" Zach inquired.

Buck grumbled, "The B-26s did some good, I guess. They are better at low altitude. My group was flying at twenty thousand feet and dropped our loads way past the beach batteries. Most bombardiers were afraid of hitting our own troops on the beach. The B-17 is not a good tactical aircraft, certainly not at twenty thousand feet. The US Navy big guns saved the day by taking out most of the German heavy gun batteries."

Dex then spoke to the crew. "Major Wheeler's squadron did manage to hit St. Lou just south of the beaches in July, and once the big brass listened to Ike and let us go after transportation centers, we did real good."

"By transportation centers, Dex means railroad yards, marshaling centers, and bridges between Normandy and the German reserves beyond the Seine and Loire Rivers," Buck explained.

Hamburg, Ruhr, and Ardennes

Zach looked at the map. "What's next, Buck? Hamburg?"

"Yup, a very popular target about seven hundred miles from here, a little less than three hours in this beautiful weather. We'll fly over Holland. The British really plastered Hamburg in 1941, but the real Battle of Hamburg happened in 1943 when we got into it."

"You had some trouble with flak as I heard it."

"Oh yes, but on many of those seventeen thousand Allied sorties, the German night fighters were a larger problem."

Two hours later, Zach and the ground crew passengers saw close up and firsthand the appalling destruction of Hamburg. As the plane cruised slowly over mile after mile of horrifying devastation, the pale-faced flyers talked in subdued voices as a sense of monstrous obscenity came over them.

"What have we done here?"

"Did it have to come to this?" Zach whispered.

"Yeah, let's get out of here," Dex murmured.

*****

Once above it all, the big plane did a 180 and headed southeast toward the Ruhr Valley.

"There's a lot more of this mess if you'd like to see Mannheim, Frankfurt, Hanover, and Kassel," Gallant said softly. He checked the instruments. "We'd better feed this bird or she's gonna sit down. Bremen is only sixty miles, and we can refuel there."

"You're the navigator, Dex. Give me a heading."

"You should know it. Didn't you bomb Bremen back in '43?"

"December, I think. We went after the big Focke-Wulf aircraft factory."

"Were you successful?" Zach asked.

"Yes, but we paid for it. We had our first fighter escorts, P-47 Thunderbolts, carrying extra gas tanks, but the tanks didn't work and they had to turn back. As soon as they were gone, wave after wave of ME-109s hit us and then followed us almost all the way back to England."

Zach gasped. "I'm afraid to ask."

"We started with 115 B-17s, lost sixteen, and another forty or fifty limped home. I was very happy to see the longer-range P-51 Mustangs in 1944."

"Bremen dead ahead, Major."

"Got it. Looks better than Hamburg, doesn't it? Guess we didn't hit it as hard as I thought."

The big flying fortress sat down in Bremen. The makeshift crew stretched their legs while the plane was refueled.

"What's next, Lieutenant Gallant?" one of the ground crew passengers asked.

"We're off to Germany's giant Ruhr Valley, a huge industrial center. You'll see some famous targets like Recklinghausen, Essen, and Cologne. Buck hit them all more than once, and Zach Gates attacked them from the ground."

"The guys will be interested in Gates's take on all of this," Buck added.

From Bremen, the Ruhr was about 250 miles, less than an hour in the smooth running B-17. First target was Recklinghausen and Buck got on the intercom. "Okay, crew. We're at the north end of the industrial Ruhr Valley. We'll travel about ninety miles of it to Cologne. I first hit Recklinghausen and Hulls in June 1943 aiming at a synthetic rubber plant. By the looks of things below, we hit it pretty good. Most of these Ruhr runs by the 8th and 9th Air Force were in '44 and '45. The RAF started hitting it in 1940. I'll let our history professor, Lieutenant Gallant, tell you about that."

"Okay. The 1940 raids were called the Battle of the Ruhr. Gates says it was 1945 for the ground troops. The RAF made forty-three attacks all through this area during twenty days in June 1940. They dropped fifteen hundred bombs and lost one thousand airplanes."

Zach shook his head in disbelief. "Dex, did you say one thousand planes?"

"Right, doughboy."

"And I wanted to go air corps…my hat's off to you flyboys."

Dex interrupted the quiet. "Check the big dam below us. It is one of three damaged by a daring, low-level run by eighteen RAF bombers." Buck banked for a better view. Dex continued. "These guys were armed with the new bouncing bombs. They were dropped ahead of the target and were designed to explode several seconds after a bounce. The bounce then carried them directly into the face of the dam. It worked. The whole place was flooded, but the price was high. Eight of the eighteen Lancasters were lost."

Dex turned the intercom back to Buck. "We're coming up on Dortmund. We hit that target along with the RAF. It was the biggest bombing attack in the ETO, isn't that right, Dex?"

"I think so. That must have been just before Gates entered the city."

Again Buck took over. "I remember Dortmund because it was the first time we dropped the Grand Slam—a hairy, twenty-two hundred pound bomb. Hang on, we're heading back east toward Dusseldorf and then south to Cologne. Off on the left is Wuppertal of firestorm fame. Tell them about that, Dex."

"Buck tells me he first saw the phenomenon in Hamburg. It is, from all reports, a nightmare on the ground. Wuppertal, hit by tons of incendiary bombs on a warm, dry night looked like a charcoal grill gone crazy—no flames, just one big, terrible red glow, and a hurricane wind howling itself into an inferno. The destruction below tells half of the story. The loss of life was staggering."

"Worse than Hamburg?" Zach asked.

"Oh yes. Eight square miles were burned literally to the ground in less than eight hours, taking out thirty-five thousand homes and an estimated forty-two thousand people."

Buck cleared his throat. "I read in the *London Times* that when Churchill saw the devastation he asked, 'Are we beasts? Is it time to desist?'"

The silent, low-flying B-17 headed south toward Cologne. Buck's voice returned on the intercom as a subdued crew recovered from the initial shock of seeing the ravages below. "In '44 and '45, the first double hits started. We had the 9th and 12th Air Force in Africa and Italy, but the RAF would fly across Germany, hit targets in the south, and continue across the Mediterranean to Algeria, refuel, reload, and then hit Italy on the way back to England."

A voice from the center of the plane shouted, "Why in the hell didn't the Germans give it up?"

"I'll let our bookworm L-4 pilot try that one," Dex laughed. Zach wasn't sure how to respond. "Zach, what did the doughboys say?" Dex asked in a quieter voice.

Zach emitted an audible moan. "Truth is, most of the doughs didn't know or say anything. I got nervous when I saw the V-2 and V-3 rockets up close. I remember the V-2 was forty-six feet long and weighed thirteen tons. Their jet aircraft also boosted German morale and lowered ours."

Dex intervened. "Let me help. I talked to an OSS guy who interviews a lot of German POWs. He said they reported a serious plan to containerize V-2s and V-3s and tow them with U-boats into New York harbor."

The plane was still processing that shocker when Palmeri called out, "Zach, did you see any jets?"

"I saw only two jets fly low over our columns—real morale busters. Did they have many of them, Dex?" Zach asked.

"Oh yeah, five hundred or more in the air and many more on assembly lines."

Buck added, "That's only the ME-262s. They also had an Arado-234 jet bomber and a real scary rocket plane."

"Right, Buck, that was the ME-163B," Dex explained.

Zach cleared his throat. "I guess many of the Wehrmacht I met really believed their Führer would pull a rabbit out of a hat. After all, they saw their rockets and jets overhead."

Buck's voice dropped to an ominous pitch. "I've been privy to the classified pictures of Hiroshima...if they'd beat us to the A-bomb..." The silence was broken when Dex shouted, "Cologne ahead!"

"Lord, all I see is the cathedral!" sounded a voice from the rear. Another shocked voice asked, "Sergeant Gates, how did it look from the ground?" Zach was shaking his head. "All I saw was the cathedral and utter destruction all around me, but it's worse from the air. You get a sick feeling from the sheer magnitude of it all."

In a gutteral voice, Buck intoned, "A grim example of a one-thousand-plane saturation bombing. Cologne was hit with everything: Halifaxes, Lancasters, Stirlings, Liberators, B-17s, anything that could fly."

Zach felt a pang of sorrow for the crushed cathedral city. Mostly to escape looking at the carnage below, he studied the charts and changed the subject. "Dex, how much trouble to head southeast to Liege and then Bastogne?"

Equally relieved to leave Cologne, Dex answered directly, "Not a big deal. We have plenty of fuel. Any place else I can take you?"

"Can you steer us sixty miles south of Bastogne to the Saar-Moselle Triangle at Saarburg? My division had some heavy fighting there."

"We can do that," Buck replied.

Zach pointed at the chart. "Will that give us time to take in Metz and Pont-a-Mousan before Reims?"

"We'll take time," Buck said flatly.

Within minutes, Liege, Belgium appeared on the right wing. This time the crew was less startled by the devastation below, for they had seen worse in the German Ruhr.

"Sergeant Gates will be your tour guide; he's been in all of these places."

"I'll try. The destruction below was caused, in part, by the German V-1 rockets. I watched them flying overhead when I was in Holland. I also saw my first V-2 back then, but I think it was headed for Antwerp. Buck tells me the first jet bomber mission in history was flown here. Sixteen German bombers hit Liege. What were they, Buck?"

"They were the twin jet Arado 234s I mentioned earlier. We called 'em Blitz Bombers. That was last Christmas. They hit Allied marshaling yards on the same run. Thank God there were not a lot of them."

Buck banked the big bomber and headed forty-five miles due south into the Ardennes and Bastogne, Belgium. Zach resumed. "Most of you know the heroic story of the 101st Airborne. However, as an armored guy, I want you to know that two combat commands of armor also helped save the day, Command A from the 9th Armored and Command B from the 10th."

"How big is a combat command, Zach?"

"It's one third of a division."

"Where were you?"

"My division was sent to the Saar area to defend against the expected second thrust. If Bastogne had fallen, we would have been center stage. Patton sent the 4th and the rest of the 10th Armored to relieve Bastogne and sent my division to the Saar-Moselle Triangle to attack and defuse the large German force deployed there."

Buck flew another circle around Bastogne and headed southeast to Saarburg some forty-five or fifty miles away. Zach continued. "The area below you is German. It's called the Triangle because of the large, delta-shaped geography formed by the junction of the Saar and Moselle Rivers just below.

"The bloody battle fought here was mostly ignored by the news people, since Bastogne was of primary concern. German forces I met here were a mean bunch led by Heinrich Himmler himself. My division took a lot of casualties, but we broke up any thought the Germans had of a second punch. The foot infantry took over from us and Patton was forced to give up my division to the 9th Army which was then answering to Montgomery. Then we raced all the way up the east side of the Bulge through Luxembourg and on to Holland where we relieved the famous British 7th Armored Desert Rats."

From Saarburg, Buck headed the plane toward Metz and Pont-a-Mousan.

Zach continued. "We had more hairy days in this region. Village fighting in the snow was a real bitch. We also learned about trench foot." Zach paused. "Buck, I can't believe these short distances by air. It seemed so much farther on the ground."

"Hell, yes, it's forever when you're slugging it out on the ground, but then air travel is a lot longer when you're being shot at."

The plane turned north and slowly winged three hundred miles to Rhineberg, Germany. Buck cleared his throat. "This is where *Tahoe Lady* was shot down." The occupants of the plane became very quiet. "Palmeri and Dex chuted into the British sector. The rest of the crew dropped in German-held territory."

A recent air corps replacement asked, "Major, where did you come down?"

"I landed in the middle of no man's land. Sergeant Gates and his squad saved my life—not without great sacrifice. One of his men was killed, another so badly wounded he never returned to duty."

The crew turned silent, then after a while began to talk quietly amongst themselves. Palmeri broke the awkward moment and shouted, "Let's hear it for Sergeant Gates!" When the cheering stopped, Zach just waved. In a restrained voice Dex announced, "Next stop, Maastricht, Holland."

*****

Buck looked at his chart. "We're getting close, Dex. Where do we set down?"

"About six kilometers north of the city. It's a tactical strip but a long one. They have fuel but no ground crew to handle B-17s. They only know P-51s and P-47s."

"No problem. We have our own experts on board."

"That's what I told them. Also, they do not have lights."

"We won't need 'em," Buck said matter-of-factly.

The crew and passengers were in a grim and cheerless mood after viewing all of the chaotic destruction followed by the poignant crash-and-rescue review. As the plane approached Maastricht, Major Wheeler tried to change the mood. "Fellow airmen, we are about to initiate an experiment in landing techniques. Sergeant Zachary Gates, a famous L-4 pilot, is going to land his first B-17 while demonstrating his skill at soft landings."

The plane erupted in spontaneous laughter from all points.

"He used to fly a tank, didn't he?"

"Will we be in the *London Times*?"

"We love you, Major Wheeler—please!"

Amid all of the laughter and wisecracks, the experienced pilot put the big bird down in a perfect landing. Buck taxied *Tahoe Revenge* up to the nearest building. The men quickly dismounted, some looking for the fuel truck, others crawling all over the airplane making sure everything was up-to-speed.

Since this tactical airstrip was operating at less than half strength, billets were readily available. The mess hall was shut down this Friday afternoon, but the crew intended to party in nearby Maastricht anyway.

Buck called his pickup crew to order. "Okay, men, listen up. I found a six-by-six and a jeep, so clean up and you can howl in Maastricht. Zach Gates can tell you about the hot spots. He helped free this whole area."

LAST RESPECTS

Dex Gallant patted Zach on the shoulder. "I'm taking these bozos to town."

Buck went to the jeep. "Are you ready for Maastricht, old buddy?"

Zach hesitated and took a deep breath. "Buck, I'd like to make one more stop. Let me take the jeep and I'll catch up with you."

Buck's uncertain expression changed as he empathized with Zach's pain. "Hell, no. I don't need to go to town with that wild ass-group. I'm a married man. Where to?"

"Diergaarde Monastery," Zach said softly.

"We're going to a monastery?" Buck asked, his eyes wide.

"Yeah...Buck, these folks put my company up at great risk to themselves. We fought a major battle in Heide Woods right behind them. I'd like to pay my respects."

Buck smiled agreeably. "I can be religious, especially after today. I'll drive. Which way?"

"Just ahead. Cadier-en-Keer I think is what the village is called."

"What kind of a monastery is it?"

"Catholic, but I never asked what order. The father superior, or whatever he's called, spoke English."

As the jeep approached a chateau-like complex, Buck asked, "Is this it?" Zach opened his mouth to speak, but no words came out as a flood of memories rushed over him. The jeep slid to a stop at the yawning entryway. "Zach, is this the place?" Buck repeated.

"Yes," Zach said softly, as a deep sadness laced with remorse and guilt gripped him.

Buck ground the jeep slowly into the large common. The area was surrounded by barns and buildings of various sizes, all built hard on three of the walls. On the fourth stood a large chapel with adjoining quarters for the monks and brothers who manned the dairy farm—all much as Zach remembered it. He felt his muscles tighten as Buck eased the jeep up to the chapel where an elderly priest waited in the fading sun to greet them. In near perfect English he said, "Welcome, my American sons. I have been expecting you."

Taken aback by the unexpected greeting, Zach was overcome by a near mystical experience. "Come closer, my son." Father Anselm studied Zach's scarred face. "I remember you, Zachary…you have been wounded."

Zach's heart raced while Buck stood transfixed by the emotion-laden interaction. Zach gathered his thoughts and found his voice. "Yes, Father, but I am fine now." His body trembled as he awkwardly extended his hand. "You housed my squad during the war. This is my friend, Major Buck Wheeler from the 8th Air Force."

The good priest shook hands and made the sign of the cross. "*Deo gratias.* And Zachary, what of your friends who visited?"

Zach stared at the priest—a sense of bewilderment overcame him. He quavered, "You have a long memory, Father Anselm."

Father Anselm smiled. "In those rushed and harsh times, you were the only soldiers who had time for a formal goodbye."

Zach rallied and intoned, "We spoke for our whole company, Father. None will forget your kindness."

"Yes, yes, but what of your friends?"

Zach's heart raced. His words came slowly. "Tom Sander went unscathed, John Brenner was wounded—" Zach paused and his eyes grew moist. "Ken Whedder was killed in action just across the Rhine."

"I am so sorry…I will pray for Private Whedder…but what of the rest of your squad?"

Zach bit his upper lip and reported tearfully, "Father…seven men were lost forever and ten were wounded."

Father Anselm genuflected and spoke with a heavy voice. "All those brave young men…my son, these men did not die in vain. They liberated Holland and many other countries. Men are free again, thanks to their great sacrifice." He put his arm around Zachary. "Come inside, gentlemen. You must stay awhile. Have you had anything to eat?"

"No, Father, but—"

"No buts! The novitiates are just getting ready to dine. They would be so pleased to have you join them, since they are all trying to learn English. We have much to talk about, Sergeant Gates."

Zach looked at Buck who, awestruck by the visceral interaction, shrugged an okay.

"First, you two must refresh yourselves. We are honored to have you brave Americans join us."

A chorus of familiar voices echoed through Zach's head as he wiped his hand across his tear-stained face. "We are honored, Father Anselm. There *is* much to talk about. It has been a long, tragic war."

Father Anselm made the sign of the cross. "So many young American boys…go, refresh. We will talk at dinner."

*****

The novitiates knew enough English to understand most of what was being said and were thoroughly enjoying their English and history lessons. Zach painfully recounted the highlights of the battle for Roermond, the attack across the Roer, and the push across the Rhine. Father Anselm recounted his earlier days with the British 2nd Army who could not move the determined German troops out of Holland. He described the feelings of relief when, after five years of occupation, the 9th Army finally drove out the invaders. The most poignant part of the evening came when Father Anselm told how he and his monks and brothers joined the American grave detail to help locate the bodies of so many of the men now buried at Margraten.

By now, Zach and Buck had learned this was a Cistercian Monastery with novitiates who were tireless. The discussions went on into the night. Buck looked at his watch. "It's 2400 hours, Sergeant Gates. I'd like to get home before the men."

The two Americans shook hands all around and received the blessings of Father Anselm and everyone else, or so it seemed. Before Zach left the building, Father Anselm shouted, "Wait," and sent a novitiate to the wine cellar. "This," he said proudly, "is our secret Cistercian Brandy. It is restricted to the order and a few of our dearest friends." Zach accepted the heavily sealed bottle with an embarrassed look.

Father Anselm embraced both men. "May God be with you."

Feeling weak, Zach again heard a symphony of lost voices—Cooper, White, Paxton, Franier, Wing, Ken Whedder, and on and on. He climbed into the jeep. "I'm ready, Buck—let's go."

*****

On the trip back to the airstrip, Zach apologized for keeping Buck from seeing Maastricht. "Forget it, Gates. This was an experience I'll never forget, and I learned a lot more about you. You're quite a piece of work."

Zach attempted to redirect the heavy interchange. "Yeah, but I didn't fly seventy missions."

"Piece of cake next to some of the stories I heard tonight. Judas Priest, the Netherlands were occupied for five years. You earned that bottle of brandy."

*****

Sleep did not come easily for Zach in this place where so many terrible, painful battles had been fought. Each objective, each city, and each small village in this panhandle of Holland had been a test of courage and resolve. They marched through his mind in a random order, each one its own nightmare—Echt, Posterholt, Schilberg, the Roer River, Roermond, Linne, St. Odilenberg, Spielmanshof, Heide Woods, Merbeck, Amern-St. Georg, the list went on and on. All of this happened west of the Roer River. The battleground from the Roer to the Rhine was yet another litany of foreign names and places, each one producing its own special feeling of foreboding ranging from agitation and cowardice to outright panic. Zach's torment was abruptly halted when he became aware of his own voice and the fact that his body was being gently shaken.

"Wake up, Zach. You're having a bad dream."

"Sorry, Buck. I was fighting every damn battle over again."

"It's part of the tempering process, soldier. I still fly old missions."

"I want it to end," Zach pleaded.

"Zach, it never ends but it gets easier as time passes. You helped save the world—now go back to sleep."

"Thanks, Buck. Good night."

Zach stretched out but his eyes refused to close. The faces of the men he lost haunted him. *Those poor bastards, unsung, buried in a foreign land to be forgotten all too soon. Why am I here and not out there with them?* His sessions with Dr. Ryder rattled through his brain. It was a long, restless night.

*****

The next morning, the crew elected to make the five-mile trip to the large American cemetery at Margraten. Many air corps men were also buried there. At the cemetery entrance they were met by the sergeant of the guard.

"Sergeant, I'm Major Wheeler. You should have orders regarding our visit."

"Yes, sir. A Lieutenant Dex Gallant made arrangements. Feel free to look around, but be careful of the open graves."

Sergeant John Palmeri looked shocked. "You mean you are still burying our dead?"

"Yes. This was a major battleground. We are still finding bodies—British, German, and American."

Zach felt pangs of anguish as he mustered the courage to ask, "Where will we find the 9th Army men?"

A cryptic military response followed. "All over. This is primarily a 9th Army cemetery, and it is the only American cemetery in the Netherlands."

"Thanks. I'm looking for 18th Armored men."

"I'd guess on the right side. Most of the rows have signs on them."

A court of honor leading into the 560-acre cemetery was being built by the graves unit. In one of the temporary buildings, huge, rough tablets recorded the names of the dead. The identifiable dead numbered eight thousand to date. Another tragic sign carried the names of American dead whose bodies were so blown apart they could not be matched to their names. Their graves for now were marked simply *Unknown.* A Catholic monk was busy chiseling a future tablet with the doleful words, "Here rests in honored glory a comrade in arms known but to God." The sentry told the group this cemetery had more than three times as many unknowns as any of the other eleven in Europe.

The cemetery was divided into sixteen plots, the temporary grave makers arrayed in somber, symmetrically invariant curves. The crew quietly spread out looking for familiar names on the wooden grave markers.

Buck followed Zach to the first few curved rows where Zachary stood frozen in place. For an agonizing moment, Zach heard the bone-chilling crashes of artillery, the gong-like sounds of mortars, the morale-killing Screaming Meemies, the canvas-tearing sound of a Schmeisser machine gun, the awesome rumble of a Tiger Royal.

Buck put his hand on his friend's shoulder. "Zach, are you all right?"

"Buck, there are so many friends in these graves."

Buck choked out his next words. "Any of your own squad?"

Zach felt his knees shake and his gut tightening—he felt he was slowly drowning in a sea of white crosses. Steeling himself, he pointed to the wooden cross in front of him. "This is Corporal Jim Wing who took my place in Munchoff and was blown to pieces. I can't believe they found enough of him." He moved to the right. "These two unknowns are probably the men who were with him."

Buck followed Zach down a few rows where he found him transfixed and struggling to find his voice. "Buck, here are White and Paxton. That's six of my squad. I'm missing only Whedder," he moaned.

Buck looked over to the next curved row. In a voice laden with mixed emotions, he declared, "I think I found him, Zach."

Zach slowly ambled over and stared at the simple white wooden cross. His heart pounded and he fell to his knees where his tears were uncontrollable. Buck put his arm around his friend. "Zach, I don't know what to say…" Zach struggled to his feet. *When your number's up* sounded so hollow now. He stood frozen in place staring quietly across the huge cemetery.

The crew worked their way back to where he stood, his tear-stained face reflecting the afternoon sunlight, saying his last goodbye to the men with whom he had shared mortal combat. Palmeri uttered a hushed, "Ten hut."

Zach turned around to see the entire crew standing at silent attention, each with his arm arched in a salute of tribute. Zach, fighting back more tears, returned the salute, then did an about-face and gently touched the cross marking Ken Whedder's last resting place. He pulled himself to attention and offered one last salute to all of his heroic friends—now just a sea of small wooden stars and crosses.

EPILOGUE

World War II 3rd Squad men who were killed in action (KIA)

    S/Sgt. Henry R. Vasey KIA
    Pfc. Robert Baxter KIA
    Pfc. Raymond L. Brown KIA
    Pfc. Robert L. Crooks KIA
    Pfc. Carl W. Fields KIA
    Pfc. Orlando D. Moore KIA
    Pfc. John O. Rohwedder ASTP KIA

The rest of the twenty-seven men. Those wounded are noted with a W.

    AAC indicates Army Aviation Cadet.

    T/Sgt. Norman H. Rucks AAC W
    S/Sgt. Raymond S. Ross ASTP W
    Sgt. Frank J. Antonetti W
    Sgt. Robert Glover
    T/5 John Taylor
    Pfc. Orville A. Anderson W
    Pfc. John Ashford
    Pfc. John Bailey
    Pfc. Peter O. Becker
    Pfc. Harvey R. Breisch
    Pfc. Henry Campbell
    Pfc. John S. Cordone W
    Pfc. Herman Fletcher
    Pfc. Robert R. Hazard W

Pfc. Anthony R. Holub W
Pfc. Joseph F. Kindolin W
Pfc. Albert Ohanesian AAC
Pfc. Angelo Sandrin ASTP W
Pfc. Gordon F. Vanburen W

Next, let me name the men not already mentioned who figured prominently in this story and/or influenced what was written.

General William Simpson (himself)
General John M. Devine (Devane)
Colonel Robert J. Wallace (Hallace) POW
Lt. Colonel (later Colonel) George Artman (Hartman)
Captain Ralph J. Elias (Blackie)
Captain Edward Falberg VIII Corps
1st Lt. Walter J. McDermott W
2nd Lt. Walter O. Dahlin W
2nd Lt. Russell J. Legrid (Lt. Russ Grinnell)
2nd Lt. George F. Southern KIA
1st Sgt. Robert Kleinschmidt
S/Sgt. George Caspers W
S/Sgt. Julian O. Nettum KIA
S/Sgt. Grover C. Pack
S/Sgt. Herman Winkler
S/Sgt. Arthur Woodal
Sgt. John W. Finn ASTP
Sgt. Jack Hendrickson
Sgt. John Hokanson ASTP
Sgt. Conrad Tiller
Sgt. Charles Weller KIA
Sgt. Arthur Woodal
Cpl. James K. King (Jim Wing) KIA
Cpl. Henry J. Kwacz
Cpl. Clyde Whitford KIA
Pfc. William (Wild Bill) Adams (medic)
Pfc. Judd M. Alexander ASTP
Pfc. Samuel Aswad
Pfc. Stuart L. Greenberg ASTP
Pfc. John S. Sensenbrenner ASTP
Pfc. Wilbert Weigel ASTP
Will Wheeler (P-51 engineer)

From the army air corps:

Lt. Col. Spencer Gates
Lt. Col. Thomas Dutter
Lt. Col. Redden
Major Robert Robinson KIA-Vietnam
Major Bud Waddell
Captain Marvin Kilton
1st Lt. Cecil Crego

Finally, honorable mentions should go to the Dutch, Belgian, and Luxembourg people, then and now, who appreciate the American blood spent to free a large part of their countries. To this day they honor Old Hickory, the 30th Infantry Division, and the Thundering Herd, the 8th Armored Division. The younger generation has a large collection of restored American armor dubbed the 8th Armored Motor Pool.

And to the surviving older Ardennes citizens and their relatives who lived where many of the actual battles were fought and who have helped me remember.

Sr. Adriana
Fr. Boniface
Hendrick Fermer
Jos Kerckhofs
Tom Reckman
drs. R. H. Roef
drs. Jaak Slangen
Jeroen Sleijpen
Tom Valeriushof
J. J. H. Van der Steen
Thomas Van der Steen
Peter Von Hasael

... Miss Reichm...
  In a request
...t he would enjoyed
...t he really does
...I never in my l...
...rough

CLOVER